Infrastructure, Environment, and Life in the Anthropocene

Experimental Futures: Technological Lives,
Scientific Arts, Anthropological Voices

A series edited by Michael M. J. Fischer and Joseph Dumit

Infrastructure, Environment, and Life in the Anthropocene

Edited by KREGG HETHERINGTON

Duke University Press | *Durham and London* | 2019

Library of Congress Cataloging-in-Publication Data
Names: Hetherington, Kregg, editor.
Title: Infrastructure, environment, and life in the
Anthropocene / edited by Kregg Hetherington.
Description: Durham : Duke University Press, 2019. | Series:
Experimental futures | Includes bibliographical references and
index.
Identifiers: LCCN 2018026168 (print)
LCCN 2018034094 (ebook)
ISBN 9781478002567 (ebook)
ISBN 9781478001133 (hardcover : alk. paper)
ISBN 9781478001485 (pbk. : alk. paper)
Subjects: LCSH: Human geography. | Infrastructure
(Economics)—Environmental aspects. | Water-supply—Political
aspects. | Climatic changes—Effect of human beings on. | Sustain-
able development.
Classification: LCC GF50 (ebook) | LCC GF50 .I54 2019 (print) |
DDC 304.2—dc23
LC record available at https://lccn.loc.gov/2018026168

Cover art: "Supertrees," Gardens by the Bay, Singapore.
Photo by Natasha Myers.

CONTENTS

vii ACKNOWLEDGMENTS

1 INTRODUCTION. Keywords of the Anthropocene |
Kregg Hetherington

Part I: Reckoning with Ground

17 ONE. The Underground as Infrastructure? Water, Figure/Ground
Reversals, and Dissolution in Sardinal | *Andrea Ballestero*

45 TWO. Clandestine Infrastructures: Illicit Connectivities
in the US-Mexico Borderlands | *Shaylih Muehlmann*

66 THREE. The Metropolis: The Infrastructure of the
Anthropocene | *Gastón Gordillo*

Part II: Lively Infrastructures

97 FOUR. Dirty Landscapes: How Weediness Indexes State
Disinvestment and Global Disconnection | *Ashley Carse*

115 FIVE. From Edenic Apocalypse to Gardens against Eden: Plants and People in and after the Anthropocene | *Natasha Myers*

149 SIX. Leaking Lines | *Nikhil Anand*

Part III: Histories of Progress

171 SEVEN. Low Tide: Submerged Humanism in a Colombian Port | *Austin Zeiderman*

193 EIGHT. Oystertecture: Infrastructure, Profanation, and the Sacred Figure of the Human | *Stephanie Wakefield & Bruce Braun*

216 NINE. Here Comes the Sun? Experimenting with Cambodian Energy Infrastructures | *Casper Bruun Jensen*

236 TEN. The Crisis in Crisis | *Joseph Masco*

261 REFERENCES

293 CONTRIBUTORS

297 INDEX

ACKNOWLEDGMENTS

Thanks, first, to all the authors in this volume who entrusted me with their manuscripts and then put up graciously with all my pestering, nagging and cajoling. I couldn't have asked for a more dedicated and considerate (and brilliant) group. This edited volume is a first for me, and I was in no way ready for the many complications that arose along the way. For that, it's been a pleasure to work with the indomitable Gisela Fosado and Lydia Rose Rappoport-Hankins. Two anonymous reviewers gave us very productive feedback on early drafts, and helped shape the book's current form.

This volume originated in a workshop by the same title at Concordia University in October 2015, which was made possible by funding support from the Social Science and Humanities Research Council of Canada, the Japanese Society for the Promotion of Science, the Loyola Sustainability Research Centre, and Concordia University. The workshop was the first place where we received formal feedback from an excellent group of commentators, including Gretchen Bakke, Aadita Chaudhury, Rosemary Collard, Jill Didur, Martin French, Kathryn Furlong, Karine Gagné, Kevin Gould, Orit Halpern, Duygu Kasdogan, Liv Krause, Bettina Stoetzer, Wakana Suzuki, Kira Turner, and Jonathan Wald. Antina von Schnitzler's contribution to that workshop wasn't available for the final volume, but she was an integral part of the process.

During this entire project, from the conception of the workshop through to the final edits, I have been supported by amazing students who continue to amaze me with their originality, honesty, and organizational skills. They are Sarah Bibeau, Tristan Biehn, Jessica Cadoch, Mark Doerksen, Chantal Gailloux, Mathieu Guérin, Serhiy Homonyuk, Elie Jalbert, Sean Miller, Aryana Soliz, Émile St-Pierre, and Myriam Tardif. Thanks to Marie-Eve Drouin-Gagné and Orenda Boucher for some last-minute help with the introduction. Others who supported us behind the scenes, or were involved from a distance, were Myra Hird, Jean-François Mayer, Atsuro Morita, Valerie Olson, Peter Stoett, Adan Suazo, and Peter van Wyck. The project also grows out of many years of discussion with others in the infrastructure mode, particularly Jeremy Campbell, Penny Harvey, and Carlota McAllister.

A final thank-you goes to Kim Fortun, who helped me conceptualize the project from the beginning, anchored the discussion at the workshop, and offered advice and feedback through to the final stages of volume editing.

INTRODUCTION. Keywords of the Anthropocene

KREGG HETHERINGTON

"Kyoto Is Dead." The simple statement is scrawled across one of the busiest underpasses in downtown Montreal, only a few blocks from where the authors of this volume met in 2015. The overpass in question facilitates the use of fossil fuels to get in and out of the city, but it also straddles one of Montreal's main protest routes, addressing itself to the city's civic consciousness and appearing in many a photograph of local Earth Day parades. To many of us who live here, the words already feel nostalgic, evoking a moment when the city's once hopeful environmental movement matured into something darker. At the end of the twentieth century, Montreal had been seen by many of its residents as a center for progressive urbanism and environmental thinking. The city had rebuilt its infrastructure for Expo '67, a celebration of speculative urban planning, that included a massive geodesic dome called "Biosphere." In 1987, it gave its name to the Montreal Protocol on Substances that Deplete the Ozone Layer, a triumph of international diplomacy that many thought would provide the blueprint for future greenhouse emissions agreement (Schneider 1998; Hulme 2009). But by 2007, the infrastructure built for Expo '67 was deteriorating rapidly, known, among other things, for the lethal collapse of several concrete overpasses. The Biosphere geodome had gone up in flames.[1] And the Kyoto Protocol was collapsing as well. The quickly scrawled words, and their persistence in Montreal's precarious concrete, now seem prescient of the uncertainty that would follow, and of the sense of undoing that many call the Anthropocene.

This volume is about how that same malaise plays out in contemporary social science. Whatever we choose to call it, the social sciences and humanities are clearly experiencing an environmental moment. Global climate change is taking a larger and larger place in social theory, profoundly challenging the distinction between social and natural categories on which the social sciences were always based, and destabilizing the ground from which academics contribute to meaningful discussions of solutions. The subjects and objects of our enterprise are no longer clearly distinguishable, and the figures and grounds of our critical traditions have been undermined. In 1987, some believed we needed to protect an environmental object for the sake of human life, using ingenious new infrastructures. But somewhere between Montreal and Kyoto, the environmental objects, infrastructural solutions, and the lives at stake had all become exponentially more complex and suspect, each becoming part of the massively distributed problem at hand.

Early approaches to the mitigation of environmental harm through heroic human designs now seem dated. The common human "we," so easily deployed in twentieth-century progressive social policy is no longer easy to pinpoint, its universalism and agency are suddenly up for question (Chakrabarty 2012), and the environmental objects that define our age, such as carbon emissions and algae blooms, are neither human nor nonhuman, neither fully outside of us, nor fully inside (Morton 2013). As Timothy Mitchell (2011) has so forcefully argued, even the democratic systems through which we purport to solve our dependence on fossil fuels are themselves the product of fossil-fuel dependency. That which humans confront as the environment, that enveloping process of being that sustains us or destroys us with complete indifference, is as much the result of infrastructural history as natural history (Chakrabarty 2012; Stengers 2015). As Kim Fortun (2012) puts it, ours is an age characterized by degrading industrial infrastructure, environmental threat, and exhausted paradigms.

It is an open question whether "Anthropocene" is the right name for this moment. The term has already spawned its own industry of critiques.[2] Three problems with the name are most evident for the project in this book. First, the root "Anthropos" itself arguably makes it very difficult to think adequately beyond the human, who stands both heroically and tragically at the center of the action (Haraway 2015; Myers this volume). In a related vein, by naming Anthropos as a singular agent of environmental change, the Anthropocene tends to elide the deep colonial and capitalist inequalities among humans that are integral to the very problematic that it purports to name (Todd 2015). Third, freighted as it is with the anxieties about disaster, the Anthropocene narrates itself as crisis, both repeating well-worn Christian and environmental tropes about the Fall (Swyngedouw 2010; Wakefield and Braun, this volume) and inducing a kind of political paralysis (Masco, this volume). When the authors in this book met we were all aware of these pitfalls, and many of us were anxious to find a way to remove the term from our conversation. And yet as our discussion progressed, we continued to find it useful, and we were less concerned with trying to critique or characterize it than with the way it served as a placeholder for a certain mode of questioning the contemporary. "Anthropocene" itself is a keyword, which serves the purpose not of smoothing over contention, but of linking epochal discussions in the social sciences with those in the natural sciences and environmental movement. Part, indeed, of what we find generative about it is its continued rawness, and the way it playfully denotes something seen and not-seen (de la Cadena 2015b). It is, as a starting point, the "scene" of our discussion (Pandian 2015; Lorimer 2017), but it is not a passive backdrop, because it keeps reaching into the discussion itself to undermine our language.[3]

This book is therefore neither a catalogue of horrors, nor an attempt to define fraught concepts. The authors come from a range of analytic traditions in political economy, science and technology studies, and critical theory, and they engage with concepts quite differently from one another. Instead, the volume brings together focused ethnographic studies of the analytic mood of the

Anthropocene, and the flurry of new and repurposed concepts that it produces. Of these, we focus particularly on the way "environment," "infrastructure," and "life" are suddenly finding new purchase in social analysis. These three terms are, I propose, keywords of the Anthropocene, words that, in the tradition of Raymond Williams (1976), are important precisely because their meanings are contested and changing, even while they continue to play a central role in defining the stakes of argument. In what remains of this introduction, I offer a brief genealogy of each of the keywords, and show why we envision the concepts of environment, infrastructure, and life rearticulating in such disparate locations.

Environment (the Continuing Growing Pains of Political Ecology)

The primary conceptual problem that the Anthropocene causes for social science is that it further unsettles the relationship between nature and culture, humans and nonhumans. That unsettling was well under way before global climate change became a household concern, and it serves as the undertone for decades of debate in political ecology. In the 1980s, political ecology was still a side branch of political economy, attempting to explore the way environments figured in dramas of social and political ecology (Orlove 1980). This followed with a decade in which the dominant position was to show the myriad ways in which nature and wilderness were discursive constructions (Descola and Pálsson 1996; Cronon 1995). Many of those questions are still relevant, and in this volume they often manifest in the crossings of objects from environment to infrastructure and back again. For instance, Ballestero confronts the question of how environmental phenomena come to be objectified as natural resources (what she calls "infrastructuralizing"), and Muehlmann shows how even people, once classified as "natural," become the embodied infrastructure of new kinds of trade. In Gordillo's piece the possibility of an Argentine rurality is subsumed by a new global infrastructure he calls simply "The Metropolis."

Even while critical political ecology has shown how discursive domains around the natural continually jump around, we are still in search of an adequate language for the ways that nature acts on its own. How fitting then that anthropogenic climate change should suddenly erupt from this epistemological impasse, a nature both social and terrifyingly antisocial. To be clear, what makes the Anthropocene so conceptually unsettling is not that humans have never been faced with environmental disaster, but rather that those disasters have always appeared to have an intellectual outside, in the privileged halls of academia, from which they could be assessed using conventional categories of society and nature. Environmental problems and the people who suffered from them could always be localized, indeed often were in very predictable ways that silently reiterated colonial violence or deepened new vectors of class and racial inequalities.[4] The conceit of the Anthropocene, by contrast, even while its effects are unevenly distributed, is its claim to reach everywhere, its promise to unsettle the condition of every life, and our scholarly attempts to grapple with it are at once part of its threat (Chakrabarty 2012; Morton 2013).

So far, discussion of the Anthropocene in the humanities has leaned heavily on actor-network theory and feminist science studies, which offer a toolkit for understanding the relationship between human knowledge and nonhuman actors. Actor-network theory, in its early iterations, gave us a blunt way of dehumanizing agency (Callon and Latour 1981; Law 2004) and of bringing into the purview of scholarly concern the different forms of construction at work (Latour 2005). Feminist science studies, by contrast, drew on a longer tradition of questioning the very category of agency (Braidotti 2013) and now offered new language for talking about ecologies of practice (Stengers 2010), relational intra-action (Haraway 2008; Barad 2007), and affect and care (Puig de la Bellacasa 2012; Hustak and Myers 2012; Tsing 2015). This broadened world allowed us to continue thinking through classic questions about politics and power, inequality and justice, but now with a broader set of relations at stake that are not or not only human.

But as the category of the human becomes less distinct, so too do the grounds on which the human claims to live, relate, and fight for justice. The concept of the Anthropocene, whatever else it does, expresses this beautifully: if humans have become a geological force, how does one differentiate ground from action? The Anthropocene amplifies a conceptual dilemma within environmental studies in general: as Morton (2007: 1) puts it, "when you mention the environment, you bring it into the foreground. In other words, it stops being the environment." Not coincidentally, this problem of interpretation, of distinguishing objects from their surroundings, is also central to the recent literature on infrastructure.

Across the humanities and social sciences, infrastructure is suddenly a buzz-word of the highest and most obnoxious order. Over the past ten years, doz-ens of new volumes have emerged claiming a stake in the redefinition of this old term, offering up new objects of analytic attention, a conversation in which many of the authors in this volume have been active participants.[5] In this book we continue that conversation, not with a new program or defini-tion, but rather to ask why infrastructure, in all of its dimensions, has become such a matter of concern in the first place.

Perhaps the most obvious reason for this is that already alluded to: environ-ment and infrastructure share a great deal of conceptual territory, and the Anthropocene disturbs the distinction between them. Both terms straddle the terrain once held by concepts such as "context," and each grapple to define the spatial extension of human action into that which surrounds, subtends, precedes, or silently conditions (Carse 2012; Hetherington and Campbell 2014). The classic way of distinguishing between them places human intention in time: the environment precedes infrastructure the way a landscape survey precedes an engineer's design for a bridge, which itself precedes a bridge (Hetherington 2014). To put it crassly, in this formulation, environment is the infrastructure of infrastructure. But such a distinction no longer works when it is our infrastructures of global transportation and consumption that produce the anthropocenic environment on which infra-structures are built. Following that logic, we would have to say that carbon is the infrastructure of the infrastructure of carbon.

As material infrastructures fold in on themselves, it becomes all the more clear that infrastructure itself was always also an interpretive tactic. As Geoff Bowker (1994) famously argued, infrastructure is an analytic moment that happens precisely when one makes a distinction between figure and ground, where infrastructure appears to be the background to something else. The point, later taken up by Susan Leigh Star and others is that infrastructure only recedes into the background for those who are not busy building or repairing or analyzing it (Star 1999; Star and Ruhleder 1996). Infrastructural analysis, by extension, is the performance of a figure-ground reversal, what Bowker (1994) called "infrastructural inversion," which brings the background to the foreground. In retrospect, we can think of all sorts of critical analyses as kinds of infrastructural inversion, in which, for instance, class relations, conditions of possibility, or semiotic structures are revealed as the infrastructure subtending cultural or social phenomena on the surface (Hetherington 2014). Classical anthropology, with its project of revealing the "context" of social phenomena, makes the same move, a figure-ground reversal in which an analyst claims to reveal the grounds for social behavior, and in so doing turns those grounds into a proper object of study, such as "society" or "culture."[6] Infrastructural inversion is always, therefore "critical," in the sense that it attempts to lay bare the wires, pipes, and foundations of a phenomenon. But it is a critique that, once named infrastructural, is never transparent, always dependent on the position of the observer, and performed without guarantees. So it's perhaps not surprising that infrastructural analytics emerges precisely at the moment when critique itself seems to be in crisis (Latour 2004b).

The crisis in critique that spurs the infrastructural moment is one of the resonances of the end of the Cold War, or the rise of neoliberalism. But infrastructural concerns resonate with Cold War histories in other ways as well. The mid-twentieth century marked a great expansion in human physical intervention on the global landscape, a continuation of what Brian Larkin (2008) calls the "colonial sublime," in which the radical transformation of landscapes was a poetic enactment of imperial power. Indeed, the very distribution of cement and rebar came to characterize the uneven development of north and south, signposts of the very theory of progressive betterment that could now be taken to underwrite world history (Koselleck 2004; Harvey and Knox 2012; Mrázek 2002). To be sure, the story of development, and the way concrete comes to both mark and facilitate it, is by no means over. But development's infrastructures began to gather new layers of meaning as the landscapes of the Cold War decayed in the late 1980s, and with them the ideas of progress that underpinned that historical period (von Schnitzler 2016; Anand, this volume). By the twenty-first century, Montreal's succinct epitaph to the Kyoto protocol was also an epitaph to the concrete of the Cold War and to the very grounds of criticism itself. The history of progress seemed to be coming to an end.

The end of progress makes certain political projects harder to imagine, but it also provides space for the emergence of other histories and projects that development, humanism, and progress marginalized. If Montreal's decaying concrete in the late twentieth century made visible the rise and fall of progressive internationalism, it also made visible the ongoing racial violence of settler colonialism. In 1990, another bridge made it impossible for Montreal's settlers to forget that the land they lived on was stolen Mohawk territory. At the time the island was taken by the French, Mohawks were forced to a small enclave on the south shore of the St. Laurence River, at Kahnawà:ke. Kahnawà:ke had then been further reduced throughout the twentieth century by Montreal's infrastructural expansion—principally the construction of the St-Lawrence Seaway Canal, which expropriated the community's waterfront, and the Mercier Bridge, which bisected the reserve to connect commuters to downtown Montreal (Alfred 1995). In 1990, that same bridge became the site for one of many political inversions. In answer to a dispute in another Mohawk community, where white developers had tried to build a golf course over a forest cemetery, Kahnawa'kehro:non occupied the bridge. They drew such a disproportionate military response from the Canadian government that the ensuing showdown couldn't but stand as a spectacle for ongoing settler violence (Simpson 2014). In other words, two disputes over environment and infrastructure—turning a river into a canal and a forest into a golf course—also forced a reimagination of Montreal as colonial space. As such they could be thought of as prefiguring the anticolonial struggles over pipelines threatening the territories of the Standing Rock Sioux and Wet'suwet'en, among many others. These are the front lines of the Anthropocene, in which indigenous people not only block carbon-intensive infrastructures, but also challenge social theory, remaking histories of progress, colonialism, and carbon (Todd 2015; TallBear 2015).

The Anthropocene as infrastructural moment is one in which infrastructural inversion is itself inverted, and in which the political stakes of material structures and historical analyses fold into each other. In this volume, Masco argues we need to reclaim elements of progress and public investment in large-scale social thinking from the Cold War imaginaries that are currently in crisis. Jensen, by contrast, argues that we should pay more attention to the micropolitics of infrastructural experimentation, by which small interventions built by states, private companies, and international agencies have the capacity to multiply future possibilities. Zeiderman wonders whether the intertidal zones in Buenaventura, once reclaimed from the sea, now reclaimed by the sea, in fact offer us an opportunity for rethinking the submerged histories of humanism. If Kyoto is dead, each of these chapters argues that we need to think more carefully about what was salvageable in Kyoto-style thinking in a way that is both materially attuned and more deliberately inclusive of submerged histories.

Life (Conceptual Weeds)

Ultimately, infrastructural decay also sets up the final conceptual term for this volume, which interrogates the degree to which "life" needs to be thought beyond its human qualifications and its colonial universalism. In their chapters, both Carse and Myers suggest weeds as our point of departure in this question, weeds that grow among the cracks of concrete buildings, along the mown banks of a canal, and throughout the groomed spectacles of future life. As these two essays suggest, weeds can be read in radically opposing ways. For residents of the Panama Canal Zone, in Carse's chapter, weeds are emblematic of the decline of progress. For artist Lois Weinberger, in Myers's chapter, the indomitability of weeds stands in for some sort of hope, of resilience, and the perpetuity of life amid human control and destruction. Weeds complicate the temporalities of growth and decay, they live in the interstices between environment and infrastructure, and they are both unwanted (by definition), and the sign of life's future.

The Anthropocene is weedy, not only because out-of-place plants grow up in the cracks of old mortar and cling to the bottom of tankers, but because it profoundly complicates the categories of life on which social science has for so long depended. The dissolution of a common academic understanding of life participates in the same plot that sees critique and infrastructure in decline. World War II may have created the conditions of possibility for the technological and material booms of the Cold War. It also facilitated a theoretical transition in the social sciences from eugenics and evolutionism to a slate of theories that treated cultural humans as radically distinct from biological humans. The distinction had of course a very long genealogy that can be traced back to Aristotle, and World War II in no way meant the end of biological reasoning in the social sciences. But the wide embrace of the cultural construction of gender and race among liberal academics produced an important shift, in which the autonomy of the social was not only a methodological prerogative; it was the basis of progressive politics.

Perhaps the most interesting effect of this shift is the way that it conditioned the emergence of Foucauldian biopolitics, which looked at the way that politics attempted to direct or capture "life itself" (Foucault 1990; Rose 2001). Taking over from eugenics, biopolitics is the arena in which late liberalism imagined how to build the infrastructures of the good life (e.g., Li 2009; Ferguson 2006). For better or for worse, the biopolitical model, in both its progressive and its critical strains, has become increasingly weedy as the conventional separation of biology and culture break down once more. Now that plants communicate and rivers have rights, the specificity of human life and politics is once more in doubt.[7]

New strands of vitalism and "sociable life" are also about opening up our analyses to the complex interweaving of different relations that used to be categorized as social, biological, or physical (Hird 2009; Bennett 2010). In anthropology, where biology and culture have been most forcefully held apart, anthropologists are suddenly debating not whether but *how* life structures a specific relationship between biology, matter, and culture (Kohn 2013; Ingold 2011). In science and technology studies, the invigoration of Deleuzian vitalism, complex systems theory, and Whiteheadian pragmatism has gone along with the resurrection of the figure of Gaia as a way of characterizing planetary life force (e.g., Latour 2013; Stengers 2015).

Social movements concerned with food infrastructures, built environments, and biodiversity are increasingly invoking "life" as the baseline for a politics of resistance (Escobar 2008; Zeiderman 2013; Hetherington 2013). But here too the question of what life actually means is not at all settled. Indeed, while conservation-oriented approaches to the environment reckon with their underlying relationship to colonialism (e.g., Neumann 1998; West 2006), others struggle with their relationship to nativism, nationalism, and a place-based politics that doesn't connect easily to the planetary scale of the Anthropocene. How can the "defense of life" be understood as simultaneously local and global, conservative and newly inclusive? And how can anyone claim to defend human life at a moment when we recognize the definitions of that life as part of the very things that are imperiling us in the first place?

Humans end, of course, not just in annihilation, but in ceasing to be other-than weeds. The Anthropocene, as Anna Tsing (2015) puts it, highlights the "unruly edges" of human endeavor, the margins between the social and the natural, and the blasted aftermath of ecological violence in which weeds and scavengers thrive. We may want to seriously question the sudden proliferation of discourses of precarity and resilience that have recently made their appearance in the literature (see Masco's chapter), but we can recognize them as symptoms of our own weediness; in ecological terms we are more like dandelions than like chimpanzees. Human life, so long qualified apart from other living beings, is suddenly reconnected—analogically, ecologically and affectively—with other forms of life (e.g., Helmreich 2009; Haraway

2008; Hustak and Myers 2012). Humans end as an infrastructural inversion, where our life projects are no longer human-life projects. The Kyotos to come will be more-than-human projects, this time explicitly.

Organization of the Book

This book does not propose answers to these questions, but it does hope to show a variety of paths in and out of them. Because the chapters that follow each grapple with the volume's central themes ethnographically, I have already done them some injustice by boiling them down to key terms. To make up for this, the book is organized in such a way as to bring out cross-currents and nuances in the way each of the authors encounters these concepts. The chapters are therefore divided into three parts, organized around one of the problems that emerged, not from the concepts themselves, but from the relation between concepts.

In the first part, "Reckoning with Ground," each of the chapters describes a moment in which some set of relations switches from environment to infrastructure. Together, the chapters recapitulate the point that infrastructure is both a material and an analytic move, often both a literal and metaphorical "ground." For Ballestero, an aquifer emerges as infrastructure from the ground of indeterminate material relations as its function for human sustenance becomes clear. For Muehlmann, clandestine trade routes play on infrastructure's ambiguous relationship to knowledge, and people become infrastructural to the extent that they both facilitate and obscure the movement of goods. To end the part, Gordillo's chapter argues that the infrastructure of South American agriculture has ceased to be a local rural endeavor and became a global, urban one. In each case, the anthropocenic moment reconfigures ecological relationships as infrastructural ones and vice versa.

If in the first part we meet squelchy aquifers, indigenous fishers, and rural territories *turning into* infrastructure, in the second part, "Lively Infrastructures," we explore the kinds of beings that thrive on infrastructure's ultimate inseparability from the environment. The key metaphor here is the weed, which in Carse's chapter shows up as a plant out of place in the once "clean" grounds around the Panama Canal. In Myers's exploration of Lois Weinberger's weedy art installations, we are offered a way to think outside the staged gardens of the Anthropocene. In a reverse echo of Ballestero's functional aquifer,

Anand shows how the dysfunction of Mumbai's urban plumbing allows water to regain its indistinct, nonhuman form.

The decay of modern piping brings us to the third part of the book, "Histories of Progress," in which four chapters explore the shifting temporality and politics of the Anthropocene. Two of the chapters are constructed around reclaiming human projects that seem to be imperiled. Zeiderman starts part III by arguing that rising tides offer an opportunity for reclaiming (submerged) humanism as a project of radical equality. Wakefield and Braun's chapter, about a project to create living tidal breaks in New York Harbor, shows how the contemplation of environmental catastrophe leads inexorably toward other lessons, that life as a progressive human project needs to reckon with other life projects. For Jensen, the failure of grand, public environmentalisms is a chance to think about more modest forms of infrastructural experimentation. For Masco, though, these small conceptual opportunities are not enough; we need to reclaim the idea of crisis as something that can spur our collective, infrastructural imagination.

In the end, this volume should be read as a modest proposal to use empirical studies of infrastructure and environment to think about the difficulties of contemporary life that are partially captured by the frame of the Anthropocene. As such it is also an invitation to extend the conversation in new research directions, toward new objects and dilemmas. Each of the chapters offers a way of thinking about critique, and of mobilizing infrastructure and environment toward new ways of conceptualizing human and other forms of life. Whether because of the "crisis in crisis" (as Masco puts it), or because new material and institutional arrangements open different future possibilities (as Jensen argues), the empirical study of moments in which infrastructure and environment become conceptual problems gives social scientists an entry to engage with the entanglements of present and future lives.

Notes

1 The acrylic covering on the geodome burned in 1976, and the hollow structure has stood since then on the artificial island built for the expo with the rubble excavated for the city's new Metro system.

2 I won't enumerate the literature here, but see Donna Haraway et al. (2016); Cymene Howe and Anand Pandian (2015); Jason Moore (2017); and Jedediah Purdy (2015), for starters.

3 See also the great collection of short essays entitled "Lexicon for an Anthropocene Yet Unseen" edited by Cymene Howe and Anand Pandian (2015).

4 I'm thinking here particularly of the long literature in "environmental racism" that traces the ways environmental harms are unevenly distributed (e.g., Bullard 1993; Checker 2005; Auyero and Swistun 2009; Martinez-Alier 1997; Nixon 2011; Harrison 2011).

5 These include Hetherington and Campbell (2014); Harvey, Jensen and Morita (2016); Anand et al. (2018); and Howe and Pandian (2015). See also Brian Larkin (2013).

6 This is particularly true of the Malinowskian school of ethnography (see Dilley 1999; Strathern 1995).

7 For two brief examples from popular media, see Nic Fleming, "Plants Talk to Each Other Using an Internet of Fungus," BBC News, November 11, 2014, http://www .bbc.com/earth/story/20141111-plants-have-a-hidden-internet; "New Zealand River First in the World to Be Given Legal Human Status," March 15, 2017, BBC News, http://www.bbc.com/news/world-asia-39282918?SThisFB%3FSThisFB.

Part I.
Reckoning with Ground

ONE. The Underground as Infrastructure?

Water, Figure/Ground Reversals,
and Dissolution in Sardinal

ANDREA BALLESTERO

As we stood in a circle, Joan sat on a bucket, notebook and pen in hand, ready to jot down the numbers that Fernando would eventually give her. We all looked expectantly into the small hole that William had carved out of thick, humid, and dark soil. William had poured fifteen liters of water into the hole. We stood ready to time the speed with which the water seeped down and disappeared into the vast subsurface world (figure 1.1). The formation we had sculpted out of empty space, liquid, and time lay peacefully, unaware of our presence, despite owing its existence to our laboriousness. Well, mostly to William's, since he dug the hole and carried the water container from the car into its temporary earthly receptacle. While we conversed, regularly looking down into the hole, the water level started going down very, very slowly.

Figure 1.1. Inscribing water's dissolution into the underground. Photo by the author.

We were witnessing how gravity patiently pressed water against layers of rock, clay, and soil that were considering whether to welcome water's intruding presence or push back to keep it at bay.

As we timed the duration of water's struggle to permeate the subsurface, the temporality of politics and the speed of the conflict that led us there that morning seemed to belong to a totally different register. That is, until all of a sudden, a pickup truck with about fifteen community members arrived to check on us. Somebody had alerted them that unknown people were doing unusual things in the area. The political atmosphere in Sardinal, the area we were at, made any atypical event suspicious, as the conflict over the potential use of underground water for "luxury" housing had reached a fever pitch.[1]

When people jumped off the pickup truck and approached us to check on our "unusual" activities, there was a sudden shift in mood. "Ah, son de SAS" (Oh, they are from SAS), a woman in her forties said. I was relieved by the swift change. The aggressive, defiant, and mostly female bodies that confronted us loosened, turning into curious and inquisitive subjects asking for specifics about our presence. "When are these tests going to yield results? Are we going to finally know if there is enough water? They can't take it if there is not enough for us! We will not let them rob us of our water!"

As we discussed the conflict, reflected on the global and local politics of water, and dissected the *longue durée* of structural economic inequalities in Guanacaste, the province where Sardinal is located, the water in the hole continued pressing downward. While Fernando, William, and I talked to our sentinels, Joan held the notebook, pen, watch, and measuring tape all on her own, while she recorded the speed with which water receded into the sub-surface and initiated its migration into the aquifer. After about half an hour of conversation, the water had seeped through the bottom and sides of the hole, and the women, children, and few men who had instructed us on Sardinal water politics left in the same pickup truck they had arrived in. Both figures, the combative community and the water, had dissolved into their backgrounds.

Our doings that morning followed a well-established protocol for preliminary infiltration tests, a set of procedures designed to measure the speed with which water dissolves into the ground. These tests are critical for determining how quickly aquifers recharge and how much water can be sustainably extracted from them, questions that were at the center of the whirlwind that enveloped the people of Sardinal, the aspirations of transnational investors, and the aquifer we were trying to understand that morning.

After packing our equipment and loading our cars, we continued to our next stop in the data collection route my coinvestigators had planned. We followed the same protocol in three different locations across the upper Sardinal Basin. Digging a hole, dumping water in it, waiting and taking notes on time and distance. No more neighbors came to supervise our activities, though. At the end of that day in 2009, we had started a new study to characterize—to "conceptually model," hydrogeologists and courts would say—the Sardinal aquifer.

Our fieldwork that morning was not a singular event. Different governmental agencies had begun visiting Sardinal more often than usual about half a year before, when the tension between local residents and the water utility, AyA, began to escalate. By the time we were running our infiltration tests, the political environment was crisped. Just a few weeks earlier, the head of the water utility and the environment minister were prevented from delivering their speeches at a public meeting convened to discuss what was already known as "the Sardinal crisis." Quietly, although angrily, the public officials had to listen to the complaints of the community as the discussion got more and more heated until police officers awkwardly escorted the institutional representatives to their cars and then managed to drive off, but not before a couple of rocks landed on their windshields.

Maneuvering across a politics of time—delaying or moving forward legal procedures to their convenience—and a politics of space (Kirsch 2014)—verifying or disproving environmental or human harm—people involved in the Sardinal case were caught in a dynamic of trust and mistrust. Tension escalated to its highest point when town residents saw the pipes that would move water fifteen kilometers from storage tanks to the Ocotal–El Coco coastal region. With their deep metallic darkness, the pipes embodied the depth of conflicting economic interests, different senses of morality, and the push of capital for the expansion of profit that entwined corporations, bureaucracies, and residents into an explosive hydrolithic arrangement.

Luckily, our infiltration tests were enfolded by a different kind of political appreciation. The governmental agency that Joan, William, and Fernando work for, SAS, is responsible for the study and planning of underground water in Costa Rica and is held in high esteem by many local citizens.[2] Generally, people perceive the information SAS produces to be fair, though many activists criticize the agency's inability to police the drilling of water wells more systematically. The technical resolutions and studies performed by SAS have been pivotal in approving or rejecting water use permits and construction licenses for projects planning to rely upon underground water in Costa Rica. The science SAS produces is structurally shaped by the politics of public interest. The institution's everyday work is grounded in an understanding that the facts it produces are always much more than mere unequivocal truths, an awareness that many public officials share (Ballestero 2012a; Ballestero 2012b). The tests we performed that day in 2009 were no different. Commissioned by an interinstitutional committee that included AyA, the Environment Ministry, and other local and state organizations, our measurements would help determine whether the plan to supply underground water to the booming tourism development in the area was viable.

A year earlier, opponents to the project identified several gaps in existing knowledge about the aquifer. A major one, singled out by the court that ultimately mediated the conflict, was a "most alarming missing piece." According to the courts, project proponents lacked knowledge about the size, temporality, movement, and qualities of the aquifer. They lacked an adequate "conceptualization" of the aquifer. Despite the construction work, infrastructural planning, and international marketing already unfolding, the aquifer was still conceptually unknown, its technoscientific material qualities undetermined. Coming up with its technical conceptualization required not only activating infrastructural and environmental imaginaries but also mobilizing a series of legal and technoscientific tools—work permits, water use licenses, mathematical models, and calculation of an extraction rate. The court hoped that combining legal imaginaries with technical instruments would transform underground water, an entity with blurred boundaries, into a clear figure.

But aquifers can be particularly uncooperative when humans try to clearly delineate them. Few environmental entities seem so unattached from the density of life that saturates the biosphere. Due to their location under the surface of the earth, aquifers occupy a peculiar symbolic place. Their invisibility to the naked eye makes stark how embedded aquifers are in the specific political and scientific histories through which they become recognizable. At once fundamental to life and hidden from it, we often make aquifers thinkable as infrastructures; as reservoirs of water for human use.

Infrastructures have been theorized as arrangements with the capacity to produce and circulate value (Marx 1976), as entities with the power to bring about social meaning (Jakobson 1980; Kockelman 2013), and as matter with the capability to move matter (Larkin 2004). Privileging functional capacities, these infrastructural concepts have also permeated environmental imaginaries. When taken as infrastructures, environmental entities are conceived via their function: maximizing, minimizing, interrupting, or transforming life. In these function-centered imaginaries aquifers take the form of receptacles that store water; they are described as tank-like entities sitting in pause until humans use them according to our needs and desires.

But on top of these functional capabilities, infrastructures are also powerful material forms where social consciousness about desired futures and the order of political life are lived, opened up, or closed off (Coleman 2014). So when we take an aquifer as an infrastructure, we also create a space where the principles along which people organize political, material, and epistemic orders can be accessed and clarified not only analytically but also practically, in this case both by the Sardinal neighbor and the anthropologist alike. In this sense, when people privilege function as they trace the ways in which an aquifer is turned into infrastructure, we can access some of the ontological assumptions inscribed in such figuration. But it is important to not lose sight of the fact that when those assumptions become apparent, the limits and excesses that come with them are also revealed. In the case at hand, the ways in which people attempt to make underground water a clear, functioning infrastructure make apparent the difficulties in doing so, the ambiguities of dissolution that keep water embedded in its grounds, and the tendency of an aquifer to dissolve, troubling, though not necessarily preventing, our aspiration of turning it into a clearly defined infrastructural object.

This chapter is concerned with the possibility of knowing aquifers without reducing them to an infrastructural function. It highlights the moments when it is difficult to bound the aquifer as such. But I will not argue for a radically different ontological order in which aquifers are alternative earth beings (see, for example, de la Cadena 2015a). Instead, my interest is to trace the moments when the Sardinal aquifer resists being "infrastructuralized," a process that troubles efforts to single out legally and technically the function that an entity plays in sustaining life, more often than not, human life.[3] This process of infrastructuralization depends, to a large extent, on the possibility of separating figure from ground, an infrastructure from its background. Just like the water we poured into the hole we carved for our infiltration tests, underground water has a material tendency to dissolve; to confuse figure and ground. Once it moves out of sight, water becomes an aquifer that in Sardinal is activated through lack of employment, agricultural practices, state science, and transnational capital.

Attending to that material and political proclivity to dissolve requires that we think about the dissolution of water into underground worlds and about the dissolution of angry residents into historical space. In Sardinal, dissolution was most evident when data couplings broke and returned numeric accounts of what an aquifer is to the materiality of subsurface structures; when assumptions about entrepreneurial well-being were questioned and emplaced among contradicting ideas of collective life grounded in local histories; when geologic scales were revealed to be arbitrary, turned inside out, and shown as nested forms that could not be separated from each other. Rather than taking these moments as minor events with little significance, I want to stay close to them. I want to dwell in them because they challenge the seamless separation between the aquifer as a figure and the subsurface as its ground. Together those moments pose questions about the very limits of figure/ground separations as means for infrastructural analysis. They remind us of the arbitrary, yet inevitable, cuts we make as we single out an infrastructure as a figure and invite us to attend more carefully to the alternate possibilities inscribed in those cuts.

To trace this project I follow the public life of the technolegal struggle to define the Sardinal aquifer. My purpose is not to offer an ethnography of scientific practice that documents all the existing, but left aside, scientific knowledge about Guanacaste and the watershed where Sardinal is located. Instead, I am interested in the moment when select technoscientific reports, with particular visions of aquifers, are introduced into the legal struggle to turn the aquifer into a viable infrastructural figure. In what follows I remain attentive to those technoscientific reports and how the knowledge (the figures) they propose dissolve. Exploring the trouble those moments engender in the heart of the bureaucratic and technoscientific apparatus short-circuits any smooth reliance on infrastructure to make sense of the "environment."

The chapter begins by thinking through the presumptions of figure-ground reversals and their relevance for infrastructural analysis. I then provide some historical background to the Sardinal underground water crisis and its connections to the expanding luxury real estate boom that has swept over certain areas in the province of Guanacaste. With that political and bureaucratic history in place, I then return to the technical challenges of figuring the aquifer out from its background and to the ontohistorical stickiness that results from its tendency to dissolve. I do so by looking at two technical studies attempting to conceptually define the aquifer and by following some of the reactions they generated. I conclude with some thoughts on the relation between functional imaginaries, figure/ground reversals and the possibilities these open for alternative underground figurations.

A Figure and Its Ground

In his groundbreaking study of knowledge production infrastructures in the oil industry, Geoffrey Bowker (1994) proposed a shift in our analysis of how major scientific and technical innovations develop. Instead of chronicling the story of a technological innovation by focusing on how an "inventor," "scientist," or collective went about developing their technology, he argued that we needed to redirect our attention toward the standards, norms, and other techniques that made it possible to work on the generation of a new technology in the first place. He showed how bureaucratic and organizational tools—such as timelines, memos, and standards—create the necessary administrative, technical, and bureaucratic infrastructures for the figure that we finally come to recognize as an invention to emerge. Turning our attention to that infrastructure, Bowker argued, performs an analytic approach he called "infrastructural inversion." With Susan Leigh Star, Bowker (1999: 34) later expanded the idea to note that the inversion strategy entails attending to the "depths of interdependence of technical networks and standards" as well as to "the real work of politics and knowledge production practices" in the emergence of new technologies. Performing this type of inversion, the authors tell us, "foregrounds these normally invisible Lilliputian threads and furthermore gives them causal prominence in many areas usually attributed to heroic actors, social movements, or cultural mores" (Bowker and Star 1999: 34). Star and Bowker's call for infrastructural inversions has resonated widely in science and technology studies (STS) and anthropology showing us the "boring" systems that make possible so many of the technological achievements of our time. I build on this tradition to ask a related, but different question.

What if we were to begin by asking where does the possibility of an inversion come from in the first place? What presuppositions are in place in the invitation to perform figural inversions? Figure-ground reversals, with their ensuing separations, ask us to alternate between viewpoints that summon "worlds or value systems at once seemingly different from, yet also comparable to, each other" (Strathern 2002: 93). Shifts between figure and ground do more than invert orders. They index a form of meaning transformation that speaks less of the contents of the figure or ground and more about people's capacity to effect the transformation in the first place; they reveal the capacity to effect a reversal (Wagner 1987: 62). One way to think about people's capacity to perform that reversal is by searching for the existence of a sliver of space between one and the other, some level of separation between figure and ground. That separation is a trademark of modern knowledge that underlies much anthropological analysis through ideals of text and context, and event and history. We do so by presuming that at some point figure and background, text and context, do not touch, that they are separated. We place an object or subject in a larger context, culture, landscape, or history. We accept this separation almost instinctively, without worrying that were that separation to disappear, an object and the larger domain where we locate it would be nothing more than a never-ending continuum.

The renewed interest in the human sciences on materials and their properties (Bennett 2010; Ingold 2012) introduces interesting twists to our usual ways of separating figure from ground. In some circumstances the possibility of reversing them is no longer self-evident. The sliver separating an object from its background seems impossible to grasp. Here, the infrastructural inversion that Bowker and Star invite us to perform can seem difficult to enact.

This is particularly so with water, a substance that cannot escape its proclivity to change form, to seep and soak. And this is even more so for aquifers. In Costa Rica, aquifers are seldom bounded by impermeable and clear layers of rock as confined aquifers are. Their location (under the earth's surface) and their inherently dynamic form (consisting of porous boundaries facilitating ongoing movement) require a less taken-for-granted process of figuration.

Because of their direct inaccessibility to the embodied senses, underground formations, such as aquifers, are particularly uncooperative figures for those of us trying to understand their material semiotic lives. The infiltration tests we conducted in Sardinal were part of a larger effort to put such a figure together by collecting, combining, and circulating numeric data. The image those data were called to produce was not visual in the classic sense of the word. The inaccessibility of the aquifer to direct sensual perception—to sight, touch and hearing—demands another form of seeing.

Courts in Costa Rica were emphatic and explicit about this. In many of their rulings they emphasized the need to see the materiality of the aquifer "conceptually," as many hydrogeologists insisted to me during our conversations. The data we collected through our infiltration tests would help make the aquifer emerge from its dense background of engineering plans, historical dispossession, rock and salt. They would create enough separation between figure and ground so that the aquifer could be carved out of its ground.

Creating such separations is not an easy task. If we do not think of aquifers as clear containers, we begin to see them differently, maybe as sticky entities; as figures whose material separation from a background is not completely intuitive. Unconfined aquifers defy becoming straightforward figures separated from their background because they are ground themselves and for that reason are better imagined through the ambiguities of dissolution. Those ambiguities are twofold. First, aquifers are materially ambiguous because it is very difficult to find the exact point at which the water, air, rock combination that we call an aquifer ends, and another formation, maybe an impermeable border, begins. For the aquifer to remain a clear-cut figure without privileging a functionally determined existence, that border would have to be determined all around it, not only in a few locations. Seldom can such borders be specified, largely because of the high financial investment required to do so. But even if theoretically that definition is possible, in concrete cases it is rarely established. Second, aquifers also are historically ambiguous. When could we say the Sardinal aquifer begins? In its geologic origins? With the conflicts that erupted in 2008? With the legal definition of water as a public good in the 1980s? Since it is implicated in all of these sociomaterial configurations, how do we place it in time? A functionalist account would read this history via an aquifer's capacity to provide water for humans. An account that considers its historical dissolution would require data that goes beyond human use. Those ambiguities, material and historical, challenge the process of figuring out the aquifer as a clearly defined entity at the center of a legal, technical, and political conflict. Particularly, in the historic conjuncture of Sardinal, these ambiguities lead us to ask what kind of inversion could you perform if the exact contour of a figure is not fully determinable?

Underground Crises

In the province of Guanacaste, Costa Rica's driest region, underground water has long captured people's attention. Well drilling has been a secure line of business for generations. In Sardinal, for example, there are more than two hundred registered wells; the number of unregistered ones is a mystery that no one dares to quantify. Each of those wells is an opening, a threshold through which the surface and the subsurface transition into each other. As Kim de Rijke et al. (de Rijke, Munro, and Melo Zurita 2016) note, wells call attention to a "vertical dimension" that creates a three-dimensional assemblage of "relatively invisible subterranean water, technological developments and social dynamics" (3). Aquifers, and the wells through which we access them, open up this verticality and challenge the aesthetic horizontality of more familiar water bodies such as rivers, lakes, and creeks. Interrupting imaginaries of horizontal wayfaring (Ingold 2011) the cut of the well into the underground invokes a volumetric geometry of space where depth and time envelop and surround; wells highlight a vertical geopolitics that challenges planar perspectives (Braun 2000; Weizman 2003; Elden 2013b). That vertical geopolitics attunes us to the precarity of submergent forms of life such as the ones Zeiderman explores (this volume) to altogether banned forms of political insurgency through underground tunnels that resist the panoptic desires of imperial vision (Bishop 2011; Gordillo 2015). Against the precedence of the visual in panoptic politics, this politics of volume demands a form of nonvisual and circular awareness. Such awareness goes beyond seeing; it requires perception of what lies behind, above, to the sides, and below a particular point of view. It depends on deprivileging the frontal orientation that visual perception creates with its emphasis on what lies ahead in lines of sight. This volumetric politics of circular awareness invites us to understand a sense of being enfolded by our surroundings in a space that is not empty, but dense and potentially pushing against our skin if we were able to inhabit it without excavation. It entails a different form of conceptual vision.

Open toward the sky or covered with wood, zinc sheets or concrete lids, the vertical cuts wells make into the underground are the only means by which most residents of Guanacaste and the technical personnel of state agencies peek into the subterranean to begin to imagine its volumetric politics. This subsurface space is indexed by the mouth of a well, by the electric pump extracting water, and by the scientific inscriptions drawn from it. Otherwise, the underground is a resting place for friends and family and a starting point of the afterlife. Nationally, wells also index a space that in Costa Rica has not been completely colonized by extractive industries. A standing moratorium on oil exploration (in place by 2018, the moment of writing) and on open-pit mining keeps popular imaginaries of the underground detached from global mineral commodities and more often tied to water. Precisely because they invoke this geopolitics of the subsurface, the three new wells drilled near the town of Sardinal tipped what had been a long-standing conflict into what was termed by the media and public officials in 2009 as a "crisis."

But crises are never flat historical definitions. They are built on historical pivots, turning points when things went wrong, and by extension, hopes for new turning points when things can be made right (Roitman 2014: 10–12). Crisis overload can annihilate the possibility of imagining positive futurities as Masco (this volume) shows is the case for the United States, or can close off possibilities and impose a morality of urgency that telescopes history and makes some interventions seem inescapable. Among different crises, water ones are particularly powerful in restricting the topics that can be put on the table, the questions that can be asked, and what counts as a solution (imagine the difference between long-term land reform and emergency fund transfers as responses to the Sardinal crisis, for example). If there is a crisis, and life depends on water, there is no hesitation about cutting into the underground to extract water and sustain whatever is left of life. Water crises make the image of a world where plants and other beings outlive humans, as the Austrian artist Lois Weinberger (see Natasha Myers, this volume) invites us to do, anything but romantic. The path to a humanless world due to lack of water is saturated with the bodily effects of dehydration, the smelly traces left by the absence of adequate sanitation, and the unsightly images of dead animals. The path toward the annihilation of the "human" due to lack of water is a traumatic real.

Descriptions of water crisis that invoke these images, if not as actualized facts, as risks in the horizon, are powerful mobilizers. Fernando, the SAS scientist we met before, understood the political implications of crisis in so many words: "Water crises are very convenient for some people in Guanacaste," he told me. He was thinking of landowners and politicians who benefit from us "little people"—as he called concerned citizens, state officials, small farmers, and NGOs—quarreling about legality, technical studies, and ultimately water. "Fights amongst little people spare the five families that continue to own the whole province from being in the spotlight," he noted.

In such situations of water crisis, the underground becomes an infrastructural frontier, the location where hope for life can be found against its aboveground fragility. This perspective is not completely off. Globally, 99 percent of the world's freshwater reserves are underground (Kemper 2004: 4). When rains fail, aquifers support. Guanacaste confronts that failure cyclically. In August 2015, for instance, the province recorded a 70 percent deficit in rainfall. Only thanks to $18 million in emergency funds could many farmers and their livestock stay afloat. The rolling golf courses near the coast, however, remained green under the feet of tourists and expats on the verge of turning painfully red after too much golf under the stark sun of what used to be tropical dry forest.

Expansion and Improvement

Before any construction project is authorized in Costa Rica, its proponents need to secure a letter from the public utility or municipality responsible for providing water access in the area. The document, known as a "Water Availability" letter, certifies that at the moment of its writing, there is enough water for the planned construction. These letters have become hot commodities in coastal areas and are sometimes illegally sold for considerable amounts, since construction permits cannot be granted without them. In 2001, AyA, the country's largest utility stopped granting availability letters to new urbanizations, lot fractionings, or apartment complexes planning to use underground water. They made exceptions, however. If the proponents of a project conducted an "integral hydrogeological study" of the aquifer from which they planned to extract water, and if that study yielded the appropriate results, developers could be granted the letter and secure authorization to move forward.

This exception transformed hydrogeology into a vortex where multiple forces coalesced. The exception benefited large construction companies, which usually move into areas without public services to develop their projects. But despite being motivated by a desire to limit unplanned urban growth, the effects of the prohibition and its hydrological exception were mostly bureaucratic. The exception thickened the paper trail behind construction projects, but had minor effects on the real estate boom that Costa Rica experienced between 2001 and 2008, particularly in Guanacaste's coastal areas, regions that are particularly dependent on underground water.

Sardinal gets its water from an aqueduct originally built by the state in the 1960s.[4] It draws water from a local aquifer with the same name. The pipes, valves, and bills of the aqueduct are managed by a type of organization known as an Asociación Administradora de Sistemas de Acueductos y Alcantarillados Comunales (ASADA; Community Association for Aqueduct Management). In Costa Rica, there are thousands of ASADA groups responsible for supplying 35 percent of the country's population with water. They are often found outside major cities in rural areas and in the last two decades have been at the center of many controversies with developers and large scale agribusinesses. These associations are peculiar collectives. ASADAS are squarely recognized as community organizations, but they operate under the legal supervision of AyA. In practice, ASADAS are quite independent community organizations. They manage and physically maintain their aqueducts with the financial resources they collect from users. While the law dictates that AyA should provide them with technical supervision until very recently they rarely received that kind of support. Historically, ASADAS have had so little support from AyA that they commonly renounce their ties to the utility and refuse to abide by its authority, though this seemed to be changing by 2015. But at the time of the conflict, ASADAS like Sardinal's were more proud of defying AyA than of working with it.

In 2006 AyA signed a memorandum of understanding with a newly formed company called CocoWater S.A. Constituted by twenty-two private investors, mainly real-estate developers, CocoWater was created to secure water access for a series of new developments in the areas serviced by the old Sardinal aqueduct. The memorandum established that AyA and CocoWater S.A. would "collaborate" to expand the existing aqueduct and service new construction.

This memorandum is an example of how the fact that ASADAS are under the legal umbrella of AyA benefited investors. Using a legal mechanism prescribed in the Urban Planning Law adopted in the 1990s, CocoWater established a trust to manage $8 million that investors raised for the project. Article 38 of the Law allows private citizens and corporations to develop public infrastructures when they are not available in the areas where their projects would be developed. The mechanism dictates that once construction is finished the infrastructure has to be transferred to the utility for public ownership. Only under that property regime can infrastructures begin to operate. This also implies that, once active, the pipes and the accounting systems have to abide by the rules and regulations that public services are subject to. These regulations include the obligation to provide universal access to water and follow the principle of *servicio al costo* (service not for profit), a regulatory principle that outlaws utilities from profiting from public services such as water and electricity (Ballestero 2015).

Based on this legal mechanism, AyA and CocoWater promoted their project as an antiprivatization effort, even though the possibility of privatized, for-profit water infrastructures is outlawed in Costa Rica. But despite their public relations efforts, activists, Sardinal residents, and the ASADA unearthed a series of inconsistencies and illegalities that AyA and CocoWater explained as intrinsic to any innovative public-private collaboration. For instance, during the planning stage of the project the regional AyA office granted developers forty-nine water availability letters for more than two thousand new water connections to the proposed expansion. These letters effectively authorized the construction of condominiums, gated communities, resorts, and apartments that otherwise would have not received building permits. Further, CocoWater and AyA claimed their project did not qualify as a "new" development; instead, it was only an expansion of an existing infrastructure, and for that reason the project was not subject to the limitations that AyA itself had put in place in the early 2000s. Recall that at that time AyA had determined that any new project planning to use underground water required a comprehensive hydrogeological study to show the capacity of the aquifer to sustain water extraction sustainably. Using the claim that they were merely "expanding" an existing aqueduct, and despite the absence of a hydrogeological study that determined whether the Sardinal aquifer could supply these massive new developments, AyA and CocoWater moved forward with construction. By early 2008 the aqueduct pipes had been expanded by more than 70 percent and they kept moving forward, getting closer, day by day, to the town of Sardinal where they would ultimately drill a well to tap into the aquifer. Torn streets, backhoes, and mechanical diggers escorted enormous pipes whose mere dimensions were enough to enlarge the concerns of an already-irked town. The speed, scale, and efficiency with which their cranky 1960s aqueduct was being "improved" to supply "the rich and the powerful" paired with the lack of knowledge about the situation of the aquifer outraged Sardinal residents and the ASADA.

Finally, in April 2008, people from Sardinal, nearby towns, and other parts of the country took to the streets, marching to demand a halt to the project. They drew enough national attention to mobilize a series of governmental institutions, including the Office of the Ombudsman [sic], the Procuraduría de la República, ministries, and the director and managers of AyA and SAS. Something else they drew was police presence. A contingent of the Guardia Civil was deployed to protect machinery and construction workers from angry demonstrators impeding any work. Rising in prominence to become one of the main referents for water conflicts in the country, the Sardinal case continues to garner attention, prompt legal processes, and set the tone for conflicts where scarcity is no longer accepted as a fact of nature but understood as the result of inequitable distribution of resources. With construction work halted by demonstrators, legal and political maneuvers unfolded from all directions until courts decided that "knowing" the aquifer was key for deciding whether to reopen or cancel the expansion project altogether; courts asked for an appropriate conceptualization of underground water sources.

Figuring Out the Underground

Envisioning aquifers depends on numeric, metallic, and plastic tools that scientists use to generate their subterranean imaginaries. In SAS those visions are constructed by mapping the displacement of water from one underground region to another and from an underground formation into the surface. Movement allows geologists to understand rocky structures. Because of their location within the state apparatus, the numeric models, maps, and diagrams scientists use to see the unseeable also have the power to yield rights, instill conditions of illegality, and set the material content of what a public good, like water, is.

Responding to a series of judicial requests made amidst the crisis of 2008, Costa Rica's Constitutional Court found CocoWater and AyA at fault for moving forward with construction without defining the conceptual model of the Sardinal aquifer. In a reversed process, a matter of concern had never been a matter of fact (Latour 2004b) and it needed to become one so that crisis could be transfigured into ordinary, everyday water management. The aquifer had to be pulled out of its messy historical and material ground so that rights, risks, and profits could be allocated. The court's decision requiring this information had two components. First, it instructed AyA and CocoWater to stop construction. And second, it mandated the public agencies with jurisdiction over water to develop an "integral conceptual hydrogeologic model" of the aquifer. The court activated the need for seeing the aquifer conceptually; the law became hydrogeological.

Hydrogeology is a discipline that is thoroughly aware of its own sensual limitations. Because the subterranean world is not "suitably scaled to the size, strength, shape, senses and even sapience of people" (Kockelman 2012: 179), its visualization depends on models of different sorts. Mathematic or physical, quantifying underground water flows or replicating the process of infiltration for educational purposes, models perform important epistemic work that not only makes things knowable, but brings into existence that which cannot be observed as a whole. The work models do is not reduced to merely re-presenting an already existing entity. They render a particular world "visible, tangible, and workable" (Myers 2015d:18). Models are foundational for entities that do not seem self-evident to the human sensorium. Aquifers are entities of that type. They present the challenge of being neither manageable as things nor subject to inhabitation. They are never perfectly sizable, nor are they large-scale formations that encompass us, like weather, biosphere, or economy. This impossibility of directly observing them has led hydrogeologists to use conceptual models as a way of knowing without seeing visually.

But the subsurface world is vast. Certain subterranean structures (e.g., tunnels and pipes) have become familiar enough so that their presumed functions—moving materials or announcing the presence of the state—can be easily (mis)recognized. Marilyn Strathern (2002) explains that such intuitive and seamless recognition is possible due to a cultivated capacity to avoid the confusion of "focusing on this or that as figure to ground because there is one very evident 'depth' already there that appears not to depend on interpretation at all" (103) An underground pipe, for example, clearly stands out against the volumetric ground that envelops it. It is easy for us to recognize because we intuitively perceive the sliver that separates it from its ground.

That depth, that separation, is largely the result of our familiarity with its functionality as a vehicle for moving water and sewage. That does not imply that the social life of a pipe is always predictable. As Anand (this volume) shows, water lines can do many things, including "reveal the limits of modernist technologies of control, categorization, and representation."

Another discipline that is also concerned with the underground and the figures inhabiting it, albeit following a different logic, is archaeology. As a field of inquiry and a set of assumptions about the world, archaeology is committed to separating figure from ground below the surface of the earth. Paul Kockelman (2012) tells us that archaeology is interested in things that did not die, assuming that death is the act of becoming in equilibrium with an environment. The objects archaeologists pursue have to stand out from their environments (grounds) to be able to narrate histories of other objects that have become inseparable from their environment, beings that have died. For Kockelman there must be a difference in liveliness (178), however small or large, for an object to be recognizable from its environment. Or, in Strathern's terms, that differential is the condition of possibility for the necessary depth to distinguish figure from ground.

With the right amount of magnification and a cultivated, specialized form of perception, the ontological condition of standing against a background can be seen at practically any scale. We can say that it is always possible to create an environment for any object, even if the borders between them are open and ambiguous. But even if this is theoretically possible and even if we had the back-up of magnification tools and specialized concepts, some formations make the task of separating them from their environment conceptually difficult: underground water is that type of formation.

To understand water in its underground environment, and render the separation between figure and ground visible, hydrogeology has to deal with interesting dilemmas. Unlike archaeology, its objects cannot be instinctually separated from their environments because, as it were, they are the environment. There is no liveliness axis along which to separate one from the other, to separate water from soil and rock under the surface. Their material liveliness dissolves into each other, their borders are so ambiguous that they become difficult to place. Costa Rican aquifers tend to be all ground, the depth that separates them from their ground is never self-evident. Unlike the weedy infrastructures that Carse (this volume) analyzes, where the weed is available to the human sensorium, aquifers are not readily available for perception. Thus, the differential by which an aquifer becomes an object distinguishable from its ground has to be conceptually crafted. The process demands a considerable amount of interpretive energy. Now, returning to the Sardinal aquifer, a question remains: What is the aquifer standing against when it is distributed liquid across different rock densities and empty spaces? What is its environment if its borders, its lively differentials, are not distinct? And, how is that separation enacted in water conflicts that are legally and scientifically mediated?

Thinking with Sponges

While we discussed in his office the steps they were going to take to produce the conceptual model of the Sardinal aquifer courts had asked for, Fernando suggested I imagine subterranean water by thinking with sponges. Initially, this seemed to me an incredible poetic license. Sponges are extremely dynamic entities: they suck liquids in and leak their excess toward the environment; they are expanding and contracting structures. Sponges stand for water movement and changing volumes. In my unspecialized imagination, underground formations were sedentary lithic fixities. That apparent immobility, however, was due to the unavailability to our very human senses of the temporal and physical scales at which their movements occur. As our conversations continued, Fernando helped me see underground formations through spongy figures that I later realized were very dear materials and models for hydrogeologists.

Water presence under the surface of the earth tends to be imagined as sitting in pocket-like formations, as sealed tanks holding water for our enjoyment. And yet, as we have seen the spatial and volumetric existence of an aquifer can be much messier. Instead of neat and clearly delimited units, aquifers can be irregular and unwieldy structures. They can be combinations of materials (sand, rock, gravel, for example) and empty spaces that blur differences between content and container. Here, an aquifer's borders are ambiguous, determined by the movement of water across volumetric space. When we privilege these flows, and not their lithic structure, aquifers are nothing but water exceeding their supposed borders. The time frame and speed of that movement vary widely, from a few months to hundreds of thousands of years, even creating in the deep underground something people imagine as "fossil water" (Brooks 2016). Nevertheless, it is that movement, or lack thereof, across subsurface geologic space and sometimes into the surface of the earth that determines their hydrogeologic existence. This ontological indeterminacy (Schrader 2010), form being set by overflowing borders, challenges any seamless infrastructuralization of unconfined aquifers. It troubles our habit of analogizing them with tanks, it interrupts any smooth figure-ground inversion.

To make sense of the blurred boundaries of aquifers, Fernando directed me to Costa Rica's somewhat recent geologic history and how a significant part of the country's subsurface territory is constituted by volcanic rock formations with porous textures. As we sat at his desk, Fernando insisted on explaining the permeability of volcanic rocks, how they are highly permeable, and how they look a lot like kitchen sponges. Their interior is open, occupied by water and air. In those structures water migrates through variegated openings, it steps in where space becomes available, colonizing possible nooks, flowing into more open locations, saturating small particles, pushing against walls, and being pushed away (up, down, or laterally) by new molecules. Our fascinating spongy conversation unfolded while nearby Fernando's office mates continued with their daily tasks: taking calls, asking for files, and coordinating transportation for their next field trip.

But despite their structural correspondence with Costa Rican aquifers, sponges are not legitimate conceptual models for legal institutions that settle questions of profit and harm. The conceptual model that courts and to an extent also community members expected was a mathematically developed one that sidestepped the problem that blurred boundaries and flow pose for tank-like imaginaries. The vision of the aquifer they wanted was literally a figure, a number that could represent the function of the aquifer as a container that is distinct from the ground in which it sits. That figure was the water extraction rate, a clear number that is incompatible with a dissolved image of an aquifer as a sticky formation impossible to detach from its grounds. Explaining the demand for such figure, Fernando showed me a key study in the legal file of the Sardinal case in the Constitutional Court which, he thought, would clarify his point.

Figure 1.2 comes from that study. It describes the geologic profile of the Sardinal area. In it we can see the subsurface as a series of layers differentiated with different sizes of dots. Two things are intriguing here. First, note that the combination of rock, dirt, and potentially water plays a cognitive trick on us. There is no self-evident ground or figure. Water and rock, structure and

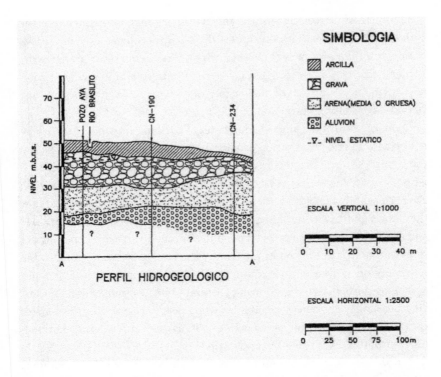

Figure 1.2. Geological profile of Sardinal Aquifer. From Schosinsky Nevermann (2008: 12).

movement, texture and border struggle for our attention with similar force. There is no self-evident figure to focus on, no self-evident way to differentiate what is background when all is ground. When saturated with water underground textures seem to become figure to a watery ground. But if we concentrate and try to privilege what would be water in the diagram, the rocky textures and layers become background. We can see in this image how figure and ground can be inverted, over and over, endlessly, and continuously. The ambiguity of the inversion reveals the difficulty in separating one from the other. The smoothness of the inversion erodes the power of the analytic maneuver. In a strange way, it reinforces the inseparability of one from the other. It makes us see the radical replaceability of one ground with another.

The second thing that draws our attention is the unknown base on which the aquifer rests. The question marks on the lower layer of the drawing announce our lack of knowledge about what underpins (?), pushes (?), upholds (?) the aquifer, leaving one to question the existence of the border in the first place. Those question marks are cognitive/material reminders of the continuity of the aquifer and our difficulty in determining the boundaries, the sliver of a separation, that allow dislodging it from its ground.

(Onto)Historical Stickiness

With sponges and mathematical models in mind we can now think about two figurations of the Sardinal aquifer that were crucial in the conflict. They come from two reports in the legal case that temporarily settled the dispute. The reports were submitted early on in the legal process communities initiated to halt the expansion of the aqueduct. As artifacts of modern knowledge (Riles 2006), the reports created distinct figures by not only embodying intense past social relations but also by scientifically and legally regimenting future actions. The reports held the power to instill particular forms of being, of seeing the architectural landscape, and of ignoring particular histories in Sardinal (Hetherington 2011; Hull 2012). And, because of their legal authority, the documents also had the capacity to materially shape the aquifers through the agencies and powers that they reinforced or weakened.

The first report was produced by the hydrogeology team of AyA and the second by a technoscientific commission comprising representatives of five public agencies. Both reports, though taking different routes, end by referring to charge and discharge rates, a volume/speed measure of water's movement in and out of the aquifer's spongy formation. The possibility of sustainable water extraction depends heavily on this figure. In the end, both studies concluded that there was enough water for the expansion of the aqueduct. But here I am interested in going beyond the issue of extraction rates to avoid reducing the aquifer to that figure, to its infrastructural function. Despite appearances, the difference between these two reports is not merely quantitative, as in allowing more or less water extraction. In each report, the aquifer remains enmeshed in grounds that go beyond the documents in which they are recorded and which cannot be dislodged through more technoscience or by arriving at a more "adequate" extraction rate. That is, the contradiction between the two reports cannot be resolved by doing "better" science and is about more than the magnitude of the extraction rate they recommend. The contradiction between the reports is about the aquifer's tendency to dissolve into its political and lithic grounds. Keeping our thinking about the aquifer enmeshed in those grounds reveals how its very materiality is not only tied to the institutional origin of their authors, but also to different forms of geological adequacy and holism, and ultimately to the difficulties inherent to delineating its presence apart from its ground. In Sardinal, the aquifer is all ground; it is all figure.

REPORT #1

The first conceptualization of the Sardinal aquifer was proposed by AyA in a report they produced soon after the 2008 conflict erupted. Here, the aquifer is figured as a single macroentity whose properties and qualities are determined at the scale of regional subterranean formations and institutional origins. Relying on data previously collected by the utility's hydrogeologists, the study places the aquifer inside an area "of interest" of 299 km². Characterizing its rock formations, the report describes the age and texture of the underground in terms of regional structures (e.g., Nicoya complex). By dissolving into an area much larger than the Sardinal basin, the aquifer is one with the geological structures it shares with neighboring territories. Hydrogeologists of the SAS found this scale and characterization inadequate because despite its concern with context it excluded from the analysis the aquifer's dynamic relation with neighboring water bodies, particularly, the impact that extracting water from Sardinal would have on neighboring Ocotal and El Coco aquifers closer to the coast. This AyA report focused on lithic continuities, determining the lively differential necessary to distinguish figure from ground by comparing rock to rock. On the other hand, the SAS hoped to see that difference as one of water on water, the relation of underground water in Sardinal with underground water in the immediately adjacent coastal area. The augmentation of territorial scale that AyA performed turned the aquifer into one with its lithic architecture, with the effect that the granularity of information produced about the specific movement of water between the Sardinal, Ocotal and El Coco aquifers was minimal.

Temporally, the report was also controversial. To determine the quantity of water available for extraction from the Sardinal aquifer, AyA used meteorological data from the early 1980s. Rainfall information is basic to calculate a sustainable extraction rate, since it constitutes the only recorded inflow of water into the aquifer. That inflow produces a "rejected" water rate, the amount of water that after saturation can no longer go into the aquifer. Ideally, the extraction rate from the Sardinal aquifer should be limited to the amount of "rejected" water to prevent depletion and secure its sustainability. But because the meteorological data lacked records of important changes in rain patterns registered in the last two decades, the conceptual model this report produced was tainted with what critics referred to as imprecision and "outdatedness." By relying on data from the 1980s, the aquifer as a concept was "old," certainly not in the geologic sense, but according to the temporality of the crisis and the legal demands of the court. This reinforced the sense some people had that AyA did not perform its due diligence when granting water availability letters.

As part of the technical consultations undertaken to evaluate AyA's study, the report was sent to an academic from the University of Costa Rica for review. His report characterized the study as "subjective" and also noted that AyA's study lacked a proper "hydrogeologic conceptualization." But what this academic saw as a lack was, in fact, a problem of adequacy. There was a conceptualization in place, just not one that was "adequate" to the hydrogeologic norms necessary for constituting a stable enough figure.

This lack of adequacy indexed another dimension along which this aquifer was especially sticky and most scandalously so: the continuity between this conceptualization, in its numeric representation, and AyA itself. Because the study was conducted by AyA hydrogeologists, and given that the utility's president had repeatedly expressed his support for the CocoWater alliance, opponents, scholars, and other governmental entities harbored profound doubts about the reports' findings. They saw the study as an extension of a group of people who institutionally, though not necessarily at a personal level, had vested interests in making the project go forward. Instead of being dissolved into notions of sustainability, the aquifer was dissolved into what many saw as AyA's suspicious support for CocoWater.

These material and historic continuities prevented the hydrogeologic model of this study from emerging out of the entangled ground on which it was enmeshed. The functionalist desire for containing the aquifer as a clear figure was confounded by old data, lack of attention to water-to-water continuities (influence of one aquifer on the next), and institutional commitments to transnational capital. This prevented the numeric figure the study proposed, the quantity of liters of water/second that can be extracted sustainably, from being recognized by the courts or community as an appropriate hydrogeologic model of the aquifer itself; as an acceptable figure.

Another attempt to produce an "integral conceptual model" of the aquifer yielded a report that was authored by the same group of AyA hydrogeologists along with technical personnel from another four institutions: SAS, the Water Department of the Environment Ministry, the National Meteorological Institute, and the protected areas and national parks administration. Ultimately, this report also supported the general findings of the first one, concluding that it was possible to extract water to supply the new developments that Coco-Water was fighting for—though it arrived at a much smaller acceptable extraction rate. This report is a fascinating combination of ambiguities. It arrives at a conclusion, yet, it also notes that for an even better conclusion to be arrived at it is necessary to better conceptualize the aquifer. The report added to AyA's regional geologic approach an analysis of the "water on water" differential that SAS was looking for. It reviewed the potential impact of increasing extraction from Sardinal on neighboring Ocotal and El Coco aquifers. These coastal formations were at high risk of saline contamination and required more sophisticated modeling to be understood. The report also considered the legal and administrative rules that applied to the trust CocoWater had established. It included a narrative of the origin of the conflict, a history of the creation and workings of a special Sardinal commission, a management plan for the Brasil and Sardinal Rivers, a meteorological data management plan (in response to the outdatedness of AyA's data), a water-quality management plan, and a detailed description of the technical standards for aqueduct expansion. Constitutional norms, international agreements, best practices, and climate change scenarios were also included.

The richness of dimensions, topics, and points of view represented in the report had the effect of blurring the borders of the aquifer along many more dimensions than the first report did. The purpose was to infuse a sense of comprehensiveness, to counterbalance the brevity of AyA's original study. This aesthetic of comprehensiveness percolated throughout the sixty-five page document.

Yet, the more dimensions added to ground the aquifer, the more questions and doubts emerged. The ambiguities that in the first report were material and historical along basically two axes, rock-on-rock differences in data and institutional continuities, were now multiplied. Those opposing CocoWater's development plans found in the report references to many of the associated questions that were brought to the table by the conflict. Concerns with employment, education, deforestation, corruption, disorganized development, political climate, climate change, and many more were now the historical grounds of the aquifer.

Here, the aquifer again resisted its total infrastructuralization by refusing to become a docile extraction rate. While in a narrow sense that figure existed—it was produced by both reports—its material, social, legal, and political existence could never be reduced to the function of providing water in the here and now. The figure of a contained tank was insufficient to approximate the aquifer. Its indeterminate borders, constant material movement, and historical embeddedness prevented its reductive interpretation as a reservoir for water extraction.

By 2010 courts ruled on the actions that had paralyzed construction. No further development could continue until an integral underground monitoring plan was launched and enough data collected to produce an adequate hydrogeological conceptualization that would yield a trustable figure in the form of an extraction rate. As a result of that legal process, SAS also decided to outsource to a Portuguese consulting firm the design of a new underground water modeling and monitoring system for another area of the country. The water resources office in the Environment Ministry, for its part, launched an initiative to centralize data on the Tempisque Basin that were disseminated in different institutions (including the Instituto Costarricense de Electricidad—the entity responsible for managing the Arenal Dam that feeds the Tempisque River—and the Organization of Tropical Studies—a research entity that has been working on conservation issues on the lower Tempisque Basin for decades). The decision also propelled a series of institutions already concerned with water management in the Tempisque Basin to pool their resources and put in place an updated monitoring system to understand and secure the sustainability of underground water sources in the broader watershed Sardinal is a part of. That process started in 2012, and by 2015 the first data from the underground monitoring network were being collected in Nicoya, another city in Guanacaste.

But more than the legal decision of 2010, it was the financial crisis what was responsible for what transpired after 2009 in Sardinal. The crisis reduced the pressures brought by golfers, surfers, and retirees on Guanacaste. Developers slowed down and in some instances abandoned their projects, leaving them unfinished. After that, the most profound drought in Guanacaste's history hit the region further busting dreams of quick "returns on investment." As a result of that drought, long-standing plans to dam water in the basin were revived, and in 2015 the government announced that the Río Piedras Dam was a priority, launching a series of technical studies to determine its viability. Today, the area is thriving with research activity, promises for new and more accurate information, and reignited fears of a new development boom that would demand communities to mobilize again.

Conclusion

While above the surface of the earth objects help humans consider their presence by insinuating themselves to our senses of sight, smell, touch, or hearing, subsurface entities have material forms that can only be inferred conceptually. Below the surface it is tricky to sense figure from ground, object from environment. When separating one from the other, functionalist assumptions become very handy. In the case of aquifers, our attention is quickly directed to their capacity to operate as infrastructures that store water for human needs; their function shapes our proclivities to see them as container-like entities. But despite the power of this logic, aquifers create difficulties for the functionalist paradigm. Their tendency to material and historical dissolution gets in the way. Aquifers are, in a sense, nothing but movement and overflowing boundaries. They are water dissolved in rocky structures with borders that are difficult to pinpoint. Historically, aquifers dissolve into geologic time and into the temporality of crisis, with its emphasis on legal and technical pivot points and events. They are entities with the capacity to dissolve in time and matter in multiple ways.

In this chapter I have opened up the relation between aquifers and infrastructure using a negative analytics. I have traced the moments in which the clarity about the function of an aquifer as a reservoir is troubled, and as a result the possibility of placing it as a figure against a distinct ground fades. I think of those moments as instances in which an aquifer resists its infrastructuralization. By first examining the necessary step of separating figure from ground, I showed how that separation is difficult to assert for aquifers, entities that require a circular awareness and vertical geopolitics both of which challenge planar perspectives and separations between object and environment. I then showed the historical and political grounds from which people try to dislodge an aquifer in the process of conceptualizing it. Economic asymmetries, transnational movements of people, and kitchen sponges help us see its ontohistorical stickiness and also reveal the technical grounds, as inscribed in two reports, to which it remains attached. As I hope to have shown, aquifers are nested figures in nested grounds that demand a form of attention that is capable of embracing not only historical but also physical dissolution.

The case of Sardinal also shows how once we resist the clear separations between figure and ground that infrastructural analyses rely upon, we need other forms of sensing and knowing that can open spaces for ways of acting that do not merely reproduce what already is. In those imaginaries, kitchen sponges, onto historical stickiness, and circular awareness can sway the sometimes narrow and often reproductive focus of infrastructural analysis.

In Sardinal, diverse groups of people demand better conceptual models of the aquifer. But those models are not to be improved by insisting on the clear figure/ground separation that the materiality and historicity of the aquifer challenges. The hope is for conceptual models that have the capacity of rendering the stickiness characteristic of underground formations. The demand is for conceptual models that avoid the artificial reduction of dynamic and dissolved material/historical worlds into something like a water extraction rate. Recognizing that aquifers are not dislodgeable from their ground does not mean that they are unknowable entities. It only entails challenging their reducibility to a figure (numeric or not), a minor demand that has the transformative potential of destabilizing blind beliefs and disbeliefs in technoscience alike—blind rebuttals of the physical limits of water as well as blind rebuttals of the sociality of aquifers. In Sardinal, the struggle over the circular awareness aquifers demand kept NGOs, technocrats, corporate actors, and courts tied to an underground only knowable through dissolution; an aquifer with the capacity to become more than it already was, an aquifer with the potentiality of precipitating new forms of water technopolitics.

Notes

1 Sardinal is part of the Tempisque River Basin of the Guanacaste province in Costa Rica.
2 I have created SAS as a pseudonym to refer to a governmental institution that participates in the study and management of underground water.
3 I want to thank Martin French for suggesting the idea of "resisting infrastructuralization."

4 Sardinal sits on the edge of the Tempisque Basin, a region tied to the fate of the Tempisque River, with its intermittent levels. The river's flow depends greatly on Costa Rica's national electricity institute and the upstream reservoir it manages near the Arenal Volcano. Releasing or withholding water according to power demands in the rest of the country, the reservoir shapes downstream water availability for farmers and wildlife in the Palo Verde National Park.

TWO. Clandestine Infrastructures

Illicit Connectivities in the US-Mexico Borderlands

SHAYLIH MUEHLMANN

I began doing research in northern Mexico in 2003, before the militarization of the "war on drugs" by the Mexican government in 2006 and before the more spectacular instances of narco-violence in the region started making international headlines. At the time I was analyzing water scarcity and a fishing conflict between an indigenous Cucapá village and the government. I was initially fairly oblivious to the physical traces of the drug trade around me, even though these traces related to the environmental devastation of the region.

But eventually the marks of the drug trade were too obvious and salient on the landscape to ignore. For instance, during the first few months of my field-work I noticed that on any dirt road that was built up through the desert—to fishing camps or smaller settlements—there were always small ditches gauged out of the surface. I found these ditches puzzling because this was the most unvegetated and uninhabited part of the Sonoran Desert located

Figure 2.1. Furrow in the desert. Photo by the author.

in the dried-up riverbed of what used to be the lush delta of the Colorado River. I also noticed that sometimes these notches were cut out of expanses of packed-down mud and desert that were not necessarily roads at all. They were clearly human made and created to make mobility difficult, for they formed hazardous mud reservoirs in the very short rainy season and were always rough on a vehicle's shocks (see figure 2.1).

When I finally asked residents what these ditches were for, they explained that they are dug out by the military to prevent illegal planes carrying drugs from landing. In this region surrounding the mouth of the Gulf of California, planes are one of the main ways to get large shipments of drugs up past the military roadblocks toward the US border. Mexican officials report that the country has destroyed nearly four thousand illegal airstrips since 2006 (O'Neill McCleskey 2012). Interestingly, the ditches also show that the state has responded to this illicit infrastructure of clandestine landing strips with a widespread infrastructure of material modifications aimed at preventing motion.

This example highlights an important theme, central to this chapter, which analyzes the human and environmental infrastructures that connect the north of Mexico with the United States in one of the most heavily trafficked narco-routes in the world. Specifically, the example shows an instance of "doubling," which refers to the ways that infrastructures, ostensibly built for one purpose, can be used for a secondary purpose. The ditches in the desert show how local infrastructures such as roads, which are built with the intention of facilitating ground traffic, are often used as drug-trafficking routes, facilitating air traffic as well.

Of course, all infrastructure can have both intended and unintended purposes and uses, and the literature on the topic certainly provides copious documentation of this (for example, see De Boeck 2012; Harvey, Jensen, and Morita 2016; Dalakoglou and Kallianos 2014). Therefore, in a general sense, the uses of infrastructure are always not merely double but multiple. However, what I will argue here is that the infrastructures that are often crucial for the transportation of illicit drugs work through a specifically dyadic interplay. The doubling that is important in drug infrastructures is an instantiation of multiplicity, which is expressed through the relationship between the visible and the invisible. So, in relation to the example above, a road can function as all sorts of other infrastructures: a makeshift market (De Boeck 2012), a spatial poetics of road narratives (Dalakoglou and Kallianos 2014), a playspace for children (Wegman 1995), or a claim to territorial sovereignty (Kernaghan 2012), to name just a few. But none of these alternate uses depend in these cases specifically on the form of the road in order to function. A clandestine airstrip, to take the example above on the other hand, needs to look like a road so that it can also function—clandestinely—as an airstrip.

Another aspect of infrastructure I will draw out in this analysis is the extent to which infrastructure is formulated as "under the surface." Common metaphors present infrastructure as a substrate: something upon which something else "runs" or "operates," underneath the surface. All of these meanings glean their specificity from the prefix "infra-," which means "beneath." In other words, infrastructures often function beneath the conscious awareness of their users.

Indeed, one of the most well-known tropes in the literature, most famously articulated by Susan Star (1999), is that users of infrastructures such as highways, sewage systems, or bridges only notice them when they break down (see also Anand 2011; Barry 2006; Elyachar 2010; Mitchell 2009; Otter 2002, 2004a). In Star's words, an enduring property of infrastructure is that it is transparent to use and "only becomes visible upon breakdown" (Star 1999: 382). This is in part because people often experience infrastructure as behind the scenes, or as the background processes that necessarily go unnoticed in order to function smoothly (Bowker and Star 1994: 234).

Geoffrey Bowker and Star (1994: 234) urged us to invert our commonsense notions of infrastructure by taking what have often been seen as background processes and bringing their contribution to the foreground. But recent work by infrastructure scholars has been careful to point out that even smoothly functioning infrastructures are not invisible to everyone all the time (Edwards 2003: 188; Larkin 2013).[1] Instead the visibility of infrastructures is situated and determined by an actor's location, their assumptions, and the nature of their work (Star and Ruhleder 1996: 113). Furthermore, as Kregg Hetherington (2016) points out, the extent to which an infrastructure is invisible depends on its location in a "geography of uneven development," whereby in some places infrastructures' invisibility is always tenuous, and breakdown and repair are the norm (see also Harvey and Thompson 2005). He argues that infrastructures are better characterized as those structures that are "*supposed* to become invisible" (2016: 62).

In the previous and opening chapter of this book Ballestero questions the limits of figure/ground separations and inversions by exploring a case in which the process of delineating an aquifer from its ground becomes arbitrary and defies its tendency toward material and historical dissolution. Ballestero invites us to attend to the alternate possibilities such delineations, and thus "infrastructural inversions" in general, foreclose. In this chapter, I continue in this project of pushing at the limits of figure/ground reversals but approach this issue from a different angle. Specifically, I argue here that the concept of the infrastructural inversion also fails to reveal the particular dynamic that exists between backgrounded and foregrounded uses of infrastructures enrolled for drug trafficking on the US-Mexico border.

The material I analyze encourages a further engagement with the topic of invisibility rather than the kind of figure-ground reversal involved in an infrastructural inversion. Instead, I heed Harvey, Jensen, and Morita's (Harvey et al. 2016) call to attend, rather, to the "patterns of invisibility and visibility" to which infrastructural systems give rise, which in this case do not map neatly onto a interplay of figure and ground as in the case of inversion. Specifically, in many of the cases I will describe invisibility is not a product of the backgrounding of processes when functioning smoothly but is rather, as I will argue, a property deliberately sought after in the technical aspects of infrastructures themselves, which allows them to function as clandestine channels. Therefore, what makes this kind of invisibility different from what Bowker and Star describe is not that visibility is conversely related to functionality. Instead, certain kinds of functionality rely on a double usage enabled through a dialectic of visibility and invisibility.

The case of the materialities, conduits, vehicles, and environments mobilized by illegal organizations to move around illicit commodities in the US-Mexico borderlands reveals this dyadic interplay of invisibility/visibility in infrastructure at several levels. I will analyze the way in which the nature of trafficking infrastructures always plays on the interplay between visibility and invisibility because these infrastructures depend on making something knowable (a route, mode of exchange, or path of communication, for example) at the same time that it remains concealed.

The phenomenon of doubling provides an example of the multiple projects at work in knowing/concealing infrastructure. I will elaborate on three cases of doubling that raise important questions about the work that goes into making infrastructures visible at particular moments. First, I'll explore the case of "infrastructural hardwares," such as local roads, which sometimes lead double lives supporting the traffic of cars and trucks for which they are originally designed but also being used as landing strips for lightweight planes that need to alight under the radar of state authorities. This is also the case for the homes, trucks, and land that form part of the networks of drug-smuggling in this region.

Second, I will argue that the "natural environment," in this case the desert, also becomes part of the material infrastructure through which drugs are transported. The land itself, in other words, has become an infrastructural component of trafficking, in the sense that, as Larkin (2013) put it, it is matter that enables the mobility of matter. This confirms what has been noted by other authors: that "nature" can become infrastructure when placed in the context of particular networks of movement and exchange (see Carse, this volume; Braun and Wakefield, this volume). Yet, because this is a geography that is hard to navigate for those who do not know its texture and complexity, traffickers often seek to hire the local indigenous Cucapá people as guides because "they know the land."

As a result, and as a final example, the Cucapá people are also "doubled" in their infrastructural capacities, serving multiple projects both in the built environment through which they navigate physically and in the phatic and identity infrastructure of the people themselves. The Cucapá people's relation to drug-trafficking territories is a poignant example of these dynamics. Their knowledge of the terrain makes certain routes visible, while their indigeneity also conceals their activities from the state. I will show how this happens because they are romanticized as a "natural" element of the landscape in various ways and therefore sometimes escape being apprehended by other actors as infrastructure. This is because first, their indigeneity gives them a certain proprietary relationship with the land that can facilitate movement across a heavily surveilled territory. Second, their conflation with the landscape also gives them a strategic inscrutability that allows them to be opaque when they want to be (as well as when they do not want to be).

In bringing together these themes, in this chapter I explore the ways in which the illicit infrastructures mobilized by narco-trafficking organizations complicate notions of invisibility and functionality raised by the literature on infrastructure. I will do so by showing how multiple drug war actors with conflicting interests and engaged in heterogeneous practices reveal infrastructures that by their very nature can never, simultaneously, function according to everyone's plans.

~~~~~~~~

The area where I have done my fieldwork has become, in the past two decades, especially since the crackdown on Colombian drug-trafficking organizations and the disruption of their traditional routes through the Caribbean and South Florida, one of the main corridors through which drugs are smuggled into the United States (see map 2.1). As I argue in *When I Wear My Alligator Boots* (2013a), one of the consequences of this traffic is that local people, indigenous and nonindigenous, have become involved in the trade, working in the lower echelons of cartels as poorly paid "mules" who often end up in jail. This is especially the case in areas that have experienced other kinds of economic and environmental pressures such as the fishing regions around the former mouth of the Colorado. What I did not get to analyze in that book is the spatiality and materiality of the infrastructure, legal and illegal, visible and invisible, mobilized by cartels to move and store the huge quantities of drugs passing through the region.

What's noteworthy about the role of infrastructure in this context is that on the one hand, these organizations use legal and visible infrastructural channels, nodes, and vehicles whose existence they appropriate for their own

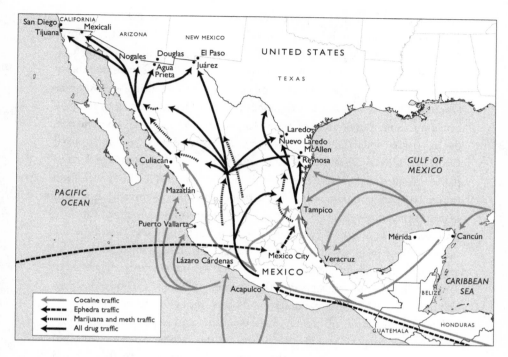

Map 2.1. Major drug-trafficking routes through Mexico.

practices. This is the phenomenon of doubling noted by several authors working in African studies, such as Achille Mbembe, whereby systems are made
to operate in variance with their purported original objective (see Mbembe
and Roitman 1995; Mbembe 2001). For example, Mbembe (2001) describes
how in South Africa, infrastructural projects often have as much to do with
patron-client rewards than with technical function. In a complementary
point, Ballestero argues (this volume) that function is often taken as an implicit starting point to understanding infrastructures. In Ballestero's analysis of
an aquifer in Costa Rica, Mbembe's work in South Africa, and drug-trafficking
infrastructures in northern Mexico, this epistemic tendency to prioritize intended use obscures the unexpected or clandestine relations that are often
co-constitutive of infrastructural forms.

In the doubling of infrastructures used in drug-trafficking routes in northern Mexico, cartels and their workers use the visible network of paved roads,
gas stations, and border crossings, facilitating mobility between Mexico and

the United States to move objects that are kept hidden from public view. This doubling has ironically been facilitated by the implementation of the North American Free Trade Agreement (NAFTA) in 1994, which in increasing legal trade between the United States and Mexico also facilitated increased illegal trade (Andreas 1995, 2009; Malkin 2001). As political scientist Peter Andreas (1996: 58) has argued, a clear example is the use of legal trucking to smuggle drugs across regular border crossings. The number of trucks crossing the border has tripled since the signing of NAFTA, and to avoid the disruption of legal forms of trade only a fraction of these trucks are inspected. Some truck companies are rumored to have been bought out by drug cartels. They still function as trucking companies but also as money-laundering enterprises as well as drug-smuggling venues. Of course, this is the kind of doubling that the drug economy has famously drawn from, creating front businesses that hide the origin of their revenue. This doubling of regular infrastructures for mobility and trade is particularly common in the case of mules who smuggle thousands of dollars tightly strapped in their bodies underneath regular clothing, and move around driving in regular roads or traveling by bus or taxis.

The appropriation of regular infrastructures and legal forms of mobility by cartels adopts a peculiar expression in the case of the so-called blind mules: people who are driving their own vehicles to cross the border and inadvertently carry drugs in them, surreptitiously placed there by members of cartels, who track the vehicle and later pick up the load. Since stories of people going to jail for carrying drugs without their knowledge were rampant, I learned to always carefully inspect my own car for hidden packages underneath the chassis prior to crossing the border back to the United States.

Yet in addition to needing to move objects across space, cartels also need an infrastructure of spaces for the temporary storage of drugs. Residents in the village where I have been doing research for the last ten years gradually told me stories about strangers who would suddenly show up at their doorsteps and ask them if they could drop off boxes or baggage for a few days or weeks. Everybody knew that saying no was not an option, and made room for those packages in their homes, no questions asked. When days or weeks later another stranger would arrive to pick up the cargo, they would give them cash or a gift in kind.

For example, I know a woman named Lupe who lived by herself in a small shack on the edge of the village. A few years ago when I went back for a visit, I learned that Lupe had gone to jail. After Lupe quarreled with one of her neighbors, the police were tipped off. They came and searched her home where they found she had a few boxes of drugs stashed. Apparently, the neighbor with whom Lupe quarreled knew the boxes were there because she had seen the drop-off happen.

In this case, the doubling of infrastructures turns ordinary people's homes into a short-term, spatially scattered, and deeply opaque infrastructure of warehouses. As I have argued elsewhere (Muehlmann 2013a), this entanglement between ordinary homes and ad hoc storage sites complicates any attempt to draw clear-cut boundaries between "involvement" and "noninvolvement" in the drug economy, in a region where few people are unaffected by its pervasive presence.

This example of doubling differs from the kinds described by Mbembe (2001) and others because in this case the relevant infrastructures are not built with alternate uses in mind. The bridges, roads, networks of trucks and truckers, and temporary storage sites are appropriations of existing infrastructures for new purposes. Here users of infrastructure perform the kind of inversion that Bowker and Star (1994) describe and take the background processes of movement and transportation to the foreground in order to capitalize on precisely the kinds of common sense that would allow "free trade" to flow relatively unperturbed. Therefore, this kind of doubling and attention to alternate uses made visible to select populations shows how actors approach infrastructure from different points of view in which different uses become visible and invisible in the process.

In addition to the appropriation of public and noticeable roads and buildings to move and store objects, drug-trafficking organizations also rely on infrastructures that are kept from view and need to remain invisible to state agents and the public in order to remain operational. The best examples are the famous and often elaborate and sophisticated tunnels that cartels have built at multiple points along the US-Mexico border to smuggle drugs, money, and weapons. In the past several decades 181 clandestine tunnels have been discovered under the US-Mexico border. Some are just big enough to crawl through. The Sinaloa cartel is known for its "supertunnels": millions of dollars to build, several months in construction, elevators, lights ventilation, and their signature arched ceilings. Most are used to funnel drugs across the border and connect to warehouses in the sprawling factory sectors of both sides, so they are very difficult to detect.

Rather than gaining their invisibility from a purported alternate use, as in the forms of doubling analyzed above, the invisibility of these tunnels relies on the intrinsic opacity of the underground (see Gordillo 2015). What makes tunnels particularly hard to detect is that the rocky materiality of the planet's crust is opaque to high-tech forms of detectability that prioritize aerial "views from above."

In February 2016, I interviewed a soldier who reflected on the difficulties of finding tunnels for precisely these reasons. He had been part of a military unit that searched out smuggling routes on the border. They had recently found a tunnel in the process of construction on the outskirts of Mexicali, in an area that predominantly comprises factories. The soldier said, "The only reason we discovered the tunnel was because there was so much going on at the site." He further explained that it was because of all the activity around an otherwise low traffic area that they investigated more fully and finally found the tunnel under a bodega. The construction had only reached a dozen meters before the tunnel dead-ended.

The soldier's emphasis on the fact that the only way the tunnel was noticeable was through the activity on the earth's surface points to the feature which allows for a tunnel's invisibility in the first place, which is that it is powerfully camouflaged by the earth.[2] This is the same invisibility that allowed the Sinaloa cartel to build a mile-long, and highly sophisticated tunnel to free the famous narco Joaquín Guzmán Loera ("El Chapo") from the maximum-security Mexican prison he was held in in July 2015. El Chapo, the leader of the Sinaloa cartel, is one of the most famous figures in the war on drugs. The way in which his most recent tunnel facilitated escape has been imagined and contested is relevant here because it highlights one dimension of the double lives of infrastructures in this region.

The official story of El Chapo's escape has been remarkably consistent since it was first reported in the news: "El Chapo escaped through a tunnel that was dug under the walls of the prison. It opened in a small hole in the floor of the shower of his cell. He went down the hole, down a ladder[,] climbed on to a motor bike that was attached to rails built into the tunnel, rode it off and disappeared" (Reel 2015). According to this account, it was just a few guards in the jail who were bought off in order for all this to happen.

However, while generally tunnels remain invisible because their infrastructural properties are hidden from everyone but their users, as the soldier's account above indicated the invisibility of tunnels is not absolute. The residual activity on the earth's surface created in the construction and use of tunnels destabilizes this node in the network of drug-trafficking activity.

For instance, forty-one-year-old Roberto, a fisherman and local business owner living near Mexicali, elaborated a theory of why El Chapo's escape tunnel must have been a fraud. His theory focused precisely on such a surplus of activity that cannot be contained by the obstruction made possible by the earth's surface. Roberto identified the "problem of the dirt." He pointed out that in El Chapo's last escape, the tunnel was 1.5 kilometers long and it "emerged in a little ranchito surrounded by other little ranchitos." Roberto emphasized that if there were a *real* tunnel, it would have generated a tremendous amount of activity because even though you cannot see the work happening underground the workers have to get there and then, most important, they have to get rid of all that dirt they dig out of the ground. "Think of all the *tierra* that tunnel would have created," he said. "That's enough dirt to fill forty ranchitos like this one" (motioning to the house we were talking in). "Think of all the trucks coming and going," he urged. "Where would they put all that dirt? Dirt is a hard thing to smuggle around."

I was intrigued by Roberto's theory about the insurmountable excess in dirt that would potentially reveal the activities of tunnel building and subsequently investigated this issue quite extensively on the internet and in several newspaper archives after our conversation. From one report I was surprised to learn that the land around the ranchito from which El Chapo's tunnel emerged was several feet higher than on adjacent properties. The implication that the dirt Roberto spoke of was spread out over the property in order to camouflage its removal, whether or not this is accurate, seems a fitting solution for hiding the evidence of a tunnel that is also hidden, in principle itself, by the powerful opacity of the earth in the first place.

The network of improvised landing sites and tunnels in the Sonora Desert near my field site are also examples of an infrastructure for mobility that while exposed to the light of day, is relatively hidden from state scrutiny by its immersion in much wider geographies that camouflage their presence. Rather than becoming visible when they "break down" (Star 1999), these clandestine infrastructures of landing areas, tunnels, and ad hoc storage sites "break down" when they become visible to the state. Drug-smuggling tunnels are no longer useful once authorities discover them, in the same way that landing strips are no longer operational when they are detected and damaged with ditches.

Because infrastructures of illicit transport depend on their invisibility to the state, one of the most effective ways in which the regional environment is made to play an infrastructural role in the re-creation of smuggling routes in the rugged geography of the desert is through the use of indigenous residents who know the land well. And in the northern deserts of Baja California and Sonora *los indios* (the Indians) are often touted as "knowing the land" better than anybody else.

"Because We Know the Land"

Sometimes I would accompany Esperanza, a seventy-four-year-old woman I was particularly close to, on walks out into the desert to visit different sacred sites. Her familiarity with the landscape was a powerful reminder of why residents' knowledge of the area is so useful for those wishing to navigate the region. Esperanza scoured the desert floor with remarkable intensity, immediately recognizing every stone that was rare or out of place. As we walked, the desert floor would crunch under our feet as we broke the salty crust of the surface. Esperanza would keep talking the whole way about how thoroughly transformed the landscape was from when she was a child. "It's so much uglier now than it was," she would often remark, "All the salt, so little water." One day, as Esperanza and I were walking through the desert, she suddenly stopped still in her stride and pointed to fresh footprints in the sand that wound out into the desert. Then, she showed me the tracks left by soldiers. She explained that the soldiers wait in the mountains because of the shipments that pass through there. She shook her head in dismay. We stood for a moment looking out beyond the tracks to the mountains Esperanza was referring to. Then we turned around and headed home.

Before massive dams were built upstream in the mid-twentieth century, the delta of the Colorado River in Mexico was an expanse of wetlands covering more than two million acres. The delta provided subsistence for the residents of the region and habitat for wildlife and marine fisheries in the Gulf of California. Now, as a result of the overdevelopment of the watershed in the United States, the river no longer reaches the sea. The area has one of the highest rates of species extinction and endangerment on the continent (Bergman 2002: 29) and, as Esperanza emphasized, the land is almost unrecognizable from what it once was. Further, the desert is regularly marked by the traces of the actors who have turned the region into a major drug corridor.

The region where Esperanza lives at the end of the Colorado River has historically been dominated by agriculture and a large fishing economy. The impact of water scarcity on the Colorado Delta's ecosystem has left the residents of this region and in particular many Cucapá fishermen with greatly reduced means of subsistence. Since legal restrictions set up in 1993, residents no longer have fishing rights in the delta under the Federal Environmental Protection Agency's fishing ban and through the creation of a nationally protected "Biosphere Reserve" (Alarcón-Cháires 2001; Gómez and Alfredo 1994; Gómez and Alfredo 2000).

The environmental crisis affecting the region and the decline of fishing as a viable source of livelihood created a fertile ground for cartel operations. Local people in northern Mexico are drawn to the drug trade for complex reasons. Only some are economic. Others are affective, epitomized by the glamor projected onto famous narcos who are openly celebrated in popular music. The indigenous and mestizo people I met in my fieldwork had become a target labor force for the same geographic and economic reasons that other local populations have: they are poor enough to take on the risks of trafficking and strategically located in a major trafficking corridor near the border. But what sets them apart, in the eyes of cartels, is their indigeneity and knowledge of a terrain perceived as rugged and opaque. Other indigenous people on both sides of the border, such as the Tarahumara (in Mexico) and the Tohono O'odham (in Arizona), have been targeted for similar reasons.

Indigenous people become an infrastructural component of drug trafficking because they achieve opacity through two principal characteristics. First, they are essentialized in colonial narratives as being at "one with the land" in ways that makes them effectively invisible by portraying them as "part of nature." And second, their knowledge of the land is reified in various ways through these same narratives and as a result becomes "black boxed" and inaccessible to outsiders. I will explore the ways these two characteristics are monopolized by drug-trafficking networks in what follows.

According to my interviews, Cucapá people's involvement is generally solicited for drug smuggling in the same ways and for the same reasons that people often work as guides for activities such as hunting and cultural tourism. Specifically, individuals are hired on as trackers or guides to help lead people through the desert or to deliver packages that need to travel across difficult territory. Local indigenous people are hired because they know the best routes, how to avoid checkpoints, and how to ensure that a party won't get lost in the dessert. Local indigenous Cucapá people are also residents and often communal land title holders on traditional Cucapá indigenous territory. Sometimes people are hired on a one-time basis to lead a single smuggling trip, and other times locals become involved in more long-term capacities.

Because the vast stretches of dessert in this area are a known thruway for illicit drugs, the Mexican Army has a regular presence in the region patrolling and surveilling all known routes in search for smugglers. I heard of and witnessed several encounters in which Cucapá people challenged the soldiers who stopped them by claiming that they are "Indians" and therefore have an inherent right to be there, on their own land. On one occasion a group of us were deep in the bush collecting arrowweed to use for building ceremonial structures for a festival when a truck full of soldiers approached us and began questioning the group about its activities and what was in our two pickup trucks. One of the most politically active fisherwomen in the group, named Adriana, engaged with the soldiers very assertively. She started by saying, "You're on Cucapá land" and then explained that we were engaged in traditional indigenous foraging activities. They kept asking about the trucks but Adriana pushed back, finally motioning to me saying that they had a witness from Canada to see how the government treats indigenous people in Mexico "on their own land." I was surprised to see that the soldiers backed off without even searching the trucks. While most confrontations between the military and indigenous people may not resolve so quickly, this example did seem to indicate that there is an acknowledgment that indigenous people do have an entitlement to the land that nonindigenous locals do not or at least a more convincing rationale for traveling through this area. Indeed, several people told me that they had evaded officials while smuggling precisely because they were seen to have a claim to the territory.

On another occasion, a Cucapá elder named Inez explained to me how this kind of entitlement might play out in an everyday interaction in this region. She said, "Sometimes you go out in the sierra or in the desert, and the soldiers are there and they won't let you pass. They stop you, pointing their guns at you on your own land. And they ask you about your business. At times like this, the kids simply say, "soy indio" in Spanish and then in Cucapá "go fuck yourself!" In hearing them utter an incomprehensible word in an indigenous language, the soldiers immediately relent and let them go, saying, "oh, pásale," "go ahead." This encounter reveals that a marker of indigeneity (the indigenous words that the soldiers do not understand) was enough to authenticate them as Indians and also explain and justify their presence in this part of the desert. The fact that the soldiers are often out in the desert when Cucapá people are hunting, tracking, or traveling through this land indicates how heavily militarized the region is. Armored vehicles full of soldiers and armed lookouts are both a persistent aspect of the landscape and a constant reminder of the narco-presence and the resulting militarization of the regional space. Yet local indigenous people are allowed a certain degree of mobility that cartels also seek to use to their own advantage, particularly involving the knowledge of hidden paths. Elsewhere, I have argued that this example is part of a larger discourse portraying the inscrutability of the indigenous subject who perpetuates colonial imaginaries of the Indian as impenetrable and exotic (Muehlmann 2008).

In this context, we can see how, like the doubling I referenced earlier, this essentialized view of indigenous people portrays them as part of the landscape and thus the infrastructure of drug trafficking. On one hand, this claim implies that Cucapá people have a connection to the land that is deeper than your average Mexican in the region. This is a familiar idea in contemporary imaginings of indigenous people. In anthropology, there is certainly a large literature focused on how indigenous peoples' "traditional ecological knowledge" (TEK) can be used for sustainable resource management as well as a more critical literature on how indigenous people have been incorporated into economic markets through programs of sustainable entrepreneurship and ecotourism projects. In both cases, their "indigenous" knowledge of the land is naturalized. Likewise, the enlistment of Cucapá people into the drug trade for this reason shows that mainstream assumptions about their relationship to the land because they are indigenous are largely the same.

Indigenous people in the border regions have not just been recruited into the ranks of the "war on drugs" to work for the narco-sector. On the flip side, they have also joined antismuggling operations. This is the case, for instance, for some of the Tohono O'odham in both the US and Mexico who have been enlisted to help track drug smugglers because of their skills (Archibold 2007). Increasingly DEA officers are also incorporating indigenous tracking techniques in their arsenal of low-tech surveillance technology. This is not a new trend. The "Shadow Wolves," for example, are a US federal law enforcement unit of Indian officers who has operated since the early 1970s on the indigenous land straddling the Mexican border. Similarly, at least one Cucapá man I interviewed had worked as a military guide for the Mexican government. He described the assistance he provided in tracking smugglers through the Sierra on Cucapá land and also claimed that others from the area had worked in this capacity, though no one else volunteered similar stories.

The terrain in which indigenous trackers and guides operate to facilitate the mobility of drugs is particularly hard to read and decipher for newcomers to this region. Beyond the settlement where I did my fieldwork, the Colorado Delta stretches out in desert and salt flats. On some days, the only people to be seen for miles are military patrols on guard. The sheer vastness of this desert, to me at least, meant that it appeared almost entirely homogenous. I would sometimes follow along on fishing trips near the Biosphere Reserve at the Gulf of California, which is about an hour-long truck ride from the main paved road that cuts through the Sonoran Desert. The route to the fishing zone is completely unmarked. But on any given day during the fishing season, there are crosscuts of tracks from pickups heading in multiple directions. These were the traces of the channels of motion of illegal commodities. And these were traces built into the natural environment of the sand, rocks, and desert.

Locals have little problem navigating this geography without getting lost. When traveling with residents through the desert, I would ask at such junctures, "How do you know which way to go?" My question hoped to illicit some expression of "local knowledge." I imagined that the answer would have to do with the angle of the sun, perhaps calibrated with the location of the Sierra in the distance or the direction of the breeze. Instead people highlighted that navigating that terrain and recognizing its forms was a matter of embodied habit. Routinely the answer was "I know which way to go, because that's the way to the fishing camp" or "I've been driving this route since I was six years old." Sometimes, I would get the sarcastic reply "Porque soy indio!" ("Because I'm an Indian!"). What was evident was that what allows people to navigate this route is not easily translatable into other forms explicable knowledge. It is this very opacity in addition to the fact that TEK is proprietary that makes this knowledge of routes and passageways difficult to translate into modern knowledge systems. It is clear that Cucapá fisherman have this knowledge and skills, but it is not possible to fully see how they function and therefore these are skills that are not easily transferred to other actors such as members of drug-trafficking organizations. Therefore, indigenous people are able to stand in, and indeed double, as the agents of illicit movements and transfers.

The question "How do you know which way to go?" in this context taps into a whole spectrum of other issues regarding indigenous people and local or "traditional" knowledge. Place has been central to the very concept of what constitutes indigenous identities, at least in the West in the past several decades. This is partially because of the fact that indigenous people are often defined as groups that existed in a given territory prior to the arrival of European settlers or state actors (Gray 1996). But it is also due to a recent tendency to project onto indigenous people what has been called a "stable spatiality" (Gordillo 2011), which emphasizes that indigenous identities are grounded in, and defined by, bounded territories infused with meanings produced throughout generations of residence there (see, for example, Basso 1996; Lee 2006). In its most romanticizing version, this depiction of indigenous peoples' relationship to place portrays indigenous people and their landscapes as being virtually inseparable.

In part, this tendency to essentialize the relationship between indigenous identity and bounded territories has been a response to the fact that residing in a given territory is central to the experiences of many indigenous people across the globe, and this has shaped recent land title disputes and conflicts over natural resources. But the conflation of indigenous identity and place also obscures a whole range of other indigenous experiences brought on by increasing urbanization and exemplified by indigenous diasporas around the world. A number of authors have shown that a "sense of place" is not necessarily the defining feature of actors who self-identify as indigenous (Clifford 2007; Gordillo 2011; Harvey and Thompson 2005; Ramirez 2007; Smith 2006; Watson 2010). Other authors have analyzed how this ideology of indigenous people as one with the land has been used against them in myriad ways (Braun 2002; Muehlmann 2013b; Povinelli 2002).

What we find in this case, however, is that many Cucapá people do identify with the idea that they have a unique connection to the land. This has been articulated both in their claims to fishing rights and in their rationalization for their work in the narco-sector. This is also a case where the idea that they are rooted to this territory has been used both by them and against them. For instance, in the conflict over their fishing rights, their ancestral occupancy of the region, and particularly the river, has been used to argue that they should not get differential rights to fish in the mouth of the river because this is the area where the river meets the sea. If they are indeed "people of the river," as the Cucapá claim, then those rights should not extend, according to environmental officials, to fishing in brackish waters.

At the same time, there have been myriad government-sponsored economic ventures that have often been encouraged as a substitute for fishing that commodify the Cucapá's familiarity with the region in other contexts. There have been NGO initiatives to create projects for Cucapá youth to map the land, and tourist initiatives to enlist Cucapá tour guides, and it is common for recreational hunters to hire Cucapá guides to lead them through the bush and the desert. Many Cucapá fisherpeople argue that the same skills that the government and NGOs have been touting to discourage illegal fishing may be more lucratively commodified for the drug economy.

The way in which some Cucapá people become part of the infrastructure of drug smuggling resonates in several ways with AbdouMaliq Simone's description of "people as infrastructure" (2004). Simone argues that certain contexts in Johannesburg are characterized by flexible and provisional intersections of residents who operate as infrastructure even without clear notions of how the city is to be inhabited and used. As an example, Simone describes a transport depot. The depot is full of hundreds of young men who work as steerers, baggage loaders, ticket salespersons, hawkers, drivers, petrol pumpers, and mechanics. Focusing in specifically on the role of "steerers," Simone describes how the depot functions as a network of constantly shifting connections among them. Each boy who steers passengers to a particular company makes a rapid assessment of their wealth, personal characteristics, and the reason for their journey. This assessment determines where the steerer will lead prospective passengers, who will sell their tickets, who will load their baggage, who will seat them, and so on. There are no explicit rules or forms of payment for steerers, but their engagement, improvisation, and collaboration combine to maximize the efficiency of each passenger's path. Simone goes on to argue that in this case infrastructure is dependent on the selective disclosure of human infrastructural capacities. In that sense, people who function as infrastructures can decide when and how they want to do so.

This is similar to the indigenous knowledge that Cucapá people can both logistically and strategically draw on to facilitate drug-smuggling networks or military operations. Here, too, people become infrastructure of a certain kind. In their capacity to extend or track down a network of smuggling, this case also differs from Simone's in important ways. While Simone's "people as infrastructure" work in a scenario in which individuals make temporary arrangements, in this account, the Cucapá people and their knowledge and usefulness as infrastructure always already depend on an existing network of relations between such powerful entities as the state and military, on the one hand, and the drug cartels, on the other. Their knowledge also depends on their prior connections and relations to the land that require a certain familiarity and connection to the region. These systems of knowledge—rather than being contingent, shifting, and improvisational as Simone describes—

are instead inscribed in and essentialized as inherent features of local indigenous people.

Knowledge is often characterized as needing to be made accessible and
standardized in order to function as infrastructure (Elyachar 2012; Bowker
and Star 1994). The implicit theory of knowledge at work here is that it is hidden and needs to be uncovered, especially the intransient infrastructures of the
poor. In this case, however, what renders the infrastructure indigenous trackers stable is in part the opacity that makes that knowledge uniquely "indigenous." Indigenous knowledge is seen as impenetrable and nontransferable
because it is linked to "tradition" and to an inalienable relationship to the
land. This opacity then, hinges both on a reification of that knowledge but
also an essentialization of the relationship between indigenous people and
the land.

These channels of communication embodied by traditional knowledge
of the land are similar to other kinds of "phatic labor" and communicative connectivity that scholars of infrastructure have described. For example,
Julia Elyachar (2012) shows the ways in which communicative channels relate signers to interpreters so that signs of all kinds can be interpreted, an account that focuses on the channels of communication rather than the people
doing the communicating, as for example in Simone's account. However, in
this case the essentializing links between people, land, and knowledge are
precisely how indigenous drug-trafficking practices become stable nodes in
the network. Indeed, in this case, knowledge needs to be black-boxed as "indigenous" or "traditional" in order to function smoothly as an infrastructural
system.

The links between land and people here also facilitated an infrastructuralization of land itself. As others such as Ballestero (this volume) Helen Verran
(2011), Atsuro Morita (2016), and Ashley Carse (2012) have shown, in some
situations it is "nature" that is enrolled to do the jobs otherwise associated with
infrastructure. In this case, like the aquifers that Ballestero describes, there
is a potential for the route through the desert to dissolve into the background.
The path to the fishing grounds can quite easily fade into the background of
the desert, as it does for some attempted users or those along for the ride.
Despite attempts to delineate the path being taken, the route to the fishing
grounds required the capacity of these fisherpeople to differentiate the path
from the wide expanses of the delta.

Conclusions

For some Cucapá people, the turn to smuggling and trafficking drugs was a response to being denied the right to fish. Alvaro, a man I came to know well during my fieldwork, was outraged when marines confiscated his nets after catching him fishing in the Biosphere Reserve. According to Alvaro, it was not long after that incident that he began smuggling drugs with his boat instead. As he explained in an ironic tone: "What else can I do with a boat and no nets?" (Muehlmann 2013b). While he said this in part as a jab at local environmental politics, his comment also indicated some of the ways that the infrastructure in place for the fishing economy and for trade across the US-Mexico border can easily double as an economy that moves drugs instead of fish.

The apparent "failure" or "breakdown" of the infrastructure for fishing, such as boats and nets, makes other infrastructural possibilities visible. Left without the crucial component of nets, Alvaro saw the opportunity for other kinds exchange (De Boeck 2012). This complicates the very idea of a "breakdown" of infrastructure and also highlights that infrastructural elements that might be invisible from the perspective of a fisherman, for example, would be highly visible from the perspective a smuggler looking to move drugs.

Because in this case, actors themselves draw on the tension between invisible and visible uses of infrastructures, my discussion here also complicates some of the assumptions in the scholarly project to perform infrastructural inversions. As some scholars have pointed out, inversions assume a sharp distinction between the analytic and the ethnographic as they focus on the view of the analyst and what the analyst is able to see (Harvey, Jensen, and Morita 2016; Jensen 2014). In this case, in contrast, the inversions in question are part of the empirical condition of infrastructural use. Drug-trafficking infrastructures show how actors are able to perform their own infrastructural inversions in order to capitalize on the way infrastructures are socially constructed as networks designed for specific uses and not others.

Interestingly, the drug trade has thrived primarily as a result of the apparent failure of the border as an infrastructure designed to slow down or stop the flow of "illegal" people and goods between the United States and Mexico. In this case it is opacity, rather than transparency, that allows for the constant flow of illegal drugs through various channels, some well worn and intended for other matter such as NAFTA-approved merchandise, and some invisible and clandestine, such as tunnels, designed for illegal goods from the start. This case study highlights that the constitution of many forms of infrastructure hinges on a delicate interplay between making visible and making invisible.

Notes

1 Brian Larkin (2013), for instance, has pointed out that many systems of infrastructure are actually built to be seen and noticed as symbols of state power and modernity.
2 Camouflage's human history is long and well researched, especially in its relation to visual technology and film and in the context of military history, while beyond the scope of my discussion here, see Hannah Rose Shell's (2012) analysis and review of this literature.

THREE. The Metropolis

The Infrastructure of the Anthropocene

GASTÓN GORDILLO

In May 2003, I drove for the first time along the foot of the Argentine Andes in the province of Salta, a region where the mountains meet the lowlands of the Gran Chaco region. As I was heading north toward the town of Las Lajitas amid a landscape dominated by agricultural fields, the roads were in terrible shape. The pavement was riddled with potholes and cracks, which forced me to drive my car carefully, zigzagging to avoid bumps or collisions. Adding to the sense of decaying infrastructure, decrepit railroads lay silently parallel to the roads—the result of privatization schemes that had terminated the passenger trains a decade earlier. The roads I was driving on were the main if precarious infrastructure that allowed for mobility to and from Las Lajitas. What struck me the most about the roads, however, was not their disrepair but the heavy traffic of trucks moving along them. The trucks advanced slowly, carefully sensing the damaged asphalt, but their motion was persistent and was part of long caravan of vehicles that, I soon learned, was converging on a cluster of large silos that had emerged in the 1990s south of

Figure 3.1. Silos in Piquete Cabado, south of Las Lajitas. Bags hermetically sealed for grain storage (*silobolsas*) can be seen on the ground. Photo by the author.

Las Lajitas (figure 3.1). The silos poured streams of soybeans into the trucks, which then turned around and drove to the southeast for over 1,300 kilometers to the shores of the Paraná River around the city of Rosario, the third largest in the country and soon to be called Argentina's "soy capital." There, crushing factories turned the soybeans into oil and soymeal, which were loaded onto ships that headed downstream the Paraná toward the ocean and then ports across the world, mostly in Asia and Europe.

In the seemingly mundane motion of those trucks navigating roads in bad shape, in retrospect, I was witnessing, first, the materialization of the record-breaking soybean harvest of 2003 and the beginning of "the Argentine soy boom," which in a few years turned this country into the third-largest producer of soy in the world after the United States and Brazil. More significantly, Argentina became the first global exporter of soymeal and oil, made possible by the existence of an enormous cluster of crushing factories around Rosario. In those early days of the boom, however, the flow of trucks and the large silos around Las Lajitas surprised me. I was not aware that agribusinesses were so active in that area of Salta, a northern province seemingly removed from the agricultural core of central Argentina. In the 1970s, Las Lajitas was a sleepy village surrounded by forests and with little infrastructure except for the railways. The region was inhabited by campesinos and rural workers: gauchos, or cowboys of mestizo background who raised cattle "in the bush." By 2003, a good part of that physical and social geography was clearly gone. While forests remained in the foothills and in the interior of the Chaco, around Las Lajitas they had been replaced by corporate, mechanized farms operating through fields, roads, and silos to respond to the global commodity boom triggered by China's rapid urbanization. Amid the growing demand for land to plant soy, deforestation north and east of Las Lajitas was then accelerating. In my early weeks in the region, I was struck not only by the traffic of trucks on the road but also by the flipside of their momentum: the bulldozers crushing forests and myriad life forms in order to create even more soy fields (see Gordillo 2014).[1]

In the following thirteen years (2003–2016), I returned to Las Lajitas multiple times and witnessed how the combined effect of deforestation, eviction of campesino residents, and the expansion of infrastructures generated a more urbanized terrain.[2] The first infrastructures to be upgraded were the roads, the main medium that allows for the extraction of the soybeans away from Salta and toward Rosario, the gateway to the ocean. On my second visit in 2004, I began encountering crews and heavy equipment replacing the damaged asphalt. By 2007, the regional roads had been turned into smooth, rapid channels of connectivity. All gas stations were renovated and now offer Wi-Fi to a growing volume of vehicles. At the entrance of Las Lajitas, modern buildings house the companies that sell inputs to farmers, from Monsanto herbicides to John Deere tractors. A few meters away, the upscale Las Lajitas Hotel attracts mostly male and white managers, engineers, or Cargill agents who meet to discuss how to plant, harvest, store, sell, and transport soybeans and other crops to Rosario. Most of them are Argentines from other parts of the country, primarily "the south" (Córdoba, Rosario, or Buenos Aires). These men are often on their phones, tablets, and laptops, attentive to the pulses coming from across the world that may affect their strategies and profit margins. Some of them manage farms whose fields look "rural." But the farms are mechanized, are sprayed with herbicides, and are part of the networks of infrastructures that expanded with deforestation.

As I witnessed the expansion of urbanized infrastructures produced by corporate elites who are newcomers to this area of Argentina, it was apparent that Las Lajitas's dramatic transformation did not involve the growth of a self-referential, bounded object. On the contrary, those assemblages of roads, machinery, vehicles, and silos were all designed to facilitate the transportation of soybeans and their industrialized derivatives to densely populated urban centers across the world. In investigating how the soy supply chains process and move their products from northern Argentina to a planetary network of urban centers, I gradually learned to view the infrastructures around Las Lajitas as an *entry-point*, a *path* into something much larger, planetary in scale, and therefore very difficult to apprehend: what Timothy Morton (2013) would call a "hyper-object" but that I prefer to think of as a vast assemblage: a wildly diverse, differentiated, yet interconnected constellation of nodes and conduits repetitively moving objects, bodies, energy, and information across national borders and continents. In this chapter, I draw from the case of the soy supply chains to analyze this plurality in motion as "the metropolis."

The most important thinkers of the metropolis have been radical theorists and activists, chiefly Antonio Negri (2018), Alberto Toscano (2004, 2011, 2014), and the collective The Invisible Committee (2009, 2015). Negri conceptualizes the metropolis as "the general structure that capitalism assumes in its imperial phase" but also as the urban spatiality that has replaced the factory as the main site of struggle and emancipation (Toscano 2004: 210). Influenced by Negri, the writings by Toscano and The Invisible Committee, in turn, dissect the infrastructures of the metropolis to reveal the power of logistics in global capitalism. In the words of Toscano, "The metropolis has the intensification and expansion of supply lines as its precondition, and logistics becomes its primary concern, its foremost product, and the basic determinant of its power" (2011: 6).

In what follows, I build from these ideas to conceptualize the metropolis in more depth and along more materialist and ethnographic lines, especially through an examination of how the soy supply chains connect Argentina to urban constellations worldwide. In particular, I draw from Henri Lefebvre (2003, 2004) and the literatures on infrastructures, logistics, and planetary urbanization to decompose the metropolis into its constitutive multiplicities and fractal differentiations. The metropolis, in this regard, is *not* a figure of the One: a totalizing object, an extended version of "the city," or a homogenous whole; rather, it is motion guided by capitalist-imperial patterns of accumulation and the infrastructures that make it possible; it is a rhizomatic multiplicity of encounters and friction; it is a heuristic, *concrete* abstraction to name the materiality of the continuum that moves matter from one continent to another in order to reproduce and expand the metabolism of the largest urban agglomerations on Earth. The metropolis's infrastructures are therefore "the secret weapon of the most powerful people in the world"

(Easterling 2014: 15). And logistics becomes "capital's art of war" (Bernes 2013: 203).

Conceptualizing the metropolis along these lines is an ambitious and complex task, chiefly because it evokes the controversial idea of totality. With the rise of poststructuralist, posthuman, and actor-network sensibilities, the idea of totality has come to symbolize to many, as Alberto Toscano and Jeff Kinkle put it, "totalitarianism at worst, or paranoid criticism at best," a concept "corrupted by the metaphysical desire for coherence and the hubris of intellectual mastery" (2015: 24). Yet understanding the daunting scale of an urbanized and interconnected world in the era of climate change cannot be done without a critical understanding of totality in the most immanent sense of the term. As Theodor Adorno insisted, "Totality is not an affirmative but rather a critical category," which seeks to identify "the whole of social relations" not to reify them but to *negate* them (cited in Vouros 2014: 179). And the main source of a nontotalizing understanding of the urban totality is Lefebvre, who wrote that "the urban phenomenon can only be comprehended as a totality, but its totality cannot be grasped. It escapes us. It is always elsewhere" (2003: 186). The metropolis, likewise, is an ungraspable, nonrepresentable totality that escapes our capacity to make sense of it. And what makes it partly opaque to thought is both its planetary scale and that it is permanently redefined by practices woven locally and regionally.

There are therefore countless dimensions of human and nonhuman life in both urban and nonurban spaces that escape the reach and control of the metropolis. Each node in urbanized planetary networks is also a place with a distinct history, texture, and political flavor, and is irreducible to this transnationality, even in highly globalized urban centers such as London, Dubai, or Shanghai. This is more so the case in regions with strong nonurban traditions. Most residents of Las Lajitas still celebrate the gauchos as icons of the region and view the agribusiness elites as arrogant newcomers with little love for the land. And in this and other towns, large multitudes go in pilgrimage to shrines in the forest and in places in ruins to venerate dark-skinned virgins believed to be miraculous (Gordillo 2014). The regional experiences, in this regard, are shaped by memories, relations, and dispositions that far exceed the rhythms of for-export agribusiness. Yet the latter's impact on this region forced me to interrogate the ways in which this place is *also* part of an intricate, physical planetary formation. This connectivity has global implications at an even larger scale. Industrial agriculture is one of the main sources of global warming and environmental ruination in the world, due to its obliteration of tropical forests, its reliance on toxic pesticides, and its subordination to the demands of animal farming—for most soybeans in South America are grown not for direct human consumption but to create animal feed. And this is why the question of the metropolis is also that of the Anthropocene, which I view, rather than as a generic "era of humans," as the era of climate change and severe environmental disruptions produced by capitalism (see Moore 2015).

In the first section, I argue why a conceptual shift away from "globalization" and toward the metropolis can help us better appreciate both the global continuum and the differences that structure supply chains. I subsequently examine the metropolis not from its most densely populated and northern nodes of agglomeration but *from its edges* in the "global South": in our case, in areas in which urbanizing infrastructures encounter and destroy forests inhabited by campesinos who actively defend them from the advance of bulldozers. In the last sections, I show how the violence of the supply chains reveals the imperial hierarchies that structure the metropolis, the salience of national differences in it, as well as the struggles and nonhuman forces that interrupt its rhythms. These interruptions bring to light that the metropolis is also a generative space of collective encounters that offers the potential to reinvent the commons.

From Globalization to the Metropolis

In the 1990s, scholars tried to make sense of the new world order created by the collapse of communism, the planetary expansion of a triumphant capitalism, and the rise of new communication technologies as a process of "globalization." As noted by Stuart Rockefeller (2011), this early work engaged the question of globalization largely through a disembodied notion of "flows," emblematic in the influential work of Arjun Appadurai (1996) on "ethnoscapes" and of Manuel Castells (2011) on "the information age." The work of Saskia Sassen (2001) on "global cities" was important for thinking globalization along more spatial lines: as a process that redefined the nature of urbanization by creating tightly interconnected and powerful urban nodes that structure financial transactions worldwide, such as New York, London, and Tokyo. Yet as argued by Ananya Roy (2009), the focus on "global cities" re-created a Euro-American gaze that overlooked the urbanizing networks of "the global South," which can no longer be dismissed as irrelevant to globalization (see Ong and Roy 2011; Simone 2004). Neil Brenner adds that "global cities" are insufficient to understand planetary urbanization, which also mobilizes "vast grids of accumulation and spatial regulation that cascade along intercontinental transportation corridors" as well as "large-scale infrastructural, telecommunications, and energy networks" (2013: 88).

The more recent research on infrastructures and logistics, in this regard, has been important to redefine these questions in more materialist terms, especially through the analysis of the assemblages, objects, and movements that make global capitalism possible (Barry 2013; Cowen 2014; Easterling 2014; Larkin 2013). And the literature on "urban metabolism," in turn, brought into focus how urban nodes attract through their infrastructures (and expel as waste) flows of water, energy, food, and myriad commodities (Gandy 2004; Kennedy, Cuddihy, and Engel-Yan 2007; see Anand 2017, this volume).

Yet amid the literatures tackling the infrastructures of globalization, the work on "planetary urbanization" led by Brenner, Christian Schmid, and Andy Merrifield has been the most ambitious effort to conceptualize the urban form of the metropolis, even if without using this concept. Profoundly influenced by Lefebvre, these authors argue that the globalized nature of urbanization in the twenty-first century forces us to move beyond the idea of "the city" as a localized, bounded object and examine, rather, the complex ways in which urban processes are, in the words of Merrifield (2013: xx), "decoupling from their traditional city forms" and becoming "formless" and "inevitably polycentric," "stretched and torn up, sprawled and ghettoized." Brenner and Schmid (2014), in particular, write that urban forms can no longer be restricted to their agglomeration in urban centers, for they also include what they call "extended urbanization": infrastructures and networks that extend into zones of extraction, such as those transformed by mining in the Andes (Arboleda 2016). This spatial extension demands for Brenner (2014) an "urban theory without outside," which dissolves the urban-rural divide and looks at the differentiated, varied ways in which even the ocean and the mountains are traversed by infrastructures.

This body of work has been criticized by postcolonial and feminist scholars for being too "totalizing" and for failing to account for the everyday, difference, locality, and struggles in the making of the urban (Derickson 2015; Buckley and Strauss 2016; Peake 2016). Some of these critics raise important questions that help us think of the limits of the metropolis, as we shall see. Yet as Kanishka Goonewardena (2018) argues, the use of the term "totalizing" to dismiss the work on planetary urbanization reproduces a problematic equation between the philosophical idea of totality and totalitarianism and determinism. Goonewardena shows that there is a long tradition not only in Marxism but also in radical feminism and postcolonial thinking that views "the social totality" *relationally*: that is, not to downplay differences but as a political injunction to "think holistically" and understand differences amid wider relations of domination. Understood in this sense, the totality posed by planetary urbanization is crucial for thinking holistically about the Anthropocene.

In proposing to name this fraught constellation of urban agglomerations and extensions "the metropolis," this chapter nonetheless goes beyond Merrifield, Schmid, and Brenner and engages the theorizations on this concept by Negri, Toscano, and the Invisible Committee. And what this latter set of authors adds to these debates is their insistence on the *imperial* dimensions of global capitalism and the metropolis, something I examine in the next section. The Invisible Committee introduces an important concept into the discussion: that the motion of these infrastructural networks defines the metropolis as "a global continuum" (2009: 52). The question of this continuum is that of what Lefebvre (2003) called "the urban form," the main concept through which he sought to move past the often fetishized ideology of "the city." This urban form is much more than a "system," a term Lefebvre disliked because it "implies fulfillment and closure." The urban form "cannot achieve closure" because it is "made manifest as movement" (2003: 173–174). Further, as Lefebvre put it, "the urban is most forcefully evoked by the constellations of light at night, especially when flying over a city" (118). These constellations capture that the urban form combines the agglomerations and extensions identified by Brenner and Schmid (2014). Yet they also show a continuum of *textured urban materials* (asphalt, cement, steel, glass, plastic, timber) through which people, vehicles, and energy move, congregate, and disperse. If the nocturnal view of the urban terrain from an airplane is zoomed out much farther to what satellite images show, we see a form that is vaster: for instance, the European peninsula crisscrossed by high-density clusters of light and rhizomatic lines forming a nebulous continuum across borders. To paraphrase Lefebvre, it is in those images that the urban forms of the metropolis as a continuum are most forcefully evoked.

But this image of continuous urban connectivity is, at the same time, misleading. In order to avoid falling into what Donna Haraway (1988) would call the "God trick" of looking at satellite images from above and from nowhere, it is crucial to examine the uneven textures of the metropolis at the ground level. This quickly reveals that the metropolis's continuum is highly selective, differentiated, and never wholly continuous. Its infrastructures are closely policed and made violently *discontinuous* by the efforts by states and corporations to restrain the mobility of undesired and racialized populations and the flow of illicit goods. The rise to power of Donald Trump in the United States, the Brexit vote in the United Kingdom, and the surge of xenophobic nationalisms confirm that borders and nation-states are far from withering away. But it is precisely the perceived erosion of borders by transnational and subaltern mobilities that is creating calls for the militarization of borders and the rise of infrastructures of separation. The metropolis, in this regard, is a decentered structuration of motion and acceleration *and also* a structuration of containment, stasis, and slowness by closely surveilled walls and fences.

When Brian Larkin (2013: 329) wrote that "infrastructures are matter that enable the movement of other matter" he was referring, in this regard, to the policed and uncoded motion of the metropolis's continuum. In its extremely diverse expressions, this continuum requires technical standardizations, made possible by infrastructures such as the strips of asphalt that allow roads to smooth out rugged terrain (Kernaghan 2012; Harvey and Knox 2015); the power grids and pipelines that channel electricity, gas, and oil across borders (Bennett 2010; Barry 2013); or the submarine cables through which internet data flow from one continent to the next (Blum 2012). This continuum is also made possible by logistical standardizations, such as the use of what Hannah Appel (2012) calls "modular" ways of outsourcing services and the use of same-size containers that are transportable by ship, train, and truck (Cowen 2014). Currents of illegal objects are part of the continuum, which includes narco-trafficking organizations moving drugs in disguise through public infrastructures and through clandestine infrastructures of their own making, such as the myriad tunnels underneath the US-Mexico border fence (Muehlmann 2013a, this volume).

Yet the metropolis's continuum, for all its seemingly unstoppable momentum, is a networked connectivity that can easily break down locally and regionally as soon as its components cannot be properly assembled. In September 2017, the severe disruptions that several hurricanes inflicted on the infrastructures of Houston, Florida, Puerto Rico, and several Caribbean islands are a clear example of the power of climate change to disrupt key nodes of the metropolis and their patterns of motion by preventing airplanes, airports, ships, ports, roads, grids, and people from being assembled in a particular way. The idea of assemblage is crucial in this regard to make sense of the intrinsic multiplicity of the metropolis; this is why the concept has long been used in the literature on infrastructures to highlight that the latter are not homogeneous entities but associations of different materialities and technologies (see Collier and Ong 2005). As Manuel De Landa (2006) put it, assemblages have no essence and do not constitute a totality because they are the temporary aggregation of a multiplicity. The metropolis, in short, is not an already-formed object but something that demands for its existence the articulation of countless materials.

These assemblages bring together not only infrastructures and human bodies but also the terrain of the planet in its solid, liquid, and atmospheric expressions (see Gordillo 2018). The ocean and the atmosphere, in particular, have been turned into spaces of global connectivity without which the metropolis would not exist. The continuum of roads, railroads, or pipelines operating on land continue by other means at the most important and long-range nodes of planetary transport: ports and airports. Departing from and converging on those nodes, the metropolis's continuum is re-created by the thousands of ships and airplanes that at any given time are moving across the ocean and the sky. This continuum is also made possible by the numerous satellites circling the earth and the flows of data traversing the metropolis via submarine cables, computers, and ATMs, like the ATMs in Las Lajitas through which I get cash from my bank account in Canada.

Yet this connectivity is not only discontinuous but also fragmented, disjointed, and extremely diverse in the uneven urban densities that define it. Some of the most powerful nodes of the metropolis are certainly what Saskia Sassen (2001) called "global cities" that structure financial flows worldwide. In the case of the soy supply chains, this includes the prominent influence of Chicago, the home of the Chicago Board of Trade, where the future prices of soy and grains are set. Yet the nodes of power of the metropolis have become so globalized that the old distinction between "core" and "peripheral" nations articulated by Immanuel Wallerstein (1974) has been spatially dispersed and made more fractal, nebulous. Urban nodes based in South America and Asia such as São Paulo, Buenos Aires, Rosario, Shanghai, or Beijing all exert various degrees of influence on the configuration of the soy supply chains. Often within these highly urbanized nodes of power, the metropolis is also made up of large zones of urban poverty served by poor or derelict infrastructures, embodied in the shantytowns of many megacities the world over.

As one moves away from the metropolis's most dense nodes of agglomeration, the spatially extended urbanization created by infrastructures usually becomes more capillary, dispersed, and rural. In areas of the world heavily populated by small farmers living in poverty, such as many areas of Latin America, Africa, and South Asia, the rhythms of the metropolis encounter

and are constrained by local rhythms of a different nature, which while affected by and entangled with urban forms are *not* urban in origin, for they
draw from an affective, tactile engagement with agrarian, forested, and moun-
tainous terrains. Brenner's idea of an "urban theory without outside" highlights
that these places are part of our globalized present but at the cost of silencing that
much of what happens in those places is not reducible to urbanization, as critics point out (Buckley and Strauss 2016). In his response to critics, Brenner
(2018) in fact concedes that he is happy to abandon the idea of urban theory
"without outside" for the sake of conceptual precision.

This is a crucial point. The metropolis is a nontotalizing totality, first,
because there are myriad places "outside" of it. While the metropolis has
been created by a capitalist system that affects the totality of the planet, its
urban textures form a configuration of a scale smaller than the world. That is,
if by "outside" of the urban we mean *nonurban textures and rhythms*, the world
is full of outsides of the metropolis, which are nonetheless "the outsides of a
world without outside": that is, they are areas that may be beyond the direct
reach of grids and infrastructures, for instance in the still-forested heart of
the Argentine Chaco, yet are *not* beyond the reach of capital. This is clear
in the worldwide impact of climate change and in the destructive effects of
agribusiness in the forests of South America.

For all its power, the metropolis therefore becomes thinner and more diffused
in those areas of the world it does not fully regiment. The latter, however, are
neither a pristine "nature" nor a rurality disconnected from the metropolis,
for "to miss the city's relation to nature and the country is in fact to miss
much of what the city is" (Cronon 1991: 19; see Williams 1973). And authors
such as Carse (2012, 2014, this volume) and Wakefield and Braun (this volume) have shown that "nature" is regularly mobilized by infrastructures. The
salience of the ocean in supply chains is a clear example of this inseparability.
But rather than "nature" or "rural" places, what the rhythms of the metropolis disrupt are nonurban terrains, such as the forests of Argentina.

On the Edge of the Metropolis

The infrastructures and urbanized networks that agribusinesses have recently
created around Las Lajitas, in this regard, can be said to be "on the edge of
the metropolis" because they tensely coexist with forested areas inhabited by

campesino families and still largely defined by rural and peasant rhythms. Ninety kilometers east of Las Lajitas, the urban forms brought about by industrial farming fade away and encounter an edge or threshold in the physical sense of the term. At kilometer ninety, the gravel road originating in Las Lajitas comes to an end; it is replaced by a dirt road in terrible shape. By then, the fields have been replaced by forests. The dirt road takes you through heavily forested terrain that is beyond the reach of electricity grids or cell-phone coverage. Here, residents have lived *en el monte*, "in the bush," raising cattle in an artisanal way for generations. They identify as gauchos, the mestizo cowboys who settled the area once the Argentine Army defeated and displaced local indigenous people in the early 1900s (Gordillo 2014). Their subaltern rurality, in this regard, is not primordial but was created by the territorial expansion of the state. Yet while they are not "outside" of the nation their distance from the infrastructures around Las Lajitas places them on an edge of sorts. This is a porous and elastic edge, clear in that most residents have cell phones for when they go to Las Lajitas and that their land is affected and threatened by the soy frontier. This is why this area where fields give way to campesino forests is more than an edge; it is a zone of what Anna Tsing (2005) calls "friction."

Around Las Lajitas, the expulsion of campesino residents by the expansion of industrial agriculture began in the late 1970s and 1980s, when agricultural firms based in other parts of Argentina began investing in the area attracted by tax benefits. Until then, Las Lajitas was a village with a strong gaucho identity that had coalesced in the 1940s around a train station. For decades, the main infrastructure were the railways, inaugurated in the 1930s, as well as dirt roads that became impassable after heavy rains. The cattle raised in this region were taken west on caravans to slaughterhouses in cities in Salta and Jujuy and in Chile. While connected to regional urban centers through the railroads, Las Lajitas was surrounded by forests and for decades maintained a low-paced rhythm. The first wave of evictions and deforestation in the 1980s and subsequently the "soy boom" destroyed this spatial configuration, turning Las Lajitas into an agribusiness hub that expanded its reach toward the Chaco. Led by companies from other areas of Argentina, this was a textbook example of "land grabs" that took advantage that many residents lacked titles to the land despite having lived there for generations. Despite multiple resistances that I briefly describe later, many evictions prevailed because they were legitimized by courts and officials and violently enforced by the police or armed civilians.

Figure 3.2. A local activist is documenting the recent destruction of forests by bulldozers near Palma Sola, lowland Jujuy, August 2016. Photo by the author.

The destruction of these expropriated forests subsequently follows a methodical plan, which begins with what Kregg Hetherington (2014) calls a foundational infrastructural practice: the surveying of the land. First, engineers reduce the complex, dense texture of the forested terrain to a Euclidian geometry of straight lines and angles. The Salta government then draws from these surveys to authorize *el desmonte*, the bulldozing of forests, which is subcontracted to companies that specialize in this task. In addition to bulldozers and drivers, these companies assemble RVs where the drivers will reside, tanks with fuel, and the main tool of destruction: an extremely heavy chain that is more than one hundred meters long and whose steel knots are twenty centimeters thick.

In order to obliterate a relatively large section of forest, bulldozers operate in pairs connected through the chain, forming an assemblage whose action is called *cadenear*, or "chaining." As the bulldozers pull in unison parallel to each other, the chain steadily crushes everything on its path, not only trees but also large amounts of wildlife and even cattle. Once the forest has been flattened, the debris is set ablaze. Manual workers then dig, remove, axe, drag, pile up, and reburn all stumps and remains, further disintegrating them in order to smooth out the terrain and turn it into agricultural fields (figure 3.2).

The fields then become the medium of a mechanized production that demands very few workers, for the planting of seeds, the spraying of pesticides, and the harvesting is done by combines, some of which are automated and controlled by satellite. The use of agrichemicals is crucial to the whole process, for making the fields grow soy demands spraying them with herbicides aimed at killing all plants growing there except the one genetically modified by Monsanto or Syngenta to resist their toxicity. The devastation created by agribusiness in the Chaco region, in short, does not stop with deforestation and continues every farming season, killing small animals, contaminating water supplies, and negatively impacting the health of residents in nearby areas, something that has been widely documented by scientists, activists, and ethnographers in many parts of Argentina (Rulli 2009; Lapegna 2016a, 2016b; Vazquez et al. 2017). Yet this is a destruction that has been silenced by the corporations and state officials who celebrate the value of the commodity, soybeans, that once produced in those fields is inserted in supply chains.

At harvest time in April and May, caravans of trucks intensify their march from Salta to Rosario, where the soy boom created a real estate boom that dramatically expanded the city vertically through the construction of skyscrapers and horizontally through the industrialization of the shores of the Paraná. Between 2003 and 2006, the giants that dominate the global market of food and logistics as well as Argentine corporations built around Rosario the largest concentration of crushing factories and private ports in the world, a process that evicted thousands of working-class residents from the shores of the river.[3] Today, the twenty factories and nineteen ports around Rosario generate half of the soymeal in the world. The largest factories can process one thousand trucks per day. But at harvest time the volume of trucks is such that thousands of them clutter the surroundings of the factories, often waiting in line for days on end before dropping off their load. Further confirming the transnational nature of this infrastructural zone, the factories around Rosario attract not only the soybeans produced in Argentina but also those that descend the Paraguay and Paraná Rivers on barges from Paraguay, Bolivia, and southern Brazil.

The urbanization generated by the soy boom in this part of Argentina also expanded into the vast farming region west of Rosario: the *pampas*, or prairies, that in the twentieth century became the agricultural and cattle-raising heart of the nation. Settled by European immigrants, these prairies were for decades devoted to producing beef and wheat for domestic consumption as well as exports, but in the 1990s they became the epicenter of soy farming in Argentina (Gras and Hernández 2013a, 2013b, 2016). Valeria Hernández (2009) has shown that this expansion of industrial agriculture has transformed the towns of these prairies into "agro-cities": modernized urban centers that are surrounded by mechanized farms and infrastructures serving agribusiness (roads, silos, gas stations, banks) and based on urban patterns of consumption (see also Hernández, Riglos, and Muzi 2013a, 2013b). A similar transformation has been noted in soy country in Brazil, which has created what Gustavo Oliveira and Susanna Hecht (2016: 268) call "a new agroindustrial urbanism." In Las Lajitas, this agroindustrial urbanism is less developed, for its growth has been limited and unequal. Most of the streets remain unpaved, and the local public hospital and schools are underfunded. In working-class neighborhoods, dark-skinned people live in poverty depending on odd jobs and social programs. It is largely around the Las Lajitas Hotel that one can see the local expression of an agroindustrial urbanism defined by modern buildings serving corporate actors attentive to the global market.

Once it is industrially processed around Rosario as feed and oil (or simply as beans), the soy originally produced around Las Lajitas is promptly loaded on ships at the ports next to the factories. Ports mark a threshold in the planet's terrain, for their presence indicates the end of landmass's solidity and the beginning of a world of water that requires a different means of transport: ships. While the Paraná is a wide river that has long been a medium of trade, it needs to be regularly dredged by heavy machinery to make it navigable for freighters. This is part of an ambitious infrastructural project called La Hidrovía (The Water Highway), which was first implemented in the 1990s by the four countries of the basin (Argentina, Uruguay, Paraguay, and Brazil) and is now the largest dredge operation in the world.[4] This infrastructural maintenance cannot be slowed down, because the sediments carried by the Paraná permanently fill back what was dredged. The motion-oriented infrastructures of the metropolis, in short, have to permanently struggle against the nonhuman motion of water and sediment flowing toward the Atlantic.

Once the ships are in the ocean, their trajectory depends on multiple factors and market fluctuations. Minor changes in the price of soy or shifting political conditions across the world may make the corporations controlling the supply chains change the trajectory of ships mid-course, redirecting them to slightly more profitable destinations (Oliveira and Schneider 2016: 173). A good percentage of the ships that leave the ports on the Paraná River dock in the ports of southeastern China, which serve one of the most urbanized, industrialized, and heavily populated zones of the metropolis. The soymeal is then distributed to thousands of farms to feed half of the world's population of pigs. The Chinese working class whose increasingly pork-based diet is partly produced with soy from South America then assemble the phones, computers, and countless other stuff that are then shipped in containers, through those same ports, to the world. In Vancouver, where I live, one can regularly see container ships arrive from China and head to the port, the largest in Canada and yet another logistical node moving matter through the metropolis.

The United Republic of Soy: Zones of Imperial Extraction

In August 2016, to my initial surprise, I came across in the streets of Las Lajitas a group of about ten men of East Asian appearance getting off two vans. What gave them away as foreigners, in addition to their facial features, was that they were more formally dressed than locals. All wore dark dress pants and white shirts, and some wore jackets. A few Argentine men were with them. I initially assumed they were from one of the largest state-run companies from China, China National Cereals, Oils, and Foodstuffs Corporation (COFCO). This company had recently arrived in Argentina by purchasing Nidera (a domestic leader in seeds and trade) and the agribusiness branch of Noble, a Hong Kong–based logistical giant that controlled many facilities in the country including a silo near Las Lajitas. A few days earlier, I had seen COFCO flags at this local silo formerly owned by Noble, publicly signaling the arrival of Chinese capital in the region. Later that afternoon, however, I met those men again at the Las Lajitas Hotel and learned they were not from COFCO but from another major Chinese corporation, China Machinery Engineering Corporation (CMEC). Following a deal signed between China and Argentina, CMEC was in the process of investing billions of US dollars to repair and upgrade the decaying railroads connecting northern Argentina to the crushing factories and ports around Rosario. This has been a long-standing demand by the local business elites, for the high cost of transporting beans and grains by truck to Rosario makes farms in Salta less competitive than those in central Argentina. The Chinese team visiting Las Lajitas was made up of engineers who were inspecting, guided by Argentine officials, the state of decay of the regional railways in preparation for their radical makeover. While they had dinner a few meters away from me, half of them were on their smartphones, communicating with urban centers located thousands of kilometers away and taking advantage of the metropolis's continuum.

While the Chinese investment in this region of Argentina is still relatively thin, the presence of those engineers as well as the recent acquisition of silos near Las Lajitas by COFCO signal that some of the regional infrastructures of the supply chains are owned and repaired by actors and capital based in Asian nodes of the metropolis. And it was not a coincidence that the Chinese delegation stayed at Las Lajitas Hotel, sharing the restaurant with this hotel's regular clientele: a few North American and European visitors but mostly Argentine white men who stay for a few days, usually coming from Salta, Córdoba, Santa Fe, or Buenos Aires to oversee farms administered or serviced by their companies or to sell farmers seeds and herbicides and buy their crops. The hotel and the modern buildings that surround it, in this regard, have become crucial political nodes that encapsulate the new hierarchies that exist in Las Lajitas. While most locals descend from gauchos who once raised cattle in the forest, the power in the town council, the hospital, the agrotechnical school is held by white men and women who came from other parts of Argentina. This elite regularly holds meetings at "the hotel," which is viewed by residents as the embodiment of the new relations of power that connect Las Lajitas with the world. And these relations are not only capitalist but also respond to spatial hierarchies of an imperial nature.

In their book *Empire*, published in 2000, Michael Hardt and Antonio Negri argued that the globalizing expansion of capitalism that followed the collapse of communism marked the weakening of the sovereignty of nation-states, the withering away of nationally based imperialisms, and the rise of the planetary and decentered system of capitalist sovereignty "without outside" that they called "Empire" (Hardt and Negri 2000). This provocative argument created a flurry of debate and many authors were quick to criticize the idea of "Empire" as a totalizing abstraction unable to explain the heterogeneous complexity of the world and the ongoing power of nation-states and nationally based imperialisms (Brennan 2003; Reyna 2002; Ong 2012). Anna Tsing, in particular, argued that the idea of an Empire "without outside" reduces global capitalism to a "unitary, homogeneous object" and misses that supply chains often depend on differences and local specificities that are not based on capitalist relations (2012: 37–38; see also 2015: 65). The phenomenal rise of China and the parallel popularity of xenophobic nationalisms, further, reveal that the world is more disjointed than *Empire* could have foreseen. Yet despite the limits of their analysis, what Hardt and Negri bring to light, and is worth redefining along more materialist lines, is that capitalist globalization has an imperial dynamic that is more decentered than the ones that defined classical, nationally based imperialisms. Rather than speaking of "Empire," however, I prefer to outline the *imperial* dimensions of the supply chains, that is, that they are structured by *long-range* spatial hierarchies that capture resources for powerful nodes in the world at the expense of zones of sacrifice.

That urban nodes based on different continents such as Rosario, Shanghai, and Chicago profit from the devastation of the forests of South America suggest that while nation-states and imperialism are indeed part of these networks, they are subsumed to the imperial constellation that exceeds them and constrains them: the metropolis. Anna Tsing (2012, 2015) wrote that studying how supply chains operate on the ground provides "an antidote" to the abstractions of Hardt and Negri's Empire. But it could be argued that the local texture and trajectories of supply chains—especially those of planetary reach—can help us better appreciate the imperial nature of globalization, whose extended forms of urbanization could be described as imperial apparatuses of capture. These apparatuses are akin to "a hostile environment" that in some parts of the world acquires more physical density that in others (Tiqqun 2011: 171). This density creates what I call "zones of imperial extraction": areas of the planet with a high density of infrastructures created to satisfy, as Mumford once put it, "the voracious mouth of the metropolis" (1989: 539).

These zones are discontinuous from each other and are scattered around the world: the Tar Sands in Canada; the open-pit mines in the Andes, Appalachia, or Papua New Guinea; or the vast nodes of oil extraction in the Gulf of Africa, the Gulf of Mexico, or western Amazonia. Andrew Barry (2006) highlighted the technical standardization of these areas by calling them "technological zones." But these zones foster a distinctly imperial type of territoriality, for while they are constrained by their host nation-states they are more subsumed than other zones to the power of global capital. Stuart Elden (2010, 2013a) articulated a theory of territory that conceives it not as a "space" but as political-legal *technologies* (such as laws, surveys, census, map-making) for the control of terrain. In the case of zones of imperial extraction, the main legal-territorial technologies for their expansion have been the free-trade and neoliberal deregulations and privatizations of the past decades, which have maximized capital's power to control terrain by overruling the rights of local people and governments. But a more physical set of territorial weapons have been used to create these zones: infrastructures and logistics.

The roads, silos, and farms around Las Lajitas, in this regard, are part of one of the largest zones of imperial extraction on Earth: lowland South America. This zone expanded rapidly across the continent after Argentina authorized Monsanto in 1996 to sell in the country its genetically modified soy seeds together with its star herbicide Roundup, one of the first in the world to do so. Using Argentina as a beachhead, in a few years Monsanto's seeds and pesticides expanded toward, and took over, much of lowland South America (Robin 2010). Enjoying the support of both the neoliberal and center-left governments of the continent, this zone of extraction was the child of the chemical companies that dominate the global market of GM seeds and pesticides: Monsanto, Syngenta, Bayer, Dow, DuPont, and BASF, a group that is going through a rapid process of further concentration. The recent fusion between Dow and DuPont, the purchase of Monsanto by Bayer, and the purchase of Syngenta by ChemChina signal the further tightening of this oligopoly and the growing presence of the Chinese state among the myriad actors that profit from this zone.

This agribusiness zone in the heart of South America forms a vast archipelago that extends north from central Argentina all the way to Amazonia in Brazil and is the main source of soy on the planet, generating almost 60 percent of the global output. In a well-known advertising campaign, the Swiss-based agrichemical giant Syngenta (now controlled by ChemChina) captured the existence of this transnational zone with an imaginary map of "the United Republic of Soy" covering much of Argentina, Uruguay, Brazil, Paraguay, and lowland Bolivia, with the heading "soy knows no borders." This vast zone is geographically and culturally very diverse and certain subregions cultivate specific modalities of soy farming (Mier y Terán Giménez Cacho 2016). Yet the soy farms around Las Lajitas operate in ways that are similar to those in Brazil or central Argentina, for they all plant genetically modified seeds, use large amounts of pesticides, and rely on mechanized operations that hire very few workers (see Oliveira and Schneider 2016).

Whereas in zones of imperial extraction that involve open-pit mining the production of ore is usually carried out by multinational corporations, in the "United Republic of Soy" the farming of soybeans is largely in the hands of Argentine, Brazilian, or Uruguayan companies and farmers. Yet the action of these domestic actors is constrained by one of the most powerful corporate conglomerates in the world: the trading and logistical companies that control the supply chains of soybeans and grains and that sell farmers their inputs (seeds, pesticides, insurance, technical assistance) and buy their crops.

The most powerful of these highly globalized companies are ADM (Archer Daniel Midlands), Bunge, Cargill, and Dreyfus, a group known collectively as "ABCD." These companies played a decisive role in helping create this zone of extraction in the 1990s, when neoliberal deregulations allowed them to take over much of the crushing, trade, and logistics sector in South America, eroding the prior prominence of domestic companies and the state on this market (Oliveira and Hecht 2016: 257). The more recent arrival in the supply chains of companies based in Asia, led now by COFCO, are further decentering these globalized forms of power.

As noted by Tsing (2015), global traders need to engage in a work of cultural translation in order to work with the diverse social actors they interact with at different stages of the supply chains. In other words, the assembling of supply chains is not a mechanical, top-down process but demands a sensibility to local specificities and cultural differences. In South America, several ethnographers including myself have noted this sensibility among the local agents of corporations such as Cargill or Bunge. These agents try to gain the trust of potential clients by adapting to their practices and cultural rhythms and by contributing to local institutions through donations and the organization of social events (Wesz 2016; Leguizamón 2016; Oliveira and Hecht 2016). Yet these localized adaptations, as Valdemar João Wesz Jr. (2016) and Amalia Leguizamón (2016) show, do not change the fact that these global traders operate in Brazil and Argentina in very similar ways. They all impose oligopolic practices that leave farmers and midsize farming companies with little space for maneuver. This is why most farmers and administrators I talked to tend to resent the globalized conglomerates that control the market.

Understanding how these trading companies operate across the multiplicity of the planetary terrain is key to appreciating the imperial nature of their strategies. All of these companies share a strategy of vertical integration through which they control the different stages of the chain in dozens of different countries. Once they purchase crops from farmers, the ABCD group as well as other companies mobilize their vast networks of ports, ships, and silos to arrange for their storage, industrial processing, and transport to their destination in Asian, European, or African nodes of the metropolis (figure 3.3). Throughout the process, these companies are guided by a planetary field of vision that is clearly articulated, for instance, on the website of Noble Group, the logistics corporation based in Hong Kong. In 2013, when it owned a silo near Las Lajitas before it sold it to COFCO, Noble was number 73 in the Fortune 500 ranking and stood out among the logistics giants because it was the

Figure 3.3. A truck receiving its load of soybeans at COFCO's *planta de acopio* (collecting facility) in Piquete Cabado. Photo by the author.

first to be based in Asia. For Noble, the soy it stored in its facility near Las Lajitas is just one of the many commodities—from iron ore to natural gas and oil—it transports and processes across the world. The company's website boasted about the planetary and hierarchical trajectories mobilized by silos such as those in Argentina: "We connect low cost producing countries with high demand growth markets." The website also highlighted that the company's geographical "diversification," by which it meant *spatial multiplicity and planetary reach*, is "crucial" to overcome "times of uncertainty": "As an example, we can source agricultural products at anytime from Argentina or the Ukraine, iron ore products from India, Mongolia, or Brazil, coal products from Colombia, Australia, or Indonesia."[5] This is what logistics corporations call "agility" (Bernes 2013). This "agile" spatiality is imperial because of its capacity to *move* at any time *any* commodity almost anywhere in the world.

As Deborah Cowen (2014) shows, this means that global logistics prioritize *the security of global currents* over national forms of control, therefore pushing for imperial, transnational forms of oversight. "Rather than territorial borders at the edge of the national space guaranteeing the sovereignty of the nation-state, a new cartography of security aims to protect global networks of circulation" (69). And while borders do not disappear, they "are superseded by transnational networks, flows, and urban nodes" (69). In the case of the soy supply chains, the destruction created in forested areas of South America by the practices and infrastructures that Bunge, Cargill, or COFCO mobilize to extract and transport soymeal across the world respond to so many transnational actors that it cannot be said to respond to "US imperialism" or "Chinese nationalism." To be clear, imperialist and nationalist agendas standing in tension with each other are part and parcel of the disjointed currents of the metropolis. The US government, for instance, permanently lobbies South American nations to favor Monsanto and other US-based corporations. And the state-run companies from China active in the soy supply chains, such as COFCO and ChemChina, follow (unlike their private competitors) the nationalist agenda of the Chinese state and its goal to guarantee food self-sufficiency.[6] Yet lowland South America has been transformed into a zone of imperial extraction not by particular nation-states but by a more transnational, dispersed, and nebulous constellation of actors and logistical operations that seek to capture cheap animal feed, oil, and beans regardless of the environmental and social cost. These corporations are so entangled with each other that they often cooperate rather than compete. China's investment in the repair of the railways between Las Lajitas and Rosario, after all, will benefit not just Chinese consumers but also the whole commodity chain.

As Aihwa Ong (1999) has argued, local actors and nation-states can definitively have an impact in shaping the spatial patterns of globalization. Likewise, zones of imperial extraction are profoundly affected by national differences. The explosive rise of an infrastructural cluster of factories and ports around Rosario in 2003–2006, for instance, was the product of the efforts by the center-left administration of President Néstor Kirchner (2003–2007) to create a crushing industry on Argentine soil. In particular, his government created a differential tax policy on soy exports, which slightly lowered taxes on soymeal and oil in relation to unprocessed soybeans. This lower tax on industrialized soy succeeded in attracting heavy investment in crushing factories by global conglomerates and in rapidly turning Argentina into the world's lead exporter of soymeal and oil. Brazil, in contrast, exports most of its much larger soy output as beans for the reverse reason: its taxes are lower for nonindustrialized exports (Wesz 2016: 292). This territorial policy by the Brazilian state means that soybeans harvested in Amazonia are crushed in factories in Asia, confirming how national differences affect the composition of the supply chains.

Revealing the agency of domestic actors in these chains, some Argentine corporations have become crucial players in the subordination of this area of South America to the metropolis. In Las Lajitas, for instance, despite the strong presence of Cargill and Bunge in the area, the main buyer of local crops is the Argentine corporation AGD, Aceitera General Deheza. And the main local seller of GM seeds is Don Mario, an Argentine company that holds the right to produce Monsanto technology in seeds. Further, these companies have developed a transnational strategy that has made them expand operations to neighboring countries such as Brazil and work closely with the corporations that dominate the global market (Craviotti 2016). Something similar occurs in Brazil, where the most powerful agribusiness in the country, Amaggi, has built a port near Rosario. In short, the infrastructures of these apparatuses of capture in South America are also produced and controlled by corporations that are based on the continent.[7]

This overlap within Argentina of different technologies of territorial control by national companies, transnational corporations, and the state often leads to conflicts. In March 2016, for instance, Monsanto began to set up checkpoints at the gates of factories and ports around Rosario to subject the trucks arriving there to the type of controls usually carried out by officials or the police. In these checkpoints, Monsanto agents tested the beans looking for traces of their Intacta soybeans (genetically modified to resist insects) and billed farmers if they had not paid royalties.[8] Notably, they did so in collaboration with the companies that own the crushing facilities. This corporate appropriation of the right to police, however, proved too controversial and the outcry from farmers and officials forced Monsanto to back down. Yet the backstory was Monsanto's efforts to force a change in the Argentine legislation on seeds, which in contrast to North American or Brazilian law does not allow corporations to claim GM seeds as private property subject to royalties. Ironically, while Argentina is a crucial node in this zone of imperial extraction, it is (at least for now) one of the last bastions of the principle that seeds should be part of the commons: owned by none, usable by all. And this key difference within "the United Republic of Soy" exists because of the social movements that have fought hard to keep seeds unpatented.

In the first decade of the century, the administrations of Néstor and Cristina Kirchner encouraged the soy boom as a source of national progress, development, and social justice. And they redistributed part of the wealth generated by the export taxes on soy, which funded the social programs that sustained their popularity among the poor, at least during the early boom years. When they were in power, Cristina Kirchner and other center-left presidents in South America such as Lula da Silva in Brazil thereby celebrated the expansion of agribusiness as a source of national pride defined against "US imperialism." But their complicity with the high levels of dispossession, violence, and destruction in the indigenous and mestizo heart of the continent has made of former presidents Kirchner and Lula what could be called "anti-imperialists for Empire": that is, leaders who may have put limits to US imperialism in South America but did so by embracing the extractive rhythms of the metropolis.

The openly right-wing government that has ruled Argentina since late 2015 has embraced extractivism further by immediately lowering taxes on soy exports and identifying the interests of agribusiness as official policy. Yet the negative legacy of two decades of deforestation, evictions, violence, and poisoning has also generated vibrant social movements committed to confronting the powerful agribusiness lobby.

Interrupting the Soy Supply Chains

The fact that the different stages of the supply chain require the reproduction of localized assemblages means that protests against agribusinesses in Argentina have attempted to interrupt and disarticulate the assemblages themselves. In forested areas of the Chaco, the attempts at interruption start as soon as the bulldozers seek to move forth against the forest and people's homes. Struggles against evictions are fought on multiple fronts, involving courts, the media, and protests on the streets of nearby towns. But most people who fight deforestation do so with their own bodies, placing themselves in the path of bulldozers to demand that the drivers halt their advance. In this low-intensity warfare, residents have even burnt bulldozes to defend their homes, and many people I know remain on their land because of their determination to stay put. But others have been jailed, wounded, or killed, and twelve people have been murdered in the past few years for defending their land on the soy frontiers of northern Argentina (Aranda 2015).

Road blockades have also proliferated in protests against agribusiness. And this has included blockages to interrupt the construction of infrastructural nodes by some of the most powerful companies in the world. The most notable defeat suffered by Monsanto in Argentina, for instance, was its failure to construct what was hailed as its largest factory in Latin America: a high-end facility in the town of Malvinas Argentinas, province of Córdoba, where the company intended to produce GM corn seeds. Because of well-founded fears that the factory would spread toxic dust into their homes, residents organized and blockaded the gate and interrupted construction for three years (2013–2016). Despite the hostility of the media and attacks by the police and thugs, the determination of local men and women to defend the blockade generated a strong national and international solidarity campaign that eventually forced Monsanto to abandon the project.[9]

In the agroindustrial ring around Rosario, the unionized workers who operate the crushing factories have regularly asserted their power at this bottleneck of the supply chain by blockading access to the factories and ports during strikes, thereby shutting down the flow of beans, oil, and soymeal out of the country.[10] These protests are a reminder that infrastructures require laborers who have the power to shut down the continuum. As Toscano (2011) argues, in a neoliberal era in which most workers have been offshored and downsized, the workers in charge of logistical nodes are therefore empowered by their partial control of infrastructures (see Mitchell 2011; Cowen 2014). And around Rosario, the capacity of workers to shut down the ports has made of them among the best paid in Argentina.

Not all of the interruptions slowing down or disrupting the supply chains are the product of human political actions. In Las Lajitas, a recurring concern among farm administrators and engineers are the growing number of "super weeds" that are becoming resistant to herbicides. These nonhuman life forms have become so resilient and expansive that they threaten to overgrow the soy fields and interrupt the farms' productive rhythms. In the Paraná River, conjunctural events generated by the becoming of terrain such as the formation of a sandbank can create massive traffic jams involving dozens of 30,000-ton freighters. In March 2014, for instance, a ship stranded on the Paraná near Rosario and immobilized eighty vessels, shutting down exports for ten days.[11] These are contingent interruptions generated by encounters between human-made objects and the shifting depth of a river; yet they confirm that for all its power the metropolis is an aggregations of multiplicities that always-already involve, and are affected by, the textures of terrain.

Conclusions: The Age of the Metropolis

The idea of the Anthropocene has been important to discuss the disruptive impact of climate change because it highlights that the world is an interconnected totality. This is a totality in the immanent sense of the term, for no part of the planet and none of its life forms are immune from a warming atmosphere. The Anthropocene is another way of admitting, in other words, that "there's no outside" of the dislocations produced by climate change. In this chapter, I sought to contribute to debates about the Anthropocene by highlighting that the atmosphere is warming not just because of capitalism but because of its incarnation in the metropolis, "a flow of beings and things, a current that runs through fiber-optic networks, high-speed train lines, and video surveillance cameras, making sure that this world keeps running straight to its ruins" (Invisible Committee 2009: 58–59).

The trajectories of the soy supply chains affecting Argentina remind us that the current configuration of the metropolis was produced by China's phenomenal urbanization and its transformation into the planetary factory for global capital, and by the resulting suction of voluminous flows of resources to build up such an expansion of the urban form. The Chinese state has since adopted an even more assertive role in the expansion of the metropolis by becoming the largest builder of infrastructures the world over: from the "New Silk Road" across central Asia to massive investment in mines, ports, railways, and dams in South Asia, Africa, Oceania, and Latin America. The repair of the railways around Las Lajitas is just one sample of this planetary presence of Chinese capital. While the nationalist agenda behind China's infrastructural drive has generated friction with other global powers, it is not at all incompatible with the imperial apparatuses of capture of global capitalism. On the contrary, China is "not outside" of these apparatuses. The huge industrial zones that exist in southeastern China to produce stuff for the metropolis under conditions of intense exploitation, after all, are also zones of imperial extraction. These are zones in which the most powerful capitalists on Earth give the Chinese state the mandate to provide them with a cheap, docile, and industrious workforce. The metropolis may have today a Chinese engine, but its apparatuses of capture remain rhizomatic and imperial.

In its nonrepresentable multiplicity and vastness, the metropolis is certainly not reducible to its destructive and exploitative dimensions. Infrastructures that provide for clean water, renewable energy, sanitation, health care, education, or public transit are central to the production of collective and egalitarian forms of well-being. And as Lefebvre (2003), Negri (2018), Merrifield (2013), and David Harvey (2012) insist, the metropolis is a space of encounters full of egalitarian and revolutionary potential: a networked terrain that in putting millions of people in close proximity with each other, and in helping them communicate across borders, can create transformative solidarities. In the words of Hardt and Negri, "the metropolis is a factory for the production of the commons" (2009: 250).

In a metropolis structured by capitalist forms of acceleration, the defense of the commons has emerged with particular force in the grassroots attempts to interrupt the assembling of infrastructures that reproduce this acceleration. The politics of interruption through which people in Argentina try to disrupt the advance of bulldozers captures, in this regard, the politics of many social movements all over the world. Well-known examples are the shutdown by twenty-five thousand protesters of the port of Oakland, California, in November 2011, following the police repression of Occupy Oakland; the rise of blockades by indigenous people to interrupt the expansion of pipelines and other fossil-fuel-related infrastructures in North America, which Naomi Klein (2015) calls "blockadia"; or the blockade of oil refineries in France in 2015 by workers opposing the erosion of their labor rights. Joshua Clover (2016) has argued that the growing popularity of blockades all over the world means that the dominant anticapitalist struggle is no longer the strike but "riots" over circulation. The Invisible Committee, further, argue that insurrections should involve the blockage and sabotage of the infrastructures of the metropolis and the derailing of its restless currents of matter. In their words, "Power is logistic. Block everything!" (2015: 81).

Alberto Toscano (2011, 2014) has nonetheless criticized this overemphasis on interruption and blockade in the radical left. He argues that any attempt to move beyond capitalism will have to confront the hard fact that the supply chains cannot be just shut down, first because the livelihood of millions of people depend on their ongoing mobility. To call for a shutdown of the metropolis, he wrote, is "to make something of a fetish out of rupture" (2011: 2). The infrastructure and logistical operations of the metropolis, Toscano argues, should rather be reconfigured toward new ends: to satisfy collective uses and needs rather than private profits. In turn, Bernes criticized Toscano by counterarguing that exploitation and disruption are so constitutive to supply chains, so central to their design as imperial weapons, that their appropriation for egalitarian ends is unfeasible. But he adds that blockades are not enough. What is needed, rather, is a "delinking from the planetary factory" through which local communes organize to cut off their dependence on supply chains (2013: 11). This act of withdrawal is "a matter of survival," Bernes writes.

These debates are multifaceted and unanswerable in the abstract. But struggles against the extractivist drive of the metropolis usually involve a combination of interruptions, delinking, and positive appropriations and creations. Activists all over Argentina confront agribusiness not only through blockades but also through efforts to create different agrarian places by cutting off links with the supply chains of GM seeds, agrichemicals, and feed. They embrace an organic, socially conscious agriculture, *la agroecología*, to grow food for people living in regional towns and cities. These efforts withdraw from some supply chains but without withdrawing from the metropolis; rather, they embrace its collective potential and exploit the connectivities of its continuum in order to forge links with social movements based elsewhere in the world.

A political interrogation of the metropolis as the fast-paced infrastructure of the Anthropocene, however, confronts us with the bleak future it hints at, confirming what Hetherington and Jeremy Campbell (2014: 193) argue about infrastructures: that they are "always about the future, or different futures." Amid the worsening patterns of class polarization, racism, atmospheric disruptions, and ambient toxicity that define this early phase of the Anthropocene, it is not surprising that in films and popular culture the future evokes a catastrophe in which the grand infrastructures and skyscrapers of the metropolis are reduced to huge piles of rubble. Any collective attempt to create a future *not* defined by a planetary ruination, in this regard, has to face that the undoing of imperial and capitalist relations will require the reinvention of the metropolis as a collective constellation that does not depend for its existence on the creation of sacrifice zones.

Notes

1 In 2003–2007 alone, over a million hectares of forests were destroyed in the province of Salta (Leake, López, and Leake 2016).
2 I first carried out the fieldwork that led to my book *Rubble* in 2003–2007 (Gordillo 2014). I subsequently returned in 2010, 2011, 2013, and 2016.
3 "Rosario, aude y caída de la Argentina dorada," *El País*, October 8, 2015.
4 Héctor Huergo, "La hidrovía abona la inversión," *Clarín*, September 2, 2006.
5 Noble Group, accessed December 2013, http://www.thisisnoble.com.

6 "ChemChina Deal for Syngenta Reflects Drive to Meet Food Needs," *New York Times*, February 3, 2016.

7 "Inversión: Grupo brasileño construirá una terminal portuaria en Rosario," *Infocampo.com.ar*, June 18, 2016, accessed July 2016, http://www.infocampo.com.ar/inversion-grupo-brasileno-construira-una-terminal-portuaria-en-rosario/.

8 "Monsanto: Crece la pelea por el pago de regalías," *La Nación*, May 11, 2016.

9 "Chau Monsanto: Triunfo de los vecinos en Malvinas Argentinas," *La Vaca*, August 3, 2016.

10 "Dani, el aceitoso," *Revista Crisis* 27, November 4, 2016.

11 "Un barco varado en el Paraná impide que se exporte soja," *La Nación*, March 20, 2014.

Part II.
Lively Infrastructures

FOUR. Dirty Landscapes

How Weediness Indexes State Disinvestment and Global Disconnection

ASHLEY CARSE

"Sucia," María repeated.

We were traveling by bus to visit the ruins of Fort San Lorenzo, a Spanish colonial structure perched on a bluff overlooking the Caribbean Sea, not far from Colón. That city, Panama's second largest, is adjacent to the Atlantic (Caribbean) terminus of the Panama Canal. Today, those Spanish ruins are located in San Lorenzo National Park, which also encompasses the ruins of Fort Sherman, a former US military base. The remains of the two forts are surrounded by mangroves, wetlands, and wet forests—now protected, at least in part, due to the dangers of unexploded armaments scattered therein.[1] This was also the site of a US firing range. For tourists, the park is a place to consume history and tropical nature together. For María and other residents, however, the growth of unruly plant life in this region indexes, or points to, processes of state disinvestment and global disconnection.

No public buses entered San Lorenzo National Park, so María and I got off at the entrance and sat down on a roadside guardrail to wait for a taxi. We weren't the only ones there. Fifteen or so *peones* (day laborers) sat and stood along the guardrail's length, also waiting. As cars whizzed by, María told me that they were employed to cut the grass in parts of the park visited by tourists. Seeing the group of laborers seemed to strike a chord.

"Since the Americans left," she said, "this whole area is *sucia* [dirty]."

Her comment surprised me because our surroundings were verdant and, to my eye, beautiful. Just then, a taxi slowed to pick us up. María stepped into the front passenger seat, and I slid into the back. As the car wound through forests and past the abandoned barracks and facilities of Fort Sherman, María repeated her observation and the driver agreed.

"Sucia?" I said. "Do you mean the grounds are covered in trash?"

"Not just that," the driver said, "the *hierba* [grass] grows up and nobody keeps it *limpia* [clean]. Nobody takes care of it."[2]

That encounter took place in 2008, only a month into my fieldwork around the Panama Canal. In the years that followed, I often heard residents of the province of Colón (colonenses) describe the landscapes around the waterway in the same terms that María had. In interviews and informal conversations, Panamanians living near the canal's Atlantic terminus characterized the social, political, and economic changes of the last few decades in terms of increasing dirtiness (using the verb *encsuciar*: to become dirty). Many focused on what they described as a proliferation of unruly plant life. A common refrain was that the Panama Canal Authority—the Panamanian state institution that administers the canal and vast swaths of surrounding territory—had allowed the "clean" modern landscapes of the former US Canal Zone to become overgrown, or sucia, when the zone was transferred from the United States to Panama, a process completed in 1999. My interviewees also contrasted Colón's "dirty" landscapes with today's Panama City, where a long economic boom has produced a new oceanfront promenade, Central America's first subway, and a thicket of glass skyscrapers containing luxury hotels, banks, and corporate offices. By comparison, Colón, which has a largely Afro-Panamanian population, is poor and decaying. For many colonenses, steady work, good housing, and hope are in short supply.

It is a truism in Panama that Colón was once beautiful and is now in ruin. Although explanations of its decline vary (racism, capital flight, the reversion of the US Canal Zone, gang violence), few would dispute that life in

Colón today is a *lucha* (struggle). Despite—or, perhaps, because of—the city's proximity to the immense wealth channeled through the canal and an adjacent complex of ports, transshipment facilities, and a free trade zone, the surrounding province has the highest unemployment rate in the country, with median wages and household income levels well below the national average (Contralaría General de la República 2018). Moreover, its aging water, sewer, stormwater, and power networks reflect long-term disinvestment. Some colonenses see these problems as an indication of the shortcomings and biases of the national government, displaying the "well-known habit," as Raymond Williams put it, "of using the past, the 'good old days', as a stick to beat the present" (1973: 12). In an interview, Paulo, an Afro-Panamanian man in his nineties, chronicled a decline in regional maintenance, providing detailed descriptions of unpainted buildings and nearby lots overgrown with weeds. By way of explanation, he concluded, "The government doesn't care. They don't live here. They live in Panama City."

Given Colón's bleak economic situation, the postcolonial nostalgia that some residents expressed didn't surprise me, but their emphasis on weediness did. Why, I wondered, did people fixate on something that seems so inconsequential in a place where many were struggling just to find work, get an education, and access basic services?

For many colonenses, I argue, weediness indexes state disinvestment and global disconnection. Extending the anthropological observation that people treat infrastructures as indices of a variety of other social, economic, and political phenomena, I suggest that colonenses think and talk about weeds to make sense of spatiotemporal relationships that are not readily accessible to the senses[3] (figure 4.1). This recognition dovetails with a useful observation about economic globalization: it produces experiences of connection and disconnection (Ferguson 2006b: 239). People in formerly cosmopolitan cities such as Colón are not historically unconnected (an original condition) but actively disconnected from the global economy as a result of others' conscious choices and priorities. In Colón, US empire, global capital, and—to a lesser degree—the Panamanian state have abandoned cultural landscapes that were historically manicured and maintained. My interest in these landscapes is inspired by Anna Tsing's work on the ecological seams of empire and the unruly edges of capitalism and state control (2012, 2015). I follow her in writing a history of weediness (Tsing 2005: 171–202) that approaches boundaries and gaps—between the cultivated and the wild, subsistence and

Figure 4.1. Disconnected drainage pipes and weeds in Colón, Panama. Photo by author.

market economies, farm and forest, settlements and hinterlands, and, I would add, between infrastructure and environment—as conceptual spaces and cultural landscapes deserving ethnographic, ecological, and historical scrutiny.

Attention to weediness reveals that the infrastructure-environment boundary is not an a priori categorical distinction, but an artifact of the constant organizational work—from discursive to physical labor—necessary to establish and maintain connections in an encroaching world. Even as the political economy of late industrialism (Fortun 2012) drives rapid deforestation along resource extraction frontiers, unruly plant life thrives in the spaces left behind. Consider the phenomenon of secondary forest succession across postagrarian and postindustrial landscapes. In parts of Panama and across Latin America, recent decades have seen an increase in secondary vegetation land cover following deforestation (Bray et al. 2003; Klooster 2003; Rudel 2002; Hecht 2004; Wright and Samaniego 2008). The reasons are complex and linked to a variety of multiscalar processes, including geopolitical shifts, commodity market dynamics, national economic policies, technological change, and flows of migrants and remittances (Hecht et al. 2006). Such processes can seem abstract and placeless, but for my interlocutors—people like my friend María—the weedy results are deeply felt, because disinvestment in the maintenance of Colón's built environment is identified with the abandonment of its human occupants.

The Clean and the Dirty: From Structural Anthropology to Infrastructure Studies

What are people talking about when they talk about weeds? For colonenses, I argue, weeds—like infrastructure—render complex spatiotemporal relationships legible and conducive to analysis. Given the distinction my Panamanian interlocutors made between clean and dirty landscapes, many readers will think of Mary Douglas's structuralist work on pollution and her maxim: dirt "is matter out of place" (1966). Here, dirtiness is understood to be socially constructed within a cultural system of classification. Certainly, colonenses' weed talk involves an element of symbolic representation. As an idea, dirty landscapes assume referential power in relation to their opposite (clean). Consider Zygmunt Bauman's constructivist definition of weeds: "What makes some plants into 'weeds,' which we mercilessly poison and uproot, is their horrifying tendency to obliterate the boundary between our garden and wilderness. . . . Their 'fault' is that they have come, uninvited, to a place in which ought to be neatly cut into lawns, rose garden, vegetable plot and flower borders. They spoil the harmony we envisaged, they play havoc with our design" (1990: 57). This is a useful way to think about weeds, but what if—following the people of Colón—we shift our attention from where plants "ought to be" generally to examine the cultural politics of maintenance practices along the infrastructure-environment borderlands.

A new generation of infrastructure studies in anthropology flags a resurgent interest in structure (Larkin 2013; Harvey, Jensen, and Morita 2016), but with a new emphasis on the sociomaterial relations that undergird and enable modern life. As James Ferguson observes, "The 'infra-structure' that is of interest here is clearly not conceived as infra-structural in the Marxian sense (underlying, causally primary), nor is it imagined as a 'structure' in the structuralist sense (a symbolically integrated system awaiting decoding). We are rather closer to the domain of engineering, with infra-structure imagined as a set of (often literally) concrete arrangements that both coexist with and enable or facilitate other such arrangements" (2012: 559). The anthropology of infrastructure literature is part of an interdisciplinary infrastructure studies conversation that spans geography (Furlong 2014), media studies (Parks and Starosielski 2015), and architecture (Easterling 2014).

This volume extends the anthropology of infrastructure—which has revealed the (unexpectedly) fascinating social lives of pumps, pipes, cables, and roads—to engage with scholarly and public conversations around the environment and life. Few humanistic scholars of technology would deny that engineered infrastructures articulate with environmental processes. They are affected by abiotic phenomena (water, light, and temperature) and surrounded and even inhabited by biotic communities (plants, animals, and bacteria). Analytically, however, historical and social studies of technology have long treated the environment as a passive backdrop to social and technological change (E. Russell et al. 2011). Since the turn of the century, scholarship in STS and at the intersection of the history of technology and environmental history (envirotech) has recognized the role of nonhuman life and materials in shaping technologies, and vice versa (Benson 2015; Jørgensen 2014; Jørgensen, Jørgensen, and Pritchard 2013; E. Russell 2004; Stine and Tarr 1998). This volume's anthropological orientation represents a welcome complement to those conversations. Organized around three keywords in contemporary social analysis—infrastructure, environment, and life—the contributors think with and against the conceptual limitations of those categories in productive ways (Hetherington, this volume). In this chapter, I find it useful to think through these keywords by focusing on weeds.

I argue that the boundary between infrastructure and environment is not an a priori categorical distinction, but an artifact of the constant organizational work (discursive, scientific, technical, physical) required to make and maintain connections in a living, encroaching world. Scholars have used terms such as "infrastructuring" (Donovan 2013; Pipek and Wulf 2009) to describe the activities and practices of rendering environments as infrastructure (Blok, Nakazora, and Winthereik 2016). Here, I use the related concept of "infrastructural work" (Bowker 1994) to analyze the extension (or retraction) of infrastructure vis-à-vis the environment. My emphasis on infrastructural work echoes Gieryn's (1983) influential idea that boundaries are made and negotiated through practices: defining insides and outsides, enclosing and excluding, and so on. Like his research on the science-nonscience boundary and others' on the economy-society boundary (Callon 1998; Mitchell 2002), work practices around the infrastructure-environment boundary redistribute power and wealth.

Nature can become infrastructure through concerted investment and management (Carse 2012)—that is, infrastructural work—and, by the same token, infrastructure can revert to nature in the absence of such organizational practices. The work of maintaining a boundary between infrastructure and environment has spatial and temporal dimensions. Consider a road. As soon as its surface is laid, it is already in the process of being destroyed by rain and ice, tires and hooves, and weeds (Barak 2009; Harvey and Knox 2015; Otter 2004b). This means that without constant work—manifest in forms that range from investment, labor, and machinery to political discourse—and the institutions capable of organizing that work, there is no road. Viewed at longer temporal scales, infrastructures—even physical monuments to human progress such as the Panama Canal—are temporary and need maintenance in the face of water, earth, and life (Weisman 2007). This is true of buildings (Brand 1994), communications cables (Starosielski 2015), canals (Barnes 2014; Carse and Lewis 2017), and urban water systems (Anand 2017).

What colonenses recognize in weediness, then, is how easily infrastructures can unbundle and run in reverse if they are not maintained. Writing about communities on Paraguay's rural frontier, Hetherington (2014) observes that infrastructural investments can materialize the promise of development, slotting the landscape along a narrative of progress. He writes, "In such a narrative, infrastructure often serves as that which holds nature and culture apart, marking a temporal break between chaos and order" (196–197). But if we redirect our attention from investments in construction to investments in maintenance, we might also say that culture serves to hold infrastructure and nature apart. Because the connections that infrastructures enable are so meaningful to individuals and communities, the infrastructure-environment borderlands can become grounds for heated debate, interpretation, mobilization, and alliance building, raising questions like: What is this landscape element? How and whom should it serve? What should be here?

In the rural and periurban communities around the Panama Canal where I have worked for the past decade, residents regularly—and often heatedly—discuss the promise of new roads, power lines, and water pipes and complain about the poor condition of old ones. From experience, people recognize that the condition of a given piece of infrastructure at any moment reflects the relationship between, on the one hand, labor, capital investment, and institutional priorities and, on the other hand, biotic and abiotic process (its ecology). As a material artifact, infrastructure is just another element of the landscape. This does not mean that those infrastructures are locally bounded. As marginalized urban and rural people often know too well, roads, electrical networks, and waterworks transcend localities, linking them to extensive networks, projects, and processes organized by governments, corporations, and other institutions.[4]

As this suggests, it is difficult to write about infrastructure and environment independent of ideologies of progress. Consider the contributors to this volume. For Wakefield and Braun, progress is a trap. For Masco, it's something important that we've lost. For Jensen, it remains an interesting experimental opportunity. Weediness plays havoc with modern landscapes and subjectivities. It indexes how the ideologies of progress that infrastructure materializes on the landscape can run in reverse. Structures can become rubble (Gordillo 2014), and the gap between nature and culture can be overgrown, confounding expectations of modernity. What people make of weediness and how they respond depends on material and imaginative relations to the built environment forged over time. How did Panamanians living around the canal come to associate modernity with a manicured landscape aesthetic? To understand, we need to go back a century.

Cutting the Grass: Empire, Modernity, and Work at the Infrastructure-Environment Boundary

In the US Canal Zone, which existed from 1904 to 1979, administrators treated the construction and maintenance of infrastructures and the management of the environments as deeply intertwined. These projects were also linked at moral and affective registers due to the modernist association between development and sanitation. When colonenses talk about today's overgrown landscapes, they often compare them to those they knew in the past—particularly the manicured short-grass landscapes of the former Canal Zone. During one interview, for example, I asked an older Afro-Panamanian man what he meant when he described an ideal landscape as limpia. He paused and then replied, "Limpia is when it looks beautiful, like the gringos had it: a savannah, green, neatly cut."

A defining feature of infrastructure—its "infra" quality—is that can become "sunk" beneath social arrangements and its functionality (or lack thereof) taken for granted (Star and Ruhleder 1996). Infrastructural norms and expectations are learned as part of group membership, shaping subjectivities and, in some cases, marking moments when people are enrolled in communities of aspiration (Hetherington 2014: 198). Those aspirational communities can, as this essay shows, be remarkably durable, persisting as points of reference among the ruins of unrealized futures. This illustrates a key point: through the communities that coalesce around infrastructures, people can become committed to or advocates for particular enactments of the environment—commitments with moral connotations and material consequences (Carse and Lewis 2017; Jørgensen 2013).

The US government "built" the Panama Canal between 1904 and 1914. Since then, canal construction has been held up as a technoscientific conquest of nature (Carse et al. 2016). On the ground, most of the construction work was done by tens of thousands of migrant laborers, mostly of Afro-Caribbean origin (Greene 2009). The US government's political, economic, and technoscientific ambitions in Panama were more expansive than building a waterway. The canal project involved urban planning, housing, security, food provisioning, and public health initiatives. Many of these second-order projects involved what we now call environmental management and sought to transform a place labeled the "pest hole of the world" into suitable habitat for a canal and its large foreign workforce (the health of white US citizens being the main concern). Public health projects were among the most extensive and, arguably, transformative of the myriad environmental management efforts pursued by the US government during the construction of the canal (Gorgas 1915; LePrince and Orenstein 1916). At the beginning of the twentieth century—just before the US canal effort began—scientists identified mosquitoes as the vectors of malaria and yellow fever.[5] Because building and operating an interoceanic canal required a massive and, ideally, healthy workforce (particularly "skilled" white workers from temperate countries), the public health response was to sanitize the environments—both natural and anthropogenic—conducive to mosquito habitation in order to establish healthy landscapes.

US sanitation and public health initiatives in the Canal Zone and adjacent areas in the Republic of Panama produced paved roads, water pipes, and manicured lawns that were collectively promoted with the language of cleanliness and modernity. Under William Gorgas, the canal's Department of Sanitation reduced mosquito habitat by draining, filling, or covering standing water in oil and either burning (figure 4.2) or cutting down "jungle," brush, and grass (Lindsay-Poland 2003: 30). Canal employees also fumigated houses and dumped human waste and garbage. Sanitation work extended across the

Figure 4.2. "Burning grass from side of ditch. Crude oil used as fuel. Miraflores, Canal Zone, June 1910." Source: National Archives.

Canal Zone—where disease control was used as a rationale for racially segregated settlements—and into Panamanian cities. In Panama City and Colón, US sanitarians, engineers, and inspectors worked with Panamanian counterparts to sanitize the urban environment (Sutter 2016).

American sanitary engineering in Panama extended the domestic work of cleaning up US cities by building water supply, wastewater, and solid waste disposal networks (Melosi 2000). At home and abroad, sanitation projects were not just about reengineering built environments, but making environmental subjects (Agrawal 2005). If the sanitized urban and suburban landscapes were "clean," then the things they replaced—forests, wetlands, communities—were, by implication, dirty. Thus, the US government had practical public health reasons to reengineer Panamanian cities and cut back vegetation, but the associated landscape aesthetic played an important symbolic role in the projection of imperial order and control, as it had in other US outposts overseas (Gillem 2007).

Even the everyday work of cutting grass was couched in the language of natural conquest and the defense of civilization from encroaching tropical nature. For Panama Canal administrators, grass cutting produced healthy landscapes and an aesthetic of control. During the construction era, the Department of Sanitation and Quartermaster's Department (QMD) both saw grass cutting as part of their mandates (Sutter 2007: 748–749). The QMD cut grass in zone communities to maintain a residential landscape attractive to North Americans. They focused on cutting the grass short (an inch) around canal facilities and "gold roll" (white) dwellings. Sanitarians, by contrast, were concerned with eradicating mosquito habitat (748–749). They left the grass longer (about a foot), cut less often, and focused on clearing disturbed and wet environments near "silver roll" (black) housing. Thus, grass cutting practices in the Canal Zone were racialized, like the rest of life.

Historian Paul Sutter writes, "While sanitarians trumpeted the need for precision mosquito control based on intimate knowledge of Panama's malaria vectors, they feared the ignorant administrators were most interested in the aesthetic symbolism of unruly jungle giving way to finely cropped lawn" (2007: 749). Promoted and internalized, this symbolism was of a piece with broader stories that US Americans told themselves about themselves and their distinctions from Panamanians. In this sense, the ongoing work of maintaining the boundary between jungle and lawn was inseparable from the ideological boundary work of distinguishing modern and nonmodern groups of people. Within this milieu, the mundane act of grass cutting could even be elevated to a public spectacle:

The Canal Record, "Grass Cutting Contest," September 1, 1909

A grass cutting contest will be held at 10 am, Labor Day, at Ancon. Eleven teams of two men each have been entered from the various scythe gangs of the Quartermaster's Department. Plots of ground approximately 200 square yards have been laid off for each team. In selecting the winners, speed and quality of work will be the determining factors. The following prizes will be given: First, $10 gold, and silver medal; second, $5 gold; third, $2.50 gold. This contest was proposed at the insistence of some of the Spanish scythemen from the Ancon District, who believed they were superior to men from the other districts. The contest has already excited considerable interest among the Spaniards employed in this class of work and it is believed the contest will be a close one.

The conquest of nature discourse was not confined to the Canal Zone. It was also disseminated by Panamanian politicians and elites, who associated national development with the construction of public works (particularly roads) and integration of the forested frontier (Carse 2014: 167–184). For example, a 1908 editorial in Panama's Star and Herald read:

The district for miles around Panama [City] should be alive with industry. Instead of which a few minutes' stroll from the city limits brings one to jungle or swamp where mongoose and the iguana pursue their livelihood undisturbed. . . . Without roads the resources of the most fertile area must remain untapped or be brought to market at a cost which renders operation a doubtful gain. How can the vegetable and mineral resources of this country be developed to any great extent if the areas in which they are located remain shrouded in impenetrable forest? ("Wanted—Good Roads," April 20, 1908)

As the US government worked to discipline weeds, insects, and environmental subjects around the canal, the Panamanian state pursued something similar across the nation's rural areas. From the Second World War on, the vision of a modern rural Panama was enacted through road construction and a program called the "Conquest of the Jungle."[6]

US sanitation and Panamanian agricultural development were both modernist projects that assigned economic and moral value to clearing wild vegetation. Even today, the socioenvironmental legacies of those projects persist. Panamanian campesinos invoke cleanliness to describe cultivated landscapes. Clearing the land—often by machete—is called *limpiando* (cleaning) and overgrown fields are characterized as sucia. Like the colonenses who complain that formerly maintained urban and periurban landscapes have become overgrown, rural Panamanians invoke dirtiness to point to the crumbling of local infrastructure due to disinvestment. But, in Colón, concern with dirty landscapes rehearses the self-presentation of imperial modernity to make sense of contemporary disconnection.

Infrastructure, Expectations of Modernity, and Disinvestment in Colón

My friend Eneida's lengthy descriptions of the bad state of affairs in Colón inevitably ended with the same punch line: "The Panamanian government doesn't know the word 'maintenance.'" The situation was serious, but the joke never failed to crack her up.

What happened to Colón? The city has gone through a series of boom-and-bust cycles linked to its dependence on the transit economy. Established on a mangrove island by the private US-owned Panama Railroad Company in the mid-nineteenth century, it became the Atlantic terminus of the first interoceanic railroad in the Americas. The city boomed during the California Gold Rush of the 1850s and 1860s as thousands of travelers crossed the isthmus. The bust began when the first US transcontinental line was completed in 1869, pulling US travelers bound for California away away from the Panama Railroad. What's more, the wealth created in Panama during the boom was mostly absorbed by foreign capitalists; comparatively little accumulated locally (Castillero Calvo 1973). The city boomed again during the (failed) French Panama Canal construction effort in the 1880s and, once more, during the 1904–1914 US canal construction era. Each boom was associated with a large transportation construction project that required a massive labor force. Those booms went bust as the need for labor declined and the jobs disappeared. Historically, Colón had traits that resembled a company town: most of its occupants were laborers and economic resources, including land, were controlled by foreign capitalists or governments. For the Panamanian sociologist Raul Leis and others, this historical trajectory continued as Colón became an "enclave city within an enclave" (i.e., Panama) and an "island of services for foreign currents" (Leis 1979; quoted in Lasso 2013).

From the mid-nineteenth century to present, Colón's history has turned on a tension inherent in its dual identity as a key node for the circulation of global commerce—and, thus, a site of wealth creation—and an underdeveloped settlement populated mainly by laborers of African descent. The *Zona Libre* (Colón Free Trade Zone)—arguably the first of its kind—was established in 1948 in response to capital flight and unemployment (Sigler 2013). Since then, there have been many government and private efforts to rejuvenate the city's economy. None have succeeded. In spite of the opening of the Zona Libre, wealthy residents and businesses continued to relocate to Panama City during the postwar decades. Within that context, employment opportunities in the Canal Zone became even more economically important. The zone was more than a company town. It was a settler colony.

The Canal Zone was an imperial and often-racist enclave—an affront to Panamanian sovereignty and dignity—but it came with tangible economic benefits. Canal operations and military bases provided thousands of jobs for Panamanians. As the Canal Zone was transferred to Panamanian control between 1979 and 1999, thousands of comparatively good jobs disappeared (when the canal treaty was signed in 1977, wages were three times higher in the zone than in Panama) (Sigler 2013: 7). As a result, the Zona Libre became the center of the regional economy. To make things worse for working-class colonenses, this realignment coincided with the rise of containerized shipping, which mechanized ports and reduced the need for manual labor (Levinson 2006). Without competition, firms in the Zona Libre paid less and wages fell, especially for unskilled workers (Sigler 2013: 7–8).

Today, Colón's regional economy still revolves around the Zona Libre, ports, and trans-shipment facilities. The largest free trade zone in the hemisphere and second largest in the world, it reexports goods from major exporters such as China, Taiwan, Hong Kong, and the United States to Latin American importers such as Venezuela, Colombia, and Costa Rica. A worker in the zone can expect to make a few hundred balboas (the same in US dollars) per month, if they can find a job (Sigler 2013: 7–8). The province of Colón has the nation's highest unemployment rate, and its median wage and household income levels are both significantly below the national average (Contralaría General de la República 2018).

Weeds thrive along the infrastructure-environment borderlands, including clearings formerly maintained by the state, capital, or empire. The signing of the Panama Canal Treaties in 1977 initiated the transfer of the waterway and Canal Zone from the US government to the Panamanian government by the end of 1999. Disinvestment in infrastructure and maintenance jobs during that period gave rise to a weedy landscape in areas of the former zone adjacent to Colón. As a number of colonenses explained to me during interviews, the most immediate cause was that state institutions (first US and then Panamanian) stopped hiring laborers to cut the grass and do maintenance work.

When we talk about infrastructure, the emphasis is typically construction, but maintenance work can be more important for many people's lives (Russell and Vinsel 2016). Since I began conducting fieldwork in the province of Colón in 2008, I have collected the work histories of people formerly employed in the former Canal Zone who were either employed by the US canal administration, US military, or made money by providing goods and services for Americans. This work included, but was not limited to, a number of manual labor jobs that can be broadly classified as "cleaning," including janitor, maid, laundry worker, maintenance crew, and landscaper. For men, working as a *machetero* (machete man) or otherwise cleaning landscapes for aesthetic and sanitation purposes was common.

The accounts of these colonenses link the history of grass cutting described above to contemporary concern with weeds and dirty landscapes. For many of them, weediness indexed not only the decay of infrastructure or the vigor of unmanaged plant life, but the abandonment of the communities

Figure 4.3. Water leaks from the pipes of a former US naval facility near Colón, Panama. These buildings, occupied by displaced Panamanians, are surrounded by ports and container terminals. Photo by author.

who worked for decades to maintain those landscapes (figure 4.3). All these jobs came with indignities and forms of discrimination, but they were steady work, and many older colonenses are proud of their decades of service. Work in the zone—and, in particular, cutting grass—was meaningful. And, regardless of what Panamanian laborers thought about the fact that the US government impinged upon national sovereignty, they were also enrolled in communities of aspiration attached to modern infrastructures and the manicured land-scapes that once surrounded them.

Geographer Paul Robbins (2007) has explored the formation of "turfgrass subjects" in the contemporary United States committed to the care of resi-dential lawns. Why, Robbins asks, do people go to such great lengths to main-tain attractive lawns? One answer is that people do it for their neighbors: a well-maintained lawn reflects good character and a weedy or overgrown lawn, by contrast, is something to be ashamed of. Seen in this way, weedi-ness signals how we view ourselves in relation to a community and imagine that others view us. But a focus on symbolic representation limits our abil-ity to understand the political ecology of lawns, Robbins argues, because the biology and ecology of specific species mediate social relations by requiring applications of pesticide, fertilizer, and labor to thrive in an exogenous ecosystem. We may mow for other people, but the grass makes specific demands of us. Weeds, by definition, don't need our help to thrive.

When people in the province of Colón complain about dirty landscapes—rodent infestations, piles of trash, and the ubiquitous concerns about weeds around waterways and buildings—they are also talking about the devaluation of maintenance work in a way that references historically salient landscape descriptors with moral connotations. Read against the urban and periurban landscapes of twenty-first-century Colón, weediness is a point of departure for making sense of relations with other places and times—to past aspirations and potential futures. Will the government or a private firm deliver new jobs and cut the grass? Or will the forest envelop the places people worked to establish? These are the palpable concerns that I failed to understand when, as I described in this essay's introduction, María characterized San Lorenzo National Park as dirty and our taxi driver added, "the hierba grows up and nobody keeps it limpia. Nobody takes care of it."

Enacting Environments: Or, the Where, When, and Whom of Secondary Vegetation

Elsewhere in this volume, Myers characterizes flourishing weeds as a profusion of life that can be read against the technonature of a high modernist botanical garden as a celebration of decay and decomposition. It is an interesting coincidence that her chapter on weeds is situated in Singapore and my own in Panama given the countries' similar historical geographies. Both sit on maritime shipping chokepoints. The Panama Canal connects the Atlantic and Pacific Oceans. The Strait of Malacca, just south of Singapore, links the Pacific and Indian Oceans. Panama and Singapore were colonized and reengineered in the nineteenth and twentieth centuries to service transportation. Today, they are sovereign and economically vibrant nations that promote themselves as global logistics hubs. This comparison is common in writing about the Panamanian economy. In the midst of a decade of economic growth, for example, the *Economist* published an article entitled "Panama's Economy: A Singapore for Central America" (2011). The article quotes former president Ricardo Martinelli saying, "We copy a lot from Singapore and we need to copy more."

There is a hopeful story to tell about weediness among the rising skyscrapers of Panama City, but Colón draws our attention to a different economic geography of late industrialism (Fortun 2012). As the city across the isthmus thrives, colonenses think with weeds to make sense of processes of state disinvestment and global disconnection that are not immediately accessible to the senses. Disintegration and decomposition are integral to the world. Nature will always return (Weisman 2007), but, as the situated analyses of colonenses remind us, it really matters where, when, how, and for whom it returns.

While some see Panama's secondary growth an index of disinvestment, other see potential. In a *New York Times* article entitled "New Jungles Prompt a Debate on Rainforests" (Rosenthal 2009), two senior staff scientists at the Smithsonian Tropical Research Institute (based in Panama), Bill Laurence and Joe Wright, disagree about what counts as a forest. The debate is staged in Chilibre, a periurban community halfway between Panama City and Colón, where we are also introduced to an older woman named Marta Ortega de Wing. Her land—a farm with pigs, bananas plants, and mango trees just ten years before—is "being overtaken by galloping jungle—palms, lizards, and ants" (A1). Extrapolating regional land cover change to global debates about deforestation and regrowth, Wright argues that the vegetation on Marta's farm is a "real rain forest" and "suitable habitat" with underrecognized conservation value and utility in the struggle against climate change. But Bill Laurence "scoffed as he viewed Ms. Ortega de Wing's overgrown land: 'This is a caricature of a rain forest!" he said. 'there's no canopy, there's too much light, there are only a few species'" (A1). The debate turned not simply on definitions, but how new forests in Chilibre indexed global environmental problems and, crucially, which qualities were relevant to those problems. Their utility as carbon sinks? Their capacity as biodiversity reservoirs? Significantly, the *Times* article made no mention of the flipside of succession. Beyond the (debated) ecological gains, had anything been lost?

For some people living in a region sedimented with imperial ruins and hollowed out by neoliberal governance, weediness indexes global disconnection and state disinvestment. I don't know how Marta Ortega de Wing felt about living in a "galloping jungle," but I did discuss similar landscape transitions in other rural, periurban, and urban communities nearby. Although the processes driving secondary growth on old farms and weediness across the facilities and grounds of the Atlantic terminus of the former US Canal Zone are distinct, many of the colonenses I interviewed described the process in the same way. For them, dirty landscapes don't index the arrival of new infrastructures (commercial or scientific) but the retraction of old ones, particularly those that promised development.

Notes

1 The park was created, in part, to provide a natural buffer for unexploded ordinances in the forest that remain from when the US military operated a firing range around Fort Sherman (Lindsay-Poland 2003). On the general phenomenon of former military zones becoming conservation areas, see geographer David Havlick's work (2011).

2 *Hierba* means grass in Spanish, but this usage can be translated as weeds.

3 To cite a few explicit examples, scholars argue that infrastructures index care (Rolston 2013), inequality (Howe et al. 2015), progress (Masquelier 2002), abandonment (Melly 2013), state integration (P. Harvey 2016; Reeves 2017), mode of production (Yarrington 2015), and the role of the state (Redfield 2015).

4 In fact, as I have argued (Carse and Lewis 2017), what makes the infrastructure concept distinct from historical precursors such as "public works" is that it no longer refers to a particular class of things. Rather, infrastructure is a historically emergent category (see Laura Bear's comments in Venkatesan et al. 2016: 5–7) and a form of calculative reason rooted in the bureaucracies of the international organizations created in the postwar era and rationalities of logistics that emphasized supranational spatial connection organized around standards.

5 One of the reasons that its precursor—the private French effort to build a sea-level canal across Panama in the late nineteenth century—failed was because mosquito-borne disease, particularly yellow fever, had decimated the workforce, killing an estimated twenty thousand people (McCullough 1977: 235).

6 I examine the history of this program in my book (Carse 2014: 185–204).

FIVE. From Edenic Apocalypse to Gardens against Eden

Plants and People in and after the Anthropocene

NATASHA MYERS

In the fall of 2013, I was following a friend on tour through the streets of downtown Sydney, Australia. I was there during a research sabbatical, giving a talk on the arts and sciences of plant sensing, and doing exploratory research for a new project that found me visiting botanical gardens and other significant plant sites wherever I traveled.[1] It was my first time in Australia, and that continent's distinctive flora was making quite an impression on my sensibilities, so attuned as they were to North American and European botanical forms. The plants were catching my attention everywhere I looked. My friend and I were walking across a wide square when an unlikely garden caught my eye. Plants had colonized the façade of an old building, taking root in the cracks between bricks and along narrow ledges. Delighting in the precariousness of this garden, I backed up to get in a good view, and I snapped a few pictures. When we turned to continue, my gaze was drawn across the square. There a gleaming condominium was on the rise, still under construction. We walked closer. The structure was swarming with workers laboring over its surfaces. Some were dangling from ropes and harnesses, busy planting an intricately patterned series of vertical gardens up and down the sides of the building (figures 5.1–5.4).

I swiveled back to look again at the tufts of weeds erupting from the surface of the building across the square. The dissonance between these two gardens was palpable. On one side of the square, an old building's façade had become a haphazard garden merely by offering affordances, fissures, and openings for the wandering seeds of weedy plants to take root and flourish. And on the other was this spectacular, energy- and labor-intensive display of capital (Larkin 2013)—an urban infrastructure impeccably enacting the "sustainability" aesthetic du jour. One untamed garden defied gravity; exposure to sun, wind, and rain; and the grasp of weed-hungry hands. The other was a technologically enhanced garden-in-the-making, built by workers interpreting architectural designs. This was a garden that would have to be tended, weeded, and watered to keep it thriving.

Strange, I thought. But I didn't yet know what to make of the experience. As my botanically inspired travels continued, I kept photographing plant life, especially plants taking root along walls and buildings (Berlin's facades were remarkable). It wasn't until I was introduced to artworks by Austrian artist Lois Weinberger months later in Vienna that I was able to start to make sense of divergences in the ways people both arrange and potentiate relationships with plants in urban spaces. These encounters forced me to ask the question: What is a garden? Were both of the sites I encountered in that square in Sydney gardens? And if so, what might we learn about gardens by holding these distinctive forms together?

This chapter proposes that we do not yet know what a garden is or what a garden can do. And yet, it begins with a provisional and loose definition of gardens as sites where people *stage their relationships with plants*. I try to make sense of the ways that garden designs variously inform, sediment, and disrupt the very infrastructure of plant-people relations, especially in cities. I ask: What might different gardens teach anthropologists about the ways that people stage relationships with plants? What might we learn about plants and their people by examining the aesthetics and politics of garden infrastructures? And how, in a time of massive ecological destruction, are people renegotiating their relationships with plants? How are people designing gardens to stage plant-people relations otherwise?

Figures 5.1, 5.2, 5.3, and 5.4. Vertical Gardens in Sydney. Photographs by the author.

This chapter tacks between two unlikely sites that recall the contradictions and contrasts I beheld standing in that one square in Sydney early on in my travels. Here I describe two other gardens. I take us to Singapore, where I encountered Gardens by the Bay, a spectacle that could best be described as an infrastructure for end-of-time botanical tourism. And I take us to Vienna, where artist Lois Weinberger's performances, installations, and durational works disrupt the self-evidence of garden enclosures by cultivating weeds and wastelands, and celebrating decay and decomposition (figures 5.5 and 5.6). These two sets of gardens are incommensurable in crucial ways. And yet, holding them together spurs new ways to think about the cultural norms and mores that shape people's relationships with plants today. Kim Fortun explains that juxtaposition aims not to "resolve difference nor merely celebrate diversity"; rather, it aspires to "provoke encounters across difference that produce new articulations" (2012: 455). Juxtaposition can amplify dissonances as well as resonances, and set in motion new ideas. In this way, something else might be able to "shimmer" in between (see Živković 2017).

I build on Fortun's approach to juxtaposition here while also drawing on Jacques Rancière's (2009, 2010) analysis of the relationship between aesthetics and politics. Rancière helps me to read these gardens through one another in a way that amplifies critical differences in these garden infrastructures. These gardens stage just two of many possible approaches to garden design, and yet both offer ways of responding to our current planetary predicament. One gesture is the design of a state garden as a gleaming spectacle for education and entertainment. This is a garden that positions itself as part of the solution, as a technological fix for climate change. The concreteness and permanence of this capital- and energy-intensive site for botanical tourism contrasts sharply with Lois Weinberger's "counter-gardens," which celebrate porosity, decay, and decomposition. I use this juxtaposition to open up new ways of thinking about the significance of aesthetics in analyses of infrastructures designed in response to this moment that many are still calling the Anthropocene. Weinberger's counter-gardens act as a pivot, disrupting aesthetic norms and expectations of gardens in a way that exposes the underlying logics of Singapore's excess. Most poignantly, this juxtaposition makes it possible to see that Gardens by the Bay is a garden that is *designed for* the Anthropocene; that is, it is a garden that perpetuates apocalyptic imaginaries and leaves intact the extractive logics of capitalism, colonialism, and what Kim Fortun (2012) calls "late industrialism."

Figures 5.5 and 5.6. Juxtaposition. Singapore's Gardens by the Bay (photograph by the author), and Lois Weinberger's "Garden" (courtesy of Lois Weinberger).

Held together, these gardens generate a poignant critique of the apocalyptic imaginaries incited by the very concept of the Anthropocene (see Swyngedouw 2010). If the idea of the Anthropocene foments the allure of "man's tragic detumescence," a posture that leans so precariously toward inevitable apocalypse, and promises ruin and devastation (Haraway and Kenney 2015), it is clear to me that the Anthropocene is no place to linger. How do we get out from under its shadow?

If colonialism, capitalism, and militarism are the very forces identified as accelerators of the Anthropocene (see Todd 2015; Davis and Todd 2017; Haraway 2015; Masco this volume), then Weinberger's gardens can be seen to work athwart these forces to propagate another kind of worlding. His gardens inspire me to explore the contours of an *episteme* that might help us break from Anthropocene thinking. I look to these counter-gardens to consider what might come *after the Anthropocene*.[2] The "after" in this formulation does not circumscribe a time-bound era, some later epoch, or period on the other side of apocalypse or ruination. Rather the "after" that I am after here marks what might come *in the wake of Anthropocene thinking* (Sharpe 2016). I am inspired by Timothy Choy's (2011) remarkable concept of a "conspiracy of breathers," a concept meant to activate new ways of thinking about forms of solidarities taking shape in resistance to air pollution. His approach to "conspiracy" takes seriously the root meaning of the word *con-spire* as an act of breathing together. And yet, as I consider here, such world-changing conspiracies must involve the plants: those beings who make our breath possible (Myers 2016). How might people learn to *conspire with plant life* in order to thwart the inevitabilities of apocalypse and grow livable worlds? Such conspiracies need not be deferred to some distant future. The gardens documented in this chapter and by other anthropologists show us that people are already conspiring with plants in remarkable ways (Battaglia 2017; Kawa 2016; Kimmerer 2015; Myers, 2017, 2018). It is time that anthropologists ask: How are people *involving* themselves with plants and staging relations otherwise? How might such *involutions* enable other worlds to thrive, even in the midst of the ongoing devastation (see Tsing 2015; Hustak and Myers 2012)?

I set the stage for this analysis by briefly introducing the two gardens. The chapter then takes a look at the aesthetics, politics, and moral orders of gardens in general, and of those designed in the midst of anxieties about the "end-of-time" in particular. Following a fuller elaboration that situates Singapore's and Weinberger's gardens in their broader contexts, the chapter takes a closer look at the ways that the juxtaposition between them provokes new ways of thinking about gardens, and their role in staging relationships between plants and people both *in and after* the Anthropocene.

The Simulated Eden of Gardens by the Bay

Gardens by the Bay is Singapore's billion-dollar infrastructure for botanical tourism.[3] Open to the public in 2012, this award-winning feat of environmental architecture sits on a hundred hectares of reclaimed land on the south shores of the island. It features two of the world's largest climate-controlled conservatories, the largest glass house is equivalent in size to 2.2 football fields and encloses a volume equivalent to seventy-five Olympic swimming pools. These are massive infrastructures, whose soaring curves and smooth organic forms resemble apparitions from some science fiction fantasy. One conservatory, the Flower Dome, simulates a Mediterranean climate and features plants from around the world, such as South Africa and Australia, including eight-hundred-year-old olive trees, ancient baobab trees, and flowering plants that bloom as if in perennial spring. The other conservatory is the Cloud Forest (figure 5.7), which features plants from tropical highlands and mountain regions. There, the website boasts, "fascinating orchids, delicate ferns, colourful bromeliads, dazzling begonias and menacing carnivorous pitcher plants" are nestled densely together in lush vertical gardens.[4]

I visit the Cloud Forest first. As I descend a staircase, I take note of a display of Indigenous artefacts. A plaque indicates that they hail from East Timor. I follow a long curving corridor toward the entrance. As wide glass doors slide open, I cross a climactic threshold. Moist, cooling, and fragrant air fills my lungs and licks at my skin, which is still radiating heat from Singapore's searing 34°C day. As I step into this unreal world, a forty-two-meter mountain covered in lush vegetation sweeps my gaze upward. Flowering plants spill their verdant blooms down the sides of this massive edifice. The tallest indoor waterfall in the world gushes from the top of the mountain, its powerful surge diffracting sunlight into rainbows and filling space with sound. Artificial clouds hover around Jetson-style walkways that arc and swerve around the mountain's peak.

The spectacle is overwhelming. I can barely take it all in. That is, until my eyes lock in on a body swinging through the waterfall. Tethered to a long

Figure 5.7. Cloud forest. Photograph by the author.

rope, a man reaches out and pulls himself across this lush facade, plucking leaves and shoots and stuffing them into an old rice sack attached to a belt around his waist (figure 5.8). His brown skin marks him as one of the multitude of migrants whose intensive and precarious physical labors have built this very structure and daily keep this lush garden flourishing. This is a living infrastructure that itself thrives on the energetic, material, and affective labors of marginalized people. I paid twenty-eight Singapore dollars for entry, a fee reduced for local residents with the right identity cards. Many others live and work in this city without such ready access. This moment, looking up at the man laboring in the simulated mist, crystallized for me the remarkable ways in which Singapore's green dreams are fully implicated with capitalism,

Figure 5.8. Laboring in the gardens. Photograph by the author.

Figure 5.9. Lois Weinberger, "Brandenberg Tor," 1994. Photograph by and with permission of Lois Weinberger.

neoliberalism, labor migration, colonial legacies, and neocolonial desires. From that moment on, I couldn't stop seeing forms of extractive labor in every sweeping curve of this massive structure and in each frilled petal dripping with dew.

Counter-gardens

In contrast to the showy opulence of Gardens by the Bay, other kinds of gardens flourish in the fissures of old buildings and in the cracks in the concrete. Some of these gardens take root on their own. Others are potentiated by artists or guerilla gardeners.[5] The works of Viennese artist Lois Weinberger offer a pitch-perfect counterpose to what Jacques Rancière (2010) might call the "aestheticization" of nature at Gardens by the Bay. Singapore's gardens are impeccably clean. There is no sign of decomposition or decay. Laborers, like the one swinging from the waterfall, swiftly remove decaying plant material, and replace spent plants with fresh ones poised to flower. This way, the gardens are kept in perennial bloom. Weinberger's gardens, by contrast, take root in the marginalia of wastelands (Gandy 2013; Mabey 2012), and in ruptures and fissures where bare earth is exposed (figure 5.9). His artworks celebrate the "ruderal ecologies" of disturbed and abandoned landscapes and potentiate new life in the rubble and ruins of wasted lands (Stoetzer, forthcoming).[6] By breaking up concrete, removing paving stones, or simply clearing patches of ground, Weinberger sets otherwise constrained forces free. His clearings give plants a stage to make their "subversive," untamed forces felt (Trevor 2013). His gardens take root in the most unlikely of spaces and revel in the potency, insurgency, and unstoppable force of green beings. Where Singapore's gardens almost flawlessly perform nature on the model of a precarious Eden— where nature is rendered an opulent, sessile beauty, vulnerable and in need of protection, separate and closed off from the mundane, everyday world—by contrast, the gardens Weinberger cultivates are *gardens against Eden*.

The Aesthetics and Politics of Garden Enclosures

The seeming incommensurability of these two gardens provoke the question: What makes a garden a garden? Gardens have a long and remarkable history, and they take on myriad forms. Landscape historian John Dixon Hunt locates the "etymological roots" of the term "garden" "in words denoting 'enclosure'" (Despard and Gagnon 2010: 7). In this sense, a garden is a bounded region, cordoned off and demarcated from the forest, the farm, the home, or urban environments. From allotment gardens, to container gardens on high-rise balconies, to a city's botanical gardens, gardens are, then, any enclosure sequestered for plants. These enclosures can be approached as kinds of infrastructure. And yet, thinking infrastructure through gardens requires more than an analysis of their function (see Ballestero, this volume). Garden infrastructures demand an attention to the politics of their aesthetic and moral forms, to the social and economic relations that their "poetics" set in motion (see Larkin 2013).

Alongside farms, forests, and plantations, gardens are crucial sites for examining the more-than-human dimensions of social, political and economic life, offering profound insights into forms of governance, political economy and ecology, industry, labor, and more.[7] Gardens are sites where people explicitly stage and restage their relationships with nature. According to garden historian Michel Conan, "There is no essence of a garden to be found in form, enclosure, or etymology. Gardens are simply places where a social group engages in gardening. This makes the definition of gardens contingent on the economy, environment, and culture of any group of gardeners" (1999: 183). Gardens not only serve as sources of nourishment, medicines and sites of leisure, for Conan they are also "systems of expression very much like language, music, painting, or dancing" (202). He makes the call for a "social anthropology" of gardening, one that reads gardens as cultural productions that express particular aesthetics, politics, values, and desires. Gardeners in this sense can be seen as artists with the craft knowledge and skill to work and rework the cusp between nature and artifice.

The ways that people design garden enclosures tells us something about how they understand "proper" relations among plants and people, and also how they want to intervene in reshaping those relations. Gardens stage moral orders. As sites where social facts and cultural norms are activated and sedimented, and where these norms and mores can be challenged and remade, gardens are potent sites for ethnographic observation. They are sites where anthropologists can learn about ways people define what is beautiful, good, orderly, and valuable; and they are instructive about where people's aesthetic and economic values converge and diverge. Gardens are also performative and pedagogical: they dictate how people should stand in relation to nature; how plants ought to figure in people's lives; what plants are "for"; and how one should appreciate these forms of life as beautiful, healing, nourishing, exotic, dangerous, economically productive, or ecologically significant. State gardens are a good example. Like zoos and museums, they are spectacles that offer their publics an "education in civics," sites where right relations between "man and nature" are encoded in the architecture, displays, and signage (see Haraway 1989; Hartigan 2015). Botanical gardens are sites where a nation explicitly displays its economic ambitions and colonial conquests (e.g., Brockway 1979; N. Johnson 2011). State gardens go a long way toward naturalizing imperialist forms of extraction through economic botany collections that lavishly display plantation crops with no mention of the ways these plants were made to participate in centuries of slavery, dispossession, and destruction.

It is helpful to remember, though, that this violence doesn't have to be the end of the story. It is also within the space of garden enclosures that gardeners, architects, artists, laborers, and visitors have the opportunity to subvert and redefine what counts as "proper" relations among plants and people. Artists, such as Weinberger, have staged remarkable interventions to expose the politics of plant-people relations. Their gardens can force us to confront contradictions at work within those moral economies that enforce a divide between humans and nature. Artists' gardens can propagate counternarratives and alternative aesthetics, and so serve as sites of cultural critique.[8]

It is also crucial to note that gardeners do not simply exert their power over nature, as if they could secure firm control over these wily forms of life. It is not just the plants that are "cultivated" or "cultured" in gardens; the plants also remake the people who tend, harvest, and enjoy them. In this sense, gardens can be read more generously as *naturecultures* (Haraway 2008); sites where human and more-than-human agencies (including the plants, microbes, soils, fungi, insects, chemicals, climate, and more) are thoroughly entangled and confused; spaces in which both plants and people come to cultivate and be cultivated by one another. Within the space of a garden enclosure, what counts as nature and what counts as culture are very much in the making. And yet, even as gardens can be seen as collaborations among people and plants, this cannot be understood as a symmetrical relationship. Gardeners have *designs on* vegetal life. While there are always indeterminate effects of any design, especially in the context of the design of living infrastructures like gardens, the aesthetic and pragmatic selection, arrangement, and management of plants in a garden does set in motion particular forms of labor and care, and particular forms of governance that dictate who and what lives and dies within its enclosures.

A garden's enclosure, whether it is a wall, fence, pot, or pane of glass, divides up the spaces between what lives on the inside and what does not. Boundaries mark what, where, and when to cultivate, weed, mulch, or neglect. Each garden thus enacts its own form of biopolitics. What lives and dies inside garden enclosures is a question of the specific biopolitical economy of a given garden. The politics of weeds offers a case in point, for it is on the inside of a garden enclosure that some plants come to be valued while others are weeded or reviled. In one context, goldenrod, milkweed, nettles, or yarrow will be yanked out without remorse. In another, they will be actively nurtured to service butterflies or an herbalist's apothecary. And as we will see, what is made to live inside a garden enclosure is very often what gets left to die in the *elsewhere* that is eternally relegated to the outside. Garden design can in this way be seen as explicitly political work. It is important to remember that garden enclosures are necessarily incomplete and porous, and they don't always work the ways they are intended. Weinberger's gardens, for example, disrupt the self-evidence of the function of conventional garden enclosures and, in so doing, perturb sedimented relations of power, and foment the eruption of subversive forces.

Designing Gardens for the End-of-Times

According to garden theorists Despard and Gagnon, gardens have traditionally been valued as "space[s] of seclusion set apart from the world," sites that offer "opportunities for reflection, relaxation and disinterested aesthetic appreciation" (2010: 7). Yet the gardens I grapple with here do no such thing. These gardens don't seclude; rather, they throw us into the world, induce anxiety, and get us very interested in the urgency of life and death at the cusp of collapse on a damaged planet. These gardens are evocative of ways that governments, city planners, architects, scientists, educators, artists, activists, and others are confronting the dire realities of life downstream from the tailings ponds, plantations, landfills, and chimney stacks, whose extractive "exuberance" follows the logics of late industrialism (see Murphy 2016). In a time of climate change, toxic flows, latent and immanent exposures, and new forms of precarity, the well-being of plants and their people have become a serious concern. Anxieties are on the rise as people reckon with the impacts of mining operations and deforestation; the paving over of agricultural lands, wetlands, and bogs; the deterioration of the planet's soils; and the impacts of pesticide and herbicide contamination on plants' and their allies' lives and worlds.[9]

In fall 2014 I participated in a conference called "Leaders in Conservation: Botanic Gardens and Biodiversity in the 21st Century."[10] The event gathered together directors of botanical gardens, plant taxonomists, and those leading worldwide initiatives to identify plants not-yet-known to science, to protect endangered species, save seeds, and conserve forests. All noted alarming trends, and the tone at this meeting was desperate. What role, many asked, could gardens play in the revaluation of the cultural and ecological significance of plants? Several of the keynote speakers at the conference wanted to teach people how to value plants differently and to instruct them on how to cultivate deeper relationships with plant life. They wanted to propagate new forms of care and concern among their visitors. But the task ahead, as they saw it, was challenging. One of the biggest difficulties they faced was what they called a kind of "plant blindness" that shaped Western culture. Plants are hard to get to know well: they move slowly, they are very quiet, and they tend to lack the charisma of the megafauna at zoos that incite so much attention for conservation efforts. How would they design gardens to engage broader publics in response to climate change and ecological devastation (see Hartigan 2015)? It seemed to me that Singapore's Gardens by the Bay was one of many possible responses to this very question and set of concerns. How did Singapore design its garden for the "end-of-times"?

Botanical Expertise in an Ecology of Artifice

I arrived in Singapore, the island city-state just south of the Malaysian peninsula, in the fall of 2013 to visit my sister and her partner who had recently relocated there from Toronto. An advertising executive and healthcare management consultant, these Canadians were model recruits. Singapore is known for its success luring foreign talent to bolster what Aihwa Ong (2006) calls an "ecology of expertise." This is a neoliberal economy that makes explicit exceptions to accommodate "green" values. In order to nourish and sustain its ecology of experts, Singapore has long been invested in a kind of greening policy. As early as the 1950s, the government identified the island's tropical vegetation as a significant source of aesthetic and economic value to lure foreign investment. The city's streets are flush with planted trees and gardens: lush canopies reach over roadways, and tree trunks are thick with epiphytic growth. Orchid blossoms even adorn airport baggage carousels. Singapore's extensive botanical gardens and numerous "eco" tourist sites are major attractions for both locals and visitors. Once known as a "garden city," Singapore now hails itself as a "city in a garden" and a leader in "smart" and "green" infrastructure (see also Wong 2015).

Following the plants, I first visited Singapore's Botanical Gardens, a site dedicated both to leisure (wedding parties and photographers were consuming the beauty everywhere) and to scientific research. I arranged to meet with a group of plant taxonomists whose research labs were housed in the herbarium. All were European expats lured to Singapore with the promise of ready access to their Southeast Asian field sites. These taxonomists were not the recipients of the massive investments Singapore was making into the high-tech life sciences and biological engineering industries. They were not part of the incentivized research hub Biopolis, which has been well documented by Ong (2006) and Michael Fischer (2013). They were struggling to document new and extant species, and they were doing this in the most trying times. Not only were their plants disappearing with the encroachment of climate change, extractive mining, and cash crop plantations, rules set out by the Convention of Biological Diversity were hampering their very access to the regions where they were trying to do this work (see also Lowe 2006). But the worst part, as they saw it, was that taxonomists were at that very moment confronting their own extinction. Unable to lure students away from the promises of high-tech genomics labs, they had no one to train in the arts of plant identification and nomenclature. Soon, they feared, there would be no one left with the skills to document plant species before they disappear.

During my visit to the Botanical Gardens, the taxonomists brought me to a research talk by one of their colleagues who works at Singapore's Nature Society. Tony O'Dempsey was reporting on his remarkable efforts to document the contours of Singapore's ecologies before colonization and the intensification of urban development. He was using remnant plants, historical maps, old naturalists' diaries and herbarium entries, combined with GIS data to predict and validate the contours where primeval freshwater swampland once thrived (see O'Dempsey and Chew 2011). Triangulating evidence, he was trying to chart how and when settler populations had first decimated the mangroves and swamp forests that used to cover the island. According to his calculations, the islands' vulnerable ecologies were already seriously degraded by the 1930s, as swamp forests were drained and mangroves cut down to open up land for rubber and pineapple plantations, market gardens and aquaculture, both for export and to support a rising population of plantation workers. Today much of the farmland has been paved over or replaced by malls, golf courses and driving ranges.

Following O'Dempsey's talk, a student based at the National University of Singapore presented findings from her master's thesis, which involved documenting the effects of Singapore's land reclamation projects on marine biodiversity. Concrete now contours 87 percent of Singapore's once-natural shoreline, and her research found serious reductions in biodiversity along the smooth surfaces of concrete shores (see Lai et al. 2015). Her observations spurred the design and testing of simple structures that mimic some of the structural features of natural shoreline habitats. She found that when these devices are affixed to the concrete, they create affordances for the sensitive life cycles of endemic species. During question period, the audience members audibly expressed their dismay at her suggestion that there was a technological fix for this situation. They instructed her to be wary of promoting the idea. Singapore's government, they argued, would be all too eager to invest in artificial structures like these as a means to "green" their development projects. Such a fix would give Singapore license to expand rather than restrict development.

As this twenty-first-century city surges upward and extends outward, reclaiming land from the ocean and paving over remnant forest, ecological restoration is not even a viable concept in Singapore. As O'Dempsey's talk brought home so poignantly, vestiges of the islands' original ecosystems are scarce. "Clean" and "green" environments are built from scratch over layers of rubble and concrete. If it is a "city in a garden," it could perhaps best be described a large, well-manicured, well-maintained container garden lined with rubble and enclosed in concrete.

The Technological Fix

Months after my visit to the Cloud Forest, I spoke with two architects involved in the design of Gardens by the Bay: Andrew Grant and Peter Higgins at Grant Associates' offices. In conversation with them, I learned that Gardens by the Bay was the dream of Kiat Tan, the former head of Singapore's

National Parks Board and now CEO of the gardens. A heroic figure in the eyes of these architects, Tan circumnavigated the globe several times over to collect plants and build a space for them to thrive here in spite of Singapore's searing heat. In a remarkable twist on a well-learned imperial impulse, the Gardens torque colonial forms of botanical display (see Pratt 1992). Singapore, once a British colony, could now demonstrate its own prowess by cultivating Mediterranean plants and those from cool mountain regions right here, at the equator. But this required a technological fix. The architects' primary challenge, as they framed it, was "How do we make sense of cooled, air-conditioned glass houses in the tropics?" Serious effort went into "mitigating the environmental consequences" of this massive infrastructure project. And they did well: the architects' efforts won them numerous awards for sustainable design.

Sustainability ethics materialize in these gardens in science fictional form. "Supertrees" (figure 5.10), clusters of vertical gardens modeled on tree forms, punctuate the landscape. Some are as tall as fifty meters, and one is home to an air-bound restaurant. These structures are integral elements of the garden's "smart" infrastructure: solar energy is collected to power the trees' elaborate light displays at night, and the structures vent heat and gases from incinerators that fuel the gardens by burning the city's waste biomass. In line with what Orit Halpern and her collaborators call the "test-bed" urbanism of Songdo, Gardens by the Bay is a flagship for Singapore's dreams of "smart" and "green" development (Halpern et al. 2013).

Singapore is a city fully under construction. Deep craters and pits pock the city streets, and vaulting cranes cut across the horizon at every turn. This city's ambitions for unfettered growth are everywhere palpable. Promotional material from government greening and infrastructure projects shows that this growth "ethic" is barely tamed by ecological concern. One brochure, which projects Singapore's "sustainable" urban planning initiatives through to 2030, emphasizes that what must be sustained is *growth*. This near-jubilant gloss on Singapore's garden city explains that "sustaining growth" is a key component of their model that imagines a "compact city" with "quality living," "housing for all," and "play options" (Urban Redevelopment Authority 2012). Singapore's efforts at maintaining a "clean and green" environment are imagined to pay off through more spaces for people to relax after work.

This rhetoric glides over the fact that Singapore is being built up on the backs of thousands of migrant laborers from Bangladesh, Sri Lanka, India and surrounding regions, many of whom work seven days a week. Predominantly

Figure 5.10. Supertrees. Photograph by the author.

male, these "unskilled" laborers working high-risk construction jobs account for nearly a quarter of all foreign workers in Singapore. Migrant labor in Singapore is currently under scrutiny. Life is precarious for those who risk life and limb on sites with high injury and fatality rates. Laborers receive little remuneration, live in cramped quarters, and are often denied health care (see Piper 2006; Chok 2009; Bal 2013). Their low wages prevent them from participating in the life of this city of affluence and opulence, which caters predominantly to foreign "talent" and investors.

On any given Sunday evening in Singapore's "Little India," throngs of South Asian men flood into the streets to savor their limited time off work. There they gather in groups on street corners or patches of grass, or wander through the streets hand-in-hand. Tensions have been flaring as of late. In the wake of a traffic accident that killed a migrant worker, a riot took over Little India's streets just months after my visit in 2013. Singapore's authoritarian government was quick to dismiss the event. More critical news sources around the world took this escalation of violence as an opportunity to publish exposés on exploitation, condemning the laborers' poor working and living conditions and reading the riot as an expression of profound discontent.[11]

From the architects I learned that the sensory pleasures involved in crossing the threshold into the Cloud Forest was one of the unintended effects of the design process. And yet, as I think back, it was in this very experience that I felt most palpably the audacity of the very desire to engineer such massive cooled conservatories at the equator. In our interview I asked whether the architects picked up on the irony of the garden's very breathability. Their muffled response suggested they hadn't really considered how the conservatories' glass enclosures offer perfect respite from Singapore's seasonal choking haze. This is the smoke from forest fires that are rapidly consuming the region, including the island of Borneo, that epicenter of earth's biodiversity that is now being terra-formed into a giant palm oil plantation (see Tsing 2005). In June 2013, just months before my visit, Singapore was engulfed in some of the worst haze ever reported.[12] With air quality at hazardous levels, people were required to wear gas masks outdoors for about two weeks. By the time I visited, the World Wildlife Fund had sponsored an ad campaign to educate Singapore's consumers to be wary of the palm oil contained in the majority of their supermarket products.

In a recent essay, Singaporean performance studies scholar Eng-Beng Lim describes the gardens as "a national dream and global technology" and highlights the gardens' breathability: "Visitors are quite literally inhaling the mist or conjuring by breath the air of myriad fantastic flora-scapes acting as surrogate for their actual landscapes in situ" (2014: 449). For him, the gardens stand as a "metaphor of the state's magic": its technological prowess to successfully perform a simulated ecology indoors. Indeed, but this is also a magic enacted through an infrastructure that governs not only plant life, but also, as Choy (2011) helps us see so poignantly, the very composition of the atmosphere, composing the airs not just inside this enclosure, but also in the elsewhere of its surround. This garden infrastructure thus performs a magic trick that distracts with spectacle from the slow violence of worldly undoing ongoing on the other side of its gleaming glass exterior (figures 5.11 and 5.12).

If at first appearance, Gardens by the Bay's remarkable conservatories seem to serve as giant, aestheticized cooling stations for overheated tourists, on closer inspection it becomes clear that the Cloud Forest also situates itself as a climate change education and demonstration site. Interspersed through the exuberant expanse of vegetation and vaulted beams, the themes of collapse

Figures 5.11 and 5.12. Flower Dome and Cloud Forest Conservatories. Photographs by the author.

and extinction are present but muted by the awe-inspiring aerial walkways and simulated clouds. For a full view of "The Fall" in this Edenic paradise, visitors are guided to the "Lost World" at the top of the mountain. There a display mixes rare and endangered plants with Indigenous artworks of animalized humans. Although perhaps not the architects' intended message, the Lost World is where it is possible to begin to see how the garden's efforts to make life thrive here do nothing to mitigate the forces that are both making and letting certain forms of life die everywhere else. In its collection and display of plants that are at risk of extinction, Gardens by the Bay reimagines the economic botany displays so central to the design of Western botanical gardens by figuring this garden as a form of salvage botany, and enacting some space-age dream of exit via Earth Ship.[13]

The urgency of concerns over planetary well-being is made explicit only as visitors descend to the lower levels of the Cloud Forest. There the garden's seemingly benign pleasures are interrupted as lush displays give way to dire scientific visualizations of a warming planet. The "exit through the gift shop" draws visitors through "Earth Check," a dramatic climate change data-visualization room pulsing with animated graphic displays projected on black walls. From there, visitors are channeled into a massive theater, where they are subjected to terrifying visions of total collapse. An immense double-channel video projection loops incessantly, splashing light and color across twenty-meter screens on the rear wall and floor. The video charts in vivid images, voiceovers, and an urgent soundtrack the devastating year-by-year projections of the rise in global temperature (for more on this see Myers 2015c). Visitors linger, first willingly, and then perhaps more reluctantly, as the urgency of the message grows, while untroubled children play and giggle in the dancing beams of light. It is here that visitors are forced to grapple with the death and extinction that underwrite all the life made to thrive in these gardens.

While touring that perfectly maintained space, I was drawn to one pane of glass that revealed what happens when this space is not so meticulously maintained by so many laboring hands (figure 5.13). Peering through this grungy smear blocking the view of what should be such a photogenic landscape, complete with Singapore's booming port lands, I came to realize that this is not just a garden of leisure and spectacle. It is both a living memorial to an already vanishing world, and a thriving fantasy of the earth's immanent undoing. From this view, the massive and impressive edifices of the gardens' conservatories appear more like thin, fragile envelopes enclosing a precariously simulated Eden, an garden whose very conception and construction—with its massive extraction of materials and species—seems to be accelerating the destruction.

I left the gardens feeling totally demoralized. Was it possible to thwart the apocalyptic future this garden dreams so furtively? I left wanting to amplify the fissures in this garden's logic of excess and extraction, and to subvert its narrative of inevitable collapse. My hunch was that artists might have some poignant and startling ways to upend these tired forms.

An Artist in the Garden against Eden

Nearly eight months after my trip to Singapore, I was visiting a friend's art studio in Vienna. When I told him about my research into plants, he eagerly introduced me to the works of Lois Weinberger, whom he described as one of Austria's most important plant artists. Just looking over the images on Weinberger's website, I could see immediately how his works could help me make sense of Singapore's gardens. Weinberger was based in Vienna,

Figure 5.13. Singapore's port lands and Supertrees through a dirty window. Photograph by the author.

and I was eager to meet him. He was away while I was there, but his wife, Franziska Weinberger, responded warmly to my email inquiry and invited me into their expansive home and studio to talk. Franziska is his close collaborator. She is an art historian and works with Lois in the conception and development of his many public artworks. I sat across from her at a large sunlit table surrounded by artworks and shelves heaving with books on art, ecology, and philosophy. I scribbled notes in rapt attention as she told me stories of the many lives of his remarkable body of work.

Weinberger prefers not to do in-person interviews, but he does respond to written requests, and has commented extensively on his work in print in gallery catalogues, and other publications, and several curators have written on his works. From these texts and my conversation with Franziska, I learned that he has been making plant-based installations, durational works, films, photographs, sculptures, large-scale public interventions and performances for about forty years. He is, as he puts it, "fundamentally" "interested in every kind of examination of plants or engagement with them" (Arrends, Ullrich, and Weinberger 2011: 41). Plants are, for him, both "followers and fugitives of culture" (Weinberger quoted in Trevor 2013). They hitch rides, following people on their circuitous routes; but plants also easily escape from human control and the enclosures people build for them. Plants' remarkable plasticity can make them readily available to human intervention and design, yet their wily ways also allow them to defy total governance. If gardens can be understood in part as reservoirs of people's desires, and gardeners' work as the cultivation of their hopes, dreams, visions of beauty, pleasure, leisure, and prosperity alongside the plants they tend, Weinberger's gardens show that these desires and values are anything but benign. By a working "against the aesthetics of the Pure and the True, against the ordering forces," his installations show up the otherwise invisible violence of the moral orders of conventional garden enclosures (Weinberger, quoted in Zanfi 2009: 24). His works are best understood as counter-gardens: de-commodified and de-moralized, they are "gardens against Eden."

For Weinberger, "The plant stands for the explosiveness of issues / from nutrition to the processes of migration in our time, for all systems surrounding us" (Arrends, Ullrich, and Weinberger 2011: 41). He calls attention the infrastructures we put in place to control, contain, and cultivate plants and which in turn control, contain, and culture people. It is the failures and instabilities of these systems that his works highlight so poignantly, including the fallout from colonialism, globalization, labor migration, xenophobia, and capitalism. Weinberger insists that he is "not a gardener": "my field" he says, "has to be seen as an analysis and counterproposal to the prevailing consumerism": "I use the term garden more as a disturbance, as something that could not take place this way or elsewhere" (Arrends, Ullrich, and Weinberger 2011: 44). Take the example of his series *Portable Gardens* (figure 5.14). Composed of "small carrier bags, laundry sacks or plastic containers filled with earth and ruderal plants," these works highlight the conjoined mobilities of plants and people (Trevor 2013: 221). He uses shopping bags and plants from local communities to highlight the resilience of local meanings, associations, and knowledges even in the wake of globalizing forces. According to his curator Tom Trevor, "The use of such cheap, everyday means of transportation has connotations of poverty and class politics, but also of migration and the current conditions of social mobility brought about by global economics" (2013: 220–21). It is by repurposing plastic garbage bags and other forms of waste that many of Weinberger's works offer a critique of the market externalities of capital. Composed of garbage and nurturing decay, decomposition, and weedy plants rather than lush vegetation, his gardens push up against what Rancière (2010) might refer to as the "proper" relations between humans

Figure 5.14. Lois Weinberger's *Portable Gardens*, 1994. Used by permission of Lois Weinberger.

and nature. In the process they challenge what Rancière calls "the aestheticization of life in the capitalistic world" (199).

Weinberger's gardens also challenge the moralizing discourses of "wildness" and of "native" and "invasive species" (see Mastnak, Elyachar, and Boellstorff 2014). Many of his gardens are durational works that involve leaving buckets or bags of soil out for months at a time in an urban center before moving them to another city, leaving to chance which seeds take root. In this sense, his gardens are designed to *potentiate ecologies*: they offer affordances and openings for both life and death. Weinberger insists: "Whatever wants to and can grow / should grow" (in Zanfi 2009: 78). Weinberger's works reveal a potency, energy, and force in plants that subverts the desires and designs of the conventional gardener. His gardens take root in ruptures and fissures where bare earth is exposed. The makeshift enclosures and containers he crafts are what he calls "perfectly provisional realms": "A perfectly provisional solution is a framework that just keeps from falling apart, but still works wonderfully, and doesn't cost anything" (Arrends, Ullrich, and Weinberger 2011: 44). The rubble of vacant lots and abandoned wastelands embody this quality of the "perfectly provisional." Where conventional garden enclosures often mark out a clear-cut domain and circumscribe areas for meticulous modes of attention and care, his "gardens of disregard" subvert norms of governance and the moralizing forces gardens typically set in motion (quoted in Zanfi 2009: 43–44). In this way, his works resonate with the emerging "wasteland aesthetic" that anthropologist Bettina Stoetzer (forthcoming) and geographers Matthew Gandy (2013) and Jamie Lorimer (2008) write about in their accounts of weedy, spontaneous, ruderal ecologies taking shape in urban "margins," sites such as brownfields, roadsides, postwar rubble heaps, and green roofs.

It is in Weinberger's efforts to destabilize and make uncertain the conventional boundaries around garden enclosures that his works acquire such potency. They do away with the conception of a gardener as an overbearing, controlling force with designs on nature. Instead, their gardens thrive on what Lois calls a "scrupulous lack of attention." For Lois, this practice redistributes the senses and sensibilities of conventional gardening. In contrast to the ways gardeners' attentions are so honed to distinguishing wanted plants from those relegated as weeds, he aims to foster more diffuse modes of attention. For him, the "fringes of perception" are "reservoirs for events" (in Zanfi 2009: 43–44). Franziska suggests that this mode of attention brings into relief that which is normally in the periphery. It is through this care-ful disregard, one hinging on minimalist interventions, that Lois is able to create spaces where plants are free to stage forms of life impossible within conventional garden enclosures.

Potentiated Ecologies

Some of Weinberger's works directly confront the politics of garden enclosures. *Wild Cube* is a series of works that impose permeable barriers around patches of earth, rubble, or lawn. What does the cage keep inside? The more relevant question is actually, "What does it keep out?" These large iron cages are porous to the wind, so birds and insects are invited to seed new ecologies, but human access is explicitly blocked. The cubes disrupt the seemingly inevitable aesthetics and politics of conventional garden enclosures by throwing into relief the moral economies that dictate the order of things in urban landscapes.

"Garden. A poetic fieldwork" is part of Weinberger's *Wild Cube* series, which includes long-term durational works that have taken shape over the course of more than twenty years (figures 5.15–5.17). Franziska recounted the history of this artwork for me during our meeting in their apartment. The work involved the placement of a massive rectangular metal cage on a lawn outside the University of Social and Economic Science in Innsbruck, Austria. As a large-scale public artwork, it produced outrage among city dwellers. Lois writes: "initially the target of demonstrations: right-wing populist politicians called it an eye-sore, the largest and most expensive garbage pail in all of Austria" (Arrends, Ullrich, and Weinberger 2011: 45). Unable to reach the garbage that winds had blown between the bars, and unable to tame the wild plants that began to thrive inside, the cage became an obstacle to the moral order and civilizing aesthetic of urban lawns.

But, Lois insists that "the work was not intended as a provocation, I had not counted on wild growth uncontrollability triggering such resistance and fear" (Arrends, Ullrich, and Weinberger 2011: 45). The Weinbergers and their supporters managed to keep the artwork in place, in spite of harsh criticism and ongoing efforts to force the city to remove it. Twenty years later, a wild profusion of weeds and shrubs have now taken root within the enclosure. Branches push up against its metal bars and reach out and up well beyond the perimeter of the cube. It is in this porous enclosure that Weinberger's dictum could be realized: "Whatever wants to and can grow / should grow" (in Zanfi 2009: 78). Over time, this "poetic fieldwork" began to seed forms of plant life that could not otherwise thrive on that institutional lawn. In this sense, Weinberger's artwork disrupts the normal function and aesthetic form of a garden infrastructure by interrupting human desires. This selectively porous infrastructure creates an affordance, or a clearing, in which other forms of life might take root. In a remarkable turn, this garden is now hailed as one of Innsbruck's most important artworks. As Franziska recounted, even the city's mayor, one of Weinberger's biggest critics, finally came around.

JUXTAPOSITIONS

Both Weinberger's counter-gardens and Singapore's Gardens by the Bay foreground the profound interimplication of plants and people in a time of unprecedented ecological destruction. And both build their gardens out of rubble. If Gardens by the Bay discreetly seals over the rubble of land reclaimed from the sea, with glass, metal, and concrete to simulate nature in the form of "clean," "green" environments for leisure and delight, Weinberger's gardens

Figures 5.15, 5.16, and 5.17.
Lois Weinberger's "Garden. A
Poetic Fieldwork," 1991–1999,
New University for Social and
Economic Science, Innsbruck.
Photographs by and with
permission of Lois Weinberger.

break right through the concrete and keep the rubble of wasted lands present as a provocation, a reminder of the ravages of war, industrialism, poverty, and the market externalities of capitalism. If Singapore's paved-over garden enclosures defer decay and decomposition to undisclosed elsewheres, and keep death out of view, Weinberger's counter-gardens hinge on the disintegration and decomposition that are integral to planetary survival, fostering potentiated ecologies that unfurl in the affordances made possible by minimalist, ephemeral, degradable, and porous enclosures.

These gardens are a remarkable example of how the anxieties of the Anthropocene might be better rendered as the affects of what Donna Haraway and others have named the Capitalocene (Haraway and Kenney 2015; Moore 2017). It is in this simulation of an already lost world in the form of capital-intensive entertainment for climate change education, that we can see that capital continues to profit from the very extinctions that it drives. Here it is possible to see how, in Fredric Jameson's (2003) words, "it is easier to imagine the end of the world than to imagine the end of capitalism."[14] In this regard I am swayed by geographer Erik Swyngedouw's (2010) trenchant critique of the allure of the apocalyptic imaginaries that suffuse climate change discourse. He pays close attention to the "post-political" moment when climate change can only be imagined to be mitigated through "radical techno-managerial and socio-cultural formations," crowding out any form of political dissensus or contestation. He shows how such managerial imaginaries are "organized within the horizons of a capitalist order," an order that remains "beyond dispute" (219). Gardens by the Bay emulates this postpolitical moment in its close coupling of Edenic imaginaries and naturalized capital, as for Swyngedouw, the postpolitical holds onto a "harmonious view of Nature that can be recaptured" while simultaneously "reproducing, if not solidifying, a liberal capitalist order for which there seems to be no alternative" (228). According to his analysis, "stabilizing the climate seems to be a condition" not for mitigating mass extinction, but for perpetuating "capitalist life as we know it" (222). In this way, it becomes clear that Singapore's Edenic aestheticization of both capitalism and collapse secures a vision for "proper" relations between "man and nature," relations that hinge on a fundamental split that renders nature as object and resource subject to technological management.

Holding these gardens together helps us see the relationship between aesthetics and politics, and the ways that different designs can potentiate different kinds of politics. Through Swyngedouw and Rancière, I have come to see Gardens by the Bay's Edenic simulation as a consensual, postpolitical project that leaves intact the logics of colonialism and capitalism, those forces which arguably have generated the crises the gardens are supposed to reveal. Consensus here can be understood in Rancière's (2009) terms as a particular "distribution of the sensible" that assumes a "proper" relationship between what is given to our senses and how we make sense of that given. Consensual politics follows a prescriptive ethics and moral economy that has defined in advance what is good and what is bad. Weinberger's artworks on the other hand show us what a rupture in this logics and moral economy might look like. In this sense Rancière (2009: 3) might identify Weinberger's "improper" gardens as a form of "dissensus," that is, "a perturbation in the normal relation" between what is given and how we make sense of that given. This perturbation is what Rancière calls a "redistribution of the sensible," or what his translator, Steven Corcoran describes as a process of "reorienting general perceptual space and disrupting forms of belonging." Corcoran reads Rancière to suggest that "genuine political or artistic activities always involve forms of innovation that tear bodies from their assigned places and free speech and expression from all reduction to functionality" (in Rancière 2010: 1). In this light, I see Weinberger's weedy aesthetics as a disruption of proper "forms of visibility and intelligibility" (172). As Kregg Hetherington astutely notes, these works also invite "aesthetic rejection of the chronological terms that the Anthropocene marks."[15] They are thus a lesson in learning to read infrastructures differently: if analyses of infrastructure tend to focus on function and assume progressive, linear temporalities, a shift to analyses of infrastructures' aesthetic forms, especially the modes of dissention possible within artists gardens, opens up space to see other temporalities in-the-making. If Singapore's Edenic apocalypse is the embodiment of "proper" relations between humans and natural world, relations explicitly conditioned by capitalism and colonialism, then Weinberger's improper gardens potentiate a different politics, propagate different relationships among plants and people, and different imaginaries of the past, present, and future.

It is from this vantage point that Weinberger helps me see that Gardens by the Bay is a design *for the Anthropocene*, a design locked into the very logics of anthropogenic catastrophe. It is a design that amplifies Anthropocenic imaginaries and temporalities, one that can only imagine nature as Eden caught interminably in the anticipation of apocalypse. In so doing, Weinberger inspires me to imagine what might come, not only after the apocalypse, in what

Anna Tsing (2015) might call the "ruins of capitalism," but more pressingly, what might come after the very concept of the Anthropocene has initiated its work; that is, after the shattering "revelation" of humanity's impact on the geological record. What forms of life and which infrastructures might potentiate a different future?

OPENINGS: PLANTS AND PEOPLE IN AND AFTER
THE ANTHROPOCENE

Those seeking to name the founding force of that era we still call the Anthropocene have placed the "golden spike" of this geological age at various moments in an entangled human/plant history: at the moment of invention of agriculture over fourteen thousand years ago; at the launch of colonial conquest, beginning with Columbus's voyage in 1492, and the subsequent decimation of Indigenous populations, and the enslavement and forced migration of African peoples (e.g., Todd 2015; de la Cadena 2015); at the moment of the expansion of plantation agriculture, through its practice of accumulation by dispossession (e.g., Tsing 2005, 2015); at the time of the rise of capitalism, with the industrial revolution and the expansion of global markets (e.g., Haraway 2015; Moore 2017; Davis and Turpin 2015); and even at the moment of the detonation of the first nuclear bomb in 1945, and the accumulation of radionucleotides in mutant plant ecologies (Masco 2004; Monastersky 2015). Each of these moments has been identified as the potential starting point of a bounded epoch of destruction and devastation whose end "will have been" humanity's last gasp.[16] These origin stories for the Anthropocene hinge on profound shifts in the ways people have staged their relationships with plants: from the earliest domestication of corn; to the clearing of vast amounts of land for sugar, rubber, and cotton plantations made possible through colonization; to the extraction of vast amounts of petrified photosynthetic life from reservoirs that fed the expansion of the Industrial Revolution and now fuel today's petrocapitalisms; to the Green Revolution, which continues to unfurl in a time of late industrialism with the proliferation of chemical herbicides and pesticides for industrial crops and twenty-first-century plantation agriculture. Whenever it began, the Anthropocene appears to be riddled with forms of violence and destruction that have shaped the lives of both plants and their people.

Many criticisms have been waged against these periodizations and the moniker chosen to signify the cause and effects of the destruction. Much of that criticism has to do with naming "Man" as singular agent. This move flattens differences and renders invisible other ways of doing life by lumping all humans together, as if all peoples everywhere share the same destructive tendencies (e.g., de la Cadena 2015). This name also keeps intact Western assumptions that pit "man against nature," perpetuating a fundamental split between humans and nonhumans, nature and culture. As Swyngedouw has shown, the Anthropocene has also become a postpolitical site for the co-optation of environmental action by a neoliberalism caught in the thrall of the carbon economy and the technological fix: "we" got ourselves into this mess, and "we" can get ourselves out of it through more of the same (geoengineering, sustainable infrastructures, etc.). These technological fixes do nothing to challenge the very conditions that precipitate the ongoing destruction. In all cases, the Anthropocene's singular focus on human agency forgets that *we are not alone*: there are other epic forces in our midst (Myers 2016).

If the Anthropocene has been thoroughly marked by the extractive logics of capitalism and the destructive power of colonialism, then perhaps it is in our best interests to get ourselves out from under its shadow. Perhaps the lesson of Gardens by the Bay is that it is time to stop *designing for the Anthropocene*; to stop locking ourselves into futures bound to this tragic, anthropocentric fantasy. To do this, however, we need to learn to read the tacit logics of the Anthropocene and to cultivate counterforms. Artists seem to be up to this task, which requires inventive techniques of disruption and dissention. Perhaps it is the space of artists' gardens that we might learn what might be able to take root in the *ruins of Anthropocene thinking*. Weinberger's gardens remind us that plant roots can foment fissures in what appear to be unmoving, hegemonic forms. Plants and their fungal allies teach us about decomposition, decay, and how to make compost out of what seems unbreakable (cf. Tsing 2015; Haraway 2015). Wily plants have the *involutionary momentum*, the desire and capacity to get entangled in and to catalyze all kinds of relations (Hustak and Myers 2012). By conspiring with plants to seed transformation, artists might be the ones to teach us how to design gardens for ways of doing life *after the Anthropocene*.

This formulation does not hinge on epochal formulations of time, which imagine a clear-cut beginning and end. Consider the dual meanings of the word "end": ends as in finalities, and ends as in telos or purpose. Both of these meanings converge all too easily in paralyzing, apocalyptic imaginaries of the end-of-times. Rather than signaling a temporal period *after the fact*, this formulation pivots around a generous reading of the Anthropocene's suffix "-cene." I hear "-cene" in multiple registers: both through Donna Haraway's (2015: 167) attention to the "root meanings of—cene/kainos," which she interprets as a "temporality of the thick, fibrous, and lumpy 'now,' which is ancient and not"; and in its homophonic vibrations with the terms "seen" (de la Cadena 2015; Howe and Pandian 2015) and "scene" (Pandian 2015). Indeed, the singular optics of conventional Anthropocene thinking make it hard to "see" other "scenes," especially those "anthropos-not-seen," those ways of doing life that have been decimated by the violences of colonialism and capitalism and which continue to be written out of the past, present, and future (de la Cadena 2015). In order to dream a different kind of future, perhaps we will have to design gardens with the potential to stage new scenes, and seed new ways to see the ancient and ongoing conspiracies among plants and their people (see also Myers 2018).

Crucially, the "after" that I flag in this formulation does not refer to some deferred time after some future apocalypse. Rather, it marks what is possible *in the wake of* the invention and circulation of the Anthropocene concept. It circumscribes what is already happening in the midst of an upswell of work by artists, scientists, journalists, scholars, and activists to alert wider publics to the violence of colonialism and extractive logics and to foment critical and creative rethinking of the long history and future of plant/people relations. Like the subterranean forces of roots that can rupture concrete, counter practices, techniques, and epistemic shifts can create fissures in even the most hegemonic formations. It is perhaps only after learning how to pay attention to centuries of resistance to colonialism, and to the ongoing and resurgent work involved in setting plant/people conspiracies in motion, that it may be possible to foster aesthetic forms and epistemes that can resist the hegemony of anthropocentric thinking. Designing gardens otherwise can potentiate ways of doing life that refuse the separation between nature and culture and exploitative relations among plants and their people.

In the spirit of the inventiveness and creativity that permeates many of the critiques of the Anthropocene, to conclude this chapter, I offer a playful term to mark an episteme that is already alive and well in our midst. The episteme that I want to see thriving in the ruins of the Anthropocene is what I am calling the *Planthroposcene* (see Myers 2016, 2017, forthcoming). Here I displace the singular figure of the *Anthropos* with the strangely hybrid figure of the *Planthropos* in order to amplify the profound interimplication of plants and people in every facet of life on earth. This is an aspirational episteme and way of doing life in which those still not in-the-know come to realize, as so many others have known all along, that *we are of the plants*; that *we are only because they are* (Myers 2016, forthcoming). And that now it is time to act with the knowledge that human futures are inextricably bound up with the future of plant lives and worlds. This is our moment to learn how to conspire with the plants to imagine livable futures for all of us. Weinberger's counter-gardens are just one way of imagining how we might root ourselves into a different future. Taking his gardens as an inspiration, it is time to ask, how will we design gardens for the Planthroposcene?

Notes

I am grateful to all the people I engaged in researching this article, and especially Franziska and Lois Weinberger for their generosity and close reading of this text. This project has benefited significantly from lively conversations at the Infrastructure, Environment, and Life in the Anthropocene meeting at Concordia organized by Kregg Hetherington. I would especially like to thank Joe Masco and Gretchen Bakke for their incredibly generative comments on the paper at that workshop. I also received generous feedback on this project in talks at UC Berkeley's Department of Geography (many thanks especially to Jake Kosek and Marissa Mika), UC Davis's STS Program, McMaster University's Department of Anthropology, and the University of Ottawa's Department of Sociology and Anthropology. Many thanks too to Nicholas D'Avella, Kristi Onzik, Kay Lewis-Jones, Benjamin Neimark, Denisa Kera, Christie Spackman, and Jerome Whittington for their thought-provoking readings of earlier drafts of this chapter.

1 See Myers (2013, 2015b).
2 For a recent series of articles with various approaches to this concept "after the Anthropocene," see Elizabeth Johnson et al. (2014).
3 Some of this analysis has appeared as a photo essay in Myers (2015c).
4 See "Cloud Forest," Gardensbythebay.com, accessed March 20, 2017, http://www.gardensbythebay.com.sg/en/the-gardens/attractions/cloud-forest.html#.
5 See, for example, von Zinnenburg Carroll (2018), and works by Oliver Kellhammer, Broken City Lab, Haha Collective and more documented in *Public's* special issue on Gardens (2010) edited by Erin Despard and Monika Kin Gagnon. See also Valerie Smith's (2006) documentation of *Down the Garden Path: The Artist's Garden after Modernism*, a group show she curated at the Queens Museum of art featuring works by Alan Sonfist, Robert Smithson, Gordon Matta-Clark, Tom Burr, and many others. Some of the plant artists I am thinking with include Amanda White, Alana Bartol, Ackroyd and Harvey, Jo Simalaya Alcampo, and Craig Campbell.

6   See also Gordillo (2014) and Tsing (2015).
7   See, for example, Hetherington (2013); Gordillo (2014); Pandian (2009); Kosek (2006); Mathews (2011); and Tsing (2005, 2015).
8   See note 6. See also Craig Campbell's (2018) remarkable design for a post-Soviet collective garden, and von Zinnenberg Carroll (2018).
9   See, for example, Puig de la Bellacasa (2014, 2015); Lyons (2014, 2016); Gordillo (2014 and this volume); Carse (this volume); Raffles (2010); Lowe (2006); and Myers (2015a).
10 "Leaders in Conservation: Botanic Gardens and Biodiversity in the 21st Century," organized by Katja Neves, October 23–25, Concordia University, Montreal. See https://leadersinconservation.wordpress.com/about/.
11 See, for example, Ghosh (2013); Malay (2014); Reuters (2013).
12 For example, "Singapore Haze Hits Record High from Indonesia Fires," BBC News, accessed September 7, 2015, http://www.bbc.com/news/world-asia-22998592.
13 In some ways these gardens could be seen as an aestheticized version of the Millennium Seed Bank or other kinds of "arks" or "Earth Ship" enclosures imagined not only in science fiction (such as the 1978 movie Silent Runner), but also in the form of Biosphere projects (see, for example, Sagan 1990). See also Peter Sloterdijk (2005) on glass houses as bubbles that mediate climate and atmosphere.
14 Jameson's (2003) insight is relevant here, especially given his essay discusses forms of capitalism taking shape in early twenty-first-century Singapore: "Someone once said that it is easier to imagine the end of the world than to imagine the end of capitalism. We can now revise that and witness the attempt to imagine capitalism by way of imagining the end of the world" (76).
15 Hetherington, personal communication.
16 See Povinelli (2011) on tense and the future anterior.

SIX. Leaking Lines

Plumber's Job on a Giant's Scale: Fixing New York's Drinking Straw
Ken Belson, *New York Times*, November 23, 2008

All tunnels leak, but this one is a sieve. For most of the last two decades, the Rondout–West Branch tunnel—45 miles long, 13.5 feet wide, up to 1,200 feet below ground and responsible for ferrying half of New York City's water supply from reservoirs in the Catskill Mountains—has been leaking some 20 million gallons a day. Except recently, when on some days it has lost up to 36 million gallons. . . . The city's Department of Environmental Protection has embarked on a five-year, $240 million project to prepare to fix the tunnel—which includes figuring out how to keep water flowing through New Yorkers' faucets during the repairs. . . .

For this, the city has enlisted six deep-sea divers who are living for more than a month in a sealed 24-foot tubular pressurized tank complete with showers, a television and a Nerf basketball hoop, breathing air that is 97.5 percent helium and 2.5 percent oxygen, so their high-pitched squeals are all but unintelligible. They leave the tank only to transfer to a diving bell that is lowered 70 stories into the earth, where they work 12-hour shifts, with each man taking a four-hour turn hacking away at concrete to expose the valve.

First designed and extended in the nineteenth century, modern urban water infrastructures have been key sites for the making and performance of the liberal, modernist city and its citizens (Joyce 2003). They are "mediating technologies" constitutive of persons and political histories (Furlong 2011); political devices that effect a series of constitutive splits—between nature and culture, politics and technics, and the human and nonhuman—that are key to the operations of liberal government. Nevertheless, today, urban water infrastructures are as known for their leakages as the water they deliver. For instance, newspapers now frequently report the prolific leakages of water from New York city's aging water infrastructure and those of other American and Canadian cities (Schaper 2014; Davison 2011; Belson 2008; CBC News 2009). And World Bank projects to reduce water leakage in cities of the global South have been compromised by their costs, their technologies, and their politics (Anand 2015).

As water infrastructures crumble and leak in cities and regions all over the world today, their promises—of smooth stable flows, freed of the exigencies of politics and nature—appear ever more fickle and porous. Persistent leakage is instead a stark reminder of the difficulties experts and agencies have in regulating the infrastructures and environments that they manage. As engineers, divers, and a cast of other experts grapple if only to find locations of leakage (never mind the difficulty of repairing leaks), the relentless leaks of water reveal how modernist liberal imaginaries of infrastructure steadily, consistently, and persistently mediating relations between environments and human life, are no longer as tenable to maintain (see also Carse, this volume). Instead, as water infrastructures leak into the ground in ways that challenge modernist stories of control and dominion over nature, these uncontrolled, often unknown flows reveal how humans don't rule over the environment with technologies and infrastructures. Instead, as the work of divers of the New York Department of Environmental Protection demonstrates, we uncertainly and tenuously live *through* them, as they constantly leak and rupture beneath and beyond our gaze.

In this chapter I focus on the significant leakages of water from municipal water networks in Mumbai to theorize how we know, govern, and are governed by infrastructures in the contemporary moment. As newspaper reports describe the prolific leakages of water from municipal infrastructures all over the world, I argue that the hidden, subterranean materialities of water infrastructures challenge efforts to govern at a distance. Extraordinary labor is required just to know how, where, and whether water is leaking in urban water infrastructures. As pipes continue to hemorrhage prolific volumes of water, they reveal the extraordinary and yet very mundane ways in which we have long been living through infrastructures that do make us live, while, at the same time, are constantly teetering out of control. I draw attention to the prolific leakages of water that escape city pipes in New York and Mumbai, not only to question the expectation that leaky crumbling infrastructures are metonymic of cities in the global South (Graham 2010; Roy and Ong 2011). I draw attention to the technologies and practices of detecting and repairing leakages in these two cities also to describe the difficulties that engineers have in governing infrastructures underground in different parts of the world. If the environment is the infrastructure of infrastructure (Hetherington 2016; Carse 2012), its subterranean materialities, as sedimented accretions of more-than-human forms, trouble human efforts to regulate it. Instead, as leakage events—of power, authority, and also water—occur underground, engineers are constantly managing the network not as experts, but as subjects compromised by the unknown materialities and processes taking place beyond their gaze. Their restive attempts to make water flow as H_2O (Illich 1985) through the city reveal the limits not of water to flow, but of modernist frames of politics, technology, and government in everyday life. The relentless leakages of water infrastructure display the limits of our abilities to manage and control "nature," even in a period that is now (or imminently) named after the *anthropos*. As water continues to soak, perforate and puncture the grounds of the city, it calls for new theorizations of power, responsibility, and vitality—theorizations that decenter and challenge the idea that humans have dominion over the earth (Locke 1980).

In recent years, scholars in science studies and geography have drawn attention to the vital and political materialities of infrastructural systems we live "with," and have urged we also consider nonhumans as actants in our political cultures (Haraway 1991; Latour and Weibel 2005; Braun and Whatmore 2010). For instance, Jane Bennett has urged an attention not just to the social but also the material actants that form infrastructure. She shows how electricity grids are "living, throbbing confederations" of human and nonhuman relations "that are able to function despite the persistent presence of energies that confound them from within" (2010: 24). In this chapter, I follow new materialist approaches by drawing attention to the way that urban water politics is subject not only to the political regimes of humans but also to the politics accreted in the materials and histories of urban water infrastructures (29). Yet, I argue that water and its infrastructures do not act and perform beyond the regimes of human responsibility. Indeed the appearance and disappearance of leaking water in the city demonstrate how its form cannot be disaggregated from the compromised authority that manages it in everyday life.

Knowing Leakage

As I have described elsewhere, Mumbai has recently developed a leakage problem. This is not to say that water was not leaking prolifically before. However, in recent years, the World Bank, together with the federal Ministry of Urban Development, have been compelling urban water utilities in India to reduce waste and "unaccounted for-water" (UFW), by measuring and auditing their water losses in the system (Anand 2015). If water has long been unaccounted for in Mumbai, the lack of accounting was only made into a contemporary problem in Mumbai as late as 2004 to make viable the neoliberal reform of water infrastructures in the city (Anand 2017).

Formally, the Mumbai Municipal Corporation (BMC) has reported leakage figures of approximately 25 percent. This is, in and of itself, not terrible. Water systems are characterized by leakage all over the world. New York City's water system, for example, is estimated to lose between 15 and 30 percent of its water every day. Yet, with over half of Mumbai's water meters out of service, it is unclear how this figure has been calculated. I heard the figure in several interviews with city engineers and saw it cited in city papers. During my years of fieldwork, I never learned how the water department calculated leakage when the tools and meters of measurement were silent and unreliable. For instance, most of the meters on the city's metered water connections (60 percent by one estimate) are not working. Without access to a reliable measure of how much water has been consumed by customers on these connections, water department officials frequently estimate these quantities for the purposes of billing.[1] As a result, many residents get water through unmetered connections by paying a flat rate. Second, water meters have been installed only on newer water connections. Connections that were approved and granted prior to the implementation of water meters in the 1980s are legal, but these flows aren't accounted for by volume. Instead, customers pay fixed water taxes (based on the ratable value of their property). Nevertheless, engineers in the billing office frequently tentatively pencil in numbers based on what these flows "should reasonably" be. It is these acts of estimation and reason that produce numbers of water supply billed and lost in the city.

Numerical fictions that are embedded in the protocols of measuring water flows in Mumbai are powerful, not least because they produced the city water department as a well-performing water utility, one that did not need any external assistance from the central ministry or the World Bank. Not accidentally, the fiction posing as fact was challenged when the World Bank consultants began to conduct water audits as part of the reform initiative. Yet in the absence of reliable measurement devices, the consultants, like the city engineers, were compelled to derive the quantities of leakage using speculative forms of reasoning that while more formalized continued to be estimates based on difficult assumptions (Anand 2015). Thus, even in the audits conducted by the consultants, water was more frequently estimated than measured.[2] In this respect, the consultants' extrapolations of leakage appear rather similar to the city engineers' derivations of water loss. They were brought into being, made distinct, and made visible by assumptions and ideas of human agency and the separations of society and materiality embedded in their protocols (see Anand 2015).

The battle over leakage figures in Mumbai reveals how attempts to produce quantitative facts about the city's leakage are frequently compromised by the dynamic social and material relations that form Mumbai's water supply infrastructure (see Poovey 1998). The struggles to measure leakage demonstrate that it is not just "inept" state employees who had difficulty measuring water. The World Bank's French engineering consultants also had a difficult time measuring water flows. The difficulty measuring water was not an effect of technical incompetence. Neither were the fuzzy numbers generated to measure leakage solely the result of a politically motivated ignorance (see Proctor and Schiebinger 2008; Mathews 2008). As I watched both the consultants and engineers work hard and fail to measure the degree of water leakage in the city, it seemed apparent that their difficulties were also emergent from the subterranean materialities and technologies of the city's water system. These materialities made measurements very difficult for a variety of reasons—reasons that constantly compromise the power engineers have to govern water systems.

First, measuring consumption and leakage is more difficult in systems of intermittent water supply. In Mumbai, city employees turn a series of large valves distributed across the city so that each hydraulic zone receives its daily quota of water during a few hours of the day. As such, water does not flow at constant pressures through the network at all times. With a different valve on the network redirecting water somewhere in the city every two minutes, the consultants speak of how pressures in the system are always varying and "going crazy," making water difficult to measure. With water only flowing in certain pipes at certain times, water pressure at any given location spikes and tapers throughout the day, making it difficult to measure volumes using flow calculations, calculations that are themselves based on steady pressures.

Second, water leakages cannot be effectively measured when water meters— the central instrument of measurement in water systems—are known to be unreliable across the world. For instance, a report by the International Water Association begins with a section on the importance of *reliable* metering, noting that meters themselves "require careful management" and are prone to a host of problems including encrustation, deterioration with age, and unreliable flow rates (Lambert and Hirner 2000). At times, particulate blockage can increase water pressure through the meter, causing elevated readings (Castalia 2007). In intermittent systems, meters also read and register air flowing through them, a common occurrence at the start of the daily water supply. Finally, meters are read by humans, who are a source both of deliberate and accidental error. Engineers would complain that meter readers seldom went to "the field" to read water meters and would prefer, instead, to generate consumption figures in the comfort of their offices. Yet, because meters were unreliable, engineers were unable to enforce good reading practices on their workers. Even when engineers would scrutinize bills generated by the billing department, they were unsure of when an unusual reading was due to excessive (or minimal) water use, a faulty meter, or an errant (or bribed) meter reader.

The intransigence of water meters (and their readers) are but two of many locations at which water infrastructures (composed of humans and non-humans) challenge human-centered theorizations of political agency and responsibility. How might we account for the consumption and leakage in Mumbai's water systems when the central instruments and agents of measurement are known to "act up"? How is leakage managed when its quantities are not knowable in the city? Who (or what) is responsible for the prolific leakages of water in the city? Can we attribute responsibility to the water meter for not acting as it ought?

In her work with the epistemology of physicist Niels Bohr, Karen Barad has insisted that measurement practices aren't as clear and distinct as Newtonian approaches would suggest. Barad challenges classical assumptions that objects and observers occupy distinct physical and epistemological locations and that matter, as such, is available for measurement by humans wielding tools, meters, or microscopes. She suggests that the technologies of measurement are not independent of but part of the phenomena they seek to apprehend. Water, meters, engineers, and pipes, she suggests, are but parts of "intra-acting" phenomena, in which "the objects of knowledge are participants in the production of knowledge" (Barad 1996: 163). For concepts such as leakage to appear evident, stable, and objective, a Cartesian cut that defines fixed subject, object, and context needs to be able to be performed consistently and reliably enough that the conditions necessary for measure to appear fixed, constant, and taken-as-given.[3]

Barad's insights on the labor and conditions necessary for measurement are helpful to understanding the difficulty of measuring water leakages in Mumbai. Leakage emerges as such through a particular, historical effort to govern the flow of water. Without engineered pipes, there is no such "thing" as leakage (Schrader 2010).[4] Wells don't leak. Leakage is brought into existence with a certain technology of controlling water flows. Further, even in engineered systems, the concept of leakage is not ahistorical or natural, but emerges as a "matter of concern" in Mumbai at a particular historical moment (Latour 1996). The interest in measuring and governing water leakage in Mumbai (and indeed in the world) proliferated amid projects to make things countable by neoliberal rationalities.[5] For water leakages to be made visible and measured by water meters, however, the proponents of leakage reduction need to assumed that social "agents," water flows, and their material "situation" are discrete and knowable through independent, verifiable measurement practices. They need to assume that the tools of measurement—water meters—are reliable, objective, uncontroversial devices that can apprehend and deliver reliable results through their operation.

Nevertheless, Mumbai's water infrastructure is anything but a stable, knowable form with uncontroversial flows. Engineers and consultants found it difficult to agree on the techniques of measurement, the assumptions of their measurement models, and the choice of meters that were used. Amid an unstable set of enabling conditions and technologies of measurement, both the engineers and consultants could only generate figures that were too situated, provisional, and questionable to be considered reliable.[6] Not wanting to be embarrassed by the degree of water leakages in the city that the consultants were finding, engineers relentlessly questioned the assumptions and context of the measurement models the consultants used. Their relentless questioning succeeded in straining relations between the engineers and the World Bank consultants and, by extension, the entire reform project.

Yet if the controversy over water leakages revealed the precarity of measure, it also called for a different accounting of responsibility for water leakages in the city—one in which we may consider the role of nonhuman actors.[7] In his examination of engineering and expertise in Egypt in the early twentieth century, political theorist Timothy Mitchell has critiqued the tendency in the social sciences of privileging the role of humans in our accounting of events. "One always knows in advance who the protagonists are," he protests, as he peruses histories of dam making in Egypt during this period. "Human beings are the agents around whose actions and intentions the story is written"(Mitchell 2002: 289). Yet, as Mitchell attends more closely to the histories of hydraulic engineering in Cairo, he demonstrates how engineering expertise was subject to the "ambivalent relations" between mosquitoes, wars, epidemics, famines, and fertilizers. In so doing, Mitchell demonstrates how the expertise of dam building was produced on-site, as engineers confronted and sought to mediate these different human and nonhuman forces.[8]

By suggesting that chemicals, mosquitos, and crops were historical actors, Mitchell follows scholars in STS, who have urged that we disassemble constitutive distinctions between humans and nonhumans, nature and culture, subject and object in theorizing social and political life.[9] As was evident in the water audit, the distinctions between subjects and objects are historically situated, interested ways of ordering the world. They give special status and form to human agency. The water audit succeeded in provincializing these efforts. It made evident how human bodies, water, pipes, or the water meters that are occasionally used are not already constituted subjects or objects. As water is made to flow in pipes to hydrate human lives that produce the technologies of distributing and measuring water, an attention to the iterative process reveals how infrastructures, natures, and human life are actively co-constituted through emergent relations with each other.[10]

Following a series of large infrastructural breakdowns, new materialist scholarship has suggested we think more modestly about the powers that humans have in controlling and managing the worlds that we make. Indeed even as humans play a vital role in structuring infrastructures, infrastructures are processes that are constantly productive of relations that exceed human control.[11] In Mumbai, while engineers seek to manage and control the city's water infrastructure and to make water known, visible, and flow in predictable ways, they are unable to constitute and measure water as a stable object that flows through the city's water network. Iteratively forming a technopolitical regime that responds to physical and social pressures, Mumbai's water cannot be reliably measured in the current distribution regime.[12] The city's water infrastructure does not cooperate with efforts to measure either the volumes of water distributed to different populations or the water that escapes these calculative regimes as "leakage." Instead, as a vital and yet innocuous substance, water moves easily through this regime in ways that are beyond those controlled by city engineers. Its surreptitious and unnoticed flows—into the earth or the bodies of differentiated residents—make it difficult to control with audit technologies in Mumbai.

Yet, in suggesting that water flows in ways that engineers are unable to fully control or know, I do not wish to suggest that engineers are beyond being accountable for the city's water infrastructure, nor that they are able to escape the political consequences of the inequitable distribution regime they manage (Appadurai 2015). As Hetherington points out, "responsibility is less a characteristic of people than a form of description that one offers of the relationships between different actors in an event whose causal sequences are not merely mechanical" (2013: 71). Elsewhere, I demonstrate the ways in which engineers design the city's water infrastructure to deliver less water to residents of the settlements (Anand 2017). These residents of the city would frequently hold its urban administration and its political apparatus responsible for the difficulties they had accessing water in everyday life. Here, I draw attentions to their inability to measure and control leakage to focus on what they *are* able to accomplish and *how they do act* in a system filled with social and material uncertainties that are beyond their control.

In Mumbai, engineers do not attempt to govern the network with neoliberal technologies such as those of the water audit. In their daily work in ward offices, engineers do not spend much time measuring water consumption or leakage in the city. Instead, they govern leakage by crafting heterogeneous and improvised sociotechnical practices.[13] Their work acknowledges the vitality and vibrancy of human nonhuman actors and the difficulties they have in managing them. Their work also demonstrates how material technologies are neither autonomous of human-centric notions of agency, nor are they encompassed by it. Engineers don't rule *over* the city's water system. By drawing attention to their quotidian efforts to control leakages, I argue that engineers "manage" water leakages as compromised and compromising experts. They manage leakages by making discrete and situated compromises with water's fickle flows.

Managing Leakage

As they work to address the thousands of leaks that fill their schedules every day, engineers in the city's ward offices are only too aware that governing water is difficult precisely because of the deeply ambivalent, unknown, and fungible relations between what is apparent and what is real, between what is physical and what is social. As a result, they are not too concerned about measuring leakage. Instead, they are very busy fixing leaks to keep the water system working.

Take, for instance, K-East Ward, one of twenty-four wards in Mumbai. The ward has a population of over 800,000 residents and is twenty-eight-square kilometers in area. In the process of studying the ward for their water audit, the management consultants collated the number of leakages that people *complained* about. Nearly three thousand leakages were reported throughout in one year alone; over six hundred were classified as "major joint leaks and bursts. This is to say, on average more than eight leakages were reported every day in K-East Ward alone. This figure did not include leaks from customer service lines—that also resulted in complaints. Because city engineers respond to these leakages less urgently than to bursts on larger and more significant service mains, connection leakages actually cause a greater loss of water from the system than bigger bursts (Kingdom et al. 2006).

Confronted with thousands of leaks a year, engineers speak of their department as functioning according to a "firefighting" model. Rather than attend and quench all fires, they attend only to the problems that—for social, political, and material reasons—are impossible to ignore. Nevertheless, they are challenged in their effort to do so. With their hands already more than occupied with known leakages, engineers do not spend much time looking for unknown leakages, not least because of the material and technological barriers to finding leaks. As pipes rust, break, or rupture underground, many leakages go unnoticed and unreported. Because the city is largely built on wetlands, much water leaking from the underground mains flows away without giving notice, even if engineers should try and use different technologies to apprehend these hidden flows.

For instance a common method for detecting leaks involves using sonic equipment, which, placed over pipes or valves, can isolate and register the peculiar sound made by a leaky pipe. But here too, engineers dismissed their efficacy in the peculiar "context" of Mumbai. Sonar technologies only work when there is little background noise, when no one is using the road. Yet, water largely flows in Mumbai's network during the day, at which time the streets are filled with the sounds of cars and traffic, of commuters and the city. Engineers complain that the city produces too much noise, rendering sonar technologies ineffective. Sonic technologies are harder to use at night because water doesn't flow through the pipes at night.[14] Other cities detect leakages using pressure monitors, by monitoring for sudden drops in pressure. However pressure monitors are compromised by the intermittent system, because the water pressure in the pipes is always changing. As valves are constantly opening and closing, the changing pressures stress the instruments and cause them to break down. Even when instruments work, engineers are unable to tell whether the drop in pressure is due to leakage or because of valves turning upstream or downstream of the monitors in the varying, dynamic system. Indeed, as I came to learn more and more about the water service system in Mumbai, I realized that the city's water infrastructure itself delivers and produces not known quantities of water, but approximations. In Mumbai, the materiality of the water and its infrastructures entailed these approximations. Because water infrastructure needed to be used and maintained at the same time, engineers often found it easier to leave leakages alone.

In some ways it is easier to fix water mains in a submarine breathing helium than it is to fix one thousand small, leaking service lines. Such work is not only time consuming, but it also requires engineers to know the network intimately well—to understand where leakages are without employing any technology. In Mumbai, regardless of their seniority, the city's engineers have only a partial, experiential knowledge of the distribution system and rely on field engineers to reveal its local state. I talked about the water system one day with Mr. Surve, one of the department's most senior engineers—referred to by his juniors as one of the five *rajas* of the city's water supply. However, when we met, I learned that even this king seemed to have only a partial grasp of the water system.

Always genial and friendly on the phone, it was only after months of persistence that Surve could make time to meet with me. When I arrived at his office, he was reviewing some works proposals and requested a few minutes to finish up. I utilized my time by taking in Surve's surroundings. As one of the city's rajas, his was a large office. I recognized, by now, the authority of the government-supplied, glass-topped desk (reserved for senior officers) at which he sat. The glass encased a long phone list with the cell phone numbers of all others in the department—a list essential to engineers, who delegated their responsibilities through phone calls. On the table behind him, a bundle of papers was wrapped in government-issued red cloth paper. The wall to my left displayed a large, electric model of the water network.

Working between the phone list, government documents, and network map, Surve started by telling me Mumbai's water story. This story, which I had by now heard several times before, began with the catchment of Mumbai's water several miles away. To help me understand, he did not refer to the map on the wall, but drew me one of his very own—enlarging and extending it as the story went on. The map, which he drew with some ease, was filled with pipe diameters and place-names, pumps, and filtration plants (figure 6.1). People, even the engineers, were almost entirely absent from the account. It was a story of careful management and effective control—of directing water from dammed rivers to the water treatment plant, a massive feat of technopolitical achievement by any standard.

The map, however, became considerably more complex and hard to quantify when he began to extend it into the secondary network, in which water subsequently flowed from the treatment plant to twenty-seven service reservoirs. Up until that point, water is generally counted and metered. It is this network that is actively seen by the state; this network that is most frequently regulated, extended, and known with representations like the map. By the time Surve began speaking of the tertiary network—the network that distributes water from service reservoirs to urban populations—his map had reached both the margin of the page and the margins of his knowledge. The tertiary network—comprising water mains taking water *from* the reservoirs to city neighborhoods—was not as easily representable through linear forms of representation. Engineers working in the city-planning offices use GIS software to represent the tertiary lines in two dimensions. Thus, the water network base map represents the diameter of pipes as they pass under roads through different neighborhoods of each city ward, here K-East Ward in northern Mumbai.

It is these networks that are the subject both of leakage work and reform efforts. World Bank consultants insist that these tertiary networks should be

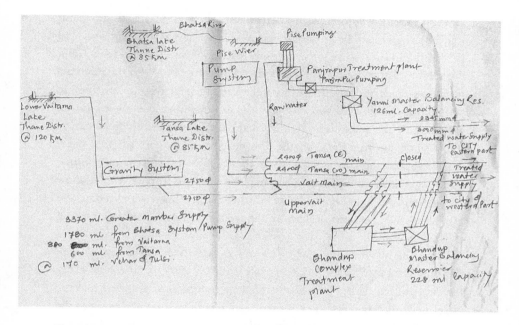

Figure 6.1. Surve's diagram of the water network. Personal communication.

continuously charged with water. But this proposition is the source of much anxiety for engineers like Surve, who know how little is known about the tertiary network. While there are indeed two-dimensional network maps of these water pipes, Surve was far from certain how best to locate them in a city whose spatial referents are always in motion along three dimensions. I quote from my field notes:

> "We just don't know the alignment of lines in the city," he said. I asked if they had maps. "Yes," he replied, "but how far and how deep from the road [the pipes are], no one knows. There is no exact GIS to tell us this. Then, we have been searching for equipment to tell us where the leaks are. There is no equipment anywhere in the world that can tell us this. Mumbai sits on reclaimed land. . . . Therefore, the [leaking] water just goes away, it does not come to the surface. . . . There are pressure monitors. . . . But for these questions the person in the field is the best judge."

Water lines frequently are laid under roads. Ward engineers are in a constant struggle to locate pipes, and their leaks, beneath the structures of the city. With much of the tertiary network underground, engineers have trouble locating exactly where its many parts were. There was little if any elevation information on these two-dimensional maps. As pipes went over and around the hilly terrain in the northern reaches of the city, engineers could not refer to maps to sufficiently apprehend the situation. With the referents of maps—roads and sidewalks themselves in constant repair, construction and motion—engineers were suspicious of any map that fixed their position in places. At the same time, they needed to know where the pipes can be found—how far from the sidewalk; how deep in the ground; whether water will climb hills and how it can do so. In the absence of this systemic information, engineers had difficulty governing the network through volume/flow calculations. Without knowledge of how much these lines were leaking, and how they could be fixed, leakage in the tertiary network risked evacuating the system of water.

Accordingly, while conducting fieldwork, I seldom noticed ward-level city engineers using these maps in their everyday work, or to enable maintenance projects. If the map is a technology to represent knowledge of the water network, engineers do not use it very much, in large part because the map does not contain the vital information that enables ward-level engineers to act. Engineers working in municipal wards instead draw on the embodied knowledges—the experience and knowledge of their colleagues in the field—for any major or minor works. They are the city's pressure monitors and geographic information systems. In a city of consistent breakdowns and hydraulic difficulties, engineers must consistently gauge and judge individual problems, and fashion solutions to each of them. Sometimes, retired engineers have been be summoned back to work—just so that they could point to where the pipes lie beneath the ground (see also Coelho 2006).

Fieldwork

Fixing leaks is hard, necessary, time-consuming work. With most of the city's network underground, water leaking from a pipe presents both material and social challenges. Engineers use their management skill not so much as authoritarian rulers, but as compromised experts subjectified by the situations of the politics, labor, and materials of the city's water infrastructure. To ensure that the system continues to function, they need to negotiate not just with the city's pipes, but also its water, residents, municipal employees, and a range of social actors who are connected to the city's pipes in a variety of ways. Thus, far from being a mechanical process, leakage maintenance makes visible the sociological and technical work that engineers are required to perform as they deploy their ingenuity and improvisational skill to manage its varied effects (Latour 1996: 33).

Like the political anthropologist, the engineer is only too aware of the ways in which his efforts to maintain the city's infrastructure is deeply situated in ambivalent social-technical environments of uncertainty, ignorance, and improvisation. As Ballestero points out in her chapter (this volume), working below the surface is challenging not least because it is difficult to distinguish figure from ground, and flow from sediment in these terrain. Working in these muddy materialities, engineers approached each problem with experience, an eye for improvisation, and a social intuition that they can only learn on the job. One afternoon, I accompanied a city water engineer to investigate a leaky main. I had been to the line previously, just a couple of weeks prior, when city workers were patching it up. A few nights before, the pipe had burst again, and residents of the neighboring ward had not received water for two days. Patankar, the engineer, told me that he had been working long hours just to locate the origin of the leak. The city's infrastructure wasn't cooperating with his efforts. The pipe lay approximately ten meters under the surface of the street, and Patankar had told me that whenever his team tried to uncover the pipe, the sodden, marshy soil would collapse over it again. As we disembarked from the bike and walked toward the troublesome pipe, we crossed over a bridge. I noticed a different pipe running alongside the bridge, with many water connections protruding from it. One small connection was leaking with high pressure into the *nalla* (canal/ drain) below. Patankar didn't even give this pipe a second glance. With his time and expertise already stretched, he walked toward the twenty-four-inch water main, where the bigger problem lay.

We arrived at the site to find water department employees and heavy machinery already at work. As we spoke, the maintenance team was trying to find a valve that could shut off the water to the burst pipe so that they could better inspect it. Patankar walked across another bridge, and, noting thick metal sheet that lay by the side of the road, asked his four men to move it to one side. As they grunted and heaved the sheet aside, they found an opening in the ground. There, about ten-feet deep, lay a layer of water, below which a manhole cover was faintly visible. Patankar asked whether it might be possible for the maintenance crew to go into the manhole, and find the valve that way. The crew members, each of whom had firm opinions about the matter, were understandably not enthusiastic. They suggested lowering a camera to find the valve that way. Patankar agreed, and wondered whether this could be accomplished during supply hours, when water was flowing through the line. The junior staff disagreed, citing the difficulty of seeing what was going on in the pipe if there was water flowing through it. Instead, they concluded that they would come back with a camera the next day. Realizing that the issue would require another day to be resolved, Patankar said a few words to the supervisor before we left the site to attend to another problem.

This everyday work of fixing water connections drew my attention to the contingency, improvisation, and social/material mediation Patankar and other engineers frequently employed to maintain the water network in working condition. To govern water pipes effectively required not only a (very contested) *metis* for repair and recovery (J. Scott 1998; Latour 1996), but also an understanding of how to handle the uncertainties and difficulties affiliated with the city's water infrastructure. As Patankar and his workers struggled to locate the leak, they were required to deal with both restive political subjects and the challenges presented by the water network—the opacity of water and earth, as well as the pipe network's corrosions, containments, and concealments.

In the absence of flexible protocols that could apprehend and direct how this leak could be known and plugged, state authority was not just improvised, but was also diffuse and actively negotiated between the experts, situations, and objects of Mumbai's water infrastructure. It was not just Patankar, the senior engineer, who was an expert of the system, but also his less formally trained workers. Fixing the unknown leak on the pipe, therefore, required not only the cooperation of the earth not to collapse onto the pipe every time it was revealed. It also required the cooperation of city workers who, while charged with maintenance works, had their own ideas about how this maintenance could be done. In order to maintain and govern the city's water network effectively, Patankar needed to know certain key facts about the line (where the leak was, how it might be found and patched) as well as how this infrastructure was situated in regimes of labor, nature, materiality, and the law. As he worked within a fickle and leaky system, Patankar possessed an acute sociotechnical knowledge of how to repair a hydraulic line that was permeated by contingency, obduracy, and the ignorance of people and things.

Conclusion

In this chapter I have described how leakage reveals the limits of modernist technologies of control, categorization, and representation. As engineers dart around the city trying to ascertain the existence and conditions of water leakage, these events confound any easy ascription of their being physical or social, real or apparent. Engineers are unable to ascertain how much water is leaking, and whether the groundwater that surrounds water pipes is social or natural. Located underground, both beyond and beneath the gaze of state officials, the materialities of leakage test the limits of new technologies of detection and repair. Thus, to repair leakages on the Rondout line, New York City recruited divers to live in a submarine and hack away at concrete for days, just to expose a valve.

New technologies—be they in Mumbai or Manhattan—to repair leakages may make these old, long-standing leakages visible anew. Yet the announcements of leakage were unable to make new forms of thought or action possible. Leakage detection efforts, for example, continue to be constrained by modernist categories of governing (or disposing) of things in the world. Rather than compel a reformulation of how to govern water with ambivalent, vibrant, and emergent socionatural relations, prolific leakages instead were sought to compel neoliberal reforms on Mumbai's water infrastructure; reforms that sought to exert even tighter regulatory constraints on the movement of water (see Bennett 2010).[15] In this chapter I attend to the practice of engineering in the field. To examine the daily practices of experts managing a system that is out of control is to ask how life is already being regulated amid political and environmental uncertainties. Where the social and material actants cannot be known in advance, a heterogeneous agnostic practice of engineering takes the unknowability of the world as its starting point to tinker with and repair. It is these practices of engineering (and not so much of the representations of engineering) that I wish to think from.

In his work on engineering, Callon has urged us to note the ways in which infrastructures and technologies are brought into being by relations not just between social actors, but also "a mass of silent others"—human and nonhuman—and their enabling environments. Engineers, he argues, are only too aware of the ways in which "technical, scientific, social, economic and political considerations are inextricably bound up" (1987: 84). As these relations always both exceed and render unstable regimes of knowledge production and practices of government (Callon 1987; Barry 2001), engineers and states are compelled to "white out chaos" from their designs (Scott 1998) in order to work. Therefore when Patankar managed the city's water infrastructure, he did so not by working *on* it, but by working *through* it, making discrete improvisations and accommodations so that it could deliver water reliably.[16] This work with the city's infrastructure is not just critical in bringing urban life into being. It also demonstrates how engineering expertise emerges from very proximate compromised relations with the materials, persons, and politics of the city's leaky infrastructure—relations that Patankar did not know everything about, nor could he fully control.[17]

Repairing leakages in this manner, Patankar and other engineers working for the city, work to bring into being a particular leaky form of authority in the city. Here, materials—valves, steel, laws, and objects—"act" in Latourian terms, together with restless human subjects, often ignoring the Water Department's authority over its pipes. As leakages exceed both the semiotics and politics of subjects and experts in the city, they appear as the nonconstitutive outside of the hydraulic state.[18] At times they are constitutive of the state and of social and political difference. At others, they interrupt and lie beside state control, dispersing power and water as they do so.

I speculate that it is this understanding, and coming to terms with this ordinary, compromised kind of rule, that will guide us through these times of climate change—times marked by uncertainty, ambivalence, and ambiguity. While Jensen and Morita (this volume) astutely call out for new paradigms of infrastructure management, these cannot continue to assume flow without leakage, ordinary breakdown, and uncertainty. Instead, as an attention to leaking modernist water infrastructures show, it is critical to account for the performance of infrastructures in everyday life. Leaks, I suggest, provide continuous moments of opening to think of infrastructure anew. Just as crises talk animated infrastructural innovations in the middle of the twentieth century (Masco, this volume), the everyday, mundane crises that surround leaking infrastructures provide compelling locations in which new infrastructures are always being created on the debris of older forms. As we live in "fractal and falling apart worlds" (Jackson 2014), worlds already structured by infrastructure (Heidegger 1977), the compromised arts of maintenance describe how infrastructures are always being made anew. Repair work reveals how infrastructures are always being remade by laboring across the constitutive divisions (of nature/ culture, material/ politics) that have structured modernist worlds (J. Scott 1998). I suggest we need to carefully follow and cultivate this creative, ambivalent expertise to imagine and remake a world that is on the verge of teetering beyond comprehension and control.

Notes

Versions of this chapter previously appeared in *Public Culture* and in *Hydraulic City: Water and the Infrastructures of Citizenship in Mumbai* (Duke University Press, 2017).

1 Paying last reliable rate.
2 Following international standards and forms, consultants bring the causes of water loss into view by qualifying leakages as real / physical or apparent / social, and speculated (based on speculations of consumption) what the quantities of these leakages were.
3 See also Latour (2005) and Poovey (1998).
4 I would like to thank Shaylih Muehlmann and Natasha Myers for drawing my attention to this.
5 During the early 2000s, new water-accounting protocols that urged urban water utilities to ensure that as much water was "visible" and billed by the water utility (a source of revenue for the water department), and not "wasted" as leakage (Kingdom, Liemberger, and Marin 2006). Accordingly, consultants in Mumbai embarked on procedures to try and identify and measure water loss by its physical and social causes.
6 See Anand (2015) for more on this controversy.
7 Here I draw on the work of Bruno Latour, who has urged that we disassemble constitutive distinctions between humans and nonhumans, nature and culture, subject and object in theorizing social and political life. For Latour, things, laws, insects, bacteria people are all actants; they emerge through relations with others in networks and act through these relations. Latour argues that actants are objects that have effects on other things through relations—they make a difference (Harman 2009; Bennett 2010). As such, Latour refuses to prioritize humans as being above or beyond nonhumans that they are in relations with. Instead, as humans and nonhumans emerge through relations with each other, it becomes difficult to consider human action/agency in a different register than other kinds of action effected by nonhumans. All these effects, Latour argues, may be theorized as political effects.
8 To the extent that dam building could be identified as a singular project, this could only be done after the different relations between human and nonhuman forces had been stabilized to produce the dam (Latour 1996).
9 Haraway (1991); Barad (1996); Schrader (2010); Latour (2005); Bennett (2010). See also Chakrabarty 2009.

10　Barad (2007); Schrader (2010: 278); Latour (1998); Nading (2014).

11　Katie Meehan has drawn on the work of scholars in object-oriented ontology to suggest that infrastructures are forceful, "capable of creating, policing, and destroying the very contours of existence" (2014: 216).

12　See Anand (2011).

13　John Law et al. (1987) have argued that the stability of engineered forms emerges out of a relation between their heterogeneous elements. By focusing on the emerging power of Portuguese ships in the fifteenth century, Law describes how the "heterogeneous engineers" of Europe drew together not only elements of ship design and technological innovations of the magnetic compass. Their success was also contingent on their ability to successfully accommodate specific temporality and directionality of the trade winds.

14　Engineers would recount to me how older city employees could find leakages using just a sounding rod and a cone. They would place the cone on the rod near a spot that had leakage and listen for the sounds of leakage. Engineers spoke of how the art was being lost among the newer employees.

15　See Jane Bennett (2010) regarding the limits of neoliberal efforts to efficiently control electricity infrastructure in the United States. As Eric Wolf warned nearly forty years ago, "by turning names into things we create models of reality, create targets for development and war" (1982: 7). I speculate this might also be the case with the scientists and engineers who are thinking of the technical solutions to regulate climate in times of the Anthropocene, where naming it as such becomes the grounds for mounting a modernist, liberal, global, and technological challenge to climate change. This response frequently elides questions of difference, history, and power anew.

16　By arguing that life and labor emerge through efforts to manage urban infrastructure, I wish to suggest that social and biological life, as such, are made possible through the very same labors that produce the expertise of the hydraulic-engineering department.

17　In doing so he revealed how the expertise of engineers does not emerge out of their ability to operate and control Mumbai's water infrastructures as objects, tools, or technologies from a distance.

18　I develop this idea of a nonconstitutive outside via a reading of Dipesh Chakrabarty's essay "Two Histories of Capital" in his book *Provincializing Europe* (2000).

Part III.
Histories of Progress

SEVEN. Low Tide

Submerged Humanism in a Colombian Port

AUSTIN ZEIDERMAN

"We reject the name Bajamar," Aurelia insisted. "We call these areas *territorios ganados al mar* (territories reclaimed from the sea)." She was objecting to the title commonly used to refer to the seaside shantytowns, built and inhabited primarily by Afro-Colombian settlers, in which about one-third of Buenaventura's 300,000 people live. Aurelia voiced her argument not only as someone advocating on behalf of the Pacific coast port-city's black communities; she herself resided in one of the waterfront settlements named explicitly for their relationship to the sea. Literally meaning "low tide," the label Bajamar invoked a precarious position relative to the fluctuating waters that interpenetrate the city on all sides. It implied that the neighborhoods given this designation were both ecologically vulnerable and legally suspect: low-lying tidal areas in Buenaventura had been identified as having the highest levels of climate-related risk, and permanent human habitation is prohibited by Colombian law within fifty meters of the high-tide line. Both implications led to the same conclusion—mandatory relocation—which activists and settlers alike passionately disputed.

This chapter focuses on territorial conflicts in Buenaventura as a window onto the racialized politics of life and death in contemporary Colombia.[1] Departing from the naming problem surrounding the seaside shantytowns commonly known as Bajamar, it examines efforts to counter displacement pressures afflicting the port-city's Afro-Colombian population. At stake is a concern for how to understand coastal precarity in the context of global climate change. Pivoting on the figure of the "human," the chapter connects recent discussions of the Anthropocene to histories of racial slavery. The coastal landscapes and seascapes once central to the dehumanization of African diasporic life throughout the Americas emerge again as key sites in which the boundaries around the human are reworked. Positioning the boundary work of activists and residents of Buenaventura's waterfront settlements alongside posthumanist thought and some of its critics, the chapter argues that a reengagement with humanism is necessary for confronting the unequal distribution of precarity in the Anthropocene.

The territorial conflicts unfolding in this Colombian port-city reflect wider debates about the exhaustion of conceptual paradigms in the face of global environmental crisis. The idea of the Anthropocene radically undermines the modernist bifurcation of the world into the separate realms of human subject and nonhuman object (Hetherington, this volume). The weakening of this divide parallels the collapsing distinction between infrastructure and the environment (Carse, this volume). By collapsing such distinctions, the Anthropocene enables (even requires) a posthumanist paradigm. Yet humanism and its categorical divisions, which appear increasingly inadequate to the ecological challenges of our times, have been essential to struggles against race, racial thinking, and racism and may remain indispensable for challenging the ongoing dehumanization and objectification of certain forms of life. In what follows, territorial conflicts in Buenaventura's seaside settlements center on the boundaries between city and sea, urban infrastructures and aquatic environments, human subjects and nonhuman objects. Yet the posthumanist imperative to blur these boundaries often compromises efforts to confront violent dispossession underpinned by racial hierarchy. As the rising tides of the Anthropocene threaten to drown the conceptual armature of antiracist politics, a submerged humanism remains timely.

The Colombian Pacific is a fluid world, with levels of rainfall surpassing even the wettest parts of the tropics and a vast system of rivers that descend from the mountains to the sea (West 1957). The city of Buenaventura was founded on an island, the Isla de Cascajal, which now hosts the commercial center, government offices, and a large percentage of the residential population, and even the more recent areas of expansion on the mainland are transected by numerous rivers and streams (Aprile-Gniset 2002). Aside from a small hillock near downtown, the city is largely flat with depressions and low-lying areas throughout. In fact, the ground is so saturated with water that from as early as 1860, building sites on the island had to be filled in with earth before construction could proceed (Gärtner 2005).

The population of Buenaventura grew in the mid-twentieth century, as Afro-Colombians migrated to the city from nearby river basins and established their settlements in a similar manner—that is, by reclaiming land from the sea. Habituated to riverine life, these migrants gravitated to the edge of the bay, or to the inlets, mudflats, and wetlands that abut and interpenetrate the city on all sides, filling them in with mollusk shells collected from nearby mangrove swamps (Mosquera Torres and Aprile-Gniset 2006; Oslender 2004). Here they built houses on stilts, adapted to the brackish estuary's tidal fluctuations, which allowed them to continue fishing, harvesting timber, and mining artisanally for gold—their primary ancestral livelihoods, all of which depend on access to the sea and its tributaries (Mosquera Torres 2010). They linked their houses together with elevated pathways and established connections to the city's electricity and water supply systems as well as to its network of sidewalks and streets. The process of reclaiming land from the sea continues to this day.

These waterfront settlements are now occupied by an estimated 110,000 inhabitants, mostly Afro-Colombian. Positioned at the interface between land and sea, they have become the vortex of the displacement pressures converging on Buenaventura. The national and local governments strive to turn Buenaventura into a "world-class port-city" and see these waterfront neighborhoods as an obstacle; after all, they occupy the very land on which urban redevelopment and port infrastructure megaprojects are slated to be built. The technical and aesthetic criteria for how a "world-class port-city" should look and function demand the relocation of the majority of Bajamar's residents. The plan to redevelop the city's waterfront and expand the port's capacity competes for space with another form of transnational commerce, which exerts its own displacement pressures. Buenaventura has recently become a primary outlet for drug shipments from Colombia to the rest of the world; its seaside shantytowns now serve as strategic locations for launching small watercraft that connect up with speedboats bound for Central America and Mexico. Vital for overseas trade, both legal and illegal, waterfront territories are now highly valuable and ferociously fought over by rival militias, who alternate between decimating each other's ranks and terrorizing the local population. A lot of money is at stake in these battles for territorial control, and not just by trafficking drugs, but by using violence, torture, and intimidation to facilitate ostensibly legal commerce. As a result, the low-lying settlements of Buenaventura's intertidal zone have become one of the most concentrated sites of racialized dispossession in the Americas today.

Aurelia's objection to the name Bajamar reflected the pernicious forces converging on the areas conventionally designated by it. Her alternative, *territorios ganados al mar*, or "territories reclaimed from the sea," linked local struggles in Buenaventura to broader efforts to confront the displacement pressures facing Afro-Colombians throughout the country.[2] She articulated both positions toward the beginning of an event entitled Encuentro Afro-Urbano (Afro-Urban Conference). Taking place in Buenaventura in 2013, the meeting brought together a number of Aurelia's neighbors and fellow activists with delegates from other urban centers, such as Bogotá, Medellín, Cali, and Cartagena. They gathered over two days to discuss the specifically *urban* dimension of the struggles currently afflicting Afro-Colombian communities.[3]

The subtext of the meeting was that Afro-Colombians' ability to confront the challenges facing them in Buenaventura and other cities was conditioned by the history of ethnoracial politics in Colombia—in particular, by how black populations have been positioned, and have positioned themselves, as legal and political subjects. Since the adoption of a new Constitution in 1991, the Colombian state has recognized itself officially as "multicultural" and "pluriethnic." The Constitution of 1991 established a number of protections for the country's ethnic and cultural diversity, including the mandate to create comprehensive legislation for the black population. The subsequent passage of Law 70, or the Law of Black Communities, in 1993 granted Afro-Colombians both symbolic recognition within the official narrative of Colombian history and rights to collective land title, to cultural protection, to the benefits of development, and to be consulted on development projects that affect them.

Crucially, Law 70 granted these rights to *comunidades negras* (black communities) officially defined as a culturally distinct ethnic group.[4] This multiculturalist codification constituted the black political subject in particular ways, which continue to shape territorial conflicts throughout the country.

In Colombia, territorial politics is entangled with the ethnoracial politics of recognition accompanying state multiculturalism, which is reflected in the Constitution of 1991 and the Law of Black Communities of 1993 (Jackson 2007; Rappaport 2005; Wade 1993). However, as security saturates the realm of the political (Rojas 2009), rights and citizenship are often also predicated on biopolitical rationalities of rule (Zeiderman 2013). But the politics of life in Colombia is also a politics of death (Ballvé 2013) and a deeply racialized one (Foucault 2003; Mbembe 2003). The capacity of certain forms of life to survive, endure, or flourish—while others are abandoned, extinguished, or left to go extinct—is distributed unevenly according to racial regimes of hierarchy and dispossession. The result is what Rinaldo Walcott (2014) calls "zones of black death," or geographical nodes throughout the Americas where forms of diasporic African life are dehumanized and devalued, and the city of Buenaventura is an extreme example.

The Afro-Urban Conference of 2013 was convened primarily by the Process of Black Communities (PCN), one of the main organizations advocating for Afro-Colombian rights. Based in Buenaventura, PCN is better characterized as an activist network than a single group, and its influence extends throughout the river basins and coastal estuaries of the Pacific lowlands (Asher 2009; Escobar 2008). Many of these communities live in resource-rich rural areas frequently under attack by paramilitary groups allied with agribusiness, mining, or energy companies. The efforts of PCN to defend Afro-Colombian territories against the threat of forced displacement reflect the political geography of multiculturalism in Colombia (cf. Bocarejo 2014, 2012).[5] As Tianna Paschel argues, the outcome of the negotiations that led to the passage of Law 70 was that "the *rural* black political subject . . . would become the prototype for granting rights to black populations" (2010: 749, emphasis added). However, as forced displacement and territorial dispossession continue to push Afro-Colombians into cities such as Buenaventura (Oslender 2007), and as these same dynamics increasingly unfold *within* cities, PCN and other Afro-Colombian activists face the question of how to orient themselves politically in an urban context.

The common dominator across their political work is the concept of "territory." As Arturo Escobar notes, this concept "has a short but complicated history in the [Colombian] Pacific" (2008: 52). On the one hand, *ordenamiento territorial* (territorial zoning) emerged from the Constitution of 1991 as central to processes of state formation and capital accumulation throughout the region (Asher 2009; Asher and Ojeda 2009; cf. Ballvé 2012). On the other hand, beginning in the 1980s, the concepts of "territory" and "region-territory" were conceptual innovations produced by Afro-Colombian activists through what Escobar calls "subaltern strategies of localization" (2008: 52–53). While social movements across Latin America once mobilized around "the peasant" as the collective subject and "land" as the object of struggle, both proved insufficient in the Colombian Pacific and by the 1990s had been replaced respectively by "black communities" and "territory" (Escobar 2008: 52). The constitutional reform process that led to Law 70, and the collective titling process that would eventually transfer over 5 million hectares of land, made territory the basis for entitlement claims. But despite its terrestrial connotation, "territory" became understood according to what social movement activists called "the logic of the river" (Oslender 2002), and the *consejos comunitarios* (community councils, the legal entities empowered to claim title) were mostly organized along fluvial lines (Oslender 2004).

For the Colombian state and for social movement activists, territory remains a contested and evolving concept at the heart of debates over development, culture, and rights throughout the region. Yet the displacement pressures mounting in Buenaventura have unsettled some of the conceptual foundations of Afro-Colombian territorial politics. Although the urban territories in question have for the most part been occupied by Afro-descendent populations for many decades, Law 70 was understood not to apply to them. Participants at the Afro-Urban Conference discussed them as *territorios y comunidades afro-urbanos* (Afro-urban communities and territories). This particular combination of ethnoracial and spatial classifications intentionally disrupted the automatic association of the black population with the rural river basins of the Colombian Pacific. Although it explicitly marked a difference between urban and rural Afro-Colombians, at stake here were their collective rights regardless of location. The geographical imaginary that once underpinned the political strategy for defending their ancestral lands would now have to be adapted to territorial conflicts unfolding in urban areas.

The location of the Afro-Urban Conference meant that much of the conversation was dedicated to concerns specific to Buenaventura. The activists, like Aurelia, playing host foregrounded the displacement pressures facing the waterfront settlements known as Bajamar. While delegates from other

Colombian cities emphasized issues such as structural racism, the majority of sessions were dedicated to what Aurelia proposed to call "territories reclaimed from the sea." Afro-Colombian social movements have often debated the concept of territory in light of the specificities of geographical location, and here again activists and residents discussed the potential efficacy of such a designation. While both the received name and its alternative belonged to what Ulrich Oslender (2004) terms "aquatic space" (the rivers, estuaries, swamps, and coastlines that are constitutive of the political organization of the social movement of black communities in the Colombian Pacific), there was a subtle but important difference between them.[6]

The name Bajamar was unanimously objectionable, since it implied that Buenaventura's waterfront settlements needed either to be rescued from their condition of ecological vulnerability or removed from their situation of regulatory illegality. Conference participants pointed out how the name belonged to a wider set of racialized assumptions, mostly held by whites and *mestizos* from the interior, that figure Afro-Colombians from the Pacific coast as either helpless victims in need of state protection or deceitful transgressors deserving of corrective discipline. Perhaps most important, the designation "low tide" was opposed for its potential to render inevitable involuntary resettlement by blurring the boundaries between city and sea, between urban infrastructure and the aquatic environment. In contrast, "territories reclaimed from the sea" was preferred as it discursively positioned these settlements within the frame of development, though of an alternative, culturally specific sort. Instead of implying that residents were either victims or transgressors, the proposed name declared them to have produced their own space of habitation just as they had in aquatic environments throughout the Pacific coast. And by reintroducing the concept of "territory" and adapting it to this context, the new title challenged the legislation authorizing collective land titling, which explicitly excluded both urban areas and intertidal zones. However, while all present seemed to agree that an alternative was needed, not everyone approved of the option on the table.

"It makes them sound like they're not respecting nature," an activist, Esteban, told me in the taxi ride back to the city center. "It doesn't reflect our collective commitment to *sustainable* development; it belongs to the same old story of humans conquering nature by domesticating it and putting it to use." Esteban went on to express his dissatisfaction with the anthropocentric implications of the proposed alternative. He objected to the modernist understanding of infrastructure and environment implied by the concept of "reclamation," whereby infrastructure denotes the technical systems human subjects autonomously create to make their lives livable and the environment refers to the purely nonhuman nature channeled through or overcome by these systems. At stake in this activist's critique of his colleague's position was the long-standing official stereotype of Afro-Colombians as "black and green"; that is, as a culturally distinct ethnic group naturally predisposed to serve as guardians of one of the world's most valuable (yet threatened) ecosystems—a stereotype that black social movements have, at times, appropriated strategically (Asher 2009).[7] He rejected the idea that the sea was a passive object that human subjects could "reclaim," which he saw as a central tenet of Euro-American paradigms of progress and development. Instead, Esteban argued that what needed emphasizing was the harmonious relationship between Afro-urban communities and the sea.

Posthumanist Disappointment and Submerged Humanism

The debate over the name Bajamar resonates with recent discussions of the Anthropocene in anthropology, geography, and science and technology studies. In particular, the critique of anthropocentrism leveled against the alternative designation "territories reclaimed from the sea" would find much support in the work of those who seek to call into question the categorical divide between humans and nature by engaging with socionatural worlds that refuse such bifurcations altogether (Latour 1993; Stengers 2005). These diverse positions can be classified as "posthumanist" for their commitment to move beyond the conceptual, ethical, and political limits of humanism and to engage with heterogeneous assemblages of people and things, both living and nonliving, and their mutually constitutive relations with one another. Posthumanism can be seen as a reaction to the new historical age called the Anthropocene, understood as a political moment in which humans have become a geological force whose impact is felt on a planetary scale (Kohn 2015: 312). For scholars and activists alike, the global environmental crisis of the Anthropocene demands a heightened sensitivity to socionatural worlds, to human-nonhuman relationships, and to political communities of living and nonliving beings (Latour 2014).

Latin America has been of particular importance to posthumanism. From the Andes to Amazonia, indigenous groups have been found to possess ways of conceptualizing and living with the nonhuman world that do not adhere to the principles of Western science, politics, and metaphysics (Descola 1996; Viveiros de Castro 2014). Latin America is also where posthumanism intersects with a "decolonial" approach that sees these principles as well as "nature" itself as modern/colonial artifacts (Escobar 2007; Dussel 2008; de la Cadena 2010). In an attempt to discover "worlds and knowledges otherwise," these studies have occasionally positioned Afro-Colombian social movements in an antagonistic, even incommensurable relationship to modernity, development, capitalism, and the state. They are seen (more or less) as autonomous socionatural assemblages with the potential to radically unsettle the "coloniality" of power through their own alternative worldviews and notions of life, territory, and nature (Escobar 2010).

Posthumanist scholars engage in "boundary work" around categories like nature/culture and human/nonhuman (Gieryn 1983).[8] This is also what activists and residents are doing when they seek to adapt their territorial politics to the specific conditions of Buenaventura's waterfront settlements by redrawing the boundary between settlers and the sea. However, their efforts do not always sit comfortably with the conceptual, ethical, and political commitments of posthumanism.[9] In line with Esteban's critique of the proposal to designate the waterfront settlements of Buenaventura as "territories reclaimed from the sea," posthumanist thought would likely find this proposal to be thoroughly and disappointingly Western, modern, and anthropocentric. In contrast to the name Bajamar, which had rendered human settlers different from but entangled with nonhuman forces (such as tides, tsunamis, and floods), focusing on "reclaiming" these "territories" from the sea emphasized the human separation from and domination of nature. However, the assertion of human agency has special significance in coastal landscapes and seascapes where African diasporic life has long been seen as less than human.

All this is magnified by climate change and by the idea of the Anthropocene. On the one hand, the ecological crisis of the present follows historical articulations of race, space, and nature (Moore, Kosek, and Pandian 2003) and legacies of environmental racism, whereby certain forms of human life are subjected disproportionately to degradation, toxicity, and hazard (Pulido 2000).[10] On the other hand, the new historical age called the Anthropocene has also unsettled received notions of humanity (Chakrabarty 2009). The planetary transformations wrought by climate change both center and decenter the figure of the "human." They center the human in that we now accept climate change to be anthropogenic (hence the charge of anthropocentrism often leveled at the idea of the Anthropocene). But they also decenter the human in that we now recognize that we do not simply "act on" the environment but are ourselves part of natural history (hence the rise of posthumanism). The dual operation of centering and decentering of the human opens up a problematic that deserves critical scrutiny. But given histories of racial slavery and the dehumanization of African diasporic life in places like the Colombian Pacific, posthumanism must be approached with caution.

The radical instability of the categories of "life" and the "human" in the Anthropocene presents both dangers and opportunities for antiracist thought and practice, which matters greatly to those who have never enjoyed full inclusion within these categories. In a recent lecture to the Royal Geographical Society, Paul Gilroy interrogates the current attractions of posthumanism and asks what a "reparative humanism" might alternatively entail.[11] If the idea of the Anthropocene forces us to rethink history beyond the human/natural divide and to embrace posthumanism, he argues, then a commitment to antiracist politics and ethics demands a continued engagement with humanism. Inspired by Frantz Fanon, C. L. R. James, and Sylvia Wynter, Gilroy sees "reparative humanism" as a helpful, indeed necessary, response to the ethical and political challenges of the Anthropocene.

For Gilroy, "reparative humanism" directly links debates over the human and its limits to struggles against racial hierarchy and to what he calls the political ontology of race. After all, for much of history, a large swath of humanity has been downgraded to the status of "sub-humans," "infra-humans," "human-animals," or "quasi-objects" and thereby relegated from the realms of full political, social, or economic personhood. The enforcement of the boundary around the human was most fully accomplished in and through the violence of racial slavery. Hence the line of thinking from classic works such as that of Sidney Mintz (1986) to more recent interventions by Katherine McKittrick (2013) that sees the plantation with slave labor as its core standing at the center of capitalist modernity. Such a recognition has been brought to discussions of climate change by Donna Haraway, Anna Tsing, and others who have endorsed the Plantationocene as an alternative name for the Anthropocene (Haraway et al. 2016; Haraway 2015).

In the journal *Nature*, Simon Lewis and Mark Maslin argue that the Anthropocene began around 1610, as the New World conquest "led to the largest population replacement in the past 13,000 years, the first global trade networks linking Europe, China, Africa, and the Americas, and the resultant mixing of previously separate biotas" (Lewis and Maslin 2015: 174). The Anthropocene, by this dating, is not only the era of global trade and biological mixing but also the era of colonial genocide and racial slavery (Davis and Turpin 2015: 8). In recognizing this, the concept of the Plantationocene responds to Gilroy's long-standing concern about the rise in popularity of antihumanism, now extended to the strains of posthumanism enabled and endorsed by the idea of the Anthropocene. Both, he implies, potentially weaken our ability to confront racial hierarchy, colonial conquest, and imperial power, past and present. A world historical moment that forces us more than ever to think about and with the nonhuman may require all the more vigilant attention to the boundaries and limits of the human.

The periodizing thrust of the idea of the Anthropocene, and the *post-humanist* thought that accompanies it, effectively render humanism out of time—lagging behind, outmoded, inadequate, or inappropriate. This implication is all the more troubling if we consider the degree to which asynchronous temporality has been central to the political ontology of race. Anthropologists have extensive experience in this domain, having contributed to some of the early, foundational schemas that placed certain people (nonwhite, non-European) out of time or behind history (Fabian 2002). But so, too, have anthropologists invested great energy in opposing and dismantling those temporal schemas. Despite their historical positioning on both sides of the problem, anthropologists today seem less reflexive about the temporal hierarchies embedded in their theorizing practices, always attuned to the emergent and the new, both empirically and conceptually (the Anthropocene is a primary example).

Theoretical positions themselves enact forms of temporal othering, which is particularly troublesome when linked to the production of racial hierarchy or complicit in its reproduction. Most scholars of the environment and climate change would acknowledge that the need to move beyond their discipline's anthropocentrism, to think past the nature/culture divide, and to account for the nonhuman in our political theories and institutions does not somehow resolve the quintessentially humanist problems of marginalization, exclusion, and injustice. In other words, once we declare ourselves posthumanists, the political ontology of race that humanists struggled against by no means disappears. Yet the periodizing thrust of posthumanism sometimes leads one to assume otherwise—that such problems, or at least the conceptual frameworks used to understand them, have become obsolete. An alternative is to follow David Scott's (1999) discussion of "Fanonian futures" as being both out of date *and* necessary for the postcolonial moment; humanism may be equally timely *and* untimely for thinking about human-environmental futures in the Anthropocene.

Chakrabarty (2009, 2012) shows what is at stake in rethinking the figure of the human in Anthropocenic times. In the contemporary humanities and social sciences, Chakrabarty identifies three images of the human: the universalist-Enlightenment human who is potentially the same everywhere; the postcolonial-poststructuralist human who is endowed everywhere with differences of race, class, sexuality, gender, history, and so on; and the human in the Anthropocene and a geophysical force on the planet, likened to nonhuman, nonliving agency, and now a threat to human civilization itself. Chakrabarty's key point is as follows: "These views of the human do not supersede one another. One cannot put them along a continuum of progress. No one view is rendered invalid by the presence of others. They are simply disjunctive. Any effort to contemplate the human condition today . . . on political and ethical registers encounters the necessity of thinking disjunctively about the human, through moves that in their simultaneity appear contradictory" (2012: 2).

To highlight such moves, Chakrabarty returns to the early days of the subaltern studies movement and to the challenge posed to it by Gayatri Spivak. He recalls: "Like Fanon, we saw the subaltern classes as claiming their humanity through revolutionary upheavals. Becoming human was for us a matter of becoming a subject" (Chakrabarty 2012: 4). Spivak challenged the very ideas of the "subject" and the "human" that so much of anticolonial thought celebrated, and invited deconstructive histories of subjecthood and humanness.[12] Again, Chakrabarty argues that these different figures of the "subject" and the "human" (organized respectively around universality and difference) were not mutually exclusive—that is, the critique of the autonomous subject did not render that figure useless or obsolete. Likewise, challenges posed to demands for inclusion in the category of the human, which questioned both the category and the imperative to belong to it, did not make the liberal, humanist, Marxist, feminist, anticolonial, antiracist, and queer struggles articulating these demands any less urgent. Hence the necessity of thinking through "contradictory figures of the human" or to "view the human simultaneously on contradictory registers" (Chakrabarty 2012: 5, 14).

The same lesson applies to the posthumanist moment. The Anthropocene may have ushered in a new figure of the human (along with new critiques of humanism), but other figures of the human have not disappeared. All of them remain operative as we consider what human agency and responsibility might mean now and in the future. Chakrabarty's conclusion can be read as a response to the questions posed by Gilroy: "The fact that the crisis of climate change will be routed through all our 'anthropological differences' can only mean that . . . there is no corresponding 'humanity' that in its oneness can act as a political agent. A place thus remains for struggles around questions of intrahuman justice regarding the uneven impacts of climate change" (2012: 14). This opens up space for the politics of climate change, and also for linking it to antiracist struggle, in places such as Buenaventura, where histories of racial slavery, plantation economies, and colonial hierarchies are not distant memories.

Caribbean poet and intellectual Kamau Brathwaite offers an alternative way of thinking about coastal precarity in landscapes and seascapes once central to the dehumanization of African diasporic life throughout the Americas.[13] Brathwaite (1984: 5–8) uses the concept of "nation language" to refer to the original languages spoken by those brought to the Caribbean as slaves and laborers. The term he prefers for understanding the fate of such languages is "submergence" for they "had to . . . submerge themselves" beneath the official languages of public discourse—English, French, Spanish, or Dutch—dictated by the colonial rulers (7). "Submerged languages" and the subjects who spoke them were considered inferior (nonhuman, in fact). They persisted, nonetheless; their rhythm, timbre, grammar, and syntax were always coursing beneath the surface, making themselves imperceptible at certain moments and perceptible at others.[14] Submerged languages were neither static nor exclusive to the subaltern; they were constantly being adapted to dominant cultural imperatives as well as influencing how official languages were spoken by both the colonizers and the colonized (Brathwaite 1984: 7–8). For Brathwaite, "submergence" is key to understanding contemporary forms of Caribbean cultural practice. In the literature, poetry, and music he analyzed, what had long been submerged was "increasingly coming to the surface" (13).

The sea is clearly important, both concretely and metaphorically, for Brathwaite's understanding of diasporic African life. Indeed, remarking on processes of historical change, Brathwaite adopts the concept of "tidalectics" as an alternative to Hegelian/Marxian dialectics, more ebb and flow than linear progression. As with his use of "submergence," the rhythms and oscillations of the tides are, for Brathwaite, central to the formation of historical consciousness in the Caribbean and, therefore, analytically appropriate for understanding its cultural forms (Sandiford 2011: 142). The work of the Saint Lucian poet and playwright Derek Walcott is a paradigmatic example. The sea features prominently in much of Walcott's writing, representing both "troubled memories and histories" and "solidarity and common experience" (Jefferson 2013: 301). Brathwaite's (1974: 64) assertion that "unity is submarine" takes this identification further by suggesting that beneath the surface of the sea, along with the bodies of slaves who died in the Middle Passage, is a submerged, contiguous political geography that unifies the peoples of the Caribbean (Jefferson 2013: 290). In the case of Afro-Colombian politics and poetics, the Pacific Ocean is at least as important as the Caribbean/Atlantic (cf. Gilroy 1993). Nevertheless, Brathwaite's engagement with the latter provides an opening for understanding Buenaventura's intertidal zone as a key site in which the boundary between the human and its others is being reworked. A submerged humanism is necessary for confronting the unequal distribution of coastal precarity in the Anthropocene.

Coastal Precarity and Resilience

The debate over the name Bajamar was only the tip of the iceberg. Much of the 2013 Afro-Urban Conference was dedicated to analyzing the problematic of "precarity" and "resilience" in Buenaventura's waterfront settlements. While recent discussions of the Anthropocene make coastal precarity seem sudden and new, the deliberations that transpired at the meeting connected it to longer histories of racial violence and transoceanic trade, which linked disparate ports, coastlines, and seas between Africa, Europe, and the Americas and were predicated on the brutal objectification of black lives. These longer histories were not invoked to discount climate change but rather to complicate the official narrative of coastal precarity and its unequal distribution in Buenaventura and throughout the Colombian Pacific. A parallel discussion interrogated resilience for its ability to render invisible actually existing adaptive strategies while legitimating plans for mass relocation, waterfront redevelopment, and port expansion. The problematic of precarity and resilience, which has come to characterize the Anthropocene, was seen to submerge humanist concerns, such as racialized dispossession, and to disable political responses to them.

A range of techniques have been used to estimate the potential impacts of climate change in Colombia, but there is now general agreement that it is likely to adversely effect Buenaventura in the years to come. According to Intergovernmental Panel on Climate Change (IPCC) predictions, the world's tropical areas will experience increased magnitude and intensity of rainfall, especially considering the possible interaction between climate change and the El Niño–Southern Oscillation, which has a major impact on Colombia's climate (Lampis and Fraser 2012: 14). There is evidence that precipitation events in some parts of Colombia have already become more intense (Aguilar et al. 2005), and increased average rainfall has been observed in Buenaventura (Amado et al. 2011: 42). Moreover, the Colombian national scientific body has reported a 2.2 millimeter rise in sea level over the previous forty years at a monitoring station in Buenaventura (IDEAM 2010).

Together, increased rainfall and rising sea levels appear to pose serious threats to the port-city. The national government's assessment of the potential impacts of climate change identified Buenaventura as among the most critical zones in the country (Lampis and Fraser 2012: 31), and the municipal government has begun to take climate-related risks into account. According to the city's recently created risk management agency, the imperative to create a resilient Buenaventura demands the removal of low-lying occupations classified as "high risk." The director of the municipal risk management agency explained why the inhabitants of *terrenos de bajamar* ("low-tide lands," as he called them) were highly vulnerable and in need of relocation:

> The national government passed Law 1523 in 2012, and this required Buenaventura to have a risk management agency. We're following the letter of the law. In terms of territorial planning, risk management has to be the first step. This is the first step in creating and implementing a master plan. Everything has to be done from the point of view of risk. Risk must prevail above everything else we do in terms of planning and development. These areas are living with risk because we didn't plan well in the past. From now on, that will have to change.

Ominous forecasts like these have also motivated plans for additional port facilities to reduce operational delays due to inclement weather and further dredging of the shipping canal to counteract sedimentation caused by higher rainfall (Amado et al. 2011: 121). The upshot of the municipal government's engagement with coastal precarity and resilience in the context of climate change is mass relocation, waterfront redevelopment, and port expansion.

At the General Maritime Directorate (DIMAR), the national authority for coastal regulation, the naval captain assigned to Buenaventura described this as a more straightforward problem of illegality: "The majority of the city is in *zonas de bajamar* [low-tide zones]. These properties are *bienes de uso público* [areas of public interest]. The residents are asking for water delivery, for electricity, for sewage, for basic services. But the regulations won't allow it, since these are invasions of public space. City Hall is supposed to do the relocation along with the police. We don't have the manpower to go in and do evictions. That's their job." While the naval captain did not resort to the logic of resilience to justify relocation, he nevertheless concurred with the municipal government's evaluation of precarity: "The *zonas de bajamar* are extremely vulnerable. In the event of a tsunami, this is the first part of the city that is going to flood."

Both within and outside of the conference, Afro-Colombian activists and residents of Buenaventura's seaside shantytowns argued that the official narrative of precarity and resilience in the intertidal zone justified displacement and dispossession. In contrast, they conceptualized the problem in rather different ways. For example, one of the members of a collective of musicians called Marcando Territorio (Marking Territory) dismissed ecological threats while emphasizing human ones. His assessment deserves quoting at length:

> Now they're talking about the risk of tsunami. They say that we have to be relocated because this is a "zone of high risk." I've lived here for four years; him five years; he's been here his whole life [pointing to other members of the collective]; others have been here for two or three generations. Now there's a tsunami threat? [All laugh.] We're not against development, but there are other interests behind all this. They say we live in "Bajamar," that we're vulnerable. They say that we're "at risk." But what about them? Are they super anti-tsunami? Are they so prepared that they don't need to worry? They say this area will flood. But a tsunami would wreck the whole city. The best option would be to negotiate with people so they can stay in their homes. Our proposal is neighborhood improvement. But we're afraid that what happened in la Imaculada [a similar settlement on the other side of the city] with the expansion of TCBUEN [port terminal] is going to happen here. You know, the paramilitaries infiltrate the barrio and say, "You have to sell or sell." [All laugh.] We know how it works. They'll say, *Para sobrevivir tienen que salir* [You have to leave if you want to survive].

In Buenaventura, this musician implied, black lives matter less than the vision of development that depends on maintaining the population in a state of protracted precarity. Yet this form of precarity differs markedly from the one identified by the municipal government's strategy of resilience.

A religious leader based in one of the "low-tide" neighborhoods introduced another possibility: "They're trying to get people out of here any way they can. I wouldn't be surprised if they eventually flood these areas and get people to move that way. After all, they need higher water levels to move the really big ships in and out of the bay, so it would serve two purposes at the same time." Here coastal precarity is linked directly to transoceanic trade. The national and local governments both envision a future in which Buenaventura will become a "world-class port-city," as is reflected in the jointly authored local economic development plan of the same name (Ministerio de Trabajo 2012). As Colombia's only Pacific Ocean port, enthusiasm for Buenaventura's rapidly rising "good fortune" is tied to projections of booming trade relations with Asia. With commentators far and wide heralding the advent of the "Chinese century," Buenaventura has been labeled "Colombia's gateway to the Pacific," which the local development plan calls the "basin of the future." Another activist connected these lucrative transoceanic fantasies, however fantastical, to the historical linkages across the Atlantic Ocean that brought Afro-descendent populations to the Colombian Pacific in the first place. Racial slavery, plantation agriculture, and gold mining in the past, he pointed out, much like drug trafficking, infrastructure development, and globalized commerce in the present, are predicated on the dehumanization of African diasporic life.

The debates that transpired during the two-day Afro-Urban Conference offered an understanding of coastal precarity that was about more than climate change. Projections of increased rainfall and rising sea levels were said to further motivate dredging operations, which had already been justified by visions of booming trade among countries of the Pacific Rim. This added additional urgency to port expansion plans bolstered previously by economic imperatives alone. Dredging subsequently increased tidal fluctuations and storm surges in the Bay of Buenaventura, making flood risk even more pronounced in waterfront areas and thereby strengthening the resolve of relocation projects in designated "zones of high risk." These combined pressures made residents of Bajamar more vulnerable to paramilitary groups fighting for control over their territories. Ultimately, the violence inflicted by rival militias made otherwise undesirable state-led relocation projects appear preferable to forced displacement carried out at gunpoint without compensation. In turn, the exodus of residents fleeing the threat of death or dismemberment fed back to encourage capital investment in port infrastructure. The coastal precarity associated with climate change was seen as inseparable from the port-city's position within transoceanic networks of exchange, past and present, and it was demanded that strategies of resilience reflect that fact.

Fluid Futures

In 2012, a respected journal of architecture and urbanism in Colombia, *Revista Escala*, organized a design competition in Buenaventura focused on climate change adaptation in coastal cities.[15] It brought together students from thirty-five architecture schools in Colombia, Mexico, Ecuador, Panama, and Venezuela to analyze existing settlement patterns, assess their vulnerability to climate risk, and propose solutions for future development. Out of the sixty-three proposals submitted at the end of the study period, not a single one endorsed the government's plan to relocate the residents of the waterfront settlements known as Bajamar. Instead, each team proposed in situ neighborhood upgrading and risk mitigation through a combination of environmental and infrastructural interventions.

Many of the proposals envisioned localized improvements throughout existing settlements combined with the restoration of the aquatic ecosystem surrounding the island. In one, an elevated network of sidewalks and streets would follow the pattern of the existing wood planks that currently connect the houses together, which themselves followed the tidal fluctuations of the bay. In another, mangrove forests, once fully established, would increase the degree to which the settlements are adapted to their environment by providing a living flood control infrastructure (cf. Braun and Wakefield, this volume). And since mangroves provide the habitat for commercially important shellfish, as well as valuable wood for construction, their restoration could be matched with a sustainable development plan based on community-led resource management. The judges praised these designs for offering promising approaches to climate change adaptation in Buenaventura, applicable to other coastal cities throughout the region. They concurred with the participating architects that the guide to resilient futures was to be found in the logic of development of the waterfront settlements themselves.

These proposals were discussed at length during the Afro-Urban Conference. Activists and residents in Buenaventura reported on their unsuccessful efforts to lobby the municipal government to consider these proposals as serious alternatives to port expansion, waterfront redevelopment, and mass relocation. Officials had refused to recognize that these settlements were already highly adapted to unpredictable climatic conditions and that environmental and infrastructural interventions could make them more so. An engineer who spoke at the conference explained these points in detail, while a representative from PCN expanded upon the economic rationale: waterfront access enabled people to shift from fishing to construction when a shipment of wood arrived and a house needed to be built, then to transportation when a group of miners needed to travel upriver, and to fall back on fishing when there was no more paid work to be found. She argued that livelihood strategies enabled by proximity to the sea were uniquely suited for ecological uncertainty.

This activist reported what the residents of the port-city's seaside settlements knew full well: that without the ability to foresee what will happen next or where tomorrow's meal will come from, work must remain flexible, diversified, opportunistic. She contrasted this elastic strategy to the inelastic official one of wagering everything on the port, and on the future of the Pacific Ocean economy, which was predicated on the displacement of waterfront residents to the city's landlocked periphery. Yet pleas from residents and activists repeatedly fell on deaf ears, and the intransigent vision of the "world-class port-city" foreclosed other possibilities. The alternatives discussed during the conference were not watertight, but they did offer creative ways of adapting to and living in Anthropocenic times.

These proposals clearly differed from the official narrative of coastal precarity epitomized by the "low tide" label, which saw Buenaventura's waterfront settlements as antithetical to the imperative of resilience. But they also stood in contrast to the alternative idea of "territories reclaimed from the sea," which positioned their inhabitants as human agents dominating nonhuman nature. The former blurred the categorical divisions of modernist paradigms, while the latter reinstated them as preconditions for intrahuman justice and equality. But as the proposals floated during the design competition were debated during the Afro-Urban Conference, both humanist and posthumanist considerations were on the table. The racialized violence and dispossession underpinning waterfront redevelopment and port expansion were challenged, as was the hierarchical value of different forms of human life. But the divides between city and sea, between urban infrastructures and aquatic environments, and between human subjects and nonhuman objects were also questioned by proposals that emphasized the mutually constitutive relationship between them. By linking the politics of climate change to antiracist struggle, these discussions pointed to the possibility of engaging disjunctively with humanism and posthumanism to confront the unequal production of coastal precarity in the Anthropocene.

Notes

1 This chapter draws primarily on interviews and site visits conducted in 2013 during two short stays of two to three weeks each in Buenaventura. One visit coincided with an event that brought together activists, community leaders, nongovernmental organizations, municipal authorities, lawyers, urbanists, and members of the interested public to discuss the question of *territorios afro-urbanos* (Afro-urban territories). The argument is based also on interviews conducted with activists, humanitarian workers, and government officials in Bogotá as well analysis of policy and planning documents, media archives, and communications materials. Approximately twenty-five interviews were conducted in total, and all names have been changed or omitted to protect anonymity. Since Afro-Colombian activists are frequently subjected to death threats and violence, I also switch gender pronouns at times to avoid personal identification. Though long-term fieldwork in Buenaventura was deemed unfeasible due to the security situation, supporting the analysis are over two years of ethnographic research in Colombia (2008–2010, with subsequent follow-up visits) on the politics of urban security. An earlier version of some of the arguments in this chapter appeared in *Antipode* (2016) as "Submergence: Precarious Politics in Colombia's Future Port-City."

2 Ethnoracial terminology is highly contested in Colombia. In this chapter, "black," "Afro-Colombian," and "Afro-descendent" are used somewhat interchangeably as forms of self-identification that are not necessarily based on traceable African origins, whereas "black communities" carries a more specific legal and policy meaning.

3 Much has been written on Afro-Colombian activism, politics, and social movements, and my analysis relies heavily on the work of others (Asher 2009; Cárdenas 2012; Escobar 2008; Oslender 2007; Paschel 2010; Restrepo 2004; Restrepo and Rojas 2004; Valencia 2011; Wade 2002). It has been recognized that geography matters greatly to ethnoracial politics in Colombia (Bocarejo 2012; Oslender 2011), and studies have examined issues facing Afro-descendent migrants and *desplazados* in cities (Arboleda 2004; Barbary and Urrea 2004; Observatorio Contra la Discriminación y el Racismo 2012). However, less attention has been paid to the problematic of Afro-Colombian *urban* politics (cf. Agudelo 2004).

4 As Tianna Paschel (2010: 730) points out, this landmark piece of legislation followed the logic of "ethnic difference" and "cultural identity" rather than "racial

equality" or "racial justice." Eduardo Restrepo refers to this process as the "ethnicization of blackness" (Restrepo 2004).

5 Law 70 recognizes "black communities" as those communities "that have traditionally occupied the uncultivated (empty) lands in the rural zones adjoining the rivers of the Pacific Basin, in accordance with their traditional cultivation practices" and grants them "the right to collective property" on these lands. Urban areas are explicitly excluded from the legislation authorizing collective land titling as are *los bienes de uso público* (areas of public interest), which include intertidal zones (see Law 70, Chapter III, Articles 6a and 6b).

6 Oslender uses "aquatic space" to "conceptualise the everyday social relationships amongst rural black communities as profoundly conditioned by various aquatic elements that the specific tropical rainforest environment in the Pacific provides, such as high levels of precipitation, large tidal ranges, intricate river networks, mangrove swamps and frequent inundations." Oslender argues that "the aquatic space has been instrumental in the spatial organising structures of these populations" and the forms of political organization they have established in these geographical locations (2004: 959).

7 Although the stance of the Colombian government was absent from the conversation, this was an instance of Kiran Asher's observation that "black movements and state interventions" sometimes use "similar discourses . . . to construct their understandings of culture, nature, and development" (2009: 20).

8 For further elaboration of Thomas Gieryn's (1983) concept of "boundary work," and the problems inherent to treating it solely as a domain of *human* action, see Ashley Carse (this volume). In this chapter, I am interested primarily in the boundary work of Afro-Colombian activists and posthumanist scholars rather than how that work coemerges alongside and in relation to nonhuman actants.

9 I am grateful here to Wakana Suzuki for pushing me to clarify how and why this might be the case.

10 The Anthropocene has also become inseparable from resurgent or emergent forms of biopolitics and biopower through which life (human and nonhuman) is governed (Boyer 2014; Dalby 2013).

11 Paul Gilroy, "Offshore Humanism," 2015, http://wp.me/p16RPC-1hI. Earlier thoughts along similar lines appear in Gilroy (2007).

12 Chakrabarty emphasizes that this was not the same as Althusserian antihumanism of the 1970s and 1980s; the postcolonial critique of the subject was a deeper turning toward the human.

13 I am most grateful to Katherine McKittrick for pointing me to the work of Kamau Brathwaite and other Caribbean writers and intellectuals, whose writings on "submergence" and the sea I have found productive and inspiring.

14 A parallel can be drawn with Edouard Glissant's "forced poetics," or the language "practiced by a community which cannot express itself directly through an autonomous activity of its members" (1976: 96). Among slaves, Glissant writes,

"expression was cautious, reticent, whispered at night." Another source of inspiration is James Scott's (1985, 1992) work on popular political expression under conditions of domination.

15 See *Convive VII—Buenaventura: Cambio Climático, Mejoramiento y Readecuación de Vivienda para Frentes Marítimos* (2012).

EIGHT. Oystertecture

Infrastructure, Profanation, and the Sacred
Figure of the Human

STEPHANIE WAKEFIELD AND BRUCE BRAUN

The life that begins on earth after the last day is simply human life.
—GIORGIO AGAMBEN, *The Coming Community*

|

It is the last weekend of summer 2015. One of us is on Governors Island, along with two young men new to the scene, crouched over a plastic-coated rebar cage that we've just spent the afternoon making. We are struggling to tie a bowline knot, which we will use to attach our oyster test stations to concrete piers located a few meters offshore. None of us have much experience with oysters. Nor with bowline knots. And certainly not here, in the long shadow of New York City's financial district. We have been hard at work since morning, having caught the first ferry along with forty others to spend the weekend learning how to care for an oyster restoration station. One of the men explains why he came: "I don't know. I was at happy hour last night and

I told my friend, 'I'm going to become an oyster farmer tomorrow, and they said 'why?!' I dunno, I said, I read a bunch of books . . . In some idyllic future I'd like to do this full time, as a farmer. It sounds peaceful." Women of all backgrounds in flip-flops and manicured nails clutch pliers, bending metal. In the background, the Freedom Tower looms over us. Along for the ride is a journalist from CBS, there to record interviews on the new "oyster mania" of which we are a part. Ann, one of the founders of Harbor School, says to him, "the future looks pretty grim, but you know when you're here now trying to bring things back to life and make a difference, you can be obsessed with the end for a while, but . . ." Her voice trails off. Although we have all just met, we make plans to monitor these stations, together, over the coming years.

A few months later, we contemplate future disasters projected for Staten Island, from a bulkhead on its exposed, southern coast. Staten Island was hit hard during superstorm Sandy, and city officials now say that people were never meant to live along its exposed shores. In 2017, it will become the site of a large-scale real-time experiment in making the city "resilient," when the state of New York—in collaboration with an unusual collection of actors, including engineers, critical infrastructure consultants, designers, and lawyers, together with oysters, concrete, steel, and computer models— will begin building two miles of artificial oyster reefs. The project is one among six winning designs in the US Department of Housing and Urban Development's "Rebuild by Design" competition, and part of a larger effort to attenuate future storm surges and remediate polluted water in Raritan Bay. "Oystertecture," or "Living Breakwaters," as the project is officially named, is today heralded as a cutting-edge replicable infrastructure adequate to the "new normal" faced by many coastal cities across the world. In the designer's projected future, the seas will continue to rise. Hurricanes will batter the city's coast with increased frequency and strength. An array of fiber optic cables will connect underwater live cams, trained on distant oyster reefs, to computer-monitoring stations on land. The plan is to use oysters to lessen the impact of waves on the coast by absorbing and diffracting their energy in the hope that disaster will be managed, even if it can never be fully stopped.

To the casual observer, the unique nature of these proposed reefs may not be immediately evident. New Yorkers have become used to the idea that oysters might return to waters from which they disappeared decades ago. Indeed, since the early 2000s the oyster has been proposed as an indicator of ecological health, and a future with oysters held out as a sign that the city can heal its relationship with nature. In city plans and artistic visions—an oft-blurred distinction—the return of the celebrated mollusks is frequently couched in an aesthetic of old-timey lifestyles connected to the harvest and consumption of maritime resources. The first public exhibition of "oystertecture"—at the Museum of Modern Art's 2010 *Rising Currents* exhibition—portrayed a fanciful plan for the Gowanus Canal Superfund site adjacent to Brooklyn's Red Hook neighborhood, pleasingly rendered by the landscape firm SCAPE and its lead architect, Kate Orff (figure 8.1).[1] Set against a postindustrial backdrop of new condos, renovated warehouses, and water taxi stations, SCAPE's design delegated to oysters the role of cleaning polluted waterways, enabling the growth of other marine life, and buffering the shores of Red Hook from occasional high water. Dominating the exhibition was the "reef-culture" oysters would help facilitate: rehabilitating a former wasteland via water-based localism, forgotten arts of oyster grilling, boardwalk jogs alongside new reefs and wetlands, and restaurants advertising oyster po' boys and Sixpoint Sweet Action beer (figure 8.2). Oystertecture was seen as a means to reconnect the city with nature, as part of an affluent, green, postindustrial urbanism: "a blue-green watery park for the next watery century," Orff announced in an exhibition video, "so get your Tevas on!" Exhibit boards pictured oyster garden cages attached to the underside of recreational boardwalks, up close and accessible to joggers and families.

Annual oyster FLUPSY parades were imagined.[2] "How much fun would it be to watch the FLUPSY parade and cheer on the oyster spats!" Orff continued, "By 2050, maybe you can 'sink your teeth into a Gowanus oyster.'" In the future, things would be better, with oysters helping to usher in "a more sustainable, a more livable, and a more delicious future."

All this would change dramatically after Hurricane Sandy hit New York City in fall 2012. Amid the poststorm wreckage a new image emerged of a fragile city menaced by myriad risks—hurricanes, rising sea levels, heat waves, technical failures—each of which threatened to interrupt transportation systems, financial institutions, and energy networks in a cascading series of uncontrollable catastrophes (for a discussion of coastal precarity in Buenaventura, Colombia, see Zeiderman, this volume). The "living breakwaters" being built today by New York State emerged in this poststorm context, as one of several efforts to buffer the city from future extreme events.[3] The same landscape design firm that designed the Gowanus Canal plan now reimagined

Figure 8.1. Installation view of "ZONE 4: Oyster-Tecture" exhibition at the Museum of Modern Art, New York, 2010. Copyright 2010 SCAPE / Landscape Architecture PLLC.

oysters in terms of "disaster preparedness," in which "letting water in" became less a touching matter of reacquainting New Yorkers with their friendly aquatic surroundings than a new strategy to respond to a changing climate and a hostile ocean. The quaint harmony of SCAPE's earlier oystertecture proposal was replaced with a focus on the project's infrastructural function; oyster shacks and sea kayaks swapped for sharp warnings about "wave velocity" and "environmental risk." Most important, oysters were reimagined as a "living, growing infrastructure" that could "drastically dissipate destructive wave energy."[4] Designs by SCAPE now propose a "necklace" of oyster reefs as "layered lines of defense" around south Staten Island. As part of the project, designers are experimenting with new cultivation techniques and designing new reef structures in which oysters can survive further offshore in "high wave action" areas. Current plans involve anchoring multiton ECOncrete® "armoring units" to the ocean floor.[5] These will be seeded with oyster spat, layered with rocks and stone, and spaced at different intervals both horizontally and vertically, with some entirely submerged and others designed to rise high enough to absorb sixteen-foot wave crests. The reefs are not meant to keep the water out; unlike a sea wall, whose purpose is to stop flooding,

Figure 8.2. Mockup of the "reef culture" imagined by design firm SCAPE as part of their 2010 "Oyster-Tecture" exhibition. Copyright 2010 SCAPE / Landscape Architecture PLLC.

block waves, or eliminate risk, the oyster reefs are intended to "make those events slower and safer," to "slow inundation," and to "take the energy out of the wave" as it passes over the breakwater (SCAPE 2014).

II

The return of oysters to New York Harbor appears to turn back the pages of history. After all, oysters and oyster reefs have long been found in the region's estuaries and bays. Before the arrival of Europeans, the Lenape had used oysters as weapons and to cover burial sites (Wissler 1909: 8; Pritchard 2002: 91). In the nineteenth and early twentieth centuries, the region became a key center of the commercial oyster industry, with oyster beds plotted as property and farmed to produce annual crops, part of a larger circulation of capital, labor, and commodities along the East Coast. During the Gilded Age, New

Yorkers could not get enough oysters, even as their habit of dumping tons of raw sewage and industrial waste into the water led to the oyster's demise. Playing on this history, SCAPE presents its plans as continuous with it.[6] But this apparent continuity masks a fundamental discontinuity. During the gilded age, oysters were valued for their *qualities* (nutrition, taste, texture, size, and color). Today's oysters are valued for what they *do*. As sea levels rise, traditional breakwaters will be increasingly less effective. It is the hope of SCAPE that its oysters will grow on top of each other, layering onto and strengthening the assemblage to which they're attached, rising "elegantly" with the seas. This, SCAPE explains, is its core concept: "'growing' climate-change infrastructure biologically now rather than relying on capital-intensive big construction projects in the distant future" (Orff 2011: 98).

It is not difficult to understand why New Yorkers are once again deeply attached to oysters. From enthusiastic volunteers at oyster restoration stations, to oyster festivals on city streets and the unexpected appearance of a woman proudly wearing an oyster hat on Staten Island, oysters have captured the imaginations, hopes, and dreams of New York residents, first in a story of harmony and sustainability, now as a buffer against the coming catastrophe. We are interested in these attachments. But we are interested also in what oystertecture tells us about infrastructure, temporality, and politics, and the relation between them, in an age of global climate change.

Stated in simple terms, oysters in New York City are notable today for being refashioned and reimagined as infrastructure. Oysters have rarely—if ever—been asked to do this before.[7] We might say that through their new infrastructural function, oysters have become "biopolitical."[8] This is true not just because oyster life is now carefully managed—though this is most certainly the case—but also because through managing the life of oysters, it is now imagined that *human* life can be managed. In an instance of biopolitical doubling, we now manage *other* life to *secure* human life.[9]

III

At first glance, then, the novelty of oystertecture lies in its use of animals as infrastructure, such that the site and definition of "critical infrastructure" is radically changed. But the use of living beings as infrastructure may be less novel than first appears. After all, animals have functioned as infrastructure before. As late as the mid-twentieth century, horses pulled boats along London's canals, their vital powers indispensable to the industrializing city. Likewise, before the development of carbon monoxide monitors, canaries served as "biosensors" in underground mines. Along with headlamps, helmets, bells and whistles, they comprised a rudimentary safety infrastructure designed to protect both workers and capital. Even humans as living beings can be considered part of a "social" infrastructure. If we accept AbdouMaliq Simone's (2004: 210) suggestion that people's heterogeneous activities constitute "mobile and provisional possibilities for how people live and make things, how they use the urban environment and collaborate with one another," then humans in and through their lives as living beings comprise something akin to a collective platform that subtends the practice of everyday life.

Yet, in important respects how oysters are enrolled as living beings *is* unusual. This has to do in part with the peculiar nature of contemporary risks. But it also has to do with the specific biology of the oyster. For residents of coastal areas, sea level rise and future storm surges are a growing risk, the consequence of our ongoing addiction to fossil fuels. Future climate is expected to be more turbulent, and extreme events more frequent. The peculiar nature of how oysters live—and die—appears the perfect antidote. Oysters begin life as one of millions of eggs released into surrounding waters by mature oysters attached to existing reefs. Not all eggs survive and transform into oysters—much depends on the first few days after they hatch. As a newborn, the oyster is little more than a tiny mobile blob of larva, nourished only by the nutrients from the egg. Within a few days, it begins to extract calcium carbonate from lime-rich waters and develops organs able to process food, and it begins to grow a thick, hard shell (Brooks 1996: 23–25). Having reached this point, it swims until it arrives at a stable surface, where it attaches and remains for the rest of its life. Unlike clams, which burrow in the mud, or mussels, which attach to outcropping of rocks, the substrate to which wild oysters attach is usually other adult oysters, or the shells of dead ones (figure 8.3). The hardening and layering of shells individually and together constitute what we refer to as a bed or a reef. As each oyster matures it releases millions more eggs, perpetuating the cycle. Over time, oyster reefs grow in an ever-expanding self-agglomeration, stuck together like glue, growing up and out, with older oysters inside and younger oysters on the exterior. In New York in the 1600s, immense reefs stretched through the Raritan Bay and its tributaries, the East River, along the Hudson River as far north as Ossining, New York, as well as throughout Arthur Kill, Jamaica Bay, and south Newark Bay (MacKenzie 1984, 1992).

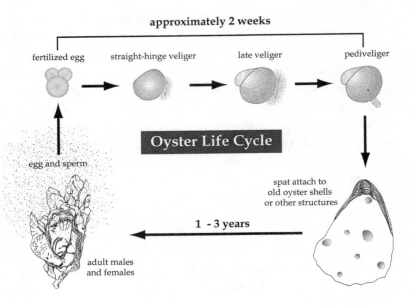

approximately 2 weeks

fertilized egg   straight-hinge veliger   late veliger   pediveliger

Oyster Life Cycle

egg and sperm

spat attach to
old oyster shells
or other structures

1 - 3 years

adult males
and females

Figure 8.3. Oyster life-cycle diagram. Copyright Karen R. Swanson/COSEE/NSF.

Today oysters are no longer found in the Hudson River, Raritan Bay, or any other location in the region. In the nineteenth century oysters in New York waters were planted, harvested, and planted again, in a mass production process that had no regard for the oysters' unique lifeworld or the cycle needed for reefs to grow. In stark contrast, the designers of the city's new "living breakwaters" seek to re-create the oyster's lifeworld and then *let it be*, seeing in the "natural functioning" of oyster reefs an inherent productivity and emergent potential that can be harnessed to protect the city from the sea (Orff 2010). It is the hope of SCAPE's designers that oysters will grow on each other, layering onto and strengthening the assemblage to which they're attached: "Designed as living systems," SCAPE's report to the Rebuild by Design jury explains, "they build up biogenically in parallel with future sea level rise" (2014: 23). Paul Greenberg (2015: 28), SCAPE member, dramatizes the fecundity of oyster life by typing out the estimated annual spawn of oyster larvae in colonial New York—300,000,000,000,000,000,000,000 (three hundred quintillion)—an almost unfathomable quantity of matter and energy that can magically organize itself into a complex, functional infrastructure. "Layer by layer," marvels Greenberg "the reef builds vertically, each new oyster generation building on the last. . . . No other bivalve builds in 3 dimensions with such architectural zeal" (28). Whereas traditional breakwaters will grow deeper and be less effective as sea levels rise, oysters "really become nature's wave attenuators" (Orff 2010).

For this infrastructure to function, then, it is the "species life" of the oyster—in its totality—that matters and continues to matter even after its death.[10] The horses that pulled boats along London's canals were certainly valued for their vital powers, such that their species life was integral to the movement of goods and people. But the death of a horse interrupted the functioning of the infrastructural system: it provided no work and produced no infrastructural value. The canary in the coal mine could be seen as part of the safety infrastructure of the mine, charged with preserving the life of the miner (or, more to the point, making sure that dangers were identified so that the laboring body could survive to work another day). Here it was not the life of the canary that mattered, but its passage into death, or at least its potential to do so. The value of the canary was realized only in the moment it showed distress or expired.[11] A dead canary, like a dead horse, had no infrastructural value.

Part of what makes the oyster-as-infrastructure unique, then, is that over the course of living its life, and passing over into death, it *builds* the infrastructure and *is* the infrastructure. Moreover, it builds the infrastructure in response to changing environmental conditions, adapting to ocean levels as they rise and fall. This in part explains oystertecture's immense appeal, for it appears as nothing short of nature's very own solution to the volatility that our activities have introduced into global climate. Nature is there to assist us, provided that we understand what it is capable of doing.

IV

For SCAPE's oysters, there is no reprieve. They are expected to work, from birth to death—and beyond death—to secure human life. What matters today is not what oysters are—their texture and taste—but what oysters *do*, individually and collectively. Oysters become infrastructure through their biological functions (for an extended discussion of the functionalism of infrastructure, see Ballestero, this volume). Yet however central the species life of the oyster is to our story, and however novel may be the idea of self-organizing, "living" infrastructure, to focus on the use of animals as infrastructure may lead us to miss the larger significance of these projects, namely, that they reveal a new relation to being, time, and politics. Oystertecture is not significant only because it enrolls nature as infrastructure, but also because with projects like oystertecture infrastructure gains a new political ontology.

This shift merits comment. When we think of infrastructure, what often comes to mind are the many roads, bridges, pipes, cables, and wires that underwrite our everyday lives, not unlike the ferry that took us to Governors Island. Much of this infrastructure is mundane, and remains in the background (e.g., Graham and Thrift 2007). But at particular historical moments, modern infrastructure has also had a spectacular dimension (Larkin 2008). Consider Michael Ondaatje's (1987) remarkable description of an ornate and imposing water treatment plant in his novel *In the Skin of the Lion*.[12] Built with great fanfare in Toronto in the 1930s, the treatment plant captivated an entire city, promising an end to water shortages and unclean drinking water.[13] Or consider the massive dams built during the New Deal era, which captured the imagination not of a single city, but an entire nation. These great engineering feats provided evidence of humanity's power to order and shape "external" nature (a power and a concept of nature that we now view in a very different light). More important, they promised the future. This promise was powerful. In the 1950s, it was common for working-class American families to take side trips to visit infrastructures. Inside shoeboxes buried at the bottom of many Americans' closets are Polaroids of parents or grandparents smiling in front of imposing dams or monumental bridges. Despite their faded colors, there remains something immensely hopeful about these images: a sense of being part of a historical movement, one of ongoing progress and improvement.

Borrowing from Hetherington (2016), we might say that modern infrastructure contains a progressive temporality, part of what Hetherington calls "development thinking." Infrastructure is not just something that fades into the background to enable other things to occur; it also creates the conditions for *another* order, or at least promises a new order to come. The tense of infrastructure is thus the future perfect, "an anticipatory state around which different subjects gather their promises and aspirations" (58). Today many infrastructure projects continue to promise the future, even if that promise is increasingly frayed: the new highway promises to facilitate mobility, new fiber optic cables promise increased connectivity and speed. The mythical time of modern infrastructure is unidirectional, irreversible and teleological, traveling, like Christian salvation, toward an assumed—and assured—end.

Oystertecture turns this temporality on its head. Rather than promising the future, oystertecture functions to *ward it off*. Moreover, it seeks to do so in perpetuity, elegantly adapting to changing conditions so as to keep all other things the same. In this sense, oystertecture is emblematic of a brand of "resilient" infrastructures being developed across America's cities that are not meant to be eventful in their own right, but to cancel out or absorb events. These do not replace modern infrastructures. Instead, they are necessitated by them. Indeed, despite their "green" characteristics—oysters, swales, reefs, and marshes—they set perfectly well alongside the proliferation of pipes, cables, wires, and roads that underwrite "modern" life. One need go no further than Raritan Bay to see this, crisscrossed as it is by some of the most important shipping routes in the US Northeast and witness to a steady parade of oil tankers to and from massive petrochemical facilities on the Jersey side of the bay. None of this is projected to go away. In their design for the reefs, SCAPE was required to incorporate these routes. As "emergent" infrastructure, oysters are not meant to *change* the world; they are tasked with adapting to a *changing world*.

We are now in a position to better understand the temporality and politics of oystertecture—and "resilient" infrastructure more generally—for it is precisely the ability of oysters to collectively adapt to changes in sea level that allows oystertecture to fulfill the political function of what Carl Schmitt (2003) called the *katechon*: the permanent management of the present to hold back the forces of chaos. Schmitt borrows the concept from the apostle Paul, who first used it when writing to the community of believers at Thessalonica, who had abandoned work in anticipation of the return of Christ. This may have been a response to Paul's earlier teaching that Christ's coming was near, an interpretation that worried the apostle. The apocalypse, Paul cautioned, would not come until the *katechon*—"he or what withholds"—would be "taken out of the way" (2 Thessalonians 2:1–12, spec. 2: 6–7).[14] It was important that the community of believers continue on with their everyday labors. Referred to ambiguously as a "who" and a "what," the concept of the katechon has since Paul's time come to mean something quite different from its original use. The early Christian theologian Tertullian, writing in the third century, identified the role and position of the katechon with the Roman Empire, which managed the earthly world, postponing the end of days until its appointed time. For Schmitt, different political authorities occupied the place of the katechon at different times: the Holy Roman Empire, the Byzantine Empire, or individual authorities such as Emperor Rudolf II of Hapsburg. Agamben (2005: 110) expands the range even further. For him, "every theory of the State, including Hobbes's—which thinks of it as a power destined to block or delay catastrophe—can be taken as a secularization of this interpretation of 2 Thessalonians 2."

To ward off the apocalypse, however, also meant warding off salvation, since in Christian eschatology the former is seen to precede the latter. Tertullian, like many others, saw the trials and tribulations of the end days as so horrific that it was preferable to hold them off, despite the cost of postponing redemption indefinitely. For Carl Schmitt, the Holy Roman Empire—and international law and order more generally (*ius publican Europaeum*)—had a similar positive function (2003: 59–60). As a force that warded off chaos, it was portrayed by Schmitt as the only possible source of sense and order in the world. Today, resilient infrastructures are asked to play this role, but with a crucial difference: whereas for Paul there still remained a promise of salvation to believe in—albeit in another time and another heavenly place—today there is no promise of future redemption. Instead there is only the endless and continuous management of crisis here on earth, in which the chaos held at bay is generated by the same order that the management of crisis seeks to preserve. Time marches on, but history comes to a stop.[15]

V

As resilient infrastructure, oystertecture is not merely physical; it is also metaphysical. It embodies and installs a particular relation to time and a particular relation to being. How might we respond to this? How might futurity be reopened, and on what terms?

In a short tract entitled *What Is an Apparatus?*, Giorgio Agamben revisits Foucault's (1980: 194–196) concept *dispositif* (apparatus) in order to explore the metaphysics of "government" or *oikonomia*, but also to explore a potential politics.[16] His is a metaphysical, rather than anthropological, investigation, since he is interested foremost in the question of "being," namely, the nature of our factical existence and, most important, the possibilities it holds for constructing worlds.[17] For Agamben, government is significant not just because it orders earthly affairs, but because it names an operation that separates us from our capacities, both from our ability to actively construct worlds, and our ability to *believe* in the worlds into which we are thrown and participate.[18] It demarcates what is possible. Take, for example, an apparatus with which many of us are intimately familiar: the university, with its ordered curriculum, divisions of knowledge, classroom architecture, and methods of evaluation, all of which encourage us to understand ourselves as if viewed from a site external to our actions: as "student," "instructor," "researcher," "administrator," and so on, and where the possibilities inherent to the tools of the trade—books, lecterns, whiteboards, laboratories—appear to be fully exhausted by the work to which they are currently put. Rather than individually and collectively grasping the possibilities of our factical conditions, our activity is governed so as to direct it toward a *particular* end, or, as in the case of apparatuses of security (e.g., resilience), to ward off the imagination or realization of any *alternative* one.[19]

Notably, for Agamben (2009), almost anything can be part of an apparatus; that is, almost anything can have a governmental dimension. Not only schools, prisons, factories, and confessions, as Foucault (1979) famously noted, but also the pen, literature, computers, and cellular phones, "literally anything that has in some way the capacity to capture, orient, determine, intercept, model, control, or secure the gestures, behaviors, opinions, or discourses of living beings" (Agamben 2009: 14). Even oysters, as we saw above, although in a rather more complicated form: in capturing the actions of oysters, it is human lives that are governed. We will see later how this "doubling up" of apparatuses to include living beings complicates Agamben's ideas, since he narrowly limits the elements of any apparatus to the inorganic.

For our purposes, what is most striking about Agamben's discussion is not only how he understands government, but also how this leads him to call for a certain relation to it, centered on the notion of profanation and an understanding of destituent rather than constituent power. Agamben begins by closely following the definition of apparatus (*dispositif*) that Foucault offered his interviewers in 1977:

> What I'm trying to single out with this term is, first and foremost, a thoroughly heterogeneous set consisting of discourses, institutions, architectural forms, regulatory decisions, laws, administrative measures, scientific statements, philosophical, moral, and philanthropic propositions—in short, the said as much as the unsaid. Such are the elements of the apparatus. The apparatus itself is the network that can be established between these elements . . . by the term "apparatus" I mean a kind of a formation, so to speak, that at a given historical moment has as its major function the response to an urgency. The apparatus therefore has a dominant strategic function. (As cited in Agamben 2009: 2; Foucault 1980: 194–196)

Most commentators of Foucault emphasize the relation between apparatuses and government, and Agamben is among them. But we can also draw out an additional point in Foucault's statement—that the governmental aspect of things is not *inherent* to the things in question; rather, it obtains from the relations into which they are drawn. There is no necessary relation between the elements, except from the perspective of administration. Ultimately, for Foucault, as for Agamben, apparatuses are ad hoc arrangements that emerge in relation to an urgent need. This insight helps us understand how oysters are drawn into apparatuses of government in the aftermath of Hurricane Sandy—how they come to be seen in terms of their function as infrastructure. It also helps us understand Agamben's initially opaque concept of profanation. For Agamben, what is notable about any apparatus is that it involves removing things from common use and placing them in a separate sphere, that of management, administration, or *oikonomia*. The effect is that the elements of an apparatus come to be thought of abstractly, as if part of a separate and preexisting plan that transcends the elements that comprise it rather than immanent in their arrangement. In other words, the magic of an apparatus is that it encourages us to see behind the apparatus a larger order, which the parts merely express.[20] By this view, the elements are sacred, insofar as they appear to have a preordained purpose. But just as the elements of an apparatus can be removed from common use, so also can they be returned to common use. That is, although we are encouraged to understand the elements of an apparatus abstractly, as part of a plan, we can begin to take on the elements of an apparatus as handy and useful, thereby disrupting or detourning their governmental function: in short, by profaning the elements of an apparatus we can begin to participate in the world, rather than conforming to its apparent order. Crucially, for Agamben, to return to common use—to profane an apparatus—does not mean to return the elements of an apparatus to their original, correct, or proper use. To do so would merely insert them within *another* apparatus, and to yet again separate action from being. To return to common use is instead to deactivate the governmental dimensions of things and turn toward the Open, what Agamben (2009) describes as "the possibility of knowing being, as such, by constructing a world" (16–17).

Elsewhere, Agamben (2014: 68–69) productively speaks of this in terms of the middle voice, verbs "that are neither active nor passive, but the two together." These verbs are rarely found in Modern English. Drawing on Émile Benveniste, Agamben notes that while the active voice "denotes a process that is realized starting from the subject and outside of it," in which the subject stands above the process as an actor, in the middle voice the subject is "internal to the process." *The subject is both the agent and the site of the action,*

being affected in its own act. What Agamben finds attractive in this formulation is its radical transformation of the subject: "Not a subject that uses an
object, but a subject that constitutes itself only through the using, the being
in relation with an other. Ethical and political is the subject that constitutes
itself in this use, the subject that testifies of the affection that it receives in
so far as it is in relation with another body." In the middle voice action is no
longer separate from being; thus, to act in the middle voice is not just the opposite of government; it deactivates government and renders it inoperative.
Crucially, this is not an attempt to return to some original order in order to
destroy it; rather, it is a destitution without refusal, in which our mode of living, not the mere fact of living, is what is at stake.

> A life that cannot be separate from its form is a life for which, in its way
> of living, what is at stake is living itself, and, in its living, what is at stake
> above all else is its mode of living. What is at stake, then, is a life in which
> the single ways, acts and processes of living are never simply *facts*, but al-
> ways and above all *possibilities* of life, always and above all potentiality. . . .
> [it is] to replace the ontology of *substance* with the ontology of *how*, an
> ontology of modality. The decisive problem is no longer "what" I am, but
> "how" I am what I am. (Agamben 2014: 73)

Ultimately, Agamben's response to apparatuses of government is not to reject
them, but to *destitute* them—to return them to common use, not in order to
govern life, but in order to live life as potentiality.[21]

VI

As a species of resilient infrastructure, oystertecture is intended to secure
a mode of life—to govern life in a particular way. Located well offshore,
secured from curious humans who might otherwise seek to collect or consume them, SCAPE's oysters are meant to manage crises, warding off the
coming catastrophe. Despite the oyster festivals and oyster parades and despite volunteers' dreams of oyster farming, New Yorkers will be forbidden
from visiting these reefs. The woman in the oyster hat will never see them,
never touch them, and never taste them. Invisible and continuously at work,
rising "elegantly" with the seas, the reefs have a simple function: holding the
seas at bay while presenting a calming image of a pacified world in which

everything is "okay." The present becomes a time of waiting, outside history and without future.

If for Agamben there is a politics to be found, it is about reanimating history. When Agamben turns to the question of use, his goal is to free us from an abstract relation to apparatuses—a relation encouraged equally by apparatuses of government and critiques thereof—in order to return us *to* the world and the *concrete* exploration of the possibilities it holds. This implies a pragmatic, experimental practice that depends upon the groups practicing it and the places where they do so. Arguably, this is consistent with a conception of use found in Foucault's work. For the Greeks, Foucault (1990) wrote, use (or nonuse) of a body was governed not by moral interdiction or code, but instead determined by a number of strategic considerations—the time of year, the weather, one's social standing and age, in addition to one's training and ability. Use was not prescribed, but neither was it arbitrary—it was determined by what was possible, and what was not, as well as when, how, and with whom. Use had determinate conditions, not all of which were "human" or "social."

Yet here we may need to go beyond Agamben, or at least extend his thought in new directions. What would it mean to profane oystertecture, or to return it to common use? Do we interpret this literally, in terms of putting oysters to *other* uses? Or is profanation more about an *orientation* to the world? And how might our analysis change when the elements of a dispositif are themselves living beings? Little if any of the growing literature on infrastructure qua government considers the question, and at least on the surface Agamben gives us few ways of thinking about it. This is not only because his interest in the animal goes no further than how the human-animal distinction is manufactured (see Agamben 2004). Nor is it only because his concept of use remains insistently anthropocentric, since for Agamben use almost always references the human.[22] Both of these matter, and we will return to them. But equally as important, Agamben limits his understanding of what an apparatus can do or become. This is evident if we return to Agamben's reading of Foucault, which is noteworthy as much for what it leaves out as for what it includes. As we saw earlier, Agamben begins by noting Foucault's initial definition of an apparatus as the elements and the system of relations that can be established between them. For Agamben, this constitutes the governmental machine that relentlessly separates action from being. But this is only the beginning of Foucault's definition. Curiously, Agamben skips over what comes next:

Secondly, what I am trying to identify in this apparatus is precisely the nature of the connection that can exist between these heterogenous elements. Thus, a particular discourse can figure at one time as the programme of an institution, and at another it can function as a means of justifying or masking a practice which itself remains silent, or as a secondary re-interpretation of this practice, opening out for it a new field of rationality. In short, between these elements, whether discursive or non-discursive, there is a sort of interplay of shifts of position and modifications of function which can also vary very widely. (Foucault 1980: 194)

We see here aspects that Agamben gestures to, but chooses to downplay. While he emphasizes that apparatuses can be profaned, he pays less attention to a different point: that apparatuses are dynamic and inherently generative. Foucault's interviewer, Élie Wajeman, presses him on precisely this point:

WAJEMAN: So an apparatus is defined by a structure of heterogeneous elements, but also by a certain kind of genesis?

FOUCAULT: Yes. And I would consider that there are two important moments in this genesis. There is a first moment which is the prevalent influence of a strategic objective. Next, the apparatus as such is constituted and enabled to continue in existence insofar as it is the site of a double process. On the one hand, there is a process of functional overdetermination, because each effect— positive or negative, intentional or unintentional—enters into resonance or contradiction with the others and thereby calls for a readjustment or a re-working of the heterogeneous elements that surface at various points. On the other hand, there is a perpetual process of strategic elaboration. Take the example of imprisonment, that apparatus which had the effect of making measures of detention appear to be the most efficient and rational method that could be applied to the phenomenon of criminality. What did this apparatus produce? An entirely unforeseen effect which had nothing to do with any kind of strategic ruse on the part of some meta- or trans-historic subject conceiving and willing it. This effect was the constitution of a delinquent milieu very different from the kind of seedbed of illegalist practices and individuals found in eighteenth-century society. What happened? The prison operated as a process of filtering, concentrating, professionalizing, and circumscribing a criminal milieu. (Foucault 1980: 195–196)

In contrast to Foucault's understanding of apparatuses as generative, Agamben's reworking of the concept is more restrictive. Apparatuses order worlds, Foucault tells us, but they also give rise to new desires, new subjects, and new politics that potentially escape to draw new lines of flight. In his own essay on the concept, Gilles Deleuze (1988) stresses precisely this aspect. For him, a *dispositif* is "a tangle, a multilinear ensemble . . . composed of lines, each having a different nature . . . subject to *changes in direction*, bifurcating and forked, and subject to *drifting*" (159, italics in original). While readers of Foucault frequently emphasize the matter of government—as does Agamben—we argue that this may be what interested him the least. Foucault was equally interested in what apparatuses were capable of becoming, the ways in which they could wander off in new directions, opening new urgencies and new possibilities for strategic elaboration (i.e., new modes of government), but also how they continuously produced elements that *escaped* such elaboration. In his discussion, Agamben nods toward this movement, noting that an apparatus can produce "elusive" elements, but he ultimately argues that today we simply witness the "incessant although aimless motion of this machine."[23] What Foucault helps us see is not only that one deactivates and returns things to common use from *within* the movement of these apparatuses, but also that one does so from *within the new desires and possibilities that they unleash*, not unlike the practical possibilities that *overspill* the imagined infrastructures analyzed by Jensen (this volume). What mattered for Foucault first and foremost was not the operations of government, but the possibilities for life that emerged within and alongside them.

We emphasize this reading of apparatus not only because it complicates the temporality and ontology of government, but also because it provides a means for thinking about the doubling up of apparatuses today: the way in which living beings are now being enrolled in the administration of "life"— the harnessing of capacities of some living beings (oysters) for the purposes of managing other living beings (humans). As apparatuses of government, oysters promise to produce certain effects—they attenuate the power of waves and storm surges, filter toxins from water, and hold together a set of underwater relations that are seen as essential for maintaining existing social and economic relations above water or on land. But are not oysters also living beings that, like humans, project themselves in and against their factical conditions? In other words, should we imagine that oysters will simply submit to their governmental function? Or will they *also* explore its possibilities to construct worlds?[24] Is this not an apparatus that is, literally, "subject to drifting"?

The point is not just that oysters may refuse to be enrolled, in a fashion similar to Michel Callon's (1986) famous scallops. Rather, the point is that oysters may use us, rather than us using them. Oysters are, after all, rather pragmatic creatures. They will affix themselves to all manner of surfaces—known as "biofouling" when it clogs up infrastructure—and will conform to the shapes of whatever surface they happened to attach to as larvae: "an oyster growing in the neck of a bottle takes the smooth, regular curve of the glass, and on the claw of a crab an oyster shell sometimes follows all the angles and ridges and spines, as if it were made of wax instead of inflexible stone" (W. Brooks 1996: 21). Nor do they conform to any particular size. Oysters can live for up to twenty years and can grow to twelve inches in length. That this surprises is only because a significant part of the oyster industry has been devoted to standardizing oysters with an eye to selling them to well-heeled consumers with discriminating tastes: not only were workers in the industry's early years employed to dilute the taste of saltwater, rinse off mud, separate oysters from each other, and scrub off any biota still clinging to the shells, but oyster farmers calibrated precise methods for growing only "pleasing" sizes and shapes, creating the now-familiar oyster we find in bars, restaurants, and food markets (MacKenzie 1992).

This leads to a key point. For Agamben, all living beings are *in* a form of life. But not all *are* a form-of-life, or have the possibility to be so. He tends to reserve the possibility of the latter for humans. Yet, there is no reason to assume that oysters do not share the same ontological conditions as do humans, whether understood in terms of "conatus," "temporality," or whatever other concept we use to capture this, nor that they do not also live in the middle voice. This is precisely the insight offered by writers such as Nigel Clark and Myra Hird (2014), who note that other living beings have lifeworlds and trajectories that are overwhelmingly unknown to us, even as we rely on them. Moreover, these beings actively use worlds we produce in order to construct worlds of their own. Unlike us, they do not have an abstract relation to the elements of an apparatus. To borrow language from Agamben, they are as just as likely to be an "elusive element" that escapes its governmental function (and that puts us to new use!) as they are to be an element put to a governmental use.[25]

At one level this returns us to a commonplace in infrastructure studies: enrolling oysters as infrastructure not only requires establishing the right conditions, but it also requires continuous maintenance. This is rarely discussed in proposals to enroll living beings in the maintenance of human life. What oysters do is assumed to be known in advance. That infrastructures work is due to no end of human labor—measuring, monitoring, maintaining and repairing, that is, all the work, knowledge and skill that is required to corral elusive elements and put them to work. Today the hope is to give oysters a new telos: instead of commodities, infrastructure. In stark contrast to the early twentieth-century oyster industry, which strove to remove oysters from their lifeworld, the wager today is that oysters as "living breakwaters" will function properly by *creating* and *maintaining* this lifeworld.

Today, New York State is spending millions of dollars to do so in a desperate bid to save New York City from rising seas. There are no guarantees that any of this will work, not only because oysters have no regard for the purposes of our all-too-human designs, but also because it may be impossible to make them live. This is a power that humans may not have, or may have long ago extinguished. Oysters today are functionally extinct through much of their original habitat. Long gone are the conditions that historically made their life in the Raritan and other waters possible: a rocky substrate, nontoxic waters, and so on. In their place exists a deserted ocean floor covered in black goo, ten feet deep in some places, cut through by shipping channels, with bottom sediments and water laden with PCBs and heavy metals, massive algae blooms, and the accretion of the 1.1 billion gallons of wastewater poured into the harbor daily (Sam Janis, personal communication, April 17, 2015; Waldman 1999: 56–57; "Water, New York Harbor, and Quality Regional Summary" 2004). Even SCAPE's designers understand that the odds are stacked against them: "What we're looking for," Kate Orff explains, "is a spark, a critical mass enough to jumpstart life again in a place that is practically speaking dead" (personal communication, May 29, 2015). With the threat of ocean acidification looming, it may be too late to get the new ecosystem off the ground and able to reproduce on its own.

If there is a possible politics to be found in oystertecture, it may not be found in profaning oysters—they do this on their own—but in a more radical recognition that returning to the world—returning things to common use—returns us to a world that exceeds us and which we do not control. If for Agamben, profanation means to refuse an abstract relation to the world, to refuse to imagine a plan that stands over and above our lives, to live in the middle voice, then perhaps we may have to give up something in exchange: the assumption of an ordered world that apparatuses themselves lead us to believe in. If apparatuses give us the appearance of an order that stands over and above its elements and its relations, then returning to the world is perhaps to return to a world in which such an order cannot be assumed. To live in the middle voice, acting so as to change ourselves in the acting, or to be "a" form of life rather than "in" a form of life, may at the same time require accepting the provisional, uncertain, and unpredictable work of entering into experimental collaborations in which the outcome cannot be known or predicted in advance. It will require not ever more resilient apparatuses to ward off the future, but rather to learn to inhabit capitalist ruins in a more-than-human world; ruins in which "we" may not stand at the center. If dispositifs of resilience leave us suspended in an eternal present, then to jump-start history may require that we be deliberately and explicitly postapocalyptic, living as if the end of times has already arrived, and with it, the end of "man" as we currently know him.[26] More than anything else, profanation may require profaning the sacred figure of the human.

This may be most in keeping with our co-volunteers as we struggle to tie oysters to oyster stations off of Governors Island. "Life," Agamben (2016: 220) writes, "is a form generated by living." It is a process of experimentation *with* the world, within its determinate conditions. Oysters as infrastructure may confront us with is a lesson that goes beyond governmental apparatuses to destitution itself: that we make worlds within a world that is not "for us," but "for itself." Ultimately, the construction of worlds—life lived in the middle voice—occurs within *this* horizon, even if we continuously fail to acknowledge it. One can be obsessed with the end for a while, but. . . .

Notes

1 The MOMA exhibit featured "soft" architectural responses to rising sea levels, infrastructural obsolescence, and the desire to reconnect NYC with its harbor. For more on *Rising Currents*, see Bruce Braun (2014).

2 The abbreviation FLUPSY is short for "Floating Upwelling System," a term for baby oyster nurseries.

3 These breakwaters can be understood as part of a *dispositif* of security that responds to the urgency of climate change. Michel Foucault (1980) understands dispositifs as ad hoc assemblages, created by bringing together diverse sites and elements in order to manage crises. Only retrospectively and with a view to the "network of relations" formed between them do those sites or practices appear as part of a plan devised in advance or as a coherent unity.

4 All kinds of new terms began to be used to describe oysters: "physical-biological infrastructure" (Greenberg 2015: 28), "living infrastructure" (Orff 2014), and "ecological infrastructure" (SCAPE 2014).

5 These "armoring units" have been engineered in Israeli laboratories by scientists attempting to mimic the composition of wild oyster reefs.

6 A video presentation of the project can be found here: "Living Breakwaters," *Rebuild by Design*, accessed March 28, 2018, http://www.rebuildbydesign.org /project/scape-landscape-architecture-final-proposal/.

7 Not unlike the "relative existence" of Pasteur's microbes (Latour 1988), oysters are now seen to have *always* had this infrastructural function, transforming the past along with the present. We are taught that oysters are a valuable infrastructure that the "moderns" destroyed: "two centuries ago, reefs composed of 3 trillion oysters were a 'natural seawall'" that created shallower bays and served as a "first line of defense for Manhattan against storms as fierce or fiercer than 2012's Hurricane Sandy," writes Paul Greenberg (*New York Post*, June 21, 2014).

8 It is tempting to analyze oystertecture as an example of "green" infrastructure. In this chapter we resist this label: as we will see, there is nothing particularly "environmental" about this infrastructure except that it mobilizes animal life to secure human life.

9 This is increasingly true with regard to "ecosystem services" more generally.

10 We borrow the distinction "species life" from Marx (see Marx and Milligan 1844), who distinguished it from "species being."

11 Canaries were considered better sentinel species than mice because, unlike mice—which might present similarly in life, sickness, and death—canaries would visibly sway on their perches before falling sick or dying. Many thanks to Peter Forman for pointing out the different qualities of sentinel species and how these are given infrastructural functions.

12 The historical reference is the palatial R. C. Harris Water Treatment Plant, which was designed in the Art Deco style and named after Harris, who served as Toronto's Commissioner of Public Works from 1912 until 1945.

13 For more on the infrastructural sublime, see Matthew Gandy (2003).

14 We follow here Patricia Dailey's translation in Giorgio Agamben (2005: 109).

15 See Masco, this volume, for a discussion of "crisis" as a counterrevolutionary idiom that stabilizes the existing present condition rather than engaging its multiple temporalities.

16 A more extended discussion would follow in 2011, with the publication of Agamben's *The Kingdom and the Glory*.

17 An "anthropological" or "historical" investigation would explore "being" in its concrete historical conditions. As we will see, for Agamben the latter becomes crucial for any politics.

18 For Agamben, "government" is bound up with the human desire for happiness, salvation, or redemption: "the capture and subjectification of this desire in a separate

sphere constitutes the specific power of the apparatus" (2009: 17). Our desire for a better life is abstracted onto an apparatus, and subsequently separated from us.

19 See, for instance, Fred Moten and Stefano Harney (2004).

20 One of the best discussions of this remains Timothy Mitchell's (1988) discussion of the "exhibition" in his book, *Colonising Egypt*.

21 Here we note the value of ethnographic studies of infrastructure and "logistical life," for what these studies reveal are the ways in which people and communities frequently "deactivate" the governmental aspects of technical systems, in order to live "as not" within them. In other cases infrastructure becomes the site of struggles for *inclusion* in an existing biopolitical order: as citizens, ratepayers, consumers. While this is not the return to "common use" that we argue for here, these struggles should not be dismissed: it is often far better to be included within a valued form of life than abandoned and placed outside it! See Anand, this volume.

22 In this sense Agamben is consistent with much of Western metaphysics. See Jacques Derrida (1994). We thank Rosemary Collard for reminding us of Derrida's trenchant critique.

23 Certainly this characterizes much of what occurs within the political rationality of "resilience" today.

24 This is precisely the possibility that Martin Heidegger (1995) refuses the animal.

25 In this sense oysters have the "potentiality to precipitate the new," much like the aquifers studied by Ballestero (this volume), but they do so in part by appropriating the worlds we incorporate them within.

26 Only the most privileged still imagine that the apocalypse lies off in the future. After the ravages of colonial capitalism, for billions of people the "postapocalyptic" is lived daily.

NINE. Here Comes the Sun?

Experimenting with Cambodian Energy
Infrastructures

CASPER BRUUN JENSEN

As if it were not already obvious from traversing Phnom Penh's scorching streets, the abundance of Cambodian sunshine was brought to my attention during a visit to the industrial outskirts of the southwest city. Sitting around the corner from the Khmer Electrical Power Co, Ltd., and a few blocks from Street Solar, this was the location of the new office and manufacturing plant of the Melbourne-based solar energy company Star8. Covered in multicolored solar panels, the building would not look out of place in a Californian innovation hub. Certainly, it offered a startling contrast to the dubious-looking garment factories surrounding it. As my Hungarian guide to the facility explained, one of the main benefits of pushing the solar agenda from Cambodia is that there is three times more sunlight than in Central Europe.

Inside the Star8 building, the lobby doubles as a high-tech showroom. It contains small model houses covered in elegantly futuristic solar panels. Also featured are solar streetlights and an assortment of more curious products. Among them, one finds what looks like a small handbag, which can be unfolded to display eight mini solar panels. Coming at a price of $250, it can be placed on top of a car and used to recharge mobile phones or other devices using a USB port. Next to it is a solar parasol cover able to provide electricity for computers and phones while sunbathing. There are solar cooking and barbecuing devices, rather scary looking, since they can't be turned off. And there are solar panels wrapped in camouflage, "for army excursions into the jungle," as helpfully explained by the guide, himself an ex-member of the UN peacekeeping mission that came to Cambodia in the early 1990s aftermath of the Khmer Rouge regime of terror.

Seated in comfortable chairs in the lobby, the general manager offers further information. Star8 is only five years old, he explains. It grew out of Australia, but presently it has offices in Singapore, Bangkok, Manila, Myanmar, and Cambodia. The Phnom Penh office opened recently, in February 2014. However, things are moving extremely quickly right now.

One does not have to take the manager's word for that. According to the United Nations Environment Programme's ninth "Global Trends in Renewable Energy Investment 2015," green energy investments increased 17 percent in 2014, to $270 billion.[1] Investments in solar power alone went up 29 percent. The leader in this surge is China, followed by the US, Japan, and several other countries: Brazil, India, South Africa, Mexico, Indonesia, Chile, Kenya, and Turkey. Only Europe lags behind.

The general manager has two explanations for why Star8 has opened an office in Cambodia. Repeating that there is a lot of sunlight in Cambodia, he adds that labor is also very cheap. This second answer makes the solar products on display in the lobby appear in a different light. Those expensive barbecues and parasol covers are of course for export. Maybe all of this has little to do with creating a platform for renewable energy in Cambodia after all.

~~~~~~~

In the grand scheme of things, solar energy is insignificant for the country. In terms of attention and investment, everything revolves around hydropower development on the Mekong and its tributaries. There have been plans to build such dams since the mid-twentieth century, but they only really began materializing in the late 1990s, when China went ahead with several dams upstream. A decade later, companies and governments are pushing ahead Lower Mekong dam projects in Laos and Cambodia.[2] Behind these projects lie dreams of energy-induced development radically different from those that invigorate proponents of solar energy.

So far, hydropower-generated electricity sets practically the whole agenda for Cambodian energy futures, while solar energy is barely a blink on the radar. This situation provides the impetus for the following discussion, which examines Cambodian energy infrastructures with a view to create some wiggle room for solar energy infrastructures to thrive. As I suggest, this depends on developing an analytics of infrastructures as ontological experiments (Jensen and Morita 2015). What comes into view is an energy landscape comprising multiple ontological test sites in which energy and people are mutually transformed via their encounters in and as infrastructure, and where solar energy could prevail, against the odds.

Energizing Social Science

It is not only in the realms of politics and business that questions of energy, its promises and dangers, are viewed with urgency. Across the social sciences, too, one can witness a surge of interest in energy infrastructures. It has become increasingly obvious that the resource arrangements that allow people, cities, countries, and regions to meet energy needs are of crucial importance not only for understanding political and economic developments but also social and cultural relations.

Recently, the anthropologist Dominic Boyer has proposed "energopower" as an analytical category to complement, if not replace, Foucault's trope of biopower. If post–World War II energy regimes were characterized, he writes: "By promises of endless growth [that] were defined above all by a remarkable integration of energic systems (transnational oil and nuclear energy) and biopolitical order (Keynesian welfarism), then since the 1970s the world has experienced an accelerating process of dis-integration in which the seams between bios and energos are increasingly taut and visible. What comes next is abundantly unclear" (Boyer 2014: 328).

Whereas the "dominant carbon energopolitical regime is increasingly disrupting and poisoning life across the world . . . at the same time we glimpse fascinating new mutations in that regime's discourse and techniques of governance with the appearance of new anthropocentric and ecocentric biopolitical imaginaries responding to climate change. Energopolitical crisis is generating biopolitical effects and vice-versa" (Boyer 2014: 328). Accordingly, as Boyer sees it, energy must move to the forefront of social scientific concerns. However, it is less clear what to do with this realization, for taking it on board requires the social scientist to move outside his or her comfort zone.

Sarah Strauss et al.'s edited volume *Cultures of Energy* (2013a) exemplifies some of the challenges. The editors are emphatic that "human use of energy is understood and experienced through cultural frameworks. . . . The enormous energy challenges facing us all are fundamentally cultural and political rather than technological" (Strauss, Rupp, and Love 2013b: 10). This leads to a focus on how people experience forms of energy, how they rely on it, and how it is harnessed "to construct socially meaningful worlds" (11).

These worthwhile questions are discussed in a range of contexts, but they are generally engaged from the point of view of peoples' experiences and political contexts. Thus, although the editorial introduction insists that "an anthropology of energy must shuttle back and forth among laws of physics, opportunities and constraints of ecological systems, and processes of culture," layers of reality that are "necessarily intertwined materially, rhetorically, and metaphorically" (2013: 12), the volume contains relatively little analysis of the technological systems, infrastructural arrangements, or material qualities of the energy sources.

In this light, the work of Leslie White, which has recently reemerged in writings on energopolitics (e.g., Boyer 2014), offers an interesting contrast. In his day, White was known not only for his battles with the Boasian school of cultural anthropology, but also for his adamant materialism, centering on the relations between energy and "the evolution of culture." Observing that "everything in the universe may be described in terms of energy," White (1943: 335) derived two "laws of cultural development." "Other things being equal," he argued, "the degree of cultural development varies directly as the amount of energy per capita per year harnessed and put to work," and, "the degree of cultural development varies directly as the efficiency of the technological means with which the harnessed energy is put to work" (338).

The obvious rejoinder was that other things were rarely equal. Nevertheless, the recent reappearance of White in the landscape of energy analytics suggests that discontents rumble under the surface of culture-centric analyses. Thus, for example, one dimension of Boyer's energopolitical reorientation is that *energy's effects* are at least as consequential as peoples' perceptions. Indeed, at a time of accelerating worries about anthropogenic global warming and the role of the oil industry, White's observation, taken from the physicist R. M. Langer's "Fast New World," sounds more plausible than ever: "The kind of civilization we might expect . . . is so different from anything we know that even guesses about it are futile" (Langer 1940, cited in White 1943: 351). Leslie White, of course, was writing at a time when it was still possible to believe in technological redemption.[3] Later would follow innumerable crises induced by technology, eventually leading to such saturation that the power of crisis to motivate action itself began to decrease (Masco, this volume).

From the present vantage point, it is only too obvious that White's depictions of energy's evolutions relied on their own dubious sociopolitical assumptions. Indeed, despite insisting on the futility of predicting the future, his immediately preceding sentences did offer estimations, which from the present vantage point seem astonishing. "The face of the earth will be changed," White quoted the physicist Langer. "Privilege and class distinctions . . . will become relics because things that make up the good life will be so abundant and inexpensive. Wars will become obsolete because of the disappearance of those economic stresses that immemorially have caused it" (Langer 1940, cited in White 1943: 351). Of these predictions, the only one still standing ominously before us is the first: "the face of the earth will be changed . . ."

In a context where all other things did indeed fail to stay equal, White's energy determinism is obviously unsatisfactory as an infrastructural analytics. Yet, anthropological studies that focus on lived experience and sense-making as if such experiences and categories were not themselves shaped by infrastructures (functioning, as it were, *as* life-worlds) are equally problematic. Accordingly, it is necessary to develop a decentered approach (Jensen 2014), capable of taking into account the material dimensions of energy infrastructures, the promissory discourses that surround them, the forms of social and political organization that support them, and the affects and experiences of people who imagine, build, or use them *all at once*.

Moreover, as Masco argues (this volume), given the current inability of crisis narratives to energize action, the varied forms of precarity catalogued by anthropologists must be supplemented by infrastructural analyses willing to take risks with articulating alternative futures. In the following, I develop one version of such an analytics by engagement with present and imagined Cambodian energy infrastructures.

Infrastructural developments are entwined with imagined futures (Hetherington 2014; Nielsen 2011), like the one in which all Cambodians will have access to cheap electricity due to hydropower development. Often, of course, such promises are dashed due to endless postponements and the inability to complete projects (Namba 2016; Weszkalnys 2016), or because the resulting infrastructures are unable to deliver the promised services.

As infrastructural promise tends to be deferred to an indefinite future, to always point just around the corner; it might be said to embed a form of Lauren Berlant's (2011) "cruel optimism." It is thus not surprising that anthropological studies of infrastructure often exhibit a narrative structure where high-minded promises give way to dismal failure. This hubris can then be juxtaposed with descriptions of the precarious lives of the people who should have benefited but never did. Such studies are very important because they capture a dynamic central to a great many infrastructure projects. At the same time, the bleak realism that makes these ethnographies so compelling is also a weakness because it often makes it very difficult to imagine any viable alternatives.

Recognition of the experimental qualities of infrastructure might be key to avoiding diminishing collective capacity to imagine and work toward such alternatives. Because infrastructures are patched together by a vast array of incongruent elements, from laws to water flows and from cement to equations, they tend to gain in complexity to the point where no one is fully able to either understand or control them (Harvey, Jensen, and Morita 2016: 7–11). Made up of transformable relations, and making new relations, they can be described as ontological sites of experimentation (Jensen and Morita 2015). On the one hand, it remains as important as ever for the anthropologist to grapple with present infrastructural realities. On the other hand, it is just as important to search for the cracks in such realities, as this is where pathways to different futures may be found.

The philosopher Paul Feyerabend (2001) offers useful guidance on this point. In advance of current preoccupations with ontology, he reminded us that a heterogeneous set of "practically effective forms of life" are always in the process of being built from incongruent elements. Such life forms, he wrote, "contain subtly articulated ontologies including spirits, Gods, dreams, animals, battles, rainbows, pains, etc. Each entity behaves in a complex and characteristic way which, though conforming to a pattern, constantly reveals new and surprising features and thus cannot be captured in a formula; it affects, and is affected by other entities and processes constituting a rich and varied universe" (Feyerabend 2001: 10). These "practically effective forms of life" can be seen as *practical ontologies* (Gad, Jensen, and Winthereik 2015), relational and transformable worlds made of such diverse things as rainbows and Gods, pains and dreams. While Feyerabend studiously avoids listing scientific or technological entities, it is clear that they *also* comprise spreadsheets, tractors, Fourier transformations, and microelectronics. If Feyerabend refrained from mentioning these kinds of things, it was probably because, contrary to dreams and spirits, their importance generally goes without saying.

Whether generated from massive dams or solar panels, energy is clearly also an ontological element, articulated with other elements in complicated, patterned ways. Some patterns appear so stable that analysts from the philosopher Manuel DeLanda (1998: 31) to the politician and solar energy activist Hermann Scheer (2004, 2012) speak of different "general energy distribution systems." Doing so, they describe decentralized, locally produced and exchanged forms of energy as starkly opposed to centralized systems that depend on complex processes of extraction and long supply chains. Yet even within this general dichotomous pattern, we might find surprises, not easily captured, as Paul Feyerabend wrote, "in a formula" (2001: 10).

Complementing Feyerabend's interest in the variety of practically effective forms of life, Vinciane Despret (2004) argues that novel experience depends on how we allow different kinds of new entities to enter our worlds. The importance of such new entities has everything to do with how we become able and willing to "attribute to [them] the power" to change us (58). Resonating with Gordillo's (this volume) characterization of infrastructures as affective assemblages, Despret's formulation encourages exploration of what solar energy might make us do. Far from a passive relation, it indicates that the capacity of solar energy to change established energy infrastructures depends both on an active imagination *and* on the active pursuance of new forms of materialization.

As Hetherington (2014: 198) suggests, such processes of affective-material transformation mark moments when people become "enrolled in a community of aspiration" (see Carse, this volume). Now, in reality, the Cambodian solar community of aspiration remains tiny, and it has hardly led to any durable infrastructural change. Yet, rather than taking this actual situation as a solid fact, I use it as a vantage point for querying what it might take to get *out of it*. In the following, accordingly, I am interested in how to move from a description of present realities to a mode of redescription that *opens toward* alternative futures that would thrive on new attitudes, imaginations, and actions pertaining to solar energy. It is precisely due to a keen awareness that the odds are *in reality* stacked against such alternative futures (see also Wakefield and Braun this volume) that I find this ethnographic-conceptual movement so important.

Hydroelectric Promises and Threats

When the Russei Chrum Krom River hydropower dam opened in January 2015, it was graced by the presence of Cambodian prime minister, Hun Sen, and the Chinese ambassador Bu Jianguo. China's official news agency, Xinhua, reported that the dam would provide a reliable source of energy to a nation desperately in need.[4] The 338-megawatt dam, stated the chairman of the China Huadian Corporation, was a historical milestone of economic collaboration between China and Cambodia. The Cambodian minister of mines and energy, Suy Sem, explained that electricity "will be sold to the state-owned Electricity of Cambodia at the price of 7.35 US cents per kilowatt-hour." He estimated it would lead to annual tax revenues of $12.5 million.

These kinds of promises have not gone unchallenged. The NGO *International Rivers* argues that all the planned dams will still only be able to deliver 6–8 percent of the projected regional power demand by 2025. Analysts and commentators, such as David Roberts writing in the *New York Times*, noted that only about 10 percent of the power from the eleven projected dams on the Lower Mekong will flow into the households and businesses of Laos and Cambodia. Most, instead, will be exported to "energy-hungry" Thailand, Vietnam, and China.[5] In its envisioned future capacity as a massive exporter of energy, Laotian minister of industry and commerce, Nam Viyaketh, has advertised Laos as "the battery of Southeast Asia."[6]

Responding to the "battery narrative," according to which Lower Mekong dams "will create a cash windfall that will open the doors to rapid development," *International Rivers* observed that "revenue does not automatically lead to economic progress."[7] Instead, "Much of the revenue will disappear as it travels from the dams to the Lao people. Laos lacks the institutions and capacity needed to manage the revenue effectively, and its government suffers from rampant corruption. Laos lacks a strong civil society and media to independently monitor how the money is spent. The Lao government has provided little information on how it intends to spend the revenue to improve people's lives. As with past hydropower projects in Laos, it is unlikely that the poorest Lao citizens living near the dams will see the benefits."

Further, whereas "energy security and economic development are legitimate goals," as David Roberts writes, the dams generally have been "conceived with little regard for their environmental consequences and socioeconomic repercussions. The proposed dams will prevent sediment from the upper stretches of the Mekong River from reaching its delta, depriving rice fields in lower Vietnam of essential nutrients. They will also disrupt the migratory patterns of fish, which will endanger the stocks on which Cambodians, especially, rely for much of their protein intake."[8] Clearly, Mekong dams are profoundly ambivalent and controversial sites. They thrive on promises of energy wealth, but *whose* wealth is disputed. They promise to bring metaphorical and electrical light to villages presently submerged in darkness, thus conjuring a particular public, yet there is little clarity about the costs of this illumination. Not least, their cumulative effect on innumerable plants, fish, and animals, from upstream Lancang to the southern delta, is also unpredictable, though the prediction that there *will be* massive effects is fairly certain.

Environmental organizations such as International Rivers, the 3S Rivers Network, and World Wildlife Fund stand together in opposition to these developments. Thus, Carl Middleton, the Mekong Program Coordinator with International Rivers, has argued that "Cambodia's free flowing rivers and abundant natural resources are invaluable assets, the health of which are vital to the well-being of Cambodia's rural population . . . . Poorly conceived hydropower development could irreparably damage these resources and undermine Cambodia's sustainable development."[9]

That is the risk inherent in development projects such as the ones taking place in the Central Cardamom Protected Forest, and the Sambor Dam planned for the Mekong mainstream. Alongside the Don Sahong Dam presently being built just on the Laotian side of the Laos-Cambodia border, the latter may accelerate the extinction of the threatened population of river dolphins (known throughout Southeast Asia as Irrawaddy dolphins) already looming on the horizon. Meanwhile EarthRights International also object to development plans for the Lower Se San 2 Dam, claiming not only that it has used coercion and intimidation against villagers to get them to agree with resettlement plans but also that it will reduce fish biomass by more than 9 percent across the entire Mekong River basin and Tonlé Sap Lake.[10]

"Then Who Will Do It for Cambodia?"

In July 2014, the diplomat Sim Vireak, stationed with the Royal Cambodian Embassy in Tokyo, responded to the overwhelmingly negative attention drawn by Cambodian dam development.[11] Writing in *The Diplomat* that the two key negative issues appeared to be "overdependence on Chinese investment" and a "relatively disproportionate focus on the environmental impacts of hydroelectric power," Vireak suggested that critics consider why Cambodia so inordinately relies on Chinese money. Japan, the biggest Cambodian donor, he noted, has not made hydroelectric investments since 1992, when they began providing official development assistance (ODA) to the country. Effectively, he argued, Cambodia is driven into the arms of China by the reluctance of other countries to invest.

Vireak drew attention to previous "bitter experiences for the Japanese government," such as the Indian Narmada Dam, and the Indonesian Koto Panjang Dam project. He ventured that it is fear of getting embroiled in similar controversies that has prompted the Japanese, as others, to stay away. Instead, he noted, the Japanese, Germans, Australians, and French involve themselves in "less sensitive projects such as electricity transmission and distribution systems."

However, he persisted, for there to be any electricity to distribute it must be generated somewhere. Presently, Cambodia relies on import of around 60 percent of its electricity, and prices are among the most expensive in the region. That situation is unsustainable, wrote Vireak, both in terms of national security and in terms of attracting international investors. The dilemma, as he described it, is that international companies locating their factories in Special Economic Zones suffer from the inflated price level and unstable supply of electricity, which thereby becomes a major bottleneck for getting more investors. In this situation, hydroelectric power generation holds significant Cambodian appeal not only due to its zero carbon footprint but also because of its cost effectiveness.

No matter the care taken in building such dams, wrote Vireak, environmental and social impacts cannot altogether be avoided. Yet, hydroelectric power is presently more a "need" than a "want" for Cambodia; and paradoxically it is a need especially in light of the need to attract foreign investments from countries, such as Japan, that refuse to get their own hands dirty. "If China does not do it," he asked, "then who will do it for Cambodia?"

The deputy executive director of the Cambodian NGO Forum, Ngy San, has insisted that "Cambodia has many choices for meeting . . . [its] electricity needs including renewable and decentralized energy options that must be explored."[12] Such alternative choices, however, received scant attention in Vireak's formula, which depicted hydroelectric dams as the core component in an upgraded Cambodia electricity network. While recognizing that biofuels, wind, and solar energy are an option for "small-scale generation," he emphasized the instability and cost of these energy forms, due to which they are not particularly attractive to the government. Comparing the situation with experiences elsewhere, he wrote that "some advanced economies have been trying to introduce these alternative energies, but successes have been modest despite enormous investments."[13]

One of the world's leading advocates of renewable energy until his death in 2010, the German politician and outspoken solar energy activist Hermann Scheer wrote of his experiences with introducing the potentials of renewable energy to leading energy experts in Cambodia's neighboring country, Vietnam. While they were all familiar with nuclear power, he reported, even in the new millennium their knowledge about renewable energy remained "at a level typical of the 1970s" (2012: 60). Whether or not this is also the case for Cambodian officials in 2015, Vireak certainly underestimated the inroads alternative energy sources have made in "advanced countries" such as Germany and Denmark, which, contrary to Cambodia, do not have year-round exposure to sunshine.

It is difficult to disagree with Scheer's assertion that it is "paradoxical that renewable energy, with its minimal external effects, is more expensive on the energy markets than our conventional energies with their high social costs" (2012: 75).[14] To resolve this paradox, Scheer argued for the necessity of completely overhauling modern energy infrastructures. Most generally, he was adamant that treating energy as a topic detached from broader social issues is an "intellectual illusion" (Jagger 2012: xii). The premise of Scheer's envisioned radical transformation, which he referred to as "100% renewable now," was thus the necessity of simultaneously democratizing and decentralizing energy systems (Jagger 2012: xiii). He further proposed to redefine the social and environmental costs of different types of energy production as embedded elements "in a social market economy" (Scheer 2012: 75).

Yet as shown by the difficulties Scheer faced in promoting his vision—even at home in Germany—there are many obstacles to such a transition. They are not diminished once one travels to Southeast Asia.

For one thing, drastic changes to energy systems are made practically difficult by the materiality of existing infrastructures and the limited resources available. For another, as exemplified by Vireak's analysis, they are also impeded by the reliance on formulaic tropes and narratives about hydropower and solar energy's respective economic and social consequences. Certainly, the practical feasibility of renewable energy on a grand scale in Cambodia presently looks bleak and *unrealistic*.

Yet, as Hermann Scheer wrote, "If analysis of the current situation indicates that the limited opportunities to act do not provide an adequate answer to the real challenges we face, then we need a different understanding of realism, one aimed at changing the parallelogram of forces to increase the room for maneuver" (Scheer 2012: 12). Rather than lose courage when faced with an apparently insurmountable *wall of reality*—in Cambodia taking the material shape of massive dams—Scheer thus insisted that such situations required a *redefinition of realism* that would make climbing the wall feasible. Writing that "the problem is not what is 'real' and what is not," but rather what occurs, and what can be *made to occur*, Feyerabend (2001: 10) would concur.

To create an appetite for what can be made to occur, it is necessary to search for Feyerabend's *surprises* within general patterns and to tease out Scheer's *room for maneuver* at the margins of established energy landscapes.

Emergent Patterns

Cambodian politicians and diplomats repeat the well-worn argument that solar energy is unsustainable, at best a small supplement to the electricity gains they hope to make via large-scale infrastructure projects. Yet, while Sim Vireak, the diplomat, looked abroad and found only modest success in spite of enormous investments, Scheer highlighted significant accomplishments in Germany and Northern Europe.

While Scheer was not speaking about the dangers of cascading dams for the Mekong Delta, but rather about those of the fossil economy for the global climate, his general conclusion is relevant: "The apologists of the fossil global economy justify their failure to make even half-hearted progress along this road with an equally tired fossil of an argument: in a world of global competition, the 'luxury' of concern for the environment must be earned through further conventional economic growth. This economic philosophy is in reality a necrosophy—the wisdom of death" (2004: 138).

In critiquing this "necrosophy," Scheer found enormous potential in solar energy, which he argued would quickly be able to outcompete conventional energy sources. Present achievements were only more impressive, he insisted, given that they had barely been subsidized, and had happened despite violent opposition from the established energy industry, including most politicians.

In 1970, Buckminster Fuller posited miniaturization as a general law of technology. "All the technical curves rise in tonnage and volumetric size to reach a giant peak," Fuller wrote, "after which miniaturization sets in. After that a more economic art takes over which also goes through the same cycle of doing progressively more with less" (1970: 73). Four decades later Scheer drew much the same conclusion, offering a formulation that might well have been about Cambodian energy politics: "We only take large seriously—a *large* project, a *large* power-plant—rather than the many small initiatives, even if their joint effect is greater" (2012: 82). Yet, he continued, when it comes to energy, small is profitable (Scheer 2012: 106, referencing Lovins 2002). Although the potentials remain vastly underestimated, a "whole spectrum of new possibilities for generating electricity [is] being opened up by photovoltaics" (Scheer 2012: 105).

From this point of view, the question is not whether but *how* existing, massive, centralized energy infrastructures can be dismantled, not whether but *how* new energy infrastructures can be shaped. Following the sociologist Oskar Negt, Scheer (2012: 110) described this is as a matter of "'sociological fantasy and learning from example': An increasing number of 'best practice' examples develop into a widespread social movement."

Although they do not presently add up to much, one can find quite a few small-scale renewable energy initiatives in Cambodia. Since 2009, the Energy and Environment Partnership with the Mekong Region, funded by the Nordic Development Fund and the Finnish Ministry of Foreign Affairs, has funded thirty-nine pilot projects. Choosing projects that hold promise to "catalyze further public and private financing in renewable energy and energy efficiency investments in the region," the partnership has supported pilots on topics such as "Solar Powered Drinking Power in Kampot Province" and the making of an "Energy Self-Sufficiency Village."[15] Taking another route, some small projects have been funded by charity fundraising websites such as *GlobalGiving*.[16] In conjunction, they illustrate an endeavor to create "a new energy mix" (Agustoni and Maretti 2012: 400).

For Alfredo Agustoni and Mara Maretti such new mixes promise not only to impact "society in terms of lifestyles and consumption patterns," but potentially to introduce "new balances in the democratic system" (400). Given the stronghold of the Cambodian People's Party on the Cambodian political system, it stretches the imagination to think that renewable pilot projects such as the ones just mention will add up to any general "re-balancing," however desirable it would be. They can nevertheless be seen as ontological experiments with future infrastructures *in miniature*.

At this point, we can return to Feyerabend's (2001: 169) argument that there is an illusory quality to experiments with new configurations of reality, precisely because they have not yet solidified into a stable pattern—like a durable infrastructure. Yet, it is *also* due to this very "illusory" quality that experiments, like solar pilot projects, can operate as test sites for alternative energy futures (Jensen 2010: 31–51; Jensen and Winthereik 2015). In the aggregate, they may eventually gather force to push existing energy infrastructures into new configurations.

That possibility, which is, of course, far from a *certainty*, gains a modicum of plausibility once it is recognized that it is not only NGOs and well-intentioned Western crowdfunders that find potentials in Cambodian sunlight. Rather, a growing number of solar energy companies, such as Star8, with which I began this chapter, are trying to raise the bar of expectations.

Writing for altenergymag.com, NRG Solutions point out that "As Cambodia is located in one of the sunniest areas of the world, solar power provides an excellent solution to the reduction in kerosene use: it's safe; reliable; and easy to use."[17] Repeating the observation that only 25 percent of the Cambodian population is connected to the centralized grid, leaving more than 10 million of people in the countryside without regular access to electricity, the article depicts a strategy that centers on "building networks of entrepreneurs," extending "their reach deeper into the remote rural areas where solar can make the most difference." Thus, for example, NRG Solutions aims to establish a solar distribution network in Kampong Thom Province that, in connection with a local microfinance institution, will offer: "custom designed 'Solar-Loan' products," via a "'Solar Shop' which will act as the management hub and will host training, stock, awareness raising, and the all-important service technicians." Contrary to export-oriented companies such as Star8, NRG Solutions is at least thinking about how to reach the elusive rural end user (cf. Wilhite 2013: 61). As I continue to discuss, however, Star8, too, seems up to more than simply extracting cheap labor.

Here Comes the Sun?

I began this chapter by describing a conversation with manager of Star8, stopping at the very moment it dawned upon me that most of the company's solar products were unlikely to be for local consumption. Similar to its neighboring garment factories, the main attraction of Cambodia seemed to be its low wages and unregulated working conditions. Let me now pick up where I left this story.

Trying to get a better sense of the situation, I press on: "Who do you think will be the buyers of the solar panels for housing?" Not at all evasive, the manager answers that it makes most sense for factories to acquire them, but there might also be a market for wealthy households. The plot thickens. Certainly, Star8's strategies are very different from the visions of local empowerment that propel NRG Solutions or the Energy and Environment Partnership. Yet, just at the point where I am ready to conclude that this is indeed nothing but exploitation in yet a new guise, the manager begins telling me about efforts to lobby the minister of the environment.

In his mid-thirties, His Excellency Say Samal is the youngest of the Cambodian ministers. Having lived in Melbourne for a decade, gone to high school, and received his university degree there, the minister is often seen to exemplify a new generation of politicians. Star8 talks to him because he "has a somewhat broader view," which is especially important since "there are many layers in Cambodian ministries and politics."

One aspect of this lobbying focuses on the use of buses in Phnom Penh and Siem Reap, home of the Angkor Wat temples, as showcases for the potentials of Cambodian solar energy. Reaching a point where this could be considered even a possibility has been a battle. As the manager explains: "Most of them knew nothing about solar power. I was asked by officials what would happen at night when the sun isn't shining. It was so dumb."[18]

Another dimension of lobbying, described by the manager as simultaneously strategic and educational, has to do with convincing government officials that solar energy is a supplement, rather than a threat, to their existing plans for national energy development. Presently, Cambodia imports more than 60 percent of its energy, so an addition of solar energy to the national grid would hardly *steal* anything from the Chinese dams. Slowly, I am told, the message that "whatever is generated by solar energy is in addition to the Cambodian grid" is starting to be understood. Officials are beginning to get that "it is simply electricity the country won't need to pay Thailand and Vietnam for."

I pursue the question of Star8's vision for Cambodian solar energy development over the next decade. The manager responds that he hopes Southeast Asian countries in general will become frontrunners of renewable energy. Just this moment, he is on the way to the Manila office, where things are quickly moving in that direction, after the Philippine government placed a huge order for solar lighting and transportation.

"When this becomes a success" (there is no "if"), the manager says—as he throws on his jacket and hurries out the door—"we will be able to say: see, they did it, and look how well it works: no pollution, no problems, and it doesn't take forever like building a dam!"

After the abrupt ending to my interview, the Hungarian guide takes me on a tour of the facilities, narrating the solar possibilities imagined by the company as we go. He proudly explains that the whole building is off-grid and generates more electricity than it needs, so the surplus is sold to the nearby electricity plant. However, off-grid electricity production and use are basic to all Star8 products. Tapping into naturally available sunshine, these products allow people to tap into *them*, feeding energy to devices or keeping it stored for later use.

In the main hall, dozens of solar vehicles are on display. There are solar-powered buses in various sizes, including those that might soon drive the roads of Phnom Penh and Siem Reap. There are solar *tuk-tuks* (three-wheel taxis), which, at a cost of $2,600–$2,800, are only a few hundred dollars more expensive than regular gasoline-powered ones. There is also a solar-powered *moto* with panels crammed onto every conceivable space. The hope is that these product lines will begin to take off, especially following the Philippine government order. But electric tuk-tuks and motos have a bright future not only in Southeast Asia, but everywhere where sun is abundant: South Asia, Africa, Central America. Certainly, this is a future that also seems to hold some commercial appeal. Coming in many shapes and colors, the vehicles are covered by Maggi, Nestle, and Coca Cola logos.

At the end of the tour, we go to the parking lot. Proudly showing a truck plugged in to collect energy from solar panels on the roof, the guide turns around and points to a small walkway in front of the main building. It, too, is made entirely of solar panels. "Step on it," he says. "See—it's very strong."

"You know what our big plan is?" he asks. "We want to put these panels all along the road between Phnom Penh and Sihanoukville." That's a 220-kilometer stretch. Smiling broadly, he continues: "The road itself would generate electricity enough for all the villages along the way and for half of Phnom Penh! An amazing thought."

"I first came here in 1993," the guide goes on. "I have lived in Phnom Penh for 18 years; this is the place for me. I have only worked for Star8 for two months. But this is special. It is big. I love working here, because this is the future."

Experimenting with Cambodian Energy Infrastructures

As noted, scholars have pointed to a fundamental discrepancy between centralized and decentralized energy systems. Thus, Hermann Scheer wrote that "the transition to renewable energy is also inevitably a conflict between two energy systems" (2012: 48), and John Urry (2014: 4, see also Wittfogel 1957) linked centralized energy systems and despotism. In the Cambodian context, where the fragility and centralization of democracy and electricity are comparable, the diagnosis seems apt. Despite the attempts of NGOs and companies such as Star8, government interest in solar energy is presently limited and a market barely exists. In the formula for national development, hydropower dams are seen to be the key, or only, variable.

In this context, Feyerabend's (2001: xi) "ontological consideration" that "worldviews interact with Being in a mutually creating fashion" is important, since it entails that "we do affect and shape 'reality.'" As Feyerabend's emphasis on "mutual creation" makes clear, this is not an argument for any rarefied kind of social construction, as if the materiality of water, sun, or cement could be ignored. Indeed, Feyerabend made explicit his keen attention to material effects by pointing to many "situations that endanger human life and that have to be dealt with." Yet he insisted that such situations are the more dangerous precisely because people tend to rely on imaginations that "'block off' what disturbs them" (2001: 4). In the context of Cambodian energy infrastructures, such "blockage" takes the form of formulaic rejections of renewable energy, not to mention of the environmental and social threats of cascading dams, in the name of short-term economic and security interests.

Even as I have tried to elucidate the capture of energy imaginations by this rigid formula, the central ambition of the chapter has not been critical. Instead, I have suggested that if one hopes to create a chance for the emergence of alternative energy infrastructures amid these grim realities, taking "an experimental attitude towards reality" (DeLanda 1998: 273) may be necessary. Thus, I have aimed to "destratify" (274) Cambodian energy reality as *it is*, in order to strengthen the capacity of sunlight for entering collective imagination and practice, opening up to what *could be*.

At this point, we can return one final time to the many-colored solar building of Star8. On the one hand, it is manifest that the success of the company depends on access to cheap labor in Cambodia and elsewhere, and on export of its high-end products. On the other hand, however, Star8 also depends on promoting an image of Cambodia as a test site, which would testify to the transformative potentials of solar energy. Working in this direction, Star8 could be characterized as aiming to prove wrong in practice what Hermann Scheer referred to as "the spurious argument that no one benefits when one country forges ahead" (2012: 50).

Among other things, this would depend on the slim possibility of getting actual solar buses and motos on the streets of Phnom Penh and Siem Reap. Even if the company obviously acts with a view to securing its own market position, it might thus be seen as *also* trying to create a room for maneuver for the making of alternative Cambodian energy futures. Rather than cynically exploitative, it could even be described as idealistic, if not naive. At the same time, my very pointing to this interpretive possibility may suggest to skeptical readers that the same terms also apply to the present argument.

As I see it, however, there is no single answer to the question of whether Star8 is cynical, naive, or both. I also do not think that determining the company's motives is the most pressing ethnographic task. For after all, as Muehlmann (this volume) notes, infrastructures that are "ostensibly built for one purpose, can be used for a secondary purpose." What matters, given the infrastructural propensity to "double," if not multiply, is finding within existing patterns the room for maneuver that makes future repurposing possible.

Such repurposing might be seen as part of the functionalist thinking critically examined by Ballestero (this volume). Yet the ease with which we can critique functionalist thinking does not subtract from the fact that infrastructures are only built in the first place because they are imagined to serve functions. Rather than rejecting the importance of function out of hand, it is important to recognize the historical emergence and variability of particular infrastructural functions. We do not yet know, for example what the "functions" of solar energy will turn out to be, either for Star8, for the Cambodian ministry of environment, for Phnom Penh tuk-tuk drivers, or for the rural population, since they will be the outcome of current infrastructural experiments.

Such, at least, has been the experimental gambit of this chapter, which has aimed to cultivate a response and disposition to solar energy futures that is equidistant from hype and critique. Such cultivation, I have suggested, is a matter of whetting an appetite for improbable, but not impossible, solar futures, giving them the chance, at least, to inhabit us, to become "preferred ways of relating to the world and to ourselves" (Despret 2004: 58).

Notes

1 FS-UNEP Collaborating Centre for Climate and Sustainable Energy Finance, 2015, Global Trends in Renewable Energy Investment 2015, accessed May 6, 2015, http://fs-unep-centre.org/publications/global-trends-renewable-energy -investment-2015.

2 Tiếng Việt, "The Lower Mekong Factsheet Text," March 28, 2013, accessed March 24, 2015, http://www.internationalrivers.org/resources/the-lower-mekong -dams-factsheet-text-7908.

3 The archetypical example is perhaps Jawaharlal Nehru's passion for dams.

4 Tian Shaohui, "Cambodia Sees Greater Electricity Supply after Chinese-Built 338MW Dam Begins Operations," January 12, 2015, Xinhua News, accessed March 24, 2015, http://news.xinhuanet.com/english/china/2015-01/12/c_1339 13817.htm.

5 David Roberts, "No More Dams on the Mekong," September 3, 2014, New York Times, accessed March 24, 2015, http://www.nytimes.com/2014/09/04/opinion /no-more-dams-on-the-mekong.html?_r=0.

6 Jared Ferrie, "Laos Turns to Hydropower to Be 'Asia's Battery,'" July 2, 2010, Christian Science Monitor, accessed March 24, 2015, http://www.csmonitor.com /World/Asia-Pacific/2010/0702/Laos-turns-to-hydropower-to-be-Asia-s-battery.

7 Tiếng Việt, "The Lower Mekong Factsheet Text," March 28, 2013, accessed March 24, 2015, http://www.internationalrivers.org/resources/the-lower-mekong -dams-factsheet-text-7908.

8 David Roberts, "No More Dams on the Mekong."

9 Foreningen for internasjonale vannstudier, "New Report Urges Better Energy Planning in Cambodia before Hydropower Dams are Developed," n.d., accessed March 24, 2015, http://www.fivas.org/sider/tekst.asp?side=192.

10 Ame Trandem, Maureen Harris, Meach Mean, and Ith Mathoura, "Human Rights Concerns over Hydropower Development in Cambodia Brought to the UN," January 2015, 12, accessed March 24, 2015, http://www.earthrights.org/media /human-rights-concerns-over-hydropower-development-cambodia-brought-un.

11 Sim Vireak, "Cambodia's Hydroelectric Question: China Power and the Environment," July 30, 2014, *The Diplomat*, accessed March 24, 2015, http://thediplomat .com/2014/07/cambodias-hydroelectric-question-china-power-and-the -environment/.

12 Foreningen for internasjonale vannstudier, "New Report Urges Better Energy Planning in Cambodia before Hydropower Dams are Developed," n.d., accessed March 24, 2015, http://www.fivas.org/sider/tekst.asp?side=192.

13 Sim Vireak. "Cambodia's Hydroelectric Question: China Power and the Environment," July 30, 2014, *The Diplomat*, accessed March 24, 2015, http://thediplomat .com/2014/07/cambodias-hydroelectric-question-china-power-and-the -environment/.

14 Masco (this volume) recalls that at the end of Jimmy Carter's presidency in 1980: "the U.S. national laboratory system was spending over 50 percent of its funds on alternative energy research." Carter also installed solar panels on the White House, which were promptly removed by Ronald Reagan. Even at this center of power, alternative energy histories have previously been in the making.

15 Energy and Environment Partnership with the Mekong Region. "EEP Mekong at a Glance," n.d., accessed May 6, 2015, http://www.eepmekong.org/about_us/eep _overview.php?reload.

16 GlobalGiving, "Renewable Energy for 15 Rural Cambodian Families," n.d., accessed May 6, 2015, https://www.globalgiving.org/projects/biogas-renewable-energy-for -15-rural-cambodian-families/updates/?subid=18418.

17 NRG Solutions, "Empowering Cambodia with Solar Lighting," November 15, 2013, Altenergymag.com, accessed May 6, 2015, http://www.altenergymag.com /content.php?post_type=2173.

18 Storage of solar and wind energy is indeed a central problem for scaling up the use of these forms of renewable energy, and much effort goes into technical innovation and improvement. At present, solar energy generated off-grid is usually stored in a local battery bank.

TEN. The Crisis in Crisis

JOSEPH MASCO

If you tune in to the mass-mediated frequency of crisis today, it quickly becomes overwhelming. News of infectious disease outbreaks (Ebola, antibiotic-resistant illnesses, measles outbreaks among purposefully unvaccinated children); wars in the Middle East, Africa, and Eastern Europe as well as new stages in the multigenerational US campaigns against drugs and terror; talk of a new Cold War between the US and Russia, or maybe one with China; the elimination of privacy to surveillance programs (run by both corporations and the security state); financial contagions; fears of economic collapse; and new extremes in global inequality; species die-offs on an unprecedented scale; mega-drought, mega-snow, mega-cold, mega-heat; proliferating toxicities and corruptions; racialized violence (state-driven, terroristic, individual); stand-your-ground laws; ocean acidification; the near-eternal longevity of plastics, peak oil, peak water, "smogocaplyse" in China; arms races (nuclear, biological, cyber)—the everyday reporting of crisis proliferates across subjects, spaces, and temporalities today and is an ever-amplifying media refrain.

This raises an important historical question about how and why crisis has come to be so dominant in our media cultures. On any given issue—disease, finance, war, or the environment—there are specific historical moments more violent than today. Yet, the configuration of the future as an unraveling, a slide into greater and greater degrees of structural chaos across finance, war, and the environment prevails in our mass media. In the United States, a 24/7 media universe offers up endangerment on a vast range of scales, making it so ever present as to dull consumer senses. The power of crisis to shock, and thus mobilize, is diminishing due to narrative saturation, overuse, and a lack of well-articulated positive futurities to balance stories of end-times. Put differently, if we were to remove crisis talk from our public speech today, what would remain? And if crisis is now an ever-present, near-permanent negative "surround," as Turner (2013) might put it, what has happened to a normative, noncrisis-riven everyday life, not to mention the conditions of possibility for positive futurisms?

In short, there is a crisis in crisis today, one that I think is diagnostic of twenty-first-century American capitalism. The United States exists in a structural contradiction, one drawn from being both a democracy and an imperially inclined superpower: since the 1980s, the federal government has increasingly exchanged domestic welfare programs for mass incarceration and permanent war rewriting the social contract in foundational ways. The infrastructures of everyday security—employment, environmental safety, justice—are no longer the primary goals of a state that relies on warfare and free markets to engineer the future. The resulting uncertainty, as well as endangerment of existing infrastructures across health, welfare, and economy, creates new forms of emerging and predictable violence that "crisis talk" attempts to manage.

This chapter examines American sensibilities about crisis, seeking to historicize and critique the collapsing of a more robust political sphere into the singular language of crisis. Crisis is, in the first instance, an affect-generating idiom, one that seeks to mobilize radical endangerment to foment collective attention and action. As Janet Roitman (2014: 82) writes in her extended study of the term, crisis is "an observation that produces meaning" by initiating critique within a given condition. It is thus a predominantly conservative modality, seeking to stabilize an existing structure within a radically contingent world. As social theorists as diverse as Reinhart Koselleck (2004), Susan Buck-Morss (2002), and David Scott (2014) have also noted, crisis and utopia have structured the modernist Euro-American project of social engineering, constituting a future caught between a narrative of collapse and one of constant improvement (see also Benhabib 1986). The language of collective social improvement has all but disappeared from political debates in the US over the last generation, a victim of a postwelfare state mentality and neoliberal economics. "Progress" is no longer tied to collective social conditions (for example, the elimination of poverty) but increasingly restricted to the boom and bust of markets and changes in consumer technology product cycles. Jonathan Crary (2013: 9) attributes the current "suspension of living" to a 24/7, always-on media and work environment, one that foments a new kind of temporality that increasingly disallows fantasies about improved collective conditions while recruiting increasing indifference to the structural violence supporting this economy.

In the twenty-first century, information technologies offer perhaps the most immediate and available sense of radical change, a sign of how far the social engineering through state planning of the twentieth century has contracted into the market engineering of consumer desires. Technological revolution in consumer electronics is now constant, creating a new kind of technosocial space marked by consumer anticipations of ever improving informational capacities and a continual transformation in the commodity form. Consider the social effects of the major communication revolutions of the past twenty years in the US—the internet, social media, and the smartphone—each of which has been integrated into everyday American life with astonishing speed and ubiquity. This experience of "revolution" in the marketplace is, however, matched by a formal political culture that is theatrically gridlocked at the national level, unable to constitute significant policy on issues of collective endangerment across the domains of finance, war, and the environment. Moreover, policy failure in each of these domains over the past generation has not produced a radical reassessment of supporting assumptions or institutions. Even as shifting information technologies secure an experience of radical structural change in every life today, formal political processes perform being unable to imagine even minor shifts in existing logics or practices, despite financial collapse, military failure, and environmental disaster. Thus, while communication has never been easier, and information about matters of collective concern never more abundant, the media spaces crafted for always-on information systems deliver largely negative portraits of the present and future.

There is, in other words, a steady invitation in American media worlds to fear the future and to reject the power of human agency to modulate even those systems crafted by industry, finance, or the security state. This marks the arrival of a new kind of governance, one based not on eliminating fears through the protective actions of the security apparatus but rather on the amplification of public dangers through inaction. It also produces a suicidal form of governance, one that cannot respond to long-standing collective dangers (for example, climate change), while generating new ones (such as the poisoning of the public water system in Flint, Michigan, in 2014 by emergency managers seeking cost savings; see also the chapter by Anand, this volume). The affective circuit of the counterterror state, for example, privileges images of catastrophic future events over such everyday violences, multiplying fears of the future while allowing everyday structural insecurities to remain unaddressed (Masco 2014). Peter Sloterdijk has suggested that the resulting psychic agitation is one important effect of a globalized economy (Sloterdijk and Heinrichs 2011: 82): "This has progressed to such an extent that those who do not make themselves continuously available for synchronous stress seem asocial. Excitability is now the foremost duty of all citizens. This is why we no longer need military service. What is required is the general theme of duty, that is to say, a readiness to play your role as a conductor of excitation for collective, opportunist psychoses." This is to say that crisis-talk serves a wide range of psychosocial purposes, creating across the domains of finance, war, and the environment an ever-expanding invitation to engage the future through negative affects. Thus, the American public can simultaneously know the US to be an unrivaled military-economic-scientific superpower, a state with unprecedented capacities, agencies, and resources, and yet feel powerless in the face of failed US military, financial, and environmental commitments. The lack of investment in infrastructure (across health, welfare, and the environment) means that everyday conditions are actually deteriorating, despite American wealth, military power, and scientific expertise. Instead of the crisis/utopia circuit that empowered the high modernist culture of the mid-twentieth century, we now have a crisis/paralysis circuit, a marker of a greatly reduced political horizon in the United States.

I am interested in this lack of political agency for those living within a hyperpower state, and wish to interrogate it via a conceptual and historical assessment of the two linked existential dangers of our time: nuclear crisis and climate crisis. Existential danger makes a claim on being the ultimate form of crisis—a mode of collective endangerment that has historically worked in the era of nation-states to define the boundaries of the community and focus the responsibilities of government. To evoke an existential danger is to call on the full powers of the state and society in the name of self-preservation. In the current moment of counterterror, financial instability, and climate change, the call to existential danger no longer functions exclusively in this way. Indeed, existential dangers are now being crafted and enhanced by both state action and inaction. After fifteen years of counterterror and geopolitical misrecognitions over weapons of mass destruction, the US nuclear complex is promoting a program to rebuild the entire US nuclear triad of bombers, missiles, and submarines and arm them with new nuclear weapons designs. Similarly, through new drilling technologies and a suspension of regulatory oversight, the US is now poised to become the world's largest energy producer by 2020—the world's number 1 petrochemical state—even as earth scientists detail the catastrophic planetary effects of releasing all that carbon from the ground. Thus, the existential security challenges of our time are not being met with programmatic efforts to move out of nuclear or petrochemical economies in the name of collective security. Rather than committing to new security and energy infrastructures, and with them generating a new geopolitics (see Clark 2014), the US is committing ever more deeply to the most well-known and collectively dangerous industrial activities.

In what follows, I interrogate the media politics around the signing of the Limited Test Ban Treaty of 1963—the first arms control agreement as well as the first environmental treaty—to consider an alternate era of crisis management. I then turn to contemporary climate science, interrogating the terms of America's current petro-state strategy. In each case, I consider how existential danger is mobilized via mass media as a collective crisis, and consider the conditions of possibility for a radical reconsideration of the terms of everyday life. Put differently, the "crisis in crisis" today marks a new political modality that can experience repeated failure as well as totalizing external danger without generating the need for structural change. "Crisis," in other words, has become a counterrevolutionary force in the twenty-first century, a call to confront collective endangerment that instead increasingly articulates the very limits of the political.

The Nuclear Danger

The period between the Soviet launch of the first artificial Earth satellite on October 4, 1957, and the signing of the Limited Test Ban Treaty (LTBT) on August 5, 1963, witnessed geopolitical and environmental crises of an astonishing range, scale, and scope: in addition to the building of the Berlin Wall, the Bay of Pigs invasion, and the Cuban Missile Crisis, the US and USSR waged fierce proxy wars in Latin America, Africa, the Middle East, and Southeast Asia. A voluntary nuclear test moratorium between the two powers in the years 1959–1960 ended suddenly in 1961, with 59 Soviet nuclear tests. The following year, the Soviets detonated an additional 79 nuclear devices, while the US exploded 96. Between the two weapons programs, this amounts to a nuclear detonation every other day for the calendar year of 1962. The speed and ferocity of nuclear detonations in 1962 belie a scientific research program, becoming instead a global theater of nuclear messaging, establishing a US and Soviet commitment to nuclear war. Most of these explosions were conducted in the atmosphere. After the atomic bombing of Hiroshima and Nagasaki in 1945, this makes 1962 probably the most dangerous year in the first two decades of the nuclear age. In addition to narrowly avoiding a nuclear war that would have destroyed North America, Europe, and much of Asia inside a few minutes of conflict (see Rosenberg and Moor 1981–1982; Scott 2014), the nuclear-testing programs were a substantial disaster for the global environment. Each of these nuclear "tests" was a planetary ecological event, one that destroyed local ecosystems and sent radioactive fallout high into the stratosphere, where it circled the earth. Aboveground nuclear explosions distributed contamination to every living being on the planet in the mid-twentieth century to a degree that is still measurable today (Masco 2006: 302).

The year 1962 thus stands as a superlative year of "crisis" in the nuclear age, involving a war fought via "test" programs and covert actions around the world that nearly became a planetary inferno. By 1962, it was well understood that aboveground nuclear explosions were a major environmental and public health risk. Beginning a decade earlier with the first hydrogen bomb tests in the Pacific, earth scientists began tracking radioactive fallout as a means of understanding ecological transport across the atmosphere, the biosphere, geology, and oceans. In 1952, the "IVY-Mike" detonation produced a mushroom cloud that rose to over 120,000 feet and was twenty-five miles wide (figure 10.1). US earth scientists used this radioactive cloud as an experimental lens, tracking the global dispersal of strontium 90 as a means of understanding stratospheric flows, showing with a new specificity how earth, ocean, ecologies, and atmosphere interact.

The fallout produced by the Mike detonation was tracked globally by Machta, List, and Hubert (1956), one of a series of studies that followed the stratospheric transport of nuclear materials produced by atmospheric testing, offering increasingly high-resolution portraits of atmospheric contamination within an integrated biosphere (figure 10.2). These wide-ranging studies directly challenged a national security concept that was no longer able

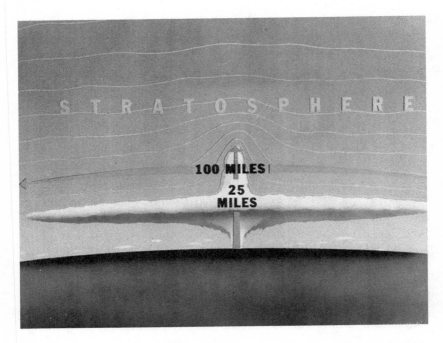

Figure 10.1. Illustration of the ɪᴠʏ-Mike Fallout Cloud. Source: US Department of Defense.

to protect discrete territories but was instead generating, in Ulrich Beck's (2009) terms, new "risk societies" united not by location, national identity, or language but rather by airborne environmental and health risks increasingly shown to be global flows (see Fowler 1960).

Radioactive fallout studies demonstrated that a new kind of species-level injury was emerging on top of the imminent threat of nuclear war; namely, that of an industrially transformed environment. Tracking the radioactive signatures of nuclear tests allowed scientists to map the biosphere as an integrated ecological space, one in which toxicity became a "flow" that connected geologies, oceans, organisms, and atmospheres in specific ways. Fallout studies required many new surveillance systems and generated major data sets for the emerging earth sciences, now formally pursued with the dual goal of understanding nuclear environmental effects and tracking Soviet nuclear progress. The early Cold War produced a massive investment in air, ocean, geology, the ice caps, and increasingly outer-space research. The US nuclear project sought to militarize nature for national advantage (see Fleming 2010;

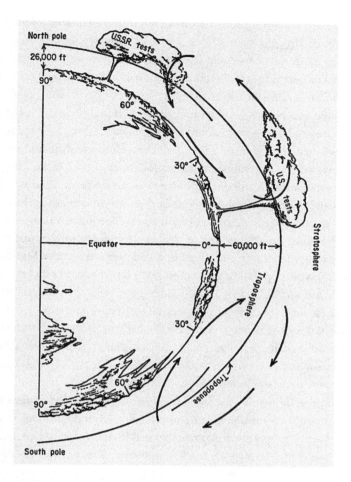

Figure 10.2. Illustration of the global travel of fallout. From Machta, List, and Fowler (1960).

Hamblin 2013) but also to understand planetary space in a new way. The resulting data sets established, as Paul Edwards (2010) has shown in detail, a new kind of global information infrastructure, allowing constantly improving portraits of earth systems to be possible. Contemporary understandings of climate change are based on the foundational scientific and big data work of this early Cold War period. In this way, the nuclear state participated in a larger militarization of the environment in the twentieth century (see Sloterdijk 2009), one that enabled new forms of ecological thinking, including a scalar multidisciplinary commitment to connecting locality with regional and global technological infrastructures and ultimately planetary-scale processes (Masco 2015).

By 1960 earth scientists could already document the stratospheric height of fallout, connect it to specific nuclear detonations, and show how US and Soviet nuclear detonations were merging the global North and global South as irradiated space. The development of US national security in the form of the hydrogen bomb was thus linked to the production of (1) an entirely new global ecological danger and (2) a new technoscientific and environmental investment in understanding ecological transport in an integrated environmental space, leading to revolutions in biomedicine, computing, geology, oceanography, and atmospheric sciences (see Masco 2010; Doel 2003; Hamblin 2013; Edwards 2010; and Farish 2010). The nuclear danger created research programs that continue to this day, including biomedical studies of exposed populations (from Hiroshima and Nagasaki to the Marshall Islands to the vast population of workers with the nuclear complex itself—see Makhijani and Schwartz 2008; Lindee 1994; and Johnston and Barker 2008). These forms of internal and external sacrifice—operating on both fast and slow scales of violence (Nixon 2011)—became embedded within Cold War national security practices raising basic questions about what kind of a human population was being created via nuclear detonations (see also Petryna 2002; Brown 2013; and Kuletz 1998).

By 1962 the US media space was filled with contradictory visions of the nuclear present and future, offering up a world of imminent danger across territories and ecologies in a manner that is difficult to appreciate today. As the Cold War civil defense programs asked Americans to practice the destruction of the nation-state in regular drills, earth scientists detailed the dangers to the human genetic pool posed by atmospheric nuclear explosions. Visions of an end of the nation-state in the flash of nuclear war were thus matched in newspaper, radio, and television accounts by portraits of a human species being transformed by the long-term genetic damage of fallout from the test programs. Consider for a moment the *New York Times*, for November 21, 1961: alongside a front-page obituary for one of the world's richest men, Axel Wenner-Gren—the philanthropist who created the Viking Fund (the future Wenner-Gren Foundation for Anthropological Research)—and an article on a United Nations vote to ban the use of the nuclear weapons and to make Africa a nuclear-free zone, was a detailed report on the Kennedy Administration's plan to "dissolve the crisis atmosphere" over atomic civil defense in the US by committing to a large-scale program to build community fallout shelters across the country. This discussion of the national panic over nuclear civil defense was followed on page A-2 by "Babies Surveyed for Strontium 90," an account of a St. Louis–based research program to collect baby teeth to measure the effects of fallout on the human body (Sullivan 1960). Publicized by ecologist Barry Commoner (see Egan and Commoner 2007), this study of strontium 90 in baby teeth continued through 1970. It projected every American family as potential casualties of nuclear testing, even as the fallout shelter program sought to protect the population at large from nuclear war by moving it underground. Alongside other fallout studies, the baby-teeth program documented accumulating strontium 90 in American infants, a startling new metric of industrial contamination. Indeed, it is difficult to imagine today in our so-called age of terror the nuclear crises of this early Cold War moment, which asked Americans to move their lives underground while also testing their children's bodies for new forms of injury created by the US national security apparatus in the name of collective defense. As a result, many new forms of activisms arose at this moment, linking issues of war and peace and environmental protection. Nuclear fear realigned race, class, and gender politics in the United States to foment a large-scale social justice movement.

The fraught discussions of this doubled planetary danger—nuclear war and radioactive fallout—in the public sphere enabled an unprecedented treaty between the United States, United Kingdom, and Soviet Union. The LTBT eliminated nuclear testing in the atmosphere, outer space, and underwater between those nuclear powers. It was the first act in a forty-year sequence of efforts to manage the global nuclear danger via diplomacy and treaties. It also stands as the first global environmental protection treaty. In his radio address to the nation announcing the treaty, President John F. Kennedy (1963) spelled out the stakes of the moment:

> A war today or tomorrow, if it led to nuclear war, would not be like any war in history. A full-scale nuclear exchange, lasting less than 60 minutes, with the weapons now in existence, could wipe out more than 300 million Americans, Europeans, and Russians, as well as untold numbers elsewhere. And the survivors, as Chairman Khrushchev warned the Communist Chinese, "the survivors would envy the dead." For they would inherit a world so devastated by explosions and poison and fire that today we cannot even conceive of its horrors. So let us try to turn the world away from war. Let us make the most of this opportunity, and every opportunity, to reduce tension, to slow down the perilous nuclear arms race, and to check the world's slide toward final annihilation.

Second, this treaty can be a step towards freeing the world from the fears and dangers of radioactive fallout. Our own atmospheric tests last year were conducted under conditions which restricted such fallout to an absolute minimum. But over the years the number and the yield of weapons tested have rapidly increased and so have the radioactive hazards from such testing. Continued unrestricted testing by the nuclear powers, joined in time by other nations which may be less adept in limiting pollution, will increasingly contaminate the air that all of us must breathe.

Even then, the number of children and grandchildren with cancer in their bones, with leukemia in their blood, or with poison in their lungs might seem statistically small to some, in comparison with natural health hazards. But this is not a natural health hazard—and it is not a statistical issue. The loss of even one human life, or the malformation of even one baby—who may be born long after we are gone—should be of concern to us all. Our children and grandchildren are not merely statistics toward which we can be indifferent.

The crisis evoked here is both of the minute and also cast into untold future generations, linking the project of nuclear deterrence to multigenerational health matters in a new way. For Kennedy, the LTBT was primarily an environmental treaty. It also was a public relations project in light of the Cuban Missile Crisis and the well-publicized scientific and environmental activist campaigns against atmospheric nuclear testing. But even with this highly detailed rendering of the violence of nuclear war, and a scientific consensus about the cumulative danger to the human genome and global environment from radioactive fallout, the LTBT did not stop the arms race or eliminate the capacity for nuclear war. Indeed, the move to underground testing consolidated the experimental regimes in the US and Soviet Union, allowing another forty years of active testing. While the fallout danger was largely eliminated from the US-USSR arms race, the vast majority of nuclear weapons on planet earth were built after the LTBT. So in this Cold War moment of existential crisis, the nuclear danger was managed rather than removed, stabilized rather than resolved, allowing the global infrastructure of nuclear war to remain firmly in place to this day. Nonetheless, the LTBT importantly made both public health and the environment national security matters. By twenty-first-century standards, the scope of the LTBT, and its important role in establishing a role for treaties and international law in managing insecurity in the global environment, remains a vital achievement, one that informs every hope and ambition for an international agreement on climate change today.

Climate Crisis

The most recent projections of the Intergovernmental Panel on Climate Change (IPCC 2013; 2014) are shocking, depicting a new kind of danger that is escalating and will play out violently over the coming centuries in every ecosystem on Earth. The extraordinary achievement of the IPCC is its radical interdisciplinarity, allowing teams of scientists across a vast range of fields to integrate huge data sets, and via computer simulations, project atmospheric effects out into the coming decades (Edwards 2010). The portrait of the coming century that the IPCC presents, however, asks us to seriously rethink industrial-age understandings of both progress and catastrophe— and restages the scale of "collective crisis." The predicted elevation in global temperature over the coming decades, the IPCC argues, will create increasingly volatile environmental conditions: melting polar ice will lead to rising ocean levels, which will flood islands and coastal cities worldwide. It will also produce a more acidic ocean leading to vast oceanic dead zones. Similarly, extreme weather patterns (producing regional droughts and flooding and heat waves) will challenge food production worldwide, while changing habitat zones on a massive scale and enabling new diseases to emerge. Moreover, human population growth, potentially rising from 7 to 9 billion people by 2050, will create ever more consumers, amplifying greenhouse gases and their reverberating effects. The resulting ecological stress could exceed what ecologists calculate is the "carrying capacity" of the global biosphere, leading to widespread scarcity or even more shocking ecological destabilizations. The worst-case vision is of future where the food chain collapses, leading to mass starvation and pushing species of all kinds toward extinction (see Kolbert 2014). In short, the industrial-age human is now formally recognized as a planetary-scale force, constituting a future of fewer species and potentially catastrophic disruptions in the food chain if consumption patterns and carbon emissions stay on their current course.

Media depictions of climate change now offer a vision of end-times to rival that of the nuclear danger. But if the global nuclear danger is characterized by its shocking immediacy (minutes of nuclear war, followed by long–term nuclear winter effects), climate danger works on an opposite temporality, constituting a slower violence that is treacherous precisely because it is so incremental that it is difficult in any given moment to sense a change in the environment or to connect discrete issues (such as sea level or drought or violent weather) to industrially generated greenhouse emissions. It is a cumulative and momentum-driven process, operating on so vast a scale that it raises basic questions about human perception, memory, and the terms of visualization necessary for a planetary-scale problem (Masco 2015). In light of climate change, geologists are now debating how to resequence planetary time to recognize the effects of human industry. The professional geological societies are formally contemplating the adoption of the term "Anthropocene" to recognize people as a new agentive force with earth systems. As Will Steffen et al. (2011) put it:

> The advent of the Anthropocene, the time interval in which human activities now rival global geophysical processes, suggests that we need to fundamentally alter our relationship with the planet we inhabit. Many approaches could be adopted, ranging from geoengineering solutions that purposefully manipulate parts of the Earth System to becoming active stewards of our own life support system. The Anthropocene is a reminder that the Holocene, during which complex human societies have developed, has been a stable, accommodating environment and is the only state of the Earth System that we know for sure can support contemporary society. The need to achieve effective planetary stewardship is urgent. As we go further into the Anthropocene, we risk driving the Earth System into a trajectory toward more hostile states from which we cannot easily return.

The 10,000-plus years of the Holocene emerges here as a temporary atmospheric condition on planet Earth, but one particularly beneficial to humans, who, living in that special air, rose to become the dominant species, inventing agriculture, writing, cars, computers, smartphones, and atomic bombs in the process. Our concept of the planetary environment is now fundamentally shifting, from literally the stable ground under our collective feet, unchangeable in its nature, to a rather fragile "life boat" in the turbulent waters of petro-capitalism.

Climate change reveals and requires a fundamentally new kind of geopolitics, one that can operate both in and above the nation-state level. Consider figure 10.3, an illustration from the *Lancet* documenting the proportion of carbon emissions by country in the top frame in relation to the health effects

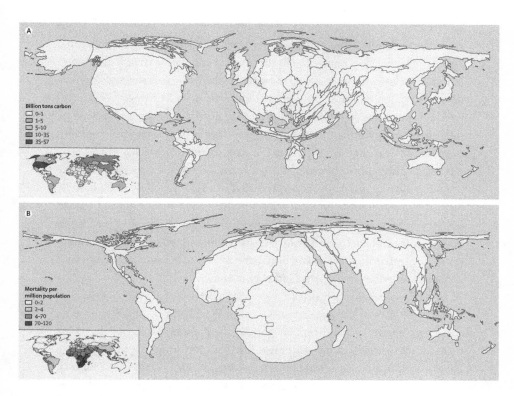

Figure 10.3. Location of carbon emission in relation to proportional health consequences of global warming. Reprinted by permission from the *Lancet*: Costello et al., "Managing the Health Effects of Climate Change," *Lancet* 373, no. 9676 (2009).

from climate change in the bottom frame (Costello et al. 2009). This chart documents an emerging relationship between the global North and global South, one played out in the conversion of carbon emissions from the north into new levels of illness in the south. This global circulation requires that one think on a planetary scale while also keeping in focus the differential effects of anthropogenic practices across nation-states and regions (see, for example, Jensen's and Wakefield and Braun's chapters in this volume). While the global North was first to industrialize and thus has put in motion the current climatic changes, the race to create consumer middle classes in the global South promises to amplify these forms of violence for all organisms on earth (see Parenti 2012).

Chakrabarty (2009) has pointed out how climate change merges human history with natural history in a new way, creating a temporality that radically undercuts long-standing logics of economic progress and development. This collapsing of human time into geological time forces us to think on unfamiliar scales—such as, the planet—and to think not of populations and nation-states but species-level impacts on earth systems involving atmosphere, glaciers, oceans, geology, and the biosphere. Climate change challenges our current political, economic, and industrial orders, requiring not only a reverse engineering of energy infrastructures to prevent declining ecological conditions but also new conceptual structures that can work on novel scales and temporalities. The built universe of things, as well as the desires that organize human consumption patterns, are revealed in climate models to be literally catastrophic. The petrochemical economy that has so revolutionized human society, creating the possibility for large-scale urbanization and the rise of nation-states and nuclear superpowers, has unintentionally generated a comprehensive environmental crisis, one that transforms the smallest of everyday consumer activities into a new kind of end-times.

Consider the everyday-ness of the metrics earth scientists use to document a starting shift in consumption patterns after World War II. Will Steffen et al. (2011: 742) have graphed human population growth in relation to global GDP, the damming of rivers, water use, fertilizer consumption, urbanization, paper consumption, cars, telephones, tourism, and McDonalds restaurants, and found a shocking parallel process: starting around 1950, each of these metrics rise exponentially, mirroring one another in an explosive rate of growth that matches fundamental changes in earth systems, including rising carbon dioxide levels, flooding, temperature change, reduction in fish stocks, forest loss, and species extinctions, among other factors. These metrics confirm a major inflection point beginning around 1950 across consumption patterns, atmospheric chemistry, temperature, and biodiversity loss. The everyday consumption patterns of each person on the planet, unremarkable in their singularity, are revealed here to be cumulatively destructive in their species totality. This makes the basic requirements for human life (including food, transportation, heating, clothing) fundamentally dangerous to the future stability of the climate if they remain embedded in the current petrochemical-based global economy. The virtues of modernization, globalization, and technological revolution have thus been turned upside down by climate change: rather than extending equality, security, and comfort, the petrochemical economy has become a slow-moving and highly negative form of geoengineering.

The conceptual implications as well as material consequences of this "great acceleration" are profound. First, it means that everyday American consumption has been a planetary force since the mid-twentieth century, indexing the US position as top historical contributor to carbon emissions. Second, it makes the American middle-class consumer economy an unprecedented force of violence in the world, one in which planned obsolescence, plastics, and petrochemical innovation have raised standards of living in North America at the expense of the collective environment as well as public health in the global South. Third, it makes climate crisis and nuclear crisis largely coterminous periods, raising important questions about perceptions of danger, the temporality of crisis itself, and the proper definition of "security." Today, the mid-twentieth century stands as the period in which people become an existential threat to themselves in two technologically mediated fashions: first, via the atomic bomb, and second, via the cumulative force of a petrochemical-based consumer economy. These dual problems are embedded within a unique military-industrial economy in the United States and operate on different temporal scales: since 1950, there has literally been a crisis *inside* of crisis structuring American modernity, one that we are only now beginning to be acknowledged in our mass media.

As a response to the oil crisis of the mid-1970s, President Jimmy Carter ordered the US national laboratories, historically devoted to national security science and the development of nuclear weapons, to convert to renewable energy research. By the end of his presidency in 1980, the US national laboratory system was spending over 50 percent if its funds on alternative energy research, promising Manhattan Projects across the renewable energy sector in the coming years. Carter also symbolically installed solar panels on the White House to demonstrate his commitment to finding a way out of a petrochemical-based energy economy. On arriving in the White House in 1981, President Ronald Reagan ordered the solar panels to be removed immediately, and then pursued one of the largest military buildups in American history, redirecting the national laboratories to resume the nuclear arms race as their primary concern. The environment and public health were explicitly delinked from national security policy in the Reagan era, allowing both unrestrained militarism and petrochemical extraction to structure American life well into the War on Terror.

Reagan was the first fully committed neoliberal; the first president to break the Cold War logic of balancing large defense budgets with welfare state programs; the first to entrust the "market" with social engineering. He entertained the thought of winnable nuclear wars and sought ultimately to end the arms race, not through disarmament, but rather by installing a space-based shield against ballistic missiles. Known as the Strategic Defense Initiative, variants of this program remain active to this day, though it has not produced a reliable defense technology despite an over $200 billion investment since 1983 (Schwartz 2012). Thus, at a key structural moment in negotiating nuclear crisis and energy crisis, the US moved from a Manhattan Project–type commitment to renewable energy research to a still fantastical quest for missile defense (one that sought to keep US nuclear weapons in place while eliminating the nuclear danger posed by Soviets arsenals). Imagine what an extra thirty years of dedicated research on renewable energy through the extensive national laboratory system might have contributed to mitigating the current climate crisis, or a redirecting of military budgets to domestic infrastructures during these decades. Here, our contemporary crisis is revealed to be the outcome of explicit policies and economic priorities, not an infrastructure in collapse but a set of values and choices that have produced multigenerational negative outcomes. The neoliberal experiment in the privatization of infrastructures and the embrace of market-based futures here makes planning for deep-time horizons increasingly impossible at precisely the moment when existential dangers require long-term plans of collective action (see also Jensen's chapter in this volume for an alternative discussion of institutions and agency).

This raises the difficult question of how ideological commitments inform understandings of crisis in the United States, and the way that crisis-talk can work to maintain a status quo. Noami Oreskes and Erik Conway (2010) have examined the techniques certain industries have used to prevent action on environmental and health matters, documenting a variety of media tactics designed to confuse the public over the scientific standing of a collective problem (see also Farrell 2016). The use of deception to defer regulation and maximize profits is often supported by more official acts as well. In 2014, the IPCC (2014) as well as the US Climate Assessment (Melillo, Richmond, and Yohe 2014) released major reports detailing a future of unprecedented ecological instability. In response, the US House of Representatives passed a bill prohibiting the Department of Defense from using any funds to respond to the wide range of security programs detailed in the reports (Koronowski 2014). What is at stake here is nothing less than the definition of "security" and the role of government in addressing the vulnerabilities, forms of violence, and uncertainties of a radically changing climate. One legacy of seventy-plus years of nuclear crisis in the US is the American tendency to believe that existential dangers can be deterred endlessly. But there are important material and temporal differences informing state-to-state confrontations mediated by nuclear weapons and the cumulative force of industrial carbon emissions across earth systems. Competing nation-states can achieve "stability" under a logic of mutual assured destruction, while global warming is a set of physical processes only gaining momentum across decades and centuries and that work on a planetary scale. The immediacy of the global nuclear crisis and the longevity of the planetary climate crisis are thus nested within one another (and have been since the mid-twentieth century), making the project of security at once one of protection, perception, and action—all terms that are in question in our current *crisis in crisis* moment.

Conclusion

The link between nuclear crisis and climate crisis is human industry: both of these existential dangers have been incrementally built over generations of labor in the pursuit of security. The nuclear complex is explicit in its goals, mobilizing the fear of mass destruction as the basis for US security in a world of competing nation-states. A changing climate is the collective effect of human industrial activity, an accumulation of a vast set of petrochemical practices dispersed across regions that have made the global economy over time. These "crises" are thus infrastructural achievements of an American modernity, modes of endangerment that are not necessary forms but rather effects of modern military and industrial systems. Following Roitman's (2014: 94) suggestion that crisis constitutes a "blind spot" that restricts narrative explanations as well as limits the kind of actions that can be taken, we could interrogate here how crisis-states have become lived infrastructures, linking imaginations, affects, and institutions in a kind of total social formation. The crisis-in-crisis from this point of view is the radical presentism of crisis-talk, the focus on stabilizing a present condition rather than engaging the multiple temporalities at stake in world of interlocking technological, financial, military, and ecological systems. As Jean-Luc Nancy argues in *After Fukushima* (2014: 30):

Fukushima is a powerfully exemplary event because it shows the close and brutal connections between a seismic quake, a dense population, and a nuclear installation (under inadequate management). It is also exemplary of a node of complex relationships between public power and private management of the installation, not to mention all the other chains of correlation that extend out from that starting point.

Put differently, there are no "natural" disasters any more, as the imbrication of technology, economy, and nature creates ever-emerging conditions for catastrophe, making crisis seem a permanent condition when it is in fact the effect of financial, technological, militaristic, and political processes interacting with earth systems.

Crisis-talk today seeks to stabilize an institution, practice, or reality, rather than interrogate the historical conditions of possibility for that endangerment to occur. In our moment, crisis blocks thought by evoking the need for an emergency response to the potential loss of a status quo, emphasizing urgency and restoration over a review of first principles and historical ontologies. In an era of complex interlocking systems of finance, technology, militarism, and ecology, unanticipated effects are inevitable and often cascading processes. In light of a postwelfare state attitude of crisis management, one that does not protect citizens but rather seeks to restore the conditions from which crisis emerged, there is much attention today to precarity as the very condition for living. Precarity and resilience are the twin logics of a neoliberal order that abandons populations in pursuit of profit, and then seeks to naturalize those abandonments as the only possible course of action (see Evans and Reid 2014). Put directly, crisis-talk without the commitment to revolution becomes counterrevolutionary.

With this in mind, how can we interrogate the "blind spots" informing nuclear crisis and climate crisis today? Despite the end of the Cold War, and the widespread politicization of "weapons of mass destruction" under the terms of the War on Terror (Masco 2014), the Department of Energy is currently planning to rebuild the US nuclear complex over the next thirty years (DOE 2013). This plan involves the first entirely new weapons designs since the 1980s, part of a strategic effort to create a nuclear arsenal and production complex that can last through the twenty-first century. These planned weapon systems will be less complicated mechanically and more robust that the Cold War designs in the current arsenal (which have been painstaking maintained part by part now for over two decades). They will also employ a new generation of weapons scientists through mid-century. These new designs will not have to be detonated, as did all prior weapons systems, before being deployed into US military arsenals thanks to the last twenty years of nuclear weapons research involving component testing, supercomputing, and simulations (see Masco 2006: 43–98). The promise of the virtual weapons laboratory now points to a permanent nuclear production capacity in the US, one that can maintain a nuclear test ban while also introducing new nuclear weapons. As the DOE's programmatic report to Congress declares (2013: 1–6): "By 2038, a new generation of weapons designers, code developers, experimentalists, and design and production engineers must demonstrate an understanding of nuclear weapons functionality using more predictive and more precisely cali- brated computer-aided design and assessment tools than are possible today. High-fidelity experimental capabilities will produce quantitative data that preclude resumption of underground nuclear testing." This commitment to building new nuclear weapons should place the recent US wars over weapons of mass destruction—both real and imagined—in a new light.

The White House's calls for a nuclear free world are now linked to a pro- jected $1 trillion investment over the coming decades in a new US nuclear complex (Wolfsthal, Lewis, and Quint 2014), which is being designed for a deep futurity. This makes current US policy a paradoxical program of pur- suing global nuclear disarmament through rebuilding a state-of-the-art US nuclear production complex and arsenal (see figure 10.4). The "crisis in cri- sis" here is the automated renewal of an infrastructure that will necessarily encourage current and future nuclear powers to pursue their own nuclear programs and undercut the collective goal of creating a world incapable of nuclear war. This program also reinvigorates nuclear fear as the coordinating logic of American geopolitics. The DOE has turned aging nuclear weapons and experts into a "crisis" requiring immediate action, rather than interrogat- ing and building a new collective security for a post–Cold War, post–War on Terror world. Alongside a new generation of nuclear experts and weapons, future nuclear crises are being built into these programs.

The governance of a warming planet has also been thoroughly politicized in the United States, a victim of national security politics (see Masco 2010) and petro-industry propaganda (see Oreskes and Conway 2010). Not coin- cidentally, the George W. Bush Administration loosened regulatory rules for domestic shale extraction in 2005 (exempting it from the Clean Air Act, the Clean Water Act, and the Safe Drinking Water Act), which, in combination with technological breakthroughs in drilling technology, opened up several large domestic shale formations for immediate exploitation. The Deepwater

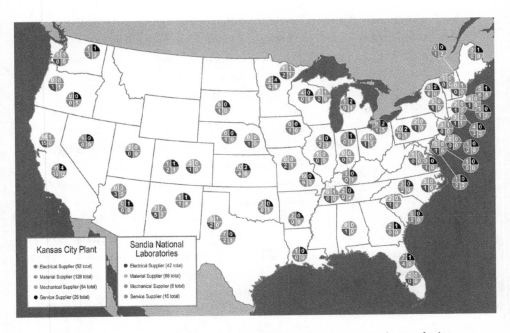

Figure 10.4. Department of Energy depiction of US nuclear weapon production facilities in 2013, which reveals the geographical scope and industrial breadth of the current nuclear complex. From DOE 2013.

Horizon oil spill (2010) in the Gulf—alongside Hurricane Katrina (2005), the Fukushima-Daiichi nuclear meltdown 2011, and superstorm Sandy in 2012—demonstrated the vulnerability of complex natural-technological-social systems and the near impossibility of environmental remediation. The boom in hydraulic fracturing has allowed the United States to increase its oil production massively even as climate scientists detail in ever-greater detail the collective environmental costs of such extraction for ice caps, atmospheric chemistry, climate, and public health. In its "Saudi America: The Economics of Shale Oil" article, the *Economist* (2014) reveals that the US has moved from producing 600,000 barrels a day in 2008 to 3.5 million a day in 2014 because of shale extractions (see figure 10.5). The *Economist* focuses on the shifting geopolitics of renewed American oil power but does not mention the consequences for the global environment of abundant, inexpensive oil. If current patterns hold, the United States will become the world's leading oil producer in 2020—the number 1 petro-state—at precisely the moment when the damage of such an achievement has been scientifically documented across the earth sciences.

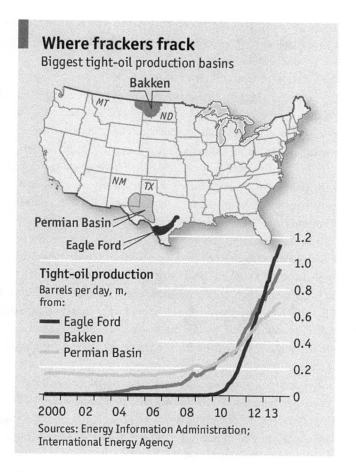

Where frackers frack
Biggest tight-oil production basins

Bakken

MT
ND

NM
TX

Permian Basin
Eagle Ford

Tight-oil production
Barrels per day, m,
from:

— Eagle Ford
— Bakken
— Permian Basin

1.2
1.0
0.8
0.6
0.4
0.2
0

2000 02 04 06 08 10 12 13

Sources: Energy Information Administration;
International Energy Agency

Figure 10.5. Location of US shale fields and extraction rates. From
the *Economist*, February 2014.

Since 2005, a vast new infrastructure of wells, pipes, and ponds, as well
as truck and train lines carrying oil and natural gas, has been built to exploit
shale formations from Texas to North Dakota to Pennsylvania. In addition
to greenhouse gas emissions, these infrastructures require vast amount of
water, create waste ponds, and also leak, raising important questions about
the environmental safety of these areas over the projected life of each well.
New York State recently banned hydraulic fracturing because of the long list
of unknown effects on water, air, and public health (New York Department
of Public Health 2014), while in Texas and North Dakota there are boom and

bust towns devoted entirely to the enterprise, and vast landscapes now covered with industrial infrastructures that produce both energy and radically uncertain environmental futures.

The deregulation of hydraulic fracturing has made petrochemical energy inexpensive and abundant by historical standards at precisely the moment when it would be most socially and environmentally sound to make it ever more expensive. If the neoliberal logics of market determinism were good at engineering a sustainable collective future, the US would not be embracing shale with such unrestrained enthusiasm. The ever-shorter profit cycle of corporate review, in other words, is diametrically opposed to the long-term investments in renewable energy, installing the perfect terms for ongoing environmental and health crises for as far into the future as anyone can imagine. Thus, one aspect of the crisis-in-crisis today is a notion of "profit" that has been so narrowly defined that a loss of the collective environment is easier to imagine that a shift in the nature of petro-capitalism.

Instead of reenergizing a collective imaginary that can engage alternative modes of living, and apply resources and agency to collective problems, governance today recommits to exactly those existentially dangerous projects that should be formally disavowed for the public good: nuclear weapons and oil. This creates a public feeling of "permanent crisis" as well as increasing vulnerabilities across a range of domestic and global issues. One perverse effect of this twenty-first-century circuit is that it encourages social theorists to focus narrowly on the endless modes of precarity that are emerging rather than articulating the alternative futures that are needed, reinforcing a generational gestalt of political gridlock and decline in the United States. It is vitally important to understand how cumulative and asymmetrically distributed industrial toxins (from carbon to plastic to nuclear materials) affect communities and individual bodies, and to articulate the ways that planetary scale flows are now remaking local conditions (see, for example, the chapters by Meyers, as well as Zeiderman, in this volume for exemplary case studies). The age of neoliberal calculation is one that naturalizes the abandonment of populations that are not immediately useful to the quarterly bottom line, and renders invisible those many others affected remotely by financial, military, or industrial policies (see Lorey 2015). It is also important to interrogate the affective recruitments to existential crisis, and the political work such recruitments do in supporting existing political structures (Masco 2014). However, it is equally important to recover the capacity to generate positive futurities—what, following Lauren Berlant (2011) we might call the not yet cruel optimisms—that can affectively charge collective action, particularly on those issues (like nuclear danger and climate danger) that have been constructed by generations of human agency, and thus are immediately available to reform.

At the end of World War II, the US embraced a new kind of technological utopianism, believing that science would solve the problem of health, welfare, and security. Designing the future for both security and prosperity was the role of the state, allowing significant investments in education, welfare state systems, and the establishment of a variety of environmental protection laws. Indeed, this mid-twentieth-century period of "crisis" is the moment when many of the key infrastructures, and generational investments in education and environmental protections, were established that inform our world today. Thus, the most dangerous moment in American history was from this point of view also one of the most productive, creating important commitments to civil rights, education, and the environment while establishing the precedents for international law and treaties to manage existential dangers.

Since the 1980s neoliberal turn in the United States, militarism has remained the project of the state but the collective future has been assigned to the marketplace, which elevates short-term profitability above all other concerns. What happened to the once-vibrant social debate about alternative futures and the commitment to making long-term investments in improving the terms of collective life? The force of global capital has absorbed the power of crisis-talk to shock, and thus mobilize, requiring a different call to action. The crisis-in-crisis today is the inability to both witness the accumulating damage of this system *and* imagine another politics. A fundamental challenge in our moment is that the key existential dangers of today—nuclear weapons and climate change—operate on different scales, creating friction between the global and the planetary, while demanding different kinds of governance (Masco 2015). Since we do not yet have planetary-scale institutions that can govern these collective problems, it is easy to focus on the emerging and amplifying forms of precarity. Instead of a more aggressive media space devoted to detailing the current and projected crises, then, perhaps what our specific historical moment requires is an explicit commitment—a critical theory commitment—to generating the nonutopian but nonetheless positive futurities that can reactivate the world-making powers of society.

Notes

An earlier version of this chapter first appeared in *Current Anthropology*. My thanks to the Wenner-Gren Foundation for continued support. Special thanks to Kregg Hetherington for convening this conversation and his editorial care.

REFERENCES

AbdouMaliq, Simone. 2004. "People as Infrastructure: Intersecting Fragments in Johannesburg." *Public Culture* 16, no. 3: 407–429.

Agamben, Giorgio. 1993. *The Coming Community*. Minneapolis: University of Minnesota Press.

Agamben, Giorgio. 2004. *The Open: Man and Animal*. Edited by Werner Hamacher. Meridian: Crossing Aesthetics. Stanford, CA: Stanford University Press.

Agamben, Giorgio. 2005. *The Time That Remains: A Commentary on the Letter to the Romans*. Translated by Patricia Dailey. Series: Meridian: Crossing Aesthetics. Stanford, CA: Stanford University Press.

Agamben, Giorgio. 2009. *What Is an Apparatus? And Other Essays*. Translated by David Kishik and Stefan Pedatella. Series: Meridian: Crossing Aesthetics. Stanford, CA: Stanford University Press.

Agamben, Giorgio. 2011. *The Kingdom and the Glory: For a Theological Genealogy of Economy and Government*. Translated by Lorenzo Chiesa with Matteo Mandarini. Series: Meridian: Crossing Aesthetics. Stanford, CA: Stanford University Press.

Agamben, Giorgio. 2014. "What Is a Destituent Power?" *Environment and Planning D: Society and Space* 32, no. 1: 65–74.

Agamben, Giorgio. 2016. *The Use of Bodies*. Translated by Adam Kotsko. Series: Meridian: Crossing Aesthetics. Stanford, CA: Stanford University Press.

Agrawal, Arun. 2005. *Environmentality: Technologies of Government and the Making of Subjects*. Durham, NC: Duke University Press.

Agudelo, Carlos Efrén. 2004. "No todos vienen del río: Construcción de identidades negras urbanas y movilización política en Colombia." In *Conflicto e (in)visibilidad: Retos en los estudios de la gente negra en Colombia*, edited by Eduardo Restrepo and Axel Rojas, 173–193. Popayán, Colombia: Universidad del Cauca.

Aguilar, Enric, et al. 2005. "Changes in Precipitation and Temperature Extremes in Central America and Northern South America, 1961–2003." *Journal of Geophysical Research: Atmospheres* 110, issue D23: 1–15.

Agustoni, Alfredo, and Mara Maretti. 2012. "Energy and Social Change: An Introduction." *International Review of Sociology* 22, no. 3: 391–404.

Alarcón-Cháires, Pablo. 2001. "Los indígenas Cucapá y la conservación de la naturaleza: El infortunio de vivir en un área natural protegida en México." *Ecología Política* 22: 117–129.

Alfred, Gerald. 1995. *Heeding the Voices of Our Ancestors: Kahnawake Mohawk Politics and the Rise of Native Nationalism*. Toronto: Oxford University Press.

Amado, Jean-Christophe, et al. 2011. "Climate Risk and Business-Ports: Terminal Marítimo Muelles el Bosque, Cartagena, Colombia, Executive Summary." International Finance Corporation, Washington, DC.

Anand, Nikhil. 2011. "Pressure: The PoliTechnics of Water Supply in Mumbai." *Cultural Anthropology* 26, no. 4: 542–564.

Anand, Nikhil. 2015. "Leaky States: Water Audits, Ignorance, and the Politics of Infrastructure." *Public Culture* 27, no. 276: 305–330.

Anand, Nikhil. 2017. *Hydraulic City: Leaks and the Infrastructures of Citizenship in Mumbai*. Durham, NC: Duke University Press.

Anand, Nikhil, Akhil Gupta, and Hannah Appel, eds. 2018. *The Promise of Infrastructure*. Durham, NC: Duke University Press.

Andreas, Peter. 1995. "Free Market Reform and Drug Market Prohibition: US Policies at Cross-Purposes in Latin America." *Third World Quarterly* 16, no. 1: 75–87.

Andreas, Peter. 1996. "US-Mexico: Open Markets, Closed Border." *Foreign Policy* 103 (Summer): 51–69.

Andreas, Peter. 2009. *Border Games: Policing the US-Mexico Divide*. Ithaca, NY: Cornell University Press.

Appadurai, Arjun. 1996. *Modernity at Large: Cultural Dimensions of Globalization*. Minneapolis: University of Minnesota Press.

Appadurai, Arjun. 2015. "Mediants, Materiality, Normativity." *Public Culture* 27, no. 2: 221–237.

Appel, Hannah. 2012. "Offshore Work: Oil, Modularity, and the How of Capitalism in Equatorial Guinea." *American Ethnologist* 39, no. 4: 692–709.

Aprile-Gniset, Jacques. 2002. *Génesis de Buenaventura: Memorias del Cascajal*. Buenaventura: Universidad del Pacífico.

Aranda, Darío. 2015. *Tierra arrasada*. Sudamericana: Buenos Aires.

Arboleda, Martín. 2016. "Spaces of Extraction, Metropolitan Explosions: Planetary Urbanization and the Commodity Boom in Latin America." *International Journal of Urban and Regional Research* 40, no. 1: 96–112.

Arboleda, Santiago. 2004. "Negándose a ser desplazados: Afrocolombianos en Buenaventura." In *Conflicto e (in)visibilidad: Retos en los estudios de la gente negra en Colombia*, edited by Eduardo Restrepo and Axel Rojas. Popayán, Colombia: Universidad del Cauca.

Archambault, Julie Soleil. Forthcoming. "'One Beer, One Block': Concrete Aspiration and the Stuff of Transformation in a Mozambican Suburb." *Journal of the Royal Anthropological Institute*.

Archibold, Randal. 2007. "In Arizona Desert, American Indian Trackers vs. Smugglers." *International Herald Tribune*, March 7.

Arrends, Bergit, Jessica Ullrich, and Lois Weinberger. 2011. "Lois Weinberger: Green Man." *Antennae* 18 (Autumn): 37–49.

Asher, Kiran. 2009. *Black and Green: Afro-Colombians, Development, and Nature in the Pacific Lowlands*. Durham, NC: Duke University Press.

Asher, Kiran, and Diana Ojeda. 2009. "Producing Nature and Making the State: Ordenamiento Territorial in the Pacific Lowlands of Colombia." *Geoforum* 40, no. 3: 292–302.

Auyero, Javier, and Débora Alejandra Swistun. 2009. *Flammable: Environmental Suffering in an Argentine Shantytown*. New York: Oxford University Press.

Bal, Charanpal Singh. 2013. *The Politics of Obedience: Bangladeshi Construction Workers and the Migrant Labour Regime in Singapore*. Perth: Murdoch University.

Ballestero, Andrea. 2012a. "The Productivity of Nonreligious Faith: Openness, Pessimism, and Water in Latin America." In *Nature, Science, and Religion: Intersections Shaping Society and the Environment*, edited by Catherine M. Tucker, 169–190. Santa Fe: School for Advanced Research Press.

Ballestero, Andrea. 2012b. "Transparency Short-Circuited: Laughter and Numbers in Costa Rican Water Politics." *PoLAR: Political and Legal Anthropology Review* 35, no. 2: 223–241.

Ballestero, Andrea. 2015. "The Ethics of a Formula: Calculating a Financial-Humanitarian Price for Water." *American Ethnologist* 42, no. 1: 262–278.

Ballvé, Teo. 2012. "Everyday State Formation: Territory, Decentralization, and the Narco Landgrab in Colombia." *Environment and Planning D: Society and Space* 30, no. 4: 603–622.

Ballvé, Teo. 2013. "Territories of Life and Death on a Colombian Frontier." *Antipode* 45, no. 1: 238–241.

Barad, Karen. 1996. "Meeting the Universe Halfway: Realism and Social Constructivism without Contradiction." In *Feminism, Science, and the Philosophy of Science*, edited by Lynn Hankinson and Jack Nelson, 161–194. Dordrecht: Kluwer Academic.

Barad, Karen. 2003. "Posthumanist Performativity: How Matter Comes to Matter." *Signs: Journal of Women in Culture and Society* 28, no. 3: 801–831.

Barad, Karen. 2007. *Meeting the Universe Halfway: Quantum Physics and the Entanglement of Matter and Meaning*. Durham, NC: Duke University Press.

Barak, On. 2009. "Scraping the Surface: The Techno-Politics of Modern Streets in Turn-of-Twentieth-Century Alexandria." *Mediterranean Historical Review* 24, no. 2: 187–205.

Barbary, Olivier, and Fernando Urrea Giraldo, eds. 2004. *Gente negra en Colombia: dinámicas sociopolíticas en Cali y el Pacífico*. Medellín, Colombia: Editorial Lealon.

Bargain, Alban. 2012. "Review of *Tuqqun*, This Is Not a Program." *Left History* 16, no. 1: 134–136

Barnes, Jessica. 2014. *Cultivating the Nile: The Everyday Politics of Water in Egypt*. Durham, NC: Duke University Press.

Barry, Andrew. 2001. *Political Machines: Governing a Technological Society*. London: A&C Black.

Barry, Andrew. 2006. "Technological Zones." *European Journal of Social Theory* 9, no. 2: 239–253.

Barry, Andrew. 2013. *Material Politics: Disputes along the Pipeline*. London: Wiley-Blackwell.

Basso, Keith H. 1996. *Wisdom Sits in Places: Landscape and Language among the Western Apache*. Albuquerque: University of New Mexico Press.

Battaglia, Debbora. 2017. "Aeroponic Gardens and Their Magic: Plants/Persons/Ethics in Suspension." *History and Anthropology* 28, no. 3: 263–292.

Bauman, Zygmunt. 1990. *Thinking Sociologically*. Hoboken, NJ: Blackwell.

Beck, Ulrich, ed. 2009. *World at Risk*. Translated by Cronin Ciaran. Cambridge, UK: Polity.

Belson, Ken. 2008. "Plumber's Job on a Giant's Scale: Fixing New York's Drinking Straw." *New York Times*, November 22.

Benhabib, Seyla. 1986. *Critique, Norm, and Utopia: A Study of the Foundations of Critical Theory*. New York: Columbia University Press.

Bennett, Jane. 2010. *Vibrant Matter: A Political Ecology of Things*. Durham, NC: Duke University Press.

Benson, Etienne. 2015. "Generating Infrastructural Invisibility: Insulation, Interconnection, and Avian Excrement in the Southern California Power Grid." *Environmental Humanities* 6, no. 1: 103–130.

Bergman, Charles. 2002. *Red Delta: Fighting for Life at the End of the Colorado River*. Golden, CO: Fulcrum.

Berlant, Lauren. 2011. *Cruel Optimism*. Durham, NC: Duke University Press.

Bernes, Jasper. 2013. "Logistics, Counterlogistics and the Communist Prospect." *Endnotes* 3: 172–201.

Bishop, Ryan. 2011. "Project 'Transparent Earth' and the Autoscopy of Aerial Targeting: The Visual Geopolitics of the Underground." *Theory, Culture and Society* 28, nos. 7–8: 270–286.

Blok, Anders, Moe Nakazora, and Brit Ross Winthereik. 2016. "Infrastructuring Environments." *Science as Culture* 25, no. 1: 1–22.

Blum, Andrew. 2012. *Tubes: Journey to the Center of the Internet*. New York: Ecco.

Bocarejo, Diana. 2012. "Emancipation or Enclosement? The Spatialization of Difference and Urban Ethnic Contestation in Colombia." *Antipode* 44, no. 3: 663–683.

Bocarejo, Diana. 2014. "Legal Typologies and Topologies: The Construction of Indigenous Alterity and Its Spatialization within the Colombian Constitutional Court." *Law and Social Inquiry* 39, no. 2: 334–360.

Bowker, Geoffrey. 1994. "Information Mythology and Infrastructure." In *Information Acumen: The Understanding and Use of Knowledge in Modern Business*, edited by Lisa Bud-Frierman, 231–247. Comparative and International Business. Abingdon: Taylor and Francis.

Bowker, Geoffrey, and Susan Leigh Star. 1994. "Knowledge and Infrastructure in International Information Management: Problems of Classification and Coding." In *Information Acumen: The Understanding and Use of Knowledge in Modern Business*, edited by Lisa Bud-Frierman, 187–216. Comparative and International Business. London: Routledge.

Boyer, Dominic. "Energopower: An Introduction." 2014. *Anthropological Quarterly* 87, no. 2: 309–333.

Braidotti, Rosi. 2013. *The Posthuman*. Cambridge: Polity.

Brand, Stewart. 1994. *How Buildings Learn: What Happens after They're Built*. New York: Penguin.

Brathwaite, Kamau. 1974. *Contradictory Omens: Cultural Diversity and Integration in the Caribbean*. Mona, Jamaica: Savacou.

Brathwaite, Kamau. 1984. *History of the Voice: The Development of Nation Language in Anglophone Caribbean Poetry*. London: New Beacon.

Braun, Bruce. 2000. "Producing Vertical Territory: Geology and Governmentality in Late Victorian Canada." *Cultural Geographies* 7, no. 1: 7–46.

Braun, Bruce. 2002. *The Intemperate Rainforest: Nature, Culture, and Power on Canada's West Coast*. Minneapolis: University of Minnesota Press.

Braun, Bruce. 2014. "A New Urban Dispositif? Governing Life in an Age of Climate Change." *Environment and Planning D: Society and Space* 32, no. 1: 49–64.

Braun, Bruce, and Sarah J. Whatmore. 2010. *Political Matter: Technoscience, Democracy, and Public Life*. Minneapolis: University of Minnesota Press.

Bray, David Barton, et al. 2003. "Mexico's Community-Managed Forests as a Global Model for Sustainable Landscapes." *Conservation Biology* 17, no. 3: 672–677.

Brennan, Timothy. 2003. "The Empire's New Clothes." *Critical Inquiry* 29, no. 2: 337–367.

Brenner, Neil. 2013. "Theses on Urbanization." *Public Culture* 25, no. 1: 85–114.

Brenner, Neil. 2014. "Introduction: Urban Theory without an Outside." In *Implosions/Explosions: Towards a Study of Planetary Urbanization*, edited by Neil Brenner, 14–30. Berlin: Jovis.

Brenner, Neil. 2018. "Debating Planetary Urbanization: For an Engaged Pluralism." *Environment and Planning D: Society and Space* 36, no. 3: 570–590. doi.org/10.1177/0263775818757510.

Brenner, Neil, and Christian Schmid. 2014. "The 'Urban Age' in Question." In *Implosions/Explosions: Towards a Study of Planetary Urbanization*, edited by Neil Brenner, 310–337. Berlin: Jovis.

Brockway, Lucile H. 1979. "Science and Colonial Expansion: The Role of the British Royal Botanic Gardens." *American Ethnologist* 6, no. 3: 449–465.

Brooks, Emily. 2016. "Fossil Water: Modeling Sustainability in Deep Time." Paper presented at the American Anthropological Association Annual Meeting. Minneapolis.

Brooks, William. 1996. *The Oyster*. Baltimore: Johns Hopkins University Press.

Brown, Kathryn L. 2013. *Plutopia: Nuclear Families, Atomic Cities, and the Great Soviet and American Plutonium Disasters*. Oxford: Oxford University Press.

Buckley, Michelle, and Kendra Strauss. 2016. "With, against, and beyond Lefebvre: Planetary Urbanization and Epistemic Plurality." *Environment and Planning D: Society and Space* 34, no. 4: 617–636.

Buck-Morss, Susan. 2002. *Dreamworld and Catastrophe: The Passing of Mass Utopia in East and West*. Cambridge, MA: MIT Press.

Bullard, Robert D. 1993. *Confronting Environmental Racism: Voices from the Grassroots*. Boston: South End.

Callon, Michel. 1986. "Some Elements of a Sociology of Translation: Domestication of the Scallops and the Fishermen of St. Brieuc Bay." In *Power, Action and Belief: A New Sociology of Knowledge?*, edited by John Law, 196–223. London: Routledge.

Callon, Michel. 1987. "Society in the Making: The Study of Technology as a Tool for Sociological Analysis." In *The Social Construction of Technological Systems: New Directions in the Sociology and History of Technology*, edited by Wiebe E. Bijker, Thomas P. Hughes, and Trevor Pinch, 83–103. Cambridge, MA: MIT Press.

Callon, Michel. 1998. "Introduction: The Embeddedness of Economic Markets in Economics." In *The Laws of the Markets*, edited by Michel Callon, 1–57. Oxford: Blackwell / The Sociological Review.

Callon, Michel, and Bruno Latour. 1981. "Unscrewing the Big Leviathan: How Actors Macro-Structure Reality and How Sociologists Help Them to Do So." In *Advances in Social Theory and Methodology: Toward an Integration of Micro- and Macro-sociologies*, edited by Aaron Victor Cicourel and K. Knorr-Cetina, 277–303. Boston: Routledge.

Campbell, Craig. 2006. "A Report from the Archives of the Monument to Eternal Return." In *Between Matter and Method: Encounters in Anthropology and Art*, edited by Gretchen Bakke and Marina Peterson. Banff, Alberta.

Campbell, Craig. 2018. "A Report from the Archives of the Monument to Eternal Return: Comgar." In *Between Matter and Method: Encounters in Anthropology and Art*, edited by Gretchen Bakke and Marina Peterson, 141–158. London: Bloomsbury Academic.

Cárdenas, Roosbelinda. 2012. "Green Multiculturalism: Articulations of Ethnic and Environmental Politics in a Colombian 'Black Community.'" *Journal of Peasant Studies* 39, no. 2: 309–333.

Carse, Ashley. 2012. "Nature as Infrastructure: Making and Managing the Panama Canal Watershed." *Social Studies of Science* 42, no. 4: 539–563.

Carse, Ashley. 2014. *Beyond the Big Ditch: Politics, Ecology, and Infrastructure at the Panama Canal*. Cambridge, MA: MIT Press.

Carse, Ashley, and Joshua Lewis. 2017. "Towards a Political Ecology of Infrastructure Standards: Or, How to Think about Ships, Waterways, Sediment, and Communities Together." *Environment and Planning A* 49, no. 1: 9–28.

Carse, Ashley, et al. 2016. "Panama Canal Forum: From the Conquest of Nature to the Construction of New Ecologies." *Environmental History* 21, no. 2: 206–287.

Castalia Strategic Advisors. 2007. "K East Water Distribution Improvement Project: Customer Service and Technical Report." Collaborative for the Advancement of the Study of Urbanism through Mixed Media.

Castells, Manuel. 2011. *The Rise of the Network Society: The Information Age: Economy, Society and Culture*. Vol. 1. 2nd ed. Oxford: Wiley-Blackwell.

Castillero Calvo, Alfredo. 1973. "Transitismo y dependencia: El caso del istmo de Panamá." *Nueva Sociedad* (March–April): 35–50.

CBC (Canadian Broadcasting Corporation). 2009. "Leaky Pipes Cost Ontario 25% of Its Drinking Water, $700M a year." *CBC News*, June 10.

Chakrabarty, Dipesh. 2000. *Provincializing Europe: Postcolonial Thought and Historical Difference*. Princeton, NJ: Princeton University Press.

Chakrabarty, Dipesh. 2009. "The Climate of History: Four Theses." *Critical Inquiry* 35, no. 2: 197–222.

Chakrabarty, Dipesh. 2012. "Postcolonial Studies and the Challenge of Climate Change." *New Literary History* 43, no. 1: 1–18.

Checker, Melissa. 2005. *Polluted Promises: Environmental Racism and the Search for Justice in a Southern Town*. New York: New York University Press.

Chok, Stephanie. 2009. "Risky Business: Death and Injury on Singapore's Construction Sites." *Journal of Project Management* 27, no. 7: 717–726.

Choy, Timothy K. 2011. *Ecologies of Comparison: An Ethnography of Endangerment in Hong Kong*. Experimental Futures. Durham, NC: Duke University Press.

Clark, Nigel. 2014. "Geo-Politics and the Disaster of the Anthropocene." *Sociological Review* 62, S1: 19–37.

Clark, Nigel Halcomb, and Myra Hird. 2014. "Deep Shit." *O-Zone: A Journal of Object-Oriented Studies* 1, no. 1: 44–52.

Clifford, James. 2007. "Varieties of Indigenous Experience: Diasporas, Homelands, Sovereignties." In *Indigenous Experience Today*, edited by Marisol de la Cadena and Orin Starn, 197–223. Oxford: Berg.

Clover, Joshua. 2016. *Riot. Strike. Riot: The New Era of Uprisings*. Brooklyn: Verso.

Coelho, Karen. 2006. "Tapping In: Leaky Sovereignties and Engineered (Dis)Order in an Urban Water System." *Sarai Reader* 6: 497–509.

Coleman, Leo. 2014. "Infrastructure and Interpretation: Meters, Dams, and State Imagination in Scotland and India." *American Ethnologist* 41, no. 3: 457–472.

Collier, Stephen, and Aihwa Ong. 2005. "Global Assemblages, Anthropological Problems." In *Global Assemblages: Technology, Politics, and Ethics as Anthropo-*

logical Problems, edited by Stephen Collier and Aihwa Ong, 3–21. New York: Wiley-Blackwell.

Conan, Michel, ed. 1999. *Perspectives on Garden Histories.* Washington, DC: Dumbarton Oaks.

Contraloría General de la Republica, Dirección de Estadística y Censo. "Indicadores Relevantes." Accessed May 21, 2018, https://www.contraloria.gob.pa/INEC /Default.aspx.

Convive VII-Buenaventura: Cambio Climático, Mejoramiento y Readecuación de Vivienda para Frentes Marítimos. 2012. Bogotá: Revista Escala.

Costello, Anthony, et al. 2009. "Managing the Health Effects of Climate Change." *Lancet* 373, no. 9676.

Cowen, Deborah. 2014. *The Deadly Life of Logistics: Mapping Violence in Global Trade.* Minneapolis: University of Minnesota Press.

Crary, Jonathan. 2013. *24/7: Late Capitalism and the Ends of Sleep.* Brooklyn: Verso.

Craviotti, Clara. 2016. "Which Territorial Embeddedness? Territorial Relationships of Recently Internationalized Firms of the Soybean Chain." *Journal of Peasant Studies* 43, no. 2: 331–347.

Cronon, William. 1991. *Nature's Metropolis: Chicago and the Great West.* New York: Norton.

Cronon, William. 1995. *Uncommon Ground: Toward Reinventing Nature.* New York: W. W. Norton.

Dalakoglou, Dimitris, and Yannis Kallianos. 2014. "Infrastructural Flows, Interruptions and Stasis in Athens of the Crisis." *City* 18, nos. 4–5: 526–532.

Dalby, Simon. 2013. "Biopolitics and Climate Security in the Anthropocene." *Geoforum* 49 (August): 184–192.

Davidson, Janet. 2011. "City Water Leaks Wasting Millions of Tax Dollars." *Canadian Broadcasting Corporation News*, November 11.

Davis, Heather, and Zoe Todd. 2017. "On the Importance of a Date, or, Decolonizing the Anthropocene." *ACME: An International Journal for Critical Geographies* 16, no. 4: 761–780.

Davis, Heather, and Etienne Turpin, eds. 2015. *Art in the Anthropocene: Encounters among Aesthetics, Politics, Environments and Epistemologies.* London: Open Humanities Press.

De Boeck, Filip. 2012. "Infrastructure: Commentary from Filip de Boeck." *Cultural Anthropology Online*, November 26. https://culanth.org/curated_collections/11 -infrastructure/discussions/7-infrastructure-commentary-from-filip-de-boeck.

de la Cadena, Marisol. 2010. "Indigenous Cosmopolitics in the Andes: Conceptual Reflections beyond 'Politics.'" *Cultural Anthropology* 25, no. 2: 334–370.

de la Cadena, Marisol. 2015a. *Earth Beings: Ecologies of Practice across Andean Worlds.* Durham, NC: Duke University Press.

de la Cadena, Marisol. 2015b. "Uncommoning Nature." In *E-Flux Journal 56th Venice Biennale*, August 22.

DeLanda, Manuel. 1998. *A Thousand Years of Nonlinear History*. New York: Zone Books.

DeLanda, Manuel. 2006. *A New Philosophy of Society: Assemblage Theory and Social Complexity*. New York: Continuum.

Deleuze, Gilles. 1988. "What Is a Dispositif?" In *Michel Foucault, Philosopher*, edited by Timothy J. Armstrong, 159–168. New York: Routledge.

Derickson, Kate. 2015. "Urban Geography I: Locating Urban Theory in the 'Urban Age.'" *Progress in Human Geography* 39, no. 5: 647–657.

de Rijke, Kim, Paul Munro, and Maria de Lourdes Melo Zurita. 2016. "The Great Artesian Basin: A Contested Resource Environment of Subterranean Water and Coal Seam Gas in Australia." *Society and Natural Resources* 29, no. 6: 696–710.

Derrida, Jacques. 1994. *Specters of Marx: The State of the Debt, the Work of Mourning and the New International*. Translated by Peggy Kamuf. London: Routledge.

Descola, Philippe. 1996. *In the Society of Nature: A Native Ecology in Amazonia*. Cambridge Studies in Social and Cultural Anthropology. Cambridge: Cambridge University Press.

Descola, Philippe, Pálsson Gísli. 1996. *Nature and Society: Anthropological Perspectives*. European Association of Social Anthropologists. London: Routledge.

Despard, Erin, and Monika Kin Gagnon, eds. 2010. "Gardens." *Public* 41 (Spring).

Despret, Vinciane. 2004. *Our Emotional Makeup: Ethnopsychology and Selfhood*. Translated by Marjolijn de Jager. New York: Other Press.

Dilley, Roy. 1999. *The Problem of Context: Perspectives from Social Anthropology and Elsewhere*. Methodology and History in Anthropology, vol. 4. Oxford: Berghahn.

DOE (Department of Energy). 2013. *Fiscal Year 2014: Stockpile Stewardship and Management Plan*. Washington, DC: Government Printing Office.

Doel, Ronald E. 2003. "Constituting the Postwar Earth Sciences: The Military's Influence on the Environmental Sciences in the USA after 1945." *Social Studies of Science* 33, no. 5: 635–666.

Donovan, Kevin P. 2013. "Infrastructuring Aid: Materializing Social Protection in Northern Kenya." Centre for Social Science Research.

Douglas, Mary. 1966. *Purity and Danger: An Analysis of Concepts of Pollution and Taboo*. London: Routledge.

Dussel, Enrique. 2008. *Twenty Theses on Politics*. Durham, NC: Duke University Press.

Easterling, Keller. 2014. *Extrastatecraft: The Power of Infrastructure Space*. London: Verso.

Edwards, Paul N. 2003. "Infrastructure and Modernity: Force, Time, and Social Organization in the History of Sociotechnical Systems." In *Modernity and Technology*, edited by Thomas J. Misa, Philip Brey, and Andrew Feenberg, 185–226. Cambridge, MA: MIT Press.

Edwards, Paul N. 2010. *A Vast Machine: Computer Models, Climate Data, and the Politics of Global Warming*. Cambridge, MA: MIT Press.

Egan, Michael, and Barry Commoner. 2007. *Barry Commoner and the Science of Survival*. Cambridge, MA: MIT Press.

Elden, Stuart. 2010. "Land, Terrain, Territory." *Progress in Human Geography* 34, no. 6: 799–817.

Elden, Stuart. 2013a. *The Birth of Territory*. Chicago: University of Chicago Press.

Elden, Stuart. 2013b. "Secure the Volume: Vertical Geopolitics and the Depth of Power." *Political Geography* 34 (May): 35–51.

Elyachar, Julia. 2010. "Phatic Labor, Infrastructure, and the Question of Empowerment in Cairo." *American Ethnologist* 37, no. 3: 452–464.

Elyachar, Julia. 2012. "Next Practices: Knowledge, Infrastructure and Public Goods at the Bottom of the Pyramid." *Public Culture* 24, no. 1: 109–129.

Escobar, Arturo. 2007. "Worlds and Knowledges Otherwise 1: The Latin American Modernity/Coloniality Research Program." *Cultural Studies* 21, nos. 2–3: 179–210.

Escobar, Arturo. 2008. *Territories of Difference: Place, Movements, Life, Redes*. Durham, NC: Duke University Press.

Escobar, Arturo. 2010. "Latin America at a Crossroads: Alternative Modernizations, Post-Liberalism, or Post-Development?" *Cultural Studies* 24, no. 1: 1–65.

Evans, Brad, and Julian Reid. 2014. *Resilient Life: The Art of Living Dangerously*. Hoboken, NJ: Wiley-Blackwell.

Fabian, Johannes. 2002. *Time and the Other: How Anthropology Makes Its Object*. New York: Columbia University Press.

Farish, Matthew. 2010. *The Contours of America's Cold War*. Minneapolis: University of Minnesota Press.

Farrell, Justin. 2016. "Corporate Funding and Ideological Polarization about Climate Change." *Proceedings of the National Academy of Sciences* 113, no. 1: 92–97.

Ferguson, James. 1999. *Expectations of Modernity: Myths and Meanings of Urban Life on the Zambian Copperbelt*. Berkeley: University of California Press.

Ferguson, James. 2006. *Decomposing Modernity: In Global Shadows. Africa in the Neoliberal World Order*. Durham, NC: Duke University Press.

Ferguson, James. 2012. "Structures of Responsibility." *Ethnography* 13, no. 4: 558–562.

Feyerabend, Paul. 2001. *Conquest of Abundance: A Tale of Abstraction versus the Richness of Being*. Chicago: University of Chicago Press.

Fischer, Michael M. J. 2013. "Biopolis: Asian Science in the Global Circuitry." *Science Technology and Society* 18, no. 3: 379–404.

Fleming, James Rodger. 2010. *Fixing the Sky: The Checkered History of Weather and Climate Control*. New York: Columbia University Press.

Fortun, Kim. 2012. "Ethnography in Late Industrialism." *Cultural Anthropology* 27, no. 3: 446–464.

Foucault, Michel. 1979. *Discipline and Punish: The Birth of the Prison*. New York: Vintage Books.

Foucault, Michel. 1980. *Power/Knowledge: Selected Interviews and Other Writings, 1972–1977*. New York: Pantheon.

Foucault, Michel. 1990. *The History of Sexuality: An Introduction*. Vol. 1. Translated by Robert Hurley. New York: Vintage Books.

Foucault, Michel. 2003. *"Society Must Be Defended": Lectures at the Collège de France, 1975–1976*. New York: Macmillan.

Fowler, John M. 1960. *Fallout: A Study of Superbombs, Strontium 90, and Survival*. New York: Basic Books.

Frenkel, Stephen. 2002. "Geographical Representations of the 'Other': The Landscape of the Panama Canal Zone." *Journal of Historical Geography* 28, no. 1: 85–99.

Fuller, Buckminister. 1970. *Education for Comprehensivity: Approaching the Benign Environment*. Tuscaloosa: University of Alabama Press.

Furlong, Kathryn. 2011. "Small Technologies, Big Change: Rethinking Infrastructure through STS and Geography." *Progress in Human Geography* 35, no. 4: 460–482.

Furlong, Kathryn. 2014. "STS Beyond the 'Modern Infrastructure Ideal': Extending Theory by Engaging with Infrastructure Challenges in the South." *Technology in Society* 38 (August): 139–147.

Gad, Christopher, Casper Bruun Jensen, and Brit Ross Winthereik. 2015. "Practical Ontology: Worlds in Anthropology and STS." *NatureCulture* 3: 67–86.

Gandy, Matthew. 2003. *Concrete and Clay: Reworking Nature in New York City*. Cambridge, MA: MIT Press.

Gandy, Matthew. 2004. "Rethinking Urban Metabolism: Water, Space and the Modern City." *City* 8, no. 3: 363–379.

Gandy, Matthew. 2013. "Marginalia: Aesthetics, Ecology, and Urban Wastelands." *Annals of the Association of American Geographers* 103, no. 6: 1301–1316.

Gärtner, Á. 2005. *Un puerto contra la voluntad del destino: Buenaventura Ciudad–Puerto*. Cali, Colombia: Sociedad Portuaria Regional de Buenaventura.

Ghosh, Palash. 2013. "Rare Riot Shows Ugly Underside of Singapore." *International Business Times*, December 10, 2013. http://www.ibtimes.com/riot-little-india-underpaid-migrant-workers-form-foundation-singapores-wealth-power-1503396.

Gieryn, Thomas F. 1983. "Boundary-Work and the Demarcation of Science from Non-Science: Strains and Interests in Professional Ideologies of Scientists." *American Sociological Review* 48, no. 6: 781–795.

Gillem, Mark L. 2007. *America Town: Building the Outposts of Empire*. Abingdon: Taylor and Francis.

Gilroy, Paul. 1993. *The Black Atlantic: Modernity and Double Consciousness*. Cambridge, MA: Harvard University Press.

Gilroy, Paul. 2007. "Offshore Humanism: Human Rights and Hydrarchy." In *Port City: On Mobility and Exchange*, edited by Maharaj Sarat, Tom Trevor, and Claudia Zanfi. Bristol: Arnolfini.

Glissant, Edouard. 1976. "Free and Forced Poetics." *Alcheringa* 2, no. 2: 95–101.

Gómez, Estrada, and José Alfredo. 1994. "Los Cucapá, las compañías colonizadoras y las tierras del Valle de Mexicali." *Calafia* 7, no. 5: 26–37.

Gómez, Estrada, and José Alfredo. 2000. "La gente del delta del Río Colorado: Indígenas, colonizadores y ejidatarios." Mexicali, Mexico: Universidad Autónoma de Baja California.

Goonewardena, Kanishka. 2018. "Planetary Urbanization and Totality." *Environment and Planning D: Society and Space* 36, no. 3: 456–473. doi.org/10.1177 /0263775818761890.

Gordillo, Gastón. 2011. "Longing for Elsewhere: Guaraní Reterritorializations." *Comparative Studies in Society and History* 53, no. 4: 855–881.

Gordillo, Gastón. 2014. *Rubble: The Afterlife of Destruction*. Durham, NC: Duke University Press.

Gordillo, Gastón. 2015. "The Insurgent Underground." *Space and Politics* (blog), August 4.

Gordillo, Gastón. 2018. "Terrain as Insurgent Weapon: An Affective Geometry of Warfare in the Mountains of Afghanistan." *Political Geography* 64: 53–62.

Gorgas, William Crawford. 1915. *Sanitation in Panama*. New York: D. Appleton and Company.

Graham, Stephen. 2010. *Disrupted Cities: When Infrastructure Fails*. London: Routledge.

Graham, Stephen, and Nigel Thrift. 2007. "Out of Order: Understanding Repair and Maintenance." *Theory, Culture and Society* 24, no. 3: 1–25.

Gras, Carla, and Valeria Hernández. 2013a. "El modelo agribusiness y sus traducciones territoriales." In *El agro como negocio: Producción, sociedad, territorios en la globalización*, edited by C. Gras and V. Hernández, 49–66. Buenos Aires: Biblos.

Gras, Carla, and Valeria Hernández. 2013b. "Los pilares del modelo agribusiness y sus estilos empresariales." In *El agro como negocio: Producción, sociedad, territorios en la globalización*, edited by C. Gras and V. Hernández, 17–46. Buenos Aires: Biblos.

Gras, Carla, and Valeria Hernández. 2016. *Radiografía del nuevo campo argentino: Del terrateniente al empresario transnacional*. Buenos Aires: Siglo XXI.

Gray, Andrew. 1996. *The Arakmbut of Amazonian Peru*. Providence: Berghahn.

Greenberg, Paul. 2015. *American Catch: The Fight for Our Local Seafood*. London: Penguin.

Greene, Julie. 2009. *The Canal Builders: Making America's Empire at the Panama Canal*. New York: Penguin.

Gupta, Akhil. 1998. *Postcolonial Developments: Agriculture in the Making of Modern India*. Durham, NC: Duke University Press.

Halpern, Orit, et al. 2013. "Test-Bed Urbanism." *Public Culture* 25, no. 270: 272–306.

Hamblin, Jacob Darwin. 2013. *Arming Mother Nature: The Birth of Catastrophic Environmentalism*. Oxford: Oxford University Press.

Haraway, Donna. 1988. "Situated Knowledge: The Science Question in Feminism and the Privilege of Partial Perspective." *Feminist Studies* 14, no. 3: 575–599.

Haraway, Donna. 1989. *Primate Visions: Gender, Race, and Nature in the World of Modern Science*. Hove: Psychology Press.

Haraway, Donna. 1991. *Simians, Cyborgs and Women: The Reinvention of Nature*. London: Free Association.

Haraway, Donna. 2008. *When Species Meet*. Minneapolis: University of Minnesota Press.

Haraway, Donna. 2015. "Anthropocene, Capitalocene, Plantationocene, Chthulucene: Making Kin." *Environmental Humanities* 6: 159–165.

Haraway, Donna, and Martha Kenney 2015. "Anthropocene, Capitalocene, Chthulhocene." In *Art in the Anthropocene: Encounters among Aesthetics, Politics, Environments and Epistemologies*, edited by Heather Davis and Etienne Turpin, 255–270. London: Open Humanities Press.

Haraway, Donna, et al. 2016. "Anthropologists Are Talking—about the Anthropocene." *Ethnos* 81, no. 3: 535–564.

Hardt, Michael, and Antonio Negri. 2000. *Empire*. Cambridge, MA: Harvard University Press.

Hardt, Michael, and Antonio Negri. 2009. *Commonwealth*. Cambridge, MA: Harvard University Press.

Harman, Graham. 2009. *Prince of Networks: Bruno Latour and Metaphysics*. Prahran, Australia: Re.press.

Harrison, Lindsay Jill. 2011. *Pesticide Drift and the Pursuit of Environmental Justice*. Cambridge, MA: MIT Press.

Hartigan, John. 2015. "Plant Publics: Multispecies Relating in Spanish Botanical Gardens." *Anthropological Quarterly* 88, no. 2: 481–507.

Harvey, David. 2012. *Rebel Cities: From the Right to the City to the Urban Revolution*. London: Verso.

Harvey, Graham, and Charles Thompson Jr. 2005. *Indigenous Diasporas and Dislocations*. Burlington, VT: Ashgate.

Harvey, Penelope. 2016. "Waste Futures: Infrastructures and Political Experimentation in Southern Peru." *Ethnos* 82, no. 4: 672–689.

Harvey, Penelope, Casper Bruun Jensen, and Atsuro Morita, eds. 2016. *Infrastructures and Social Complexity: A Companion*. London: Routledge.

Harvey, Penny, and Hannah Knox. 2012. "The Enchantments of Infrastructure." *Mobilities* 7, no. 4: 521–536.

Harvey, Penny, and Hannah Knox. 2015. *Roads: An Anthropology of Infrastructure and Expertise*. Ithaca, NY: Cornell University Press.

Havlick, David G. 2011. "Disarming Nature: Converting Military Lands to Wildlife Refuges." *Geographical Review* 101, no. 2: 183–200.

Hecht, Susanna. 2004. "Invisible Forests: The Political Ecology of Forest Resurgence in El Salvador." In *Liberation Ecologies: Environment, Development, Social Movements*, 2nd ed., 64–104. London: Routledge.

Hecht, Susanna B., et al. 2006. "Globalization, Forest Resurgence, and Environmental Politics in El Salvador." *World Development* 34, no. 2: 308–323.

Heidegger, Martin. 1977. *The Question concerning Technology.* New York: Garland.

Heidegger, Martin. 1995. *The Fundamental Concepts of Metaphysics: World, Finitude, Solitude.* Bloomington: Indiana University Press.

Helmreich, Stefan. 2009. *Alien Ocean: Anthropological Voyages in Microbial Seas.* Berkeley: University of California Press.

Hernández, Valeria. 2009. "La ruralidad globalizada y el paradigma de los agronegocios en la pampa gringa." In *La Argentina rural: De la agricultura familiar a los agronegocios,* edited by C. Gras and V. Hernández, 39–64. Buenos Aires: Biblos.

Hernández, Valeria, María F. Fossa Riglos, and María E. Muzi. 2013a. "Agrociudades pampeanas: Usos del territorio." In *El agro como negocio: Producción, sociedad, y territorios en la globalización,* edited by C. Gras and V. Hernández, 123–149. Buenos Aires: Biblos.

Hernández, Valeria, María F. Fossa Riglos, and María E. Muzi. 2013b. "Figuras socioproductivas de la ruralidad globalizada." In *El agro como negocio: Producción, sociedad, y territorios en la globalización,* edited by C. Gras and V. Hernández, 151–169. Buenos Aires: Biblos.

Hetherington, Kregg. 2011. *Guerrilla Auditors: The Politics of Transparency in Neoliberal Paraguay.* Durham, NC: Duke University Press.

Hetherington, Kregg. 2013. "Beans before the Law: Knowledge Practices, Responsibility, and the Paraguayan Soy Boom." *Cultural Anthropology* 28, no. 1: 65–85.

Hetherington, Kregg. 2014. "Waiting for the Surveyor: Development Promises and the Temporality of Infrastructure." *Journal of Latin American and Caribbean Anthropology* 19, no. 2: 195–211.

Hetherington, Kregg. 2016. "Surveying the Future Perfect: Anthropology, Development and the Promise of Infrastructure." In *Infrastructures and Social Complexity: A Companion,* edited by Penelope Harvey, Casper Bruun Jensen, and Atsuro Morita, 58–68. London: Routledge.

Hetherington, Kregg, and Jeremy M. Campbell. 2014. "Nature, Infrastructure, and the State: Rethinking Development in Latin America." *Journal of Latin American and Caribbean Anthropology* 19, no. 2: 191–194.

Hird, Myra J. 2009. *The Origins of Sociable Life: Evolution after Science Studies.* London: Palgrave Macmillan.

Howe, Cymene, and Anand Pandian. 2015. "Introduction: Lexicon for an Anthropocene Yet Unseen." *Fieldsites,* Society for Cultural Anthropology.

Howe, Cymene, et al. 2015. "Paradoxical Infrastructures Ruins, Retrofit, and Risk." *Science, Technology and Human Values* 41, no. 3: 547–565.

Huergo, Héctor. 2006. "La hidrovía abona la inversión." *Clarín,* September 2.

Hull, Matthew S. 2012. *Government of Paper: The Materiality of Bureaucracy in Urban Pakistan.* Berkeley: University of California Press.

Hulme, Mike. 2009. *Why We Disagree about Climate Change: Understanding Controversy, Inaction and Opportunity*. Cambridge: Cambridge University Press.

Hustak, Carla, and Natasha Myers. 2012. "Involutionary Momentum: Affective Ecologies and the Sciences of Plant/Insect Encounters." *Differences* 23, no. 3: 74–118.

IDEAM. 2010. *Segunda Comunicación Nacional ante la Convención Marco de las Naciones Unidas sobre el Cambio Climático*. Bogotá: Instituto de Hidrología, Meteorología y Estudios Ambientales.

Illich, Ivan. 1985. *H₂O and the Waters of Forgetfulness: Reflections on the Historicity of "Stuff."* Dallas: Dallas Institute of Humanities and Culture.

Ingold, Tim. 2011. *Being Alive: Essays on Movement, Knowledge and Description*. London: Routledge.

Ingold, Tim. 2012. "Toward an Ecology of Materials." *Annual Review of Anthropology* 41: 427–442.

Invisible Committee. 2009. *The Coming Insurrection*. Aware Journalism.

Invisible Committee. 2015. *To Our Friends*. Los Angeles: Semiotext(e).

IPCC (Intergovernmental Panel on Climate Change). 2013. "Summary for Policymakers." In *Climate Change 2013: The Physical Science Basis. Contribution of Working Group I to the Fifth Assessment Report of the Intergovernmental Panel on Climate Change*, edited by T. F. Stocker et al. Cambridge: Cambridge University Press.

IPCC (Intergovernmental Panel on Climate Change). 2014. *Climate Change 2014: Impacts, Adaptation, and Vulnerability*. Cambridge: Cambridge University Press.

Jackson, Jean E. "Rights to Indigenous Culture in Colombia." 2007. In *The Practice of Human Rights: Tracking Law between the Global and the Local*, edited by Mark Goodale and Sally Engle Merry, 204–241. Cambridge: Cambridge University Press.

Jackson, Steven. "Rethinking Repair." 2014. In *Media Technologies: Essays on Communication, Materiality and Society*, edited by Tarleton Gillespie, Pablo Boczkowski, and Kristen Foot. Cambridge, MA: MIT Press.

Jagger, Bianca. 2012. Foreword to *The Energy Imperative: 100 Percent Renewable Now*, edited by H. Scheer, xii–xv. New York: Earthscan.

Jakobson, Roman. 1980. *The Framework of Language*. Ann Arbor: Michigan Slavic.

Jameson, Fredric. 2003. "Future City." *New Left Review* 21 (May–June): 65.

Jefferson, Ben Thomas. 2013. "The Sea as Place in Derek Walcott's Poetry." *Journal of Commonwealth Literature* 48, no. 2: 287–304.

Jensen, Casper Bruun. 2010. *Ontologies for Developing Things: Making Health Care Futures through Technology*. Rotterdam: Sense.

Jensen, Casper Bruun. 2014. "Experiments in Good Faith and Hopefulness: Towards a Post-Critical Social Science." *Common Knowledge* 20, no. 2: 337–362.

Jensen, Casper Bruun, and Atsuro Morita. 2015. "Infrastructures as Ontological Experiments." *Engaging Science, Technology and Society* 1: 81–87.

Jensen, Casper Bruun, and Brit Ross Winthereik. 2013. *Monitoring Movements in Development Aid: Recursive Partnerships and Infrastructures*. Cambridge, MA: MIT Press.

Jensen, Casper Bruun, and Brit Ross Winthereik. 2015. "Test Sites: Attachments and Detachments in Community-Based Ecotourism." In *Detachment: Essays on the Limits of Relational Thinking*, edited by Matei Candea, Jo Cook, Catherine Trundle, and Tom Yarrow, 197. Manchester: Manchester University Press.

Johnson, Elizabeth, et al. 2014. "After the Anthropocene Politics and Geographic Inquiry for a New Epoch." *Progress in Human Geography* 38, no. 3: 439–456.

Johnson, Nuala C. 2011. *Nature Displaced, Nature Displayed: Order and Beauty in Botanical Gardens*. New York: IB Tauris.

Johnston, Barbara Rose, and Holly M. Barker. 2008. *Consequential Damages of Nuclear War: The Rongelap Report*. Walnut Creek, CA: Left Coast Press.

Jørgensen, Dolly. 2013. "Environmentalists on Both Sides: Enactments in the California Rigs-to-Reefs Debate." In *New Natures: Joining Environmental History with Science and Technology Studies*, edited by Dolly Jørgensen, Finn Arne Jørgensen, and Sara B. Pritchard, 51–68. Pittsburgh: University of Pittsburgh Press.

Jørgensen, Dolly. 2014. "Not by Human Hands: Five Technological Tenets for Environmental History in the Anthropocene." *Environment and History* 20, no. 4: 479–489.

Jørgensen, Dolly, Finn Arne Jørgensen, and Sara B. Pritchard. 2013. *New Natures: Joining Environmental History with Science and Technology Studies*. Pittsburgh: University of Pittsburgh Press.

Joyce, Patrick. 2003. *The Rule of Freedom: Liberalism and the Modern City*. New York: Verso.

Kawa, Nicholas C. 2016. "How Religion, Race, and the Weedy Agency of Plants Shape Amazonian Home Gardens." *Culture, Agriculture, Food and Environment* 38, no. 2: 84–93.

Kemper, Karin E. 2004. "Groundwater: From Development to Management." *Hydrogeology Journal* 12, no. 1: 3–5.

Kennedy, Christopher, John Cuddihy, and Joshua Engel-Yan. 2007. "The Changing Metabolism of Cities." *Journal of Industrial Ecology* 11, no. 2: 43–59.

Kennedy, John F. 1963. "Address to the Nation on the Nuclear Test Ban Treaty," 26 July. Signing of the Nuclear Test Ban Treaty. http://www.jfklibrary.org/JFK/JFK-in-History/Nuclear-Test-Ban-Treaty.aspx.

Kernaghan, Richard. 2012. "Furrows and Walls, or the Legal Topography of a Frontier Road in Peru." *Mobilities* 7, no. 4: 501–520.

Kimmerer, Robin. 2015. *Braiding Sweetgrass: Indigenous Wisdom, Scientific Knowledge and the Teachings of Plants*. Minneapolis: Milkweed Editions.

Kingdom, Bill, Roland Liemberger, and Philippe Marin. 2006. "The Challenge of Reducing Non-Revenue Water (NRW) in Developing Countries: How the Private Sector Can Help: A Look at Performance-Based Service Contracting." In *Water Supply and Sanitation Sector Board Discussion Paper*. Washington, DC: World Bank.

Kirsch, Stuart. 2014. *Mining Capitalism: The Relationship between Corporations and Their Critics*. Berkeley: University of California Press.

Klein, Naomi. 2015. *This Changes Everything: Capitalism vs. the Climate*. New York: Simon and Schuster.

Klooster, Dan. 2003. "Forest Transitions in Mexico: Institutions and Forests in a Globalized Countryside." *Professional Geographer* 55, no. 2: 227–237.

Kockelman, Paul. 2012. "The Ground, the Ground, the Ground: Or, Why Archeology Is So 'Hard.'" *Yearbook of Comparative Literature* 58: 176–184.

Kockelman, Paul. 2013. *Agent, Person, Subject, Self: A Theory of Ontology, Interaction, and Infrastructure*. Oxford: Oxford University Press.

Kohn, Eduardo. 2013. *How Forests Think: Toward an Anthropology beyond the Human*. Berkeley: University of California Press.

Kohn, Eduardo. 2015. "Anthropology of Ontologies." *Annual Review of Anthropology* 44: 311–327.

Kolbert, Elizabeth. 2014. *The Sixth Extinction: An Unnatural History*. London: A&C Black.

Koronowski, Ryan. 2014. "House Votes to Deny Climate Science and Ties Pentagon's Hands on Climate Change." ThinkProgress.org. May 22.

Kosek, Jake. 2006. *Understories: The Political Life of Forests in Northern New Mexico*. Durham, NC: Duke University Press.

Koselleck, Reinhart. 2004. *Futures Past: On the Semantics of Historical Time*. New York: Columbia University Press.

Kuletz, Valerie. 1998. *The Tainted Desert: Environmental Ruin in the American West*. Hove: Psychology Press.

Lai, Samantha, et al. 2015. "The Effects of Urbanisation on Coastal Habitats and the Potential for Ecological Engineering: A Singapore Case Study." *Ocean and Coastal Management* 103: 78–85.

Lambert, Allan, and W. Hirner. 2000. "Losses from Water Supply Systems: Standard Terminology and Recommended Performance Measures." The Blue Pages, International Water Association.

Lampis, Andrea, and Arabella Fraser. 2012. *The Impact of Climate Change on Urban Settlements in Columbia*. Nairobi: UN-HABITAT.

Langer, R. M. 1940. "Fast New World." *Collier's Weekly* (July 6): 18–19.

Lapegna, Pablo. 2016a. "Genetically Modified Soybeans, Agrochemical Exposure, and Everyday Forms of Peasant Collaboration in Argentina." *Journal of Peasant Studies* 43, no. 2: 517–536.

Lapegna, Pablo. 2016b. *Soybeans and Power: Genetically Modified Crops, Environmental Politics, and Social Movements in Argentina*. Oxford: Oxford University Press.

Larkin, Brian. 2004. "Degraded Images, Distorted Sounds: Nigerian Video and the Infrastructure of Piracy." *Public Culture* 16, no. 2: 289–314.

Larkin, Brian. 2008. *Signal and Noise Media, Infrastructure, and Urban Culture in Nigeria*. Durham, NC: Duke University Press.

Larkin, Brian. 2013. "The Politics and Poetics of Infrastructure." *Annual Review of Anthropology* 42, no. 1: 327–343.

Lasso, Marixa. 2013. "Nationalism and Immigrant Labor in a Tropical Enclave: The West Indians of Colón City, 1850–1936." *Citizenship Studies* 17, no. 5: 551–565.

Latour, Bruno. 1988. *The Pasteurization of France*. Cambridge, MA: Harvard University Press.

Latour, Bruno. 1993. *We Have Never Been Modern*. Cambridge, MA: Harvard University Press.

Latour, Bruno. 1996. *Aramis, or, The Love of Technology*. Cambridge, MA: Harvard University Press.

Latour, Bruno. 1998. "To Modernise or Ecologise? That Is the Question." In *Remaking Reality: Nature at the Millennium*, edited by B. Braun and N. Castree. London: Routledge.

Latour, Bruno. 2004a. *Politics of Nature: How to Bring the Sciences into Democracy*. Cambridge, MA: Harvard University Press.

Latour, Bruno. 2004b. "Why Has Critique Run Out of Steam? From Matters of Fact to Matters of Concern." *Critical Inquiry* 30, no. 2: 225–248.

Latour, Bruno. 2005. "Reassembling the Social an Introduction to Actor-Network-Theory." In *Clarendon Lectures in Management Studies*. New York: Oxford University Press.

Latour, Bruno. 2013. "Facing Gaia: Six Lectures on the Political Theology of Nature." Gifford Lectures on Natural Religion. February 18–28.

Latour, Bruno. 2014. "Agency at the Time of the Anthropocene." *New Literary History* 45, no. 1: 1–18.

Latour, Bruno, and Peter Weibel, eds. 2005. *Making Things Public: Atmospheres of Democracy*. Cambridge, MA: MIT Press.

Law, John. 2004. *After Method: Mess in Social Science Research*. London: Routledge.

Law, John, et al. 1987. "Technology and Heterogeneous Engineering: The Case of Portuguese Expansion." In *The Social Construction of Technological Systems: New Directions in the Sociology and History of Technology*, edited by Wiebe E. Bijker, Thomas P. Hughes, and Trevor Pinch, 1:111–134. Cambridge, MA: MIT Press.

Leake, Andrés, Omar López, and María C. Leake. 2016. *La deforestación del Chaco salteño*. Salta, Argentina: SMA Ediciones.

Lee, Richard. 2006. "Twenty-First Century Indigenism." *Anthropological Theory* 6, no. 4: 455–479.

Lefebvre, Henri. 2003. *The Urban Revolution*. Minneapolis: University of Minnesota Press.

Lefebvre, Henri. 2004 (1992). *Rhythmanalysis*. New York: Continuum.

Leguizamón, Amalia. 2016. "Disappearing Nature? Agribusiness, Biotechnology and Distance in Argentine Soybean Production." *Journal of Peasant Studies* 43, no. 2: 313–330.

Leis, Raúl A. 1979. *Colón en el ojo de la tormenta*. Panama City: Centro de Capacitación Social.

LePrince, Joseph A. and A. J. Orenstein. 1916. *Mosquito Control in Panama: The Eradication of Malaria and Yellow Fever in Cuba and Panama.* New York: G. P. Putnam's Sons.

Levinson, Marc. 2006. *The Box: How the Shipping Container Made the World Smaller and the World Economy Bigger.* Princeton, NJ: Princeton University Press.

Lewis, Simon L., and Mark A. Maslin. 2015. "Defining the Anthropocene." *Nature* 519, no. 7542: 171–180.

Li, Tania. 2009. "To Make Live or Let Die? Rural Dispossession and the Protection of Surplus Populations." *Antipode* 41, S1: 66–93.

Lim, Eng-Beng. 2014. "Future Island." *Third Text* 28, nos. 4–5: 443–453.

Lindee, M. Susan. 1994. *Suffering Made Real: American Science and the Survivors at Hiroshima.* Chicago: University of Chicago Press.

Lindsay-Poland, John. 2003. *Emperors in the Jungle: The Hidden History of the US in Panama.* Durham, NC: Duke University Press.

"Living Breakwaters: Rebuild by Design Competition." 2013. Scape / Landscape Architecture.

Locke, John. 1980. *Second Treatise of Government.* Indianapolis: Hackett.

Lorey, Isabell. 2015. *State of Insecurity: Government of the Precarious.* New York: Verso.

Lorimer, Jamie. 2008. "Living Roofs and Brownfield Wildlife: Towards a Fluid Biogeography of UK Nature Conservation." *Environment and Planning A* 40, no. 9: 2042–60.

Lorimer, Jamie. 2017. "The Anthropo-Scene: A Guide for the Perplexed." *Social Studies of Science* 47, no. 1: 117–142.

Lovins, Amory B., et al. 2002. *Small Is Profitable: The Hidden Economic Benefits of Making Electrical Resources the Right Size.* Boulder, CO: Rocky Mountain Institute.

Lowe, Celia. 2006. *Wild Profusion: Biodiversity Conservation in an Indonesian Archipelago.* Princeton, NJ: Princeton University Press.

Lyons, Kristina Marie. 2014. "Soil Science, Development, and the 'Elusive Nature' of Colombia's Amazonian Plains." *Journal of Latin American and Caribbean Anthropology* 19, no. 2: 212–236.

Lyons, Kristina Marie. 2016. "Decomposition as Life Politics: Soils, Selva, and Small Farmers under the Gun of the US-Colombia War on Drugs." *Cultural Anthropology* 31, no. 1: 56–81.

Mabey, Richard. 2012. *Weeds: In Defense of Nature's Most Unloved Plants.* New York: Ecco.

Machta, Lester, Robert J. List, and J. M. Fowler. 1960. "The Global Pattern of Fallout." In *Fallout: Study of Superbombs, Strontium 90, and Survival,* edited by J. M. Fowler, 26. New York: Basic Books.

Machta, L., Robert J. List, and L. F. Hubert. 1956. "World-Wide Travel of Atomic Debris." *Science* 124, no. 3220: 474–477.

MacKenzie, Clyde L., Jr. 1984. "A History of Oystering in Raritan Bay, with Environmental Observations." In *Raritan Bay: Its Multiple Uses and Abuses*, edited by A. L. Pacheco, 37–66. Sandy Hook, NJ: Sandy Hook Laboratory.

MacKenzie, Clyde L., Jr. 1992. *The Fisheries of Raritan Bay*. New Brunswick, NJ: Rutgers University Press.

Makhijani, Arjun, and Stephen I. Schwartz. 2008. "Victims of the Bomb." In *Atomic Audit: The Costs and Consequences of U.S. Nuclear Weapons since 1940*, edited by Stephen I. Schwartz, 375–431. Washington, DC: Brooking Institution Press.

Malay, Michael. 2014. "Singapore Needs to Address Its Treatment of Migrant Workers." *Guardian*, April 21.

Malkin, Victoria. 2001. "Narcotrafficking, Migration and Modernity in Rural Mexico." *Latin American Perspectives* 28, no. 4: 101–128.

Martinez-Alier, Juan. 1997. "Environmental Justice (Local and Global)." *Capitalism Socialism* 1: 91–107.

Marx, Karl. 1976. *Capital: A Critique of Political Economy*. Vol. 1. London: Penguin.

Marx, Karl, and Martin Milligan. 1844. *Economic and Philosophic Manuscripts and the Communist Manifesto*. Amherst, NY: Prometheus Books.

Masco, Joseph. 2004. "Mutant Ecologies: Radioactive Life in Post–Cold War New Mexico." *Cultural Anthropology* 19, no. 4: 517–50.

Masco, Joseph. 2006. *The Nuclear Borderlands: The Manhattan Project in Post–Cold War New Mexico*. Princeton, NJ: Princeton University Press.

Masco, Joseph. 2010. "Bad Weather: On Planetary Crisis." *Social Studies of Science* 40, no. 1: 7–40.

Masco, Joseph. 2014. *The Theater of Operations: National Security Affect from the Cold War to the War on Terror*. Durham, NC: Duke University Press.

Masco, Joseph. 2015. "The Age of Fallout." *History of the Present* 5, no. 2: 137–168.

Masquelier, Adeline. 2002. "Road Mythographies: Space, Mobility, and the Historical Imagination in Postcolonial Niger." *American Ethnologist* 29, no. 4: 829–856.

Mastnak, Tomaz, Julia Elyachar, and Tom Boellstorff. 2014. "Botanical Decolonization: Rethinking Native Plants." *Environment and Planning D: Society and Space* 32, no. 2: 363–380.

Mathews, Andrew S. 2008. "State Making, Knowledge, and Ignorance: Translation and Concealment in Mexican Forestry Institutions." *American Anthropologist* 110, no. 4: 484–494.

Mathews, Andrew S. 2011. *Instituting Nature: Authority, Expertise, and Power in Mexican Forests*. Cambridge, MA: MIT Press.

Mbembe, Achille. 2001. *On the Postcolony*. Berkeley: University of California Press.

Mbembe, Achille. 2003. "Necropolitics." *Public Culture* 15, no. 1: 11–40.

Mbembe, Achille, and Janet Roitman. 1995. "Figures of the Subject in Times of Crisis." *Public Culture* 7, no. 2: 323–352.

McCullough, David. 1977. *The Path between Two Seas*. New York: Simon and Schuster.

McKittrick, Katherine. 2013. "Plantation Futures." *Small Axe* 17, no. 342: 1–15.

Meehan, Katie M. 2014. "Tool-Power: Water Infrastructure as Wellsprings of State Power." *Geoforum* 57: 215–224.

Melillo, Jerry M., Terese Richmond, and Gary W. Yohe, eds. 2014. *Highlights of Climate Change Impacts in the United States: The Third National Climate Assessment.* Washington: US Global Change Research Program.

Melly, Caroline. 2013. "Ethnography on the Road: Infrastructural Vision and the Unruly Present in Contemporary Dakar." *Africa: The Journal of the International African Institute* 83, no. 3: 385–402.

Melosi, Martin. 2000. *The Sanitary City: Urban Infrastructure in America from Colonial Times to the Present.* Baltimore: Johns Hopkins University Press.

Merrifield, Andy. 2013. *The Politics of the Encounter: Urban Theory and Protest under Planetary Urbanization.* Athens: University of Georgia Press.

Mier y Terán Giménez Cacho, Mateo. 2016. "Soybean Agrifood Systems Dynamics and the Diversity of Farming Styles on the Agricultural Frontier in Mato Grosso, Brazil." *Journal of Peasant Studies* 43, no. 2: 419–441.

Ministerio de Trabajo. 2012. *Buenaventura, ciudad puerto de clase mundial: Plan local de empleo 2011–2015.* Buenaventura: Ministerio de Trabajo, Fundación Panamericana para el Desarrollo.

Mintz, Sidney Wilfred. 1986. *Sweetness and Power: The Place of Sugar in Modern History.* New York: Penguin Books.

Mitchell, Timothy. 1988. *Colonising Egypt.* Berkeley: University of California Press.

Mitchell, Timothy. 2002. *Rule of Experts: Egypt, Techno-Politics, Modernity.* Berkeley: University of California Press.

Mitchell, Timothy. 2009. "Carbon Democracy." *Economy and Society* 38, no. 3: 399–432.

Mitchell, Timothy. 2011. *Carbon Democracy: Political Power in the Age of Oil.* London: Verso.

Monastersky, Richard. 2015. "First Atomic Blast Proposed as Start of Anthropocene." *Nature,* January 16. https://www.nature.com/news/first-atomic-blast-proposed -as-start-of-anthropocene-1.16739.

Moore, Donald S., Jake Kosek, and Anand Pandian. 2003. *Race, Nature, and the Politics of Difference.* Durham, NC: Duke University Press.

Moore, Jason W. 2015. *Capitalism in the Web of Life: Ecology and the Accumulation of Capital.* London: Verso.

Moore, Jason W. 2017. "The Capitalocene, Part I: On the Nature and Origins of Our Ecological Crisis." *Journal of Peasant Studies* 44, no. 3: 594–630.

Morita, Atsuro. 2016. "Infrastructuring Amphibious Space: The Interplay of Aquatic and Terrestrial Infrastructures in the Chao Phraya Delta in Thailand." *Science as Culture* 25, no. 1 117–140.

Morton, Timothy. 2007. *Ecology without Nature: Rethinking Environmental Aesthetics.* Cambridge, MA: Harvard University Press.

Morton, Timothy. 2013. *Hyperobjects: Philosophy and Ecology after the End of the World*. Minneapolis: University of Minnesota Press.

Mosquera Torres, Gilma. 2010. *Vivienda y arquitectura tradicional en el Pacífico colombiano: Patrimonio cultural afrodescendente*. Cali, Mexico: Universidad del Valle, Programa Editorial.

Mosquera Torres, Gilma, and Jacques Aprile-Gniset. 2006. *Aldeas de la Costa de Buenaventura*. Cali, Mexico: Universidad del Valle.

Moten, Fred, and Stefano Harney. 2004. "The University and the Undercommons: Seven Theses." *Social Text* 22, no. 2: 101–115.

Mrázek, Rudolf. 2002. *Engineers of Happy Land: Technology and Nationalism in a Colony*. Princeton, NJ: Princeton University Press.

Muehlmann, Shaylih. 2008. "'Spread Your Ass Cheeks': And Other Things That Should Not Be Said in Indigenous Languages." *American Ethnologist* 35, no. 1: 34–48.

Muehlmann, Shaylih. 2013a. *When I Wear My Alligator Boots: Narco-Culture in the US-Mexican Borderlands*. Berkeley: University of California Press.

Muehlmann, Shaylih. 2013b. *Where the River Ends: Contested Indigeneities in the Mexican Colorado Delta*. Durham, NC: Duke University Press.

Mumford, Lewis. 1989. *The City in History: Its Origins, Its Transformations, and Its Prospects*. New York: Harcourt Brace.

Murphy, Michelle. 2016. "To What Extent Is Embodied Knowledge a Form of Science and Technology by Other Means?" Keynote lecture, Society for Social Studies of Science Annual Meeting, September. Barcelona, Spain.

Myers, Natasha. 2013. "Plant Vocalities: Articulating Botanical Sensoria in the Experimental Arts and Sciences." Unpublished paper presented at the University of New South Wales. October 15.

Myers, Natasha. 2015a. "Amplifying the Gaps between Climate Science and Forest Policy: The Write2Know Project and Participatory Dissent." *Canada Watch* 18–21.

Myers, Natasha. 2015b. "Conversations on Plant Sensing: Notes from the Field." *NatureCulture* 3: 35–66.

Myers, Natasha. 2015c. "Edenic Apocalypse: Singapore's End-of-Time Botanical Tourism." In *Art in the Anthropocene: Encounters among Aesthetics, Politics, Environments and Epistemologies*, edited by Heather Davis and Etienne Turpin, 31–42. London: Open Humanities Press.

Myers, Natasha. 2015d. *Rendering Life Molecular: Models, Modelers, and Excitable Matter*. Durham, NC: Duke University Press.

Myers, Natasha. 2016. "Photosynthesis." *Theorizing the Contemporary, Cultural Anthropology*. January 21. https://culanth.org/fieldsights/790-photosynthesis.

Myers, Natasha. 2017. "From the Anthropocene to the Planthroposcene: Designing Gardens for Plant/People Involution." *History and Anthropology* 28, no. 30: 1–5.

Myers, Natasha. 2018. "How to Grow Livable Worlds: Ten Not-So-Easy Steps." In *The World to Come*, edited by Kerry Oliver-Smith, 53–63. Gainesville: Samuel P. Harn Museum of Art, University of Florida.

Myers, Natasha. Forthcoming. "An Anthropologist among Artists in the Gardens." In *Botanical Drift: Economic Botany and Its Plant Protagonists*, edited by Khadija von Zinnenburg Carroll and Petra Lange-Berndt. Berlin: Sternberg.

Myers, Natasha. Forthcoming. "How to Grow Livable Worlds: Ten Not-So-Easy Steps." In *A World to Come*, edited by Kerry Oliver-Smith. Gainesville: Harn Museum; University Press of Florida.

Nading, Alex M. 2014. *Mosquito Trails: Ecology, Health, and the Politics of Entanglement*. Berkeley: University of California Press.

Namba, Miki. 2016. "Becoming a City: Infrastructural Fetishism and Scattered Urbanization in Vientiane, Laos." In *Infrastructures and Social Complexity: A Reader*, edited by Penny Harvey, Casper Bruun Jensen, and Atsuro Morita, 76–87. London: Routledge.

Nancy, Jean-Luc. 2014. *After Fukushima: The Equivalence of Catastrophes*. New York: Fordham University Press.

Negri, Antonio. 2018. *From the Factory to the Metropolis*. Cambridge, England: Polity.

Neumann, Roderick P. 1998. *Imposing Wilderness: Struggles over Livelihood and Nature Preservation in Africa*. Berkeley: University of California Press.

New York Department of Health. 2014. *A Public Health Review of High Volume Hydraulic Fracturing for Shale Gas Development*. New York: New York Department of Public Health.

Nielsen, Morten. 2011. "Futures Within: Reversible Time and House-Building in Maputo, Mozambique." *Anthropological Theory* 11, no. 4: 397–423.

Nixon, Rob. 2011. *Slow Violence and the Environmentalism of the Poor*. Cambridge, MA: Harvard University Press.

Observatorio Contra la Discriminación y el Racismo. 2012. *Discriminación laboral en Cali: Un acercamiento desde la desigualdad socio-demográfica en el área metropolitana*. Bogotá, Colombia: Ministerio del Interior.

O'Dempsey, Tony, and Ping Ting Chew. 2011. "The Freshwater Swamp Forests of Sungei Seletar Catchment: A Status Report." Proceedings of Nature Society, Singapore's Conference on Nature Conservation for a Sustainable Singapore, 121–166. October 16.

Oliveira, Gustavo, and Susanna Hecht. 2016. "Sacred Groves, Sacrifice Zones and Soy Production: Globalization, Intensification and Neo-Nature in South America." *Journal of Peasant Studies* 43, no. 2: 251–285.

Oliveira, Gustavo, and Mindi Schneider. 2016. "The Politics of Flexing Soybeans: China, Brazil, and Global Agroindustrial Restructuring." *Journal of Peasant Studies* 43, no. 1: 167–194.

Ondaatje, Michael. 1987. *In the Skin of the Lion*. Toronto: McClelland and Stewart.

O'Neill McCleskey, Claire. 2012. "Mexico Destroyed 4,000 Narco-Airstrips since 2006." *InSight Crime*. November 7, 2012. https://www.insightcrime.org/news/brief/4000-narco-airstrips-mexico-2006/.

Ong, Aihwa. 1999. *Flexible Citizenship: The Cultural Logics of Transnationality*. Durham, NC: Duke University Press.

Ong, Aihwa. 2006. *Neoliberalism as Exception: Mutations in Citizenship and Sovereignty*. Durham, NC: Duke University Press.

Ong, Aihwa. 2012. "Powers of Sovereignty: State, People, Wealth, Life." *Focaal: Journal of Global and Historical Anthropology* 64: 24–35.

Oreskes, Naomi, and Erik M. Conway. 2010. *Merchants of Doubt: How a Handful of Scientists Obscured the Truth on Issues from Tobacco Smoke to Global Warming*. New York: Bloomsbury.

Orff, Kate. 2010. "Reviving New York's Rivers—With Oysters!" Filmed December 2010. TEDWomen, 10:07. Posted December. https://www.ted.com/talks/kate_orff_oysters_as_architecture.

Orff, Kate. 2011. "Oyster-Tecture." In B. Bergdoll, *Rising Currents: Projects for New York's Waterfront*, 90–99. New York: Museum of Modern Art.

Orff, Kate. 2014. "Rebuilding Eco-Infrastructure." Filmed March 2014. TEDxGowanus. Posted March.

Orlove, Benjamin S. 1980. "Ecological Anthropology." *Annual Review of Anthropology* 9, no. 1: 235–273.

Oslender, Ulrich. 2002. "The Logic of the River: A Spatial Approach to Ethnic-Territorial Mobilization in the Colombian Pacific Region." *Journal of Latin American Anthropology* 7, no. 2: 86–117.

Oslender, Ulrich. 2004. "Fleshing Out the Geographies of Social Movements: Colombia's Pacific Coast Black Communities and the 'Aquatic Space.'" *Political Geography* 23, no. 8: 957–985.

Oslender, Ulrich. 2007. "Violence in Development: The Logic of Forced Displacement on Colombia's Pacific Coast." *Development in Practice* 17, no. 6: 752–764.

Oslender, Ulrich. 2011. *Comunidades negras y espacio en el Pacífico colombiano: Hacia un giro geográfico en el estudio de los movimientos sociales*. Bogotá, Colombia: Instituto Colombiano de Antropología e Historia.

Otter, Christopher. 2002. "Making Liberalism Durable: Vision and Civility in the Late Victorian City." *Social History* 27, no. 1: 1–15.

Otter, Christopher. 2004a. "Cleansing and Clarifying: Technology and Perception in Nineteenth-Century London." *Journal of British Studies* 43: 40–64.

Otter, Chris. 2004b. "Streets." In *Patterned Ground: Entanglements of Nature and Culture*, edited by Stephan Harrison, Steve Pile, and Nigel Thrift, 242–248. London: Reaktion Books.

"Panama's Economy: A Singapore for Central America?" 2011. *Economist*, July 14.

Pandian, Anand. 2009. *Crooked Stalks: Cultivating Virtue in South India*. Durham, NC: Duke University Press.

Pandian, Anand. 2015. *Reel World: An Anthropology of Creation*. Durham, NC: Duke University Press.

Parenti, Christian. 2012. *Tropic of Chaos: Climate Change and the New Geography of Violence*. New York: Nation Books.

Parks, Lisa, and Nicole Starosielski. 2015. *Signal Traffic: Critical Studies of Media Infrastructures*. Champaign: University of Illinois Press.

Paschel, Tianna S. 2010. "The Right to Difference: Explaining Colombia's Shift from Color Blindness to the Law of Black Communities." *American Journal of Sociology* 116, no. 3: 729–769.

Peake, Linda. 2016. "The Twenty-First Century Quest for Feminism and the Global Urban." *International Journal or Urban and Regional Research*. 40, no. 1: 219–227.

Petryna, Adriana. 2002. *Life Exposed: Biological Citizens after Chernobyl*. Princeton, NJ: Princeton University Press.

Pipek, Volkmar, and Volker Wulf. 2009. "Infrastructuring: Toward an Integrated Perspective on the Design and Use of Information Technology." *Journal of the Association for Information Systems* 10, no. 5: 306–332.

Piper, Nicola. 2006. "Migrant Worker Activism in Singapore and Malaysia: Freedom of Association and the Role of the State." *Asian and Pacific Migration Journal* 15, no. 3: 359–380.

Poovey, Mary. 1998. *A History of the Modern Fact: Problems of Knowledge in the Sciences of Wealth and Society*. Chicago: University of Chicago Press.

Povinelli, Elizabeth. 2002. *The Cunning of Recognition: Indigenous Alterities and the Making of Australian Multiculturalism, Politics, History, and Culture*. Durham, NC: Duke University Press.

Povinelli, Elizabeth. 2011. *Economies of Abandonment: Social Endurance and Belonging in Late Liberalism*. Durham, NC: Duke University Press.

Pratt, Mary Louise. 1992. *Imperial Eyes: Travel Writing and Transculturation*. New York: Routledge.

Pritchard, Evan T. 2002. *Native New Yorkers: The Legacy of the Algonquin People of New York*. Tulsa, OK: Council Oak Books.

Proctor, Robert, and Londa L. Schiebinger, eds. 2008. *Agnotology: The Making and Unmaking of Ignorance*. Stanford, CA: Stanford University Press.

Puig de la Bellacasa, María. 2012. "'Nothing Comes without Its World': Thinking with Care." *Sociological Review* 60, no. 2: 197–216.

Puig de la Bellacasa, María. 2014. "Encountering Bioinfrastructure: Ecological Struggles and the Sciences of Soil." *Social Epistemology* 28, no. 1: 26–40.

Puig de la Bellacasa, Maria. 2015. "Making Time for Soil: Technoscientific Futurity and the Pace of Care." *Social Studies of Science* 45, no. 5: 691–716.

Pulido, Laura. 2000. "Rethinking Environmental Racism: White Privilege and Urban Development in Southern California." *Annals of the Association of American Geographers* 90, no. 1: 12–40.

Purdy, Jedediah. 2015. *After Nature: A Politics for the Anthropocene*. Cambridge, MA: Harvard University Press.

Raffles, Hugh. 2010. *Insectopedia*. New York: Vintage.

Ramirez, Renya. 2007. *Native Hubs: Culture, Community and Belonging in the Silicon Valley and Beyond*. Durham, NC: Duke University Press.

Rancière, Jacques. 2009. "The Aesthetic Dimension: Aesthetics, Politics, Knowledge." *Critical Inquiry* 36, no. 1: 1–19.

Rancière, Jacques. 2010. *Dissensus: On Politics and Aesthetics*. Edited and translated by Steven Corcoran. London: Bloomsbury.

Rappaport, Joanne. 2005. *Intercultural Utopias: Public Intellectuals, Cultural Experimentation, and Ethnic Pluralism in Colombia*. Latin America Otherwise. Durham, NC: Duke University Press.

Redfield, Peter. 2015. "Fluid Technologies: The Bush Pump, the LifeStraw® and Microworlds of Humanitarian Design." *Social Studies of Science* 46, no. 2: 159–183.

Reel, M. 2015. "Underworld: How the Sinaloa Drug Cartel Digs Its Tunnels." *New Yorker*, August 3, 22–28.

Reeves, Madeleine. 2017. "Infrastructural Hope: Anticipating 'Independent Roads' and Territorial Integrity in Southern Kyrgyzstan." *Ethnos* 82, no. 4: 711–737.

Restrepo, Eduardo. 2004. "Ethnicization of Blackness in Colombia: Toward De-Racializing Theoretical and Political Imagination." *Cultural Studies* 18, no. 5: 698–753.

Restrepo, Eduardo, and Axel Rojas. 2004. *Conflicto e (in)visibilidad: Retos en los estudios de la gente negra en Colombia*. Popayán, Colombia: Universidad del Cauca.

Reuters. 2013. "Singapore Shocked by Worst Riots in Decades, as Migrant Workers Vent Anger." *The Guardian*, December 9. http://www.theguardian.com/world/2013/dec/09/singapore-riots-decades-migrant-workers.

Reyna, Stephen. 2002. "Empire: A Dazzling Performance according to a Simpleton." *Anthropological Theory* 2, no. 4: 489–497.

Riles, Annelise, ed. 2006. *Documents: Artifacts of Modern Knowledge*. Ann Arbor: University of Michigan Press, 2006.

Robbins, Paul. 2007. *Lawn People: How Grasses, Weeds and Chemicals Make Us Who We Are*. Philadelphia: Temple University Press.

Robin, Marie-Monique. 2010. *The World according to Monsanto: Pollution, Corruption, and the Control of the World's Food Supply*. Translated by George Holoch. New York: New Press.

Rockefeller, Stuart Alexander. 2011. "Flow." *Current Anthropology* 52, no. 4: 557–578.

Roitman, Janet. 2014. *Anti-Crisis*. Durham, NC: Duke University Press.

Rojas, Cristina. 2009. "Securing the State and Developing Social Insecurities: The Securitisation of Citizenship in Contemporary Colombia." *Third World Quarterly* 30, no. 1: 227–245.

Rolston, Jessica Smith. 2013. "The Politics of Pits and the Materiality of Mine Labor: Making Natural Resources in the American West." *American Anthropologist* 115, no. 4: 582–594.

Rose, Nikolas S. 2001. "The Politics of Life Itself." *Theory, Culture and Society* 18, no. 6: 1–30.

Rosenberg, D. A., and W. B. Moor. 1981–1982. "Smoking Radiating Ruin at the End of Two Hours: Documents on American Plans for Nuclear War with the Soviet Union, 1954–55." *International Security* 6, no. 3: 3–38.

Rosenthal, Elisabeth. 2009. "New Jungles Prompt a Debate on Saving Primeval Rain Forests." *New York Times*, January 9.

Roy, Ananya. 2009. "The 21st Century Metropolis: New Geographies of Theory." *Regional Studies* 43, no. 6: 819–830.

Roy, Ananya, and Aihwa Ong. 2011. *Worlding Cities: Asian Experiments and the Art of Being Global.* Malden, MA: Wiley Blackwell.

Rudel, Thomas K. 2002. "Paths of Destruction and Regeneration: Globalization and Forests in the Tropics." *Rural Sociology* 67, no. 4: 622–636.

Rulli, Jorge Eduardo. 2009. *Pueblos fumigados: Los efectos de los plaguicidas en las regiones sojeras.* Buenos Aires: Del Nuevo Extremo.

Russell, Andrew, and Lee Vinsel. 2016. "Hail the Maintainers." *Aeon.*

Russell, Edmund. 2004. "Introduction: The Garden in the Machine. Toward an Evolutionary History of Technology." In *Industrializing Organisms: Introducing Evolutionary History*, edited by Philip Screpfer and Susan R. Scranton, 1–18. New York: Routledge.

Russell, Edmund, Susan R. Schrepfer, and Philip Scranton. 2004. "Introduction: The Garden in the Machine. Toward an Evolutionary History of Technology." In *Industrializing Organisms: Introducing Evolutionary History*, edited by Philip Screpfer and Susan R. Scranton, 1–18. New York: Routledge.

Russell, Edmund, et al. 2011. "The Nature of Power: Synthesizing the History of Technology and Environmental History." *Technology and Culture* 52, no. 2: 246–259.

Sagan, Dorion. 1990. *Biospheres: Metamorphosis of Planet Earth.* London: Arkana.

Sandiford, Keith. 2011. *Theorizing a Colonial Caribbean-Atlantic Imaginary: Sugar and Obeah.* New York: Routledge.

Sassen, Saskia. 2001. *The Global City: New York, London, Tokyo.* Princeton, NJ: Princeton University Press.

"Saudi America: The Economics of Shale Oil." 2014. *Economist*, February 14.

SCAPE / Landscape Architecture PLLC. 2014. "Living Breakwaters Rebuild by Design Proposal Summary." Accessed May 19, 2018. http://www.rebuildbydesign.org /project/scape-landscape-architecture-final-proposal/.

Schaper, David. 2014. "As Infrastructure Crumbles, Trillions of Gallons of Water Lost." *National Public Radio.* October 29.

Scheer, Hermann. 2004. *The Solar Economy: Renewable Energy for a Sustainable Global Future.* New York: Earthscan.

Scheer, Hermann. 2012. *The Energy Imperative: 100 Per Cent Renewable Now.* New York: Eathscan.

Schmitt, Carl. 2003. *The Nomos of the Earth in the International Law of the Jus Publicum Europaeum*. Translated by G. L. Ulmen. Candor, NY: Telos Press.

Schneider, Stephen H. 1998. "Kyoto Protocol: The Unfinished Agenda." *Climatic Change* 39, no. 1: 1–21.

Schosinsky Nevermann, Gunther. 2008. "Estudio Hidrogeológico, Balance Hídrico y Modelo Conceptual Acuífero." Sardinal: SENARA.

Schrader, Astrid. 2010. "Responding to Pfiesteria Piscicida (the Fish Killer) Phantomatic Ontologies, Indeterminacy, and Responsibility in Toxic Microbiology." *Social Studies of Science* 40, no. 2: 275–306.

Schwartz, Stephen. 2012. "The Real Price of Ballistic Missile Defenses." *Nonproliferation Review*.

Scott, David. 1999. *Refashioning Futures: Criticism after Postcoloniality*. Princeton, NJ: Princeton University Press.

Scott, David. 2014. *Omens of Adversity: Tragedy, Time, Memory, Justice*. Durham, NC: Duke University Press.

Scott, James C. 1985. *Weapons of the Weak: Everyday Forms of Peasant Resistance*. New Haven, CT: Yale University Press.

Scott, James C. 1992. *Domination and the Arts of Resistance: Hidden Transcripts*. New Haven, CT: Yale University Press.

Scott, James C. 1998. *Seeing like a State: How Certain Schemes to Improve the Human Condition Have Failed*. Yale Agrarian Studies. New Haven, CT: Yale University Press.

Sharpe, Christina. *In the Wake: On Blackness and Being*. Durham, NC: Duke University Press, 2016.

Shell, Hanna Rose. 2012. *Hide and Seek: Camouflage, Photography, and the Media of Reconnaissance*. Cambridge, MA: MIT Press.

Sigler, Thomas J. 2013. "Relational Cities: Doha, Panama City, and Dubai as 21st Century Entrepôts." *Urban Geography* 34, no. 5: 612–633.

Simone, AbdouMaliq. 2004. *For the City Yet to Come: Changing African Life in Four Cities*. Durham, NC: Duke University Press.

Simpson, Audra. 2014. *Mohawk Interruptus: Political Life across the Borders of Settler States*. Durham, NC: Duke University Press.

Sloterdijk, Peter. 2005. "Atmospheric Politics." In *Making Things Public: Atmospheres of Democracy*, edited by Bruno Latour and Peter Weibel, 944–951. Cambridge, MA: MIT Press.

Sloterdijk, Peter. 2009. *Terror from the Air*. Translated by Amy Patton and Steve Corcoran. Semiotext(e) / Foreign Agents. Cambridge, MA: MIT Press.

Sloterdijk, Peter, and Hans-Jürgen Heinrichs. 2011. *Neither Sun nor Death*. Translated by Steve Corcoran. Semiotext(e) / Foreign Agents. Cambridge, MA: MIT Press.

Smith, Benjamin. 2006. "'More than Love': Locality and Affects of Indigeneity in Northern Queensland." *Asia Pacific Journal of Anthropology* 7: 221–235.

Smith, Valerie. 2006. *Down the Garden Path: The Artist's Garden after Modernism*. New York: Queens Museum of Art.

Star, Susan Leigh. 1999. "The Ethnography of Infrastructure." *American Behavioural Scientist* 43, no. 3: 377–391.

Star, Susan Leigh, and Karen Ruhleder. 1996. "Steps toward an Ecology of Infrastructure: Design and Access for Large Information Spaces." *Information Systems Research* 7, no. 1: 111–134.

Starosielski, Nicole. 2015. *The Undersea Network: Sign, Storage, Transmission.* Durham, NC: Duke University Press.

Steffen, Will, et al. 2011. "The Anthropocene: From Global Change to Planetary Stewardship." AMBIO: *A Journal of the Human Environment* 40, no. 7: 739–761.

Stengers, Isabelle. 2005. "The Cosmopolitan Proposal." In *Making Things Public: Atmospheres of Democracy*, edited by Bruno Latour and P. Weibel, 994–1004. Cambridge, MA: MIT Press.

Stengers, Isabelle. 2010. *Cosmopolitics.* Translated by Robert Bononno. Minneapolis: University of Minnesota Press.

Stengers, Isabelle. 2015. "Accepting the Reality of Gaia." In *The Anthropocene and the Global Environmental Crisis: Rethinking Modernity in a New Epoch*, edited by Clive Hamilton, Francois Gemenne, and Cristophe Bonneuil, 134–144. London: Routledge.

Stine, Jeffrey K., and Joel A Tarr. 1998. "At the Intersection of Histories: Technology and the Environment." *Technology and Culture* 39, no. 4: 601–640.

Stoetzer, Bettina. Forthcoming. *Ruderal City: Ecologies of Migration and Urban Life in Berlin.*

Strathern, Marilyn, ed. 1995. *Shifting Contexts: Transformations in Anthropological Knowledge.* ASA Decennial Conference Series: The Uses of Knowledge: Global and Local Relations. London: Routledge.

Strathern, Marilyn. 2002. "On Space and Depth." In *Complexities: Social Studies of Knowledge Practices*, edited by John Law and Annemarie Mol, 88–115. Durham, NC: Duke University Press.

Strauss, Sarah, Stephanie Rupp, and Thomas Love. 2013a. *Cultures of Energy: Power, Practices, Technologies.* Walnut Creek, CA: Left Coast Press.

Strauss, Sarah, Stephanie Rupp, and Thomas Love. 2013b. "Powerlines: Cultures of Energy in the Twenty-First Century." In *Cultures of Energy: Power, Practices, Technologies*, edited by Susan Strauss, Stephanie Rupp, and Thomas Love, 10–41. Walnut Creek, CA: Left Coast Press.

Sullivan, Walter. 1960. "Babies Surveyed for Strontium 90." *New York Times*, November 25.

Sutter, Paul S. 2007. "Nature's Agents or Agents of Empire? Entomological Workers and Environmental Change during the Construction of the Panama Canal." *Isis* 98, no. 4: 724–754.

Sutter, Paul S. 2016. "'The First Mountain to Be Removed': Yellow Fever Control and the Construction of the Panama Canal." *Environmental History* 21, no. 2: 250–259.

Swyngedouw, Erik. 2010. "Apocalypse Forever? Post-political Populism and the Spectre of Climate Change." *Theory, Culture and Society* 27, nos. 2–3: 213–232.

TallBear, Kim. 2015. "An Indigenous Reflection on Working beyond the Human/Not Human." *GLQ: A Journal of Lesbian and Gay Studies* 21, no. 2: 230–235.

Tiqqun. 2010. *Introduction to Civil War*. Translated by Alexander R. Galloway and Jason E. Smith. Semiotext(e) / Intervention. Cambridge, MA: MIT Press.

Tiqqun. 2011. *This Is Not a Program*. Los Angeles: Semiotext(e).

Tng, Serene, and Serene Tan. 2012. "Designing Our City: Planning for a Sustainable Singapore." Urban Redevelopment Authority.

Todd, Zoe. 2015. "Indigenizing the Anthropocene." In *Art in the Anthropocene: Encounters among Aesthetics, Politics, Environments and Epistemologies*, edited by Heather Davis and Etienne Turpin. London: Open Humanities Press.

Toscano, Alberto. 2004. "Factory, Territory, Metropolis, Empire." *Angelaki: Journal of the Theoretical Humanities* 9, no. 2: 197–216.

Toscano, Alberto. 2011. "Logistics and Opposition." *Mute* 3, no. 2: 30–41.

Toscano, Alberto. 2014. "Lineaments of the Logistical State." *Viewpoint Magazine*.

Toscano, Alberto, and Jeff Kinkle. 2015. *Cartographies of the Absolute*. Alresford, England: Zero Books.

Trevor, Tom. 2013. "Three Ecologies." In *Lois Weinberger*, edited by Philippe van Cauteren, 217–225. Berlin: Hatje Cantze.

Tsing, Anna Lowenhaupt. 2005. *Friction: An Ethnography of Global Connection*. Princeton, NJ: Princeton University Press.

Tsing, Anna Lowenhaupt. 2012. "Empire's Salvage Heart: Why Diversity Matters in the Global Political Economy." *Focaal* 2012, no. 64: 36–50.

Tsing, Anna Lowenhaupt. 2015. *The Mushroom at the End of the World: On the Possibility of Life in Capitalist Ruins*. Princeton, NJ: Princeton University Press.

Turner, Fred. 2013. *The Democratic Surround: Multimedia and American Liberalism from World War II to the Psychedelic Sixties*. Chicago: University of Chicago Press.

Urry, John. 2014. "The Problem of Energy." *Theory, Culture and Society* 31, no. 5: 3–20.

Valencia, Inge Helena. 2011. "Impactos del reconocimiento multicultural en el archipiélago de San Andrés, Providencia y Santa Catalina." *Antípoda* 47, no. 2: 69–95.

Vazquez, Medardo Avila, et al. 2017. "Association between Cancer and Environmental Exposure to Glyphosate." *International Journal of Clinical Medicine* 8, no. 2: 73.

Venkatesan, Soumhya, et al. 2016. "Attention to Infrastructure Offers a Welcome Reconfiguration of Anthropological Approaches to the Political." *Critique of Anthropology* 38, no. 1: 3–50.

Verran, Helen. 2011. "The Changing Lives of Measures and Values: From Centre Stage in the Fading 'Disciplinary' Society to Pervasive Background Instrument in the Emergent 'Control' Society." *Sociological Review* 59, no. 2 (suppl): 60–72.

Viveiros de Castro, Eduardo. 2014. *Cannibal Metaphysics*. Translated by P. Skafish. Minneapolis: University of Minnesota Press.

von Schnitzler, Antina. 2016. *Democracy's Infrastructure: Techno-Politics and Protest after Apartheid*. Princeton Studies in Culture and Technology. Princeton, NJ: Princeton University Press.

Von Zinnenburg, Carroll, ed. 2018. *Botanical Drift: Protagonists of the Invasive Herbarium*. Berlin: Sternberg.

Vouros, Dimitri. 2014. "Hegel, 'Totality,' and 'Abstract Universalism' in the Philosophy of Theodor Adorno." *Parrhesia* 21: 176–186.

Wade, Peter. 1993. *Blackness and Race Mixture: The Dynamics of Racial Identity in Colombia*. Baltimore: Johns Hopkins University Press.

Wade, Peter. 2002. "Introduction: The Colombian Pacific in Perspective." *Journal of Latin American Anthropology* 7, no. 2: 2–33.

Wagner, Roy. 1987. "Figure-Ground Reversal among the Barok." In *Assemblage of Spirits: Idea and Image in New Ireland*, edited by L. Lincoln, 56–62. New York: George Braziller.

Walcott, Rinaldo. 2014. "Zones of Black Death: Institutions, Knowledges, and States of Being." Antipode Lecture.

Waldman, John. 1999. *Heartbeats in the Muck: The History, Sea Life, and Environment of New York Harbor*. New York: Lyons.

Wallerstein, Immanuel. 1974. *The Modern World System*. New York: Academic Press.

"Water, New York Harbor, and Quality Regional Summary." 2004. New York City Department of Environmental Protection.

Watson, Mark. 2010. "Diasporic Indigeneity: Place and the Articulation of Ainu Identity in Tokyo, Japan." *Environment and Planning A* 42, no. 2: 268–284.

Wegman, Fred. 1995. "Influence of Infrastructure Design on Road Safety." Paper presented at the International Symposium on Traffic Safety, A Global Issue. Kuwait.

Weisman, Alan. 2007. *The World without Us*. New York: Picador.

Weizman, Eyal. 2003. "The Politics of Verticality: The West Bank as an Architectural Construction." In *Territories: Islands, Camps and Other States of Utopia*, edited by Anselm Franke. Berlin: Kunst-Werke Institute of Contemporary Art.

West, Paige. 2006. *Conservation Is Our Government Now: The Politics of Ecology in Papua New Guinea*. Durham, NC: Duke University Press.

West, Robert Cooper. 1957. *The Pacific Lowlands of Colombia: A Negroid Area of the American Tropics*. Baton Rouge: Louisiana University Press.

Wesz, Valdemar João, Jr. 2016. "Strategies and Hybrid Dynamics of Soy Transnational Companies in the Southern Cone." *Journal of Peasant Studies* 43, no. 2: 286–312.

Weszkalnys, Gisa. 2016. "Infrastructure as Gesture." In *Infrastructure and Social Complexity: A Reader*, edited by Penny Harvey, Casper Bruun Jensen, and Atsuro Morita, 284–296. London: Routledge.

White, Leslie. 1943. "Energy and the Evolution of Culture." *American Anthropologist* 45, no. 3: 335–356.

Whitington, Jerome. 2016. "Modernist Infrastructure and the Vital Systems Security of Water: Singapore's Pluripotent Climate Futures." *Public Culture* 28, no. 2: 415–441.

Wilhite, Harold. 2013. "Energy Consumption as Cultural Practice: Implications for the Theory and Policy of Sustainable Energy Use." In *Cultures of Energy: Power, Practices, Technologies*, edited by Sarah Strauss, Stephanie Rupp, and Thomas Love, 60–73. Walnut Creek, CA: Left Coast Press.

Williams, Raymond. 1973. *The Country and the City*. New York: Oxford University Press.

Williams, Raymond. 1976. *Keywords: A Vocabulary of Culture and Society*. New York: Oxford University Press.

Wittfogel, Karl. 1957. *Oriental Despotism: A Comparative Study of Total Power*. New Haven, CT: Yale University Press.

Wissler, Clark. 1909. *The Indians of Greater New York and the Lower Hudson*. Vol. 3. New York: Trustees.

Wolf, Eric. 1982. *Europe and the People without History*. Berkeley: University of California Press.

Wolfsthal, Jon B., Jeffrey Lewis, and Marc Quint. 2014. "The Trillion Dollar Nuclear Triad." Monterey: James Martin Center for Nonproliferation Studies.

Wong, May Ee. 2015. "Singapore as Garden City: The Techno-Organic Home." In *The Measure of Your Dwelling: Singapore Unhomed*, edited by Jason Wee, 62–171. Berlin: Ifa-Galerie.

Wright, Stuart Joseph, and Mirna Julieta Samaniego. 2008. "Historical, Demographic, and Economic Correlates of Land-Use Change in the Republic of Panama." *Ecology and Society* 13, no. 2.

Yarrington, Landon. 2015. "The Paved and the Unpaved: Toward a Political Economy of Infrastructure, Mobility, and Urbanization in Haiti." *Economic Anthropology* 2, no. 1: 185–204.

Zanfi, Claudia. 2009. *Lois Weinberger: The Mobile Garden*. Bologna: Damiani.

Zeiderman, Austin. 2013. "Living Dangerously: Biopolitics and Urban Citizenship in Bogotá, Colombia." *American Ethnologist* 40, no. 1: 71–87.

Živković, Marko. 2017. "Marina Abramovic and Mr. Wilson: Intersecting Worlds, Higher Dimensions, and Meta-stable Shimmerings." In *Anthropology of the Arts: A Reader*, edited by Gretchen Bakke and Marina Peterson, 363–371. New York: Bloomsbury Academic.

Zucker, Howard A. 2014. *A Public Health Review of High Volume Hydraulic Fracturing for Shale Gas Development*. New York: New York Department of Public Health.

CONTRIBUTORS

NIKHIL ANAND is an assistant professor of anthropology at the University of Pennsylvania. His first book, *Hydraulic City* (Duke University Press, 2017), explores the quotidien ways in which cities and citizens are made through the everyday management of water infrastructure in Mumbai. With Hannah Appel and Akhil Gupta, he has coedited a volume, *The Promise of Infrastructure* (Duke University Press, 2018), that demonstrates how infrastructures are a promising location from which to theorize time and politics.

ANDREA BALLESTERO is an assistant professor of anthropology at Rice University and the convener of the Ethnography Studio, an interdisciplinary space for ethnographic experimentation. Her interests include legal and political anthropology, science and technology studies, political economy, value, and liberalism. She is the author of *A Future History of Water: Rights, Commodities, and Wonder*, forthcoming from Duke University Press.

BRUCE BRAUN is professor of geography at the University of Minnesota. He is the author of *Intemperate Rainforest* (2002) and coeditor, with Sarah Whatmore, of *Political Matter: Technoscience, Democracy, and Public Life* (2010). His current work includes research on the intersection of biopolitics, urban planning, and climate change.

ASHLEY CARSE, an anthropologist, is an assistant professor of human and organizational development at Vanderbilt University. He is the author of *Beyond the Big Ditch: Politics, Ecology, and Infrastructure at the Panama Canal* (2014).

GASTÓN GORDILLO is a professor in the Department of Anthropology at the University of British Columbia. A Guggenheim scholar, he is the author of *Rubble: The Afterlife of Destruction* (Duke University Press, 2014; Honorary Mention, Victor Turner Prize for Ethnographic Writing, Society for Humanistic Anthropology) and *Landscapes of Devils: Tensions of Place and Memory in the Argentinean Chaco* (Duke University Press, 2004; winner of the Sharon Stephens Book Prize, American Ethnological Society).

KREGG HETHERINGTON is an associate professor of anthropology at Concordia University in Montreal, and director of the Concordia Ethnography Lab. He is the author of *Guerrilla Auditors: The Politics of Transparency in Neoliberal Paraguay* (Duke University Press, 2011) and is currently finishing a project on environmental regulation and life politics in industrial agriculture.

CASPER BRUUN JENSEN is a specially appointed associate professor at Osaka University and honorary lecturer at Leicester University. His present work focuses on knowledge, infrastructure, and practical ontologies in the Mekong River basin.

JOSEPH MASCO is a professor of anthropology at the University of Chicago. He is the author of *The Nuclear Borderlands: The Manhattan Project in Post–Cold War New Mexico* (2006) and *The Theater of Operations: National Security Affect from the Cold War to the War on Terror* (Duke University Press, 2014). His current scholarship considers environmental endangerment, with a particular focus on the emergence of the planetary as an object of political concern.

SHAYLIH MUEHLMANN is an associate professor and Canada Research Chair in the Department of Anthropology at the University of British Columbia. She is the author of *When I Wear My Alligator Boots* (2013) and *Where the River Ends* (Duke University Press, 2013).

NATASHA MYERS is an associate professor of anthropology at York University, director of the Plant Studies Collaboratory, convenor of the Politics of

Evidence Working Group, and cofounder of the Technoscience Salon. She is the author of *Rendering Life Molecular: Models, Modelers, and Excitable Matter* (Duke University Press, 2015), and her new work documents plant/people conspiracies in scientific laboratories, artists' studios, gardens, and ecological restoration sites.

STEPHANIE WAKEFIELD is an urban geographer and Urban Studies Foundation Research Fellow based at Florida International University. She is currently completing a book titled *Living in the Back Loop: Experimentation in Unsafe Operating Space*, and beginning a second project titled *Miami Forever: Urbanism in the Back Loop*, investigating experimental practices for living with water in Miami, Florida, and through this the emergence of a new paradigm of back loop urbanism.

AUSTIN ZEIDERMAN is an anthropologist and associate professor in the Department of Geography and Environment at the London School of Economics and author of *Endangered City: The Politics of Security and Risk in Bogotá* (Duke University Press, 2016). His research focuses on the cultural and political dimensions of cities, development, and the environment, with a specific focus on Colombia.

INDEX

ABCD group, 85
Aceitera General Deheza (AGD), 88
actants, 151
actor-network theory (ANT), 5, 70
Adorno, Theodor, 70
Africans, diasporic, 183–184
Afro-Colombians, 171–174, 178. *See also* Bajamar
Afro-Urban Conference (Buenaventura, Colombia): about, 174–175; Bajamar, emphasis on, 176–177; climate change adaptation proposals, 188–189; coastal precarity, 184, 186–187, 189–190; development, 186–187; Pacific trade, 187, 189; "territories reclaimed from the sea" term, 171, 174, 177–179, 189
Agamben, Giorgio: on animals, 208, 211; on apparatuses, 205–206, 208, 210; being, interest in, 204, 214n17; Foucault, use of, 205, 208–210; on government, 204–205, 207, 214n18; on katechon, 203; on life, 207, 211, 213; on the middle voice, 206–207; profanation concept, 206, 210, 212; on use, 208
agriculture, industrial: agro-cities, 80; and the Anthropocene, 144; and climate change, 70–71; corporations controlling, 84; and deforestation, 78–79; herbicide use, 79; Monsanto, 68, 79, 84, 87–88, 90; South American zone, 84. *See also* soybean industry, Argentinian
agro-cities, 80

agroindustrial urbanism, 80, 90
America. *See* United States of America
animals as infrastructure, 198–199, 201, 214n11. *See also* Oystertecture project
Anthropocene, the: about, 178, 248; and agriculture, industrial, 144; alternatives to, 145–146; beginning of, 144, 180–181; biopolitics, 191n10; and colonialism, 181; conceptual problems created by, 4–5; definitions of, 71; and gardens, Weinberger's, 120, 142–143, 145; and Gardens by the Bay, 118, 120, 143, 145; gardens for, 146; historical contexts of, 179; and humanism, 172, 180–181; and humans, 10–11, 145, 180, 182; as infrastructural moment, 8; and the metropolis, 71, 91, 93; and planetary urbanization, 73; versus Planthroposcene, 146–147; and plants, 120, 144–145; and posthumanism, 172, 178, 180; and slavery, 181; studies of, past, 5; technological fixes, focus on, 145, 168n15; thinking after, 120; thwarting, techniques for, 120, 145–146; ubiquity of, 5, 91; as weedy, 9. *See also* climate change
"Anthropocene" term, 3–4, 144–146
anthropocentrism, resisting, 146
anthropology: and biology, 10; and indigenous knowledge, 53, 59–60; as infrastructural inversion, 7; of infrastructure, 101–102, 181, 221; and temporal hierarchies, 181
antihumanism, 181

antiracism, 180

Appadurai, Arjun, 71

apparatuses, 204–206, 208–210, 213, 213n3

Appel, Hannah, 74

aquatic space, 177, 191n6

aquifers: about, 21; ambiguity of, 25–26, 34–35, 42; conceptual models of, 32, 42–43; extent of, 28; and figure/ground distinctions, 25, 33–34, 42–43; and figure/ground reversals, 25–26; as infrastructure, 21–22, 42; measuring, 25–26, 32; ontohistorical stickiness of, 23, 37–38, 43. *See also* Sardinal aquifer

archaeology, 33

Argentina: decay, infrastructural, 66; Monsanto in, 68, 79, 84, 87–88, 90; *pampas*, 79–80; Paraná river, 80, 90; social movements, anti-agribusiness, 89–90, 93; The Water Highway, 80; zones of imperial extraction in, 84, 87, 89. *See also* Las Lajitas; Rosario; Salta; soybean industry, Argentinian

ASADAS, 29

assemblages, 74–75

AyA water utility (Costa Rica): and ASADAS, 29–30; and CoCoWater, 29–30, 39; and infiltration tests, 20; Sardinal aquifer reports, 38–40; and Water Availability letters, 28–29, 39

Bajamar (Buenaventura, Colombia): about, 171–172; adaptability of, 189; and climate change, 172, 178–179, 188–189; posthuman perspectives on, 179; relocation from, 173–174, 176, 185–186; term debate, 171, 174, 177, 179; and violence, 187

Barad, Karen, 155

Barry, Andrew, 83

Bennet, Jane, 151, 168n15

Bernes, Jasper, 92–93

biology-culture separation, 9–10

biopolitics, 9–10, 127, 191n10, 198, 214n9

boundaries and practices, 102

Bowker, Geoff, 6, 23–24, 48

Boyer, Dominic, 218–219

Brathwaite, Kamu, 183–184

Brazil, 79–80, 84, 87–88

Brenner, Neil, 71–73, 76

Buenaventura (Colombia): about, 173; Afro-Colombians, 171–174, 178; aquatic space in, 177; and climate change, 171–172, 184–185, 188; coastal precarity of, 184–190; development plans for, 173–174, 186–187, 189; and drug trade, 174; land reclamation, 173; militias in, 174; Process of Black Communities (PCN), 175, 189; relocation in, 171–172;

resiliency of, 184–186, 188–189; territorial politics in, 175–177; "territories reclaimed from the sea" term, 171, 174, 177–179, 189; and water, 173, 188–189. *See also* Afro-Urban Conference; Bajamar

Bunge (corporation), 85, 87–88

Cambodia, hydroelectric energy in: and China, 223, 225; emphasis on, 217–218, 232; environmental impact of, 224–225; insufficiency of, 223; and Japan, 225; as need, 226; negative reactions to, 224–225; Russei Chrum Krom River dam, 223; Vireak on, 225–227

Cambodia, solar energy in: arguments against, 227; attitudes toward, changing, 233; buses, 230–231; as community of aspiration, 222–223; functions of, undetermined, 234; government interest in, lack of, 227, 232; lobbying for, 230–231; NRG Solutions, 229–230; roads, 232; and rural communities, 229–230; Star8 company, 216–217, 230–234; transportation, 230–231, 233; as unimportant, 217–218

Cambodia: electrical grid of, 229; energy, importation of, 225, 231; and Feyerabendian blockages, 232; Phnom Penh, 216–217, 230–231, 233–234; renewable energy in, 228–229, 232; Star8's relationship to, 233; sunlight, prevalence of, 216–217

Campbell, Jeremy, 93

capitalism: American, 237; the Anthropocene, as producing, 71, 145; end of, 142, 148n14; and extinction, 142, 148n14; Gardens by the Bay and, 118, 122, 143; and globalization, 82; and the metropolis, 69, 73, 76, 92; and national sovereignty, 82; Panama and, 109; and plantations, 180; undoing of, 92–93

Capitalocene, the, 142

Cargill (corporation), 68, 85, 87–88

Caribbean culture, 183–184

Carter, Jimmy, 235n14, 251

Castells, Manuell, 71

Chakrabarty, Dipesh, 182, 191n12, 249–250

chapter overviews, 8, 11–12

ChemChina, 79, 84, 87

China: and Cambodian hydropower, 223; and industrial agriculture, 84; and the metropolis, 91; rise of, 82, 91; and soybean industry, Argentinian, 68, 80–82, 87; urbanization of, 68; zones of imperial extraction in, 91

China Machinery Engineering Corporation (CMEC), 81

China National Cereals, Oils and Foodstuffs Corporation (COFCO), 81–82, 85, 87

Choy, Timothy, 120

climate change: American responses to, 252–253; and Buenaventura, Colombia, 171–172, 178–179, 184–185, 188–189; and capitalism, 142, 237; coastal precarity, 184–190; and Colombia, 171–172, 184–185; confronting, methods for, 166–167; and consumption, 250–251; and Costa Rica, 40–41; and fallout studies, 243; and forests, secondary, 113; and gardens, 118, 127–128; and Gardens by the Bay, 133–135, 142; geopolitics of, 248–249; historical contexts of, 179; human and natural history, as merging, 249–250; IPCC predictions, 247; and the metropolis, 70, 74; modernization, as inverting, 250; and nuclear crises, 247–248, 251, 253; and racial inequality, 179; and Singapore, 129; and social justice, 182–183; social theory, impact on, 2; and tropical areas, 184–185; ubiquity of, 91. *See also* Anthropocene, the
Clover, Joshua, 92
CMEC, 81
coastal precarity, 184–190
CocoWater, 29–32, 39–40
COFCO, 81–82, 85, 87
Cold War, 7, 242–246
Colón (Panama): about, 97, 108–110; twentieth-century decline of, 98–99, 109–110; dirty landscapes, concern with, 98, 101, 108, 114; economy of, 110; Free Trade Zone, 109–110; infrastructural decay, 99; Leis on, 109; public health initiatives, 106; unemployment in, 99, 110
Colón, weediness of: and aspirational communities, 111; and disconnection, 99, 113; and disinvestment, 99, 101, 110–111, 113; emphasis on, residents', 98–99; as infrastructural loss, 114; and maintenance politics, 101, 103, 112; post-canal transfer, 110–111; versus US Canal Zone, 104; and vegetation clearing symbolism, 110–112
colonialism: and the Anthropocene, 3, 120, 181; and the Caribbean, 183; and indigenous peoples, 57, 59; and Montreal, 7–8
Colorado River delta, 56–57, 60
Colombia: about, 173; Afro-Colombians, 171–174, 178–179, 190n1; black communities, 174–177, 190n2, 191n5; climate change, 171–172, 184–185; Constitution of 1991, 174–176; ethnoracial politics in, 174–175; ethnoracial terminology in, 190n2; Law, 70, 174–176; oceans, cultural importance of, 184; rivers, importance of, 176; territorial politics in, 175–176. *See also* Afro-Urban Conference; Bajamar; Buenaventura
communities of aspiration, 105, 111, 222

Conan, Michel, 125
conceptual models of aquifers, 32, 42–43
concrete, 7
consensual politics, 143
consumption patterns, 250–251
Costa Rica: ASADAS, 29; AyA water utility, 20, 28–30, 39–40; geologic history of, 35; infrastructure, development of, 30; oil exploration, 27; open-pit mining, 27; SAS agency, 20, 28, 31, 38, 40–41, 43n2; Tempisque basin, 41, 44n4; Urban Planning Law, 30; Water Availability letters, 28–29. *See also* Guanacaste; Sardinal
Cowen, Deborah, 86–87
Crary, Jonathan, 238
crises: about, 27, 237, 254; and action, 220; alternatives, need for, 258–259; and American capitalism, 237–239; Cold War, 240–241; as counterrevolutionary force, 240, 254; existential dangers, 239–240; Fukushima, 253–254; and ideology, 252–253; management of, 203–204; in the media, 236–237; and modernity, 253; as permanent conditions, 254, 258; power of, diminishing, 237; psychosocial purposes of, 239; Roitman on, 237, 253; and the social sciences, 258; of water, 27–28. *See also* climate change; nuclear weapons programs
crisis-in-crisis, 253, 258–259
crisis-talk, 237, 239, 252–254, 259
critique, 7
Cucapá people (Mexico): in drug trade, 57, 64; as infrastructure, 49–50, 57, 59–60, 63; land, connection to, 61–62; navigation abilities of, 60
culture-biology separation, 9–10

dam building, Egyptian, 156, 167n8
deforestation, 68, 77–78, 93n1
DeLanda, Manuel, 75
Deleuze, Gilles, 210
deregulation, 83, 85
Despret, Vinciane, 222
dirt, 101
dispositifs concept, 204–206, 208, 210, 213, 213n3
doubling, infrastructural. *See* Mexican drug trade and infrastructural doubling
Douglas, Mary, 101

Elden, Stuart, 83
Elyachar, Julia, 63
empire, 82–83, 89, 99, 104, 110
energopolitics, 219
energopower, 218

energy systems: centralized versus decentralized, 232; changing, 227–228; and culture, 219; hydroelectric energy, 223–224; as ontological, 222; petrochemical, 240, 256–258; politics of, 219; and scale, 228; Scheer on, 226–227; and social issues, 226; in the social sciences, 218–220; White on, 219–220. *See also* Cambodia, hydroelectric energy in; Cambodia, solar energy in; renewable energy; solar energy

engineering, 165–166

environment, militarization of, 243–244

environmental disasters, 2–3, 5. *See also* climate change; nuclear weapons programs

"environment" concept: about, 4–5; and infrastructure, 6, 21; and political ecology, 4–5

Escobar, Arturo, 175–176

Fanon, Frantz, 180–182

feminism, 5, 72–73

Ferguson, James, 101

Feyerabend, Paul, 221–222, 227, 229, 232

figure/ground distinctions: and aquifers, 25, 33–34, 42–43; in infrastructural analysis, 22, 43; and Sardinal geologic profile, 36; and the underground, 31–34, 42; and weediness, 100

figure/ground reversals: about, 24; and aquifers, 25–26; effects of, 24; and epistemology, 24; and materialism, 24; and the underground, 31–34

forced poetics, 191n14

forests, secondary, 100, 113

Fort Sherman (Panama), 97–98, 114n1

Fortun, Kim, 118

Foucault, Michel, 204–206, 208–210, 213n3

Fuller, Buckminster, 228

future, the, 93, 202, 221, 233, 237

Gandy, Matthew, 139

gardens, Weinberger's: about, 118, 124; and the Anthropocene, 120, 142–143, 145; and climate change, 140, 142; versus conventional gardens, 139; as counter-gardens, 137; as dissensus, 143; durational works, 138; enclosures, use of, 127, 138–139; versus Gardens by the Bay, 118, 140, 142–143; Hetherington on, 143; human desires, subversions of, 138–140; "perfectly provisional" aesthetic, 138–139; photographs of, *119, 123, 141*; and plant/people relations, 126; *Portable Gardens* series, 137; waste, use of, 137–138; and wasteland aesthetics, 139; *Wild Cube* series, 139–141

Gardens by the Bay (Singapore): about, 118, 121–122, 124; air quality of, 133; and the Anthropocene, 118, 120, 143, 145; architects of, 130–131, 133; and climate change, 133–135, 142; Cloud Forest, 121–122, 124, 133–135; creation of, 130–131; Flower Dome, 121; infrastructure of, 131, 133; Lost World exhibit, 134, 148n13; photographs of, *119, 122–123, 132, 134*; as postpolitical project, consensual, 143; Supertrees, 131, *132, 136*; and sustainability, 131; versus Weinberger's gardens, 118, 140, 142–143

gardens: for the Anthropocene, 146; biopolitics of, 127; in building façades, decayed, 115–117; and climate change, 118, 127–128; as cultural productions, 125–126; definitions of, 116, 125; enclosures, 127; and gardeners, 126–127; history of, 124–125; as infrastructure, 125; and moral order, 125–126; as *naturecultures*, 126; plant blindness, confronting, 128; theories of, 127

Gieryn, Thomas, 102, 191n8

Gilroy, Paul, 180–182

global cities, 71–72, 75

globalization: and connection, experiences of, 99; imperialism of, 83; materialist research on, 72; versus the metropolis, 71–76; origins of, 71; planetary urbanization, 69, 72–73; spatial patterns of, 87

Goonewardena, Kanishka, 72–73

government: and apparatuses, 204–205, 207, 210, 214n18; and infrastructural studies, 215n21; and the middle voice, 207; and things, 206–207

Guanacaste, Costa Rica, 19, 23, 26–29, 41, 43. *See also* Sardinal

Haraway, Donna, 73, 142, 146

Hardt, Michael, 82

Harvey, David, 92

Hernández, Valeria, 80

Hetherington, Kregg, 48, 93, 143, 157, 202

Holocene, the, 248

humanism, 172, 180–182

humans: in the Anthropocene, 10–11, 182, 248; categorical dilution of, 5, 182; conceptions of, 182; in the Holocene, 248; as infrastructure, 62, 199; as planetary-scale force, 247; in posthumanism, 182

Hunt, John Nixon, 124

hydroelectric energy, 223–224. *See also* Cambodia, hydroelectric energy in

hydrogeology, 32–33, 43

indigenous peoples: in colonial imaginaries, 59; knowledge of, 53, 59–60; and Mexican drug trade, 57–59; Mohawk, 7–8; and place, 58, 60–61. *See also* Cucapá people

industrial agriculture. *See* agriculture, industrial

information technology, 238

infrastructural analysis, 22, 43. *See also* infrastructural inversion

infrastructural doubling. *See* Mexican drug trade and infrastructural doubling

infrastructural inversion: Anthropocene inversion of, 8; anthropology as, 7; Bowker on, 23–24, 48; and critique, 7; definitions of, 6, 23; and doubling, 48, 53; examples of, 6–7; impact of, 24; Star on, 24, 48; by users, 64

infrastructural work, 102–103

infrastructure: animals as, 198–199, 201, 214n11; and the Anthropocene, 6; anthropology of, 101–102, 181, 221; aquifers as, 21–22; as creative, 157, 167n11; and development, 7; doubling of, 47; and environment, 6; experimental qualities of, 221, 229; failure and visibility of, 47–48; as figure and ground, 6; functions of, 233–234; and the future, 93, 202, 221, 233; importance of, 4; invisibility of, 47–49; and life, 166, 168n16; localities, as transcending, 104; maintenance, need for, 103; materialities of, 151–152; as mediating technologies, 150; oysters as, 196, 198, 201, 211–212, 213, 214n7; versus public works, 114n4; remaking of, 166–167; social aspects of, 104–105; and social consciousness, 21; in social sciences and humanities, 6–8; society, as indexing, 99, 114n3; spectacular dimension of, 202; as substrate, 47; theories of, 21; for trafficking, 49; visibility of, 47–48, 53–55, 64–65, 65n1. *See also* Mumbai's water infrastructure; water infrastructures

infrastructure/environment boundaries, 101–104

Intergovernmental Panel on Climate Change (IPCC), 184, 247, 252

International Rivers, 223–224

interruption, politics of, 92–93

The Invisible Committee, 69, 73, 92

juxtaposition, 118

katechon, 203

Kinkle, Jeff, 70

Klein, Naomi, 92

knowledge as infrastructure, 63

Kockelman, Paul, 33

Laos, 223–224

Larkin, Brian, 7, 49, 65n1, 74

Las Lajitas (Argentina): about, 66–68, 77; agroindustrial urbanism in, 80; campesino residents, 68, 71, 77; deforestation of, 68, 77–78, 93n1; edges of, 76–77; elites of, 82; gauchos in, 77; Hotel, 80–82; regional experiences in, 70; roads, 66, 68; soybean industry in, 68–69, 77, 80, 84; superweeds, 90; urbanization of, 68; as "zone of imperial extraction," 84

Latin America: Brazil, 79–80, 84, 87–88; decolonialism in, 179; and posthumanism, 178–179; social movements in, 176; South America, 84–85. *See also* Argentina; Costa Rica; Mexico; Panama

Latour, Bruno, 166, 167n7

lawns, residential, 111–112

Lefebvre, Henri, 69, 70, 72–73, 92

Leguizamón, Amalia, 85

life, "practically effective forms of," 221–222

"life" concept, 4, 9–10

lifeworlds, 200, 211–212

Lim, Eng-Beng, 133

Limited Test Ban Treaty of 1963, 240, 245–247

Living Breakwaters. *See* Oystertecture project

logistics, 70, 75, 85–87. *See also* supply chains

Lorimer, Jamie, 139

materialism and materiality: Feyerabend and, 232; and figure/ground reversals, 24; and globalization, 72; of infrastructure, 151–152; of the metropolis, 73; Mumbai's water leakages, 165; new materialism, 152, 156–157; White's, 219

measurement practices, 155

mediating technologies, 150

Mekong river dams, 223–224

Merrifield, Andy, 72, 92

metropolis, the: and the Anthropocene, 71, 91, 93; as assemblage, 74–75; and borders, 74; and China, 91; connectivity, 75; contemporary configuration of, 91; as continuum, 73–75; definitions of, 69; edges of, 76–81; egalitarian and revolutionary potential of, 92; and global cities, 75; versus globalization, 71–76; infrastructures and well-being, 91–92; and interruption politics, 92–93; logistics in, 70, 75; materiality of, 73; motion, infrastructural, 69, 73–74, 80; and nationalism, 87; as nontotalizing totality, 76; and outside areas, 75–76; regionalism in, 70; social movements disrupting, 90; standardization, need for, 74; struggles against, 92–93; and terrain, 75, 90; theories, foundational, 70–72; theories of, 69; and totalities, 70; and the urban form, 73; "zones of imperial extraction," 83–84, 87, 91

Mexican drug trade: airstrip destruction, 46; El Chapo, 54–55; draw of, 57; and indigenous peoples, 57–59, 64; local population involvement, 50; Sinaloa cartel, 53–54; trafficking infrastructure visibility, 48–49, 53–55, 64–65; tunnels, use of, 53–55; war on, 45–47, 56, 58–59

Mexican drug trade and infrastructural doubling: about, 47; of Cucapá people, 49–50, 57, 59–60, 63; of hardware, 49–53; of homes, 52–53; and inversion, 53; and NAFTA, 52; of the natural environment, 49, 60, 63; of people, 50, 52; and visibility, 64

Mexico, 38, 55–57, 60. *See also* Cucapá people

middle voice, 206–207, 211–213

miniaturization, 228

Mitchell, Timothy, 156

models, 32, 43. *See also* Sardinal aquifer

Mohawk indigenous people, 7–8

Monsanto, 68, 79, 84, 87–88, 90

Montreal, 1–2, 7–8, 12n1

Mumbai's water engineers: accountability of, 157; embodied knowledges of, 162; infrastructure, relationships to, 165–166, 168n16–17; leakage estimates, 152–153; management strategies of, 157–163; maps, as useless to, 162; and meter readings, 154; practice of, 165; social/material mediation, 163–164; as subjects, 151, 162; and World Bank consultants, 156

Mumbai's water infrastructure: approximations in, 159; governance of, 158, 164–166; intermittent supply system, 153–154, 159; maps of, 160–162; neoliberalism's impact on, 155, 165; networks comprising, 160–161; pipes, locating, 159–162; responsibility for, 157–158; and settlements, 157; as unknowable, 159–162

Mumbai's water leakages: accounting of, 152–153; audits of, 153, 156, 167n2; complaints about, 158; detecting, 159, 168n14; estimates of, 152–153; firefighting strategy, 158; fixing, 162–164, 166; in K-East Ward, 158; management of, 158–162; materialities of, 165; measuring, 154–156, 167n5; measuring difficulties, 152–155, 157, 159; rate of, 152; and reforms, calls for, 165; responsibility for, 156, 157; and state control, 166; unknown, 158–159, 161

NAFTA, 52, 64

nation languages, 183, 191n14

Negri, Antonio, 69, 82, 92

neoliberalism: and contemporary crises, 252; and critique, crisis in, 7; humans, abandonment of, 238, 254, 258; logistics workers in, 90; in Mumbai, 155, 165; precarity in, 254;

Reagan and, 251–252, 259; in Singapore, 128; and zones of imperial extraction, 83–85

new materialism, 152, 156–157

New York City: and Hurricane Sandy, 194–195; oyster farming restoration, 193–194; resiliency of, 194; Staten Island, 194, 196, 198; water leakages, 149–152, 165. *See also* oysters in New York City; Oystertecture project

Noble Group, 81, 85–86

North American Free Trade Agreement (NAFTA), 52, 64

nuclear weapons programs: activist movements resulting from, 245; and climate crises, 247–248, 251, 253; ecological impact of, 241–242; environment, as militarizing, 243–244; fallout studies, 242–245; goals of, 253; IVY-Mike detonation, 241–242; Limited Test Ban Treaty of 1963, 240, 245–247; in the media, 244–245; missile defense, 252; overview of, 240–241; production locations, American, 256; reinstatement of, 240, 254–255; results of, 244; simulations, use of, 255; Strategic Defense Initiative, 252; testing, 241–244

O'Dempsey, Tony, 129–130

Ong, Aihwa, 87, 128–129

ontohistorical stickiness, 23, 37–38, 43

ontologies, practical, 221–222

Oslender, Ulrich, 177, 191n6

oysters: as apparatuses, 205–206, 210–211; extinction of, 198, 200, 212; humans, using, 211, 219n25; as infrastructure, 196, 198, 201, 211–212, 213, 214n7; life cycle of, 199–200, 211; standardization of, 211

oysters in New York City: and ecological health, 194–195; extinction of, 198, 200; history of, 197–200; as infrastructure, 196, 198, 201, 214n7–8; restoration projects, 193–194; value of, changing, 198, 201

Oystertecture project (New York City): about, 194–195, 198; "armoring units," 196, 214n5; as disaster preparedness, 196–197; FLUPSYS, 195, 213n2; as government, 207; Gowanus Canal version, 195; Hurricane Sandy, impact of, 195; as infrastructure, resilient, 203–204, 207; as katechon, 203; oyster lifecycle, use of, 200–201; politics of, 203, 212–213; temporality of, 202–203

pampas, 79–80

Panama, US Canal Zone in: decline of, 98; grass cutting in, 106–108; maintenance in, 104; public health initiatives, 105–107; transfer of, 109–110; weeds in, 9

Panama Canal, 103, 105–106, 109–110, 112, 114n5
Panama: Chilibre, 113; "Conquest of the Jungle" program, 108; development as infrastructure, 107–108; environmental management in, 105; forests, secondary, 100, 113; Fort Sherman, 97–98, 114n1; infrastructure, discussions of, 103; Panama Canal Authority, 98; Panama City, 98, 106, 113; San Lorenzo National Park, 97–98, 112; versus Singapore, 112; US interests in, 105; vegetation clearing, symbolism of, 106–108. *See also* Colón
Paschel, Tianna, 175
people. *See* humans
petrochemical energy, 256–258
Phnom Penh (Cambodia), 216–217, 230–234
pipes, underground, 32–33. *See also* Mumbai's water infrastructure
planetary urbanization, 69, 72–73
Plantationocene, the, 180–181
Planthroposcene, the, 146–147
plants, 120, 137, 144–145, 147n5. *See also* gardens; weeds
political ecology, 4
politics, volumetric, 26–27
ports, 75, 80. *See also* Buenaventura; Colón; Rosario; supply chains
posthumanism: about, 178; and the Anthropocene, 172, 178, 180; and Bajamar, 179; boundary work, 179, 191n8; and humans, conceptions of, 182; and Latin America, 178–179; and racism, 172, 181; and social justice, 181
postpolitical, the, 142–143, 145
practical ontologies, 221–222
profanation, 206, 208, 210, 212
progress, 7, 104, 237–238

race and racism: and climate change, 179; hierarchies of, 181; and humanism, 172, 180; nuclear fear and politics, 245; political ontology of, 180–181; and posthumanism, 172, 181
Rancière, Jacques, 118, 124, 137–138, 143
R. C. Harris Water Treatment Plant, 202, 214n12
Reagan, Ronald, 251–252
renewable energy, 226. *See also* hydroelectric energy; solar energy
reparative humanism, 180
resiliency to climate change: of Buenaventura, 184–186, 188–189; infrastructure improving, 203–204; of New York City, 194. *See also* Oystertecture project
Rising Currents exhibit, 195, 213n1
Robbins, Paul, 111–112
Rockefeller, Stuart, 71

Roitman, Janet, 237, 253
Rosario (Argentina): labor movements in, 90; Monsanto checkpoints in, 88; real estate boom, 79; and soy industry, 67–68, 79–81, 87
Roy, Ananya, 71

Salta (Argentina): about, 66–67; cattle industry, 77; deforestation, 78; and soybean industry, 68, 78–79, 81. *See also* Las Lajitas
San Lorenzo National Park (Panama), 97–98, 112
Sardinal (Costa Rica): about, 43n1, 44n4; dams, use of, 41–42; geologic profile of, 35–37; SAS agency, 20, 43n2; and Tempisque River, 44n4; water infiltration tests, 17–20, 25; water sources, 26, 29, 44n4
Sardinal aquifer: conceptual models of, 32, 35, 39–41, 43; defining, struggle to, 22–23; extraction rate of, 35, 37, 41; information on, lack of, 20–21, 40–41; infrastructuralization of, 22, 41; monitoring of, 41; reports on, 22, 37–42; sponge metaphor, 34–35
Sardinal water crisis of 2008: CocoWater and, 29–32, 39–40; court findings, 31–32, 41; effects of, 31; and financial crisis, 41; origins of, 30–31; protests, 19–20, 31; reports commissioned, 37–42
Sasken, Saskia, 71, 75
SCAPE. *See* Oystertecture project
Scheer, Hermann, 222, 226–228, 232–233
Schmid, Chris, 72–73
Schmitt, Carl, 203–204
science and technology studies (STS), 10, 24, 102, 147, 156
Simone, AbdouMaliq, 62–63, 199
Singapore: air quality, 133; botanical expertise in, 128–130; ecologies, building, 130; ecologies, precolonization, 129–130; foreign talent, luring of, 128–129; greening policies, 128–131; growth, emphasis on, 131; invasive plant species, 130; Little India, 132; migrant laborers, 131–132; as neoliberal, 128; versus Panama, 112. *See also* Gardens by the Bay
Sloterdijk, Peter, 239
social engineering, 237–238, 252
social sciences, 9, 182, 218–220, 258
solar energy: in the Carter administration, 235n14; global investment in, 217; Scheer and, 226, 228; Star8, 216–217, 230–234; storage of, 231, 235n18; transformative potential of, 222. *See also* Cambodia, solar energy in
Sonoran Desert (Mexico), 38, 55–57, 60
South America, 79–80, 84–85, 87–88. *See also* Argentina

soybean industry, Argentinian: AGD corporation, 88; bean processing, 79–80; and China, 68, 80–82, 87; and climate change, 70–71; and deforestation, 78–79; exports, 80–81; in Las Lajitas, 68–69, 77, 80, 84; and national progress, 88–89; and the *pampas*, 79–80; and Paraná river, 80; in Rosario, 67–68, 79–81; and seed patents, 88; size of, 84; social movements against, 89–90; supply chain, global, 75, 79–80, 84–85; and zones of imperial extraction, 84, 87, 89
soybean industry, Brazilian, 79–80, 84, 87–88
soybean industry, South American generally, 84–85, 87–88
species life, 201, 214n10
Spivak, Gayatri, 182
Star, Susan Leigh, 24, 47–48
Star8, 216–217, 230–234
stickiness, 23, 37–38, 43
Stoetzer, Bettina, 139
Strategic Defense Initiative, 252
Strathern, Marilyn, 32–33
subaltern studies, 182
supply chains: "agility" in, 86; corporations controlling, 84–85; dependence on, human, 92; as imperial, 83, 86–87; logistics, 70, 75, 85–87; and national differences, 87; social aspects, 85; social disruptions of, 89–90; soybean industry, 75, 79–80, 84–85
Sutter, Paul, 107
Swyngedouw, Erik, 142, 145
Syngenta (ChemChina), 79, 84, 87

Tan, Kiat, 130–131
technoscientific reports, 22, 31, 37–42
TEK, 59–60
Tempisque basin (Costa Rica), 41, 44n4
temporality, progressive, 202
temporal othering, 181
territory as technology, 83
things, governmental aspects of, 206–207
tidalectics, 183
Toscano, Alberto, 69–70, 90, 92
totalities: about, 70; Anthropocene as, 91; versus assemblages, 75; criticisms of, 70, 72–73; empire as, 82; and the metropolis, 70, 76
trading companies, 84–85
traditional ecological knowledge (TEK), 59–60
Tsing, Anna, 10, 77, 82–83, 99; on empire, 82–83, 99

underground, the: and archaeology, 33; conceptual models of, 42; and figure-ground distinctions, 31–34, 42; pipes, 32–33; and volumetric politics, 26–27; water leakages,

151. *See also* aquifers; Mumbai's water infrastructure; Sardinal aquifer
United States of America: capitalism of, 237; Carter era, 235n14, 251; and climate change, 251–252, 255–256; consumer economy of, 251; contemporary crisis of, 252–253, 259; and existential dangers, 239–240; future, fear of, 238–239; governance in, 238–240, 255; hydraulic fracturing, 255–258; information technologies, effects of, 238; infrastructural crumbling in, 239; and neoliberalism, 251–252, 254, 258–259; petrochemical industry, 240; political agency, lack of, 239–240; postwar, 259; progress in, 237–238; Reagan era, 251–252; renewable energy research, 235n14, 251–252; technological utopianism in, 259. *See also* nuclear weapons programs; Panama, US Canal Zone in
urban form, 73
urbanization, 68–69, 72–73
urban metabolism, 72

Vancouver, 81
Vietnam, 223–224, 226, 231
Vireak, Sim, 225–227
volumetric politics, 26–27

Walcott, Derek, 183–184
Walcott, Rinaldo, 175
wasteland aesthetics, 139
water crises, 27–28. *See also* Sardinal water crisis of 2008
Water Highway, The (La Hidrovía), 80
water infiltration tests, 17–20, 25
water infrastructure, 150–155. *See also* Mumbai's water infrastructure
weeds: definitions of, 101; and deforestation, 100; and gardens, 127; and infrastructure, 100; and infrastructure/environment boundary, 101; and "life" concept, 9–10; subjectivity of, 104, 127; symbolism of, 111. *See also* Colón, weediness of
Weinberger, Franziska, 136, 139–140
Weinberger, Lois, 118, 135–138. *See also* gardens, Weinberger's
wells, 26–27
Wesz, Valdemar João, Jr., 85
White, Leslie, 219–220
Williams, Raymond, 99
World Bank, 150, 152–153, 160
worldviews, 179, 232

zones of black death, 175
zones of imperial extraction, 83–84, 87, 89, 91